Bellissima

Bellissima

FEMININE BEAUTY AND THE IDEA OF ITALY

STEPHEN GUNDLE

YALE UNIVERSITY PRESS
NEW HAVEN AND LONDON

For information about this and other Yale University Press publications, please contact:

U.S. Office: sales.press@yale.edu   www.yalebooks.com
Europe Office: sales@yaleup.co.uk   www.yaleup.co.uk

Set in Minion by J&L Composition, Filey, North Yorkshire
Printed in Great Britain by St Edmundsbury Press Ltd, Bury St Edmunds

Library of Congress Cataloging-in-Publication Data

Gundle, Stephen, 1956–
    Bellissima: feminine beauty and the idea of Italy/Stephen Gundle.
       p. cm.
    Includes bibliographical references and index.
    ISBN 978–0–300–12378–6 (alk. paper)
    1. Feminine beauty (Aesthetics)—Italy—History—20th century. 2. National characteristics.
Italian.   I. Title.
    HQ1220.I8G86 2007
    306.4'613—dc22

                                                                                2006037320

A catalogue record for this book is available from the British Library

10 9 8 7 6 5 4 3 2 1

To the memory of
Patrick McCarthy

CONTENTS

List of Illustrations   viii

Acknowledgements   xi

Introduction   xv

 1   Italy, the Land of Beauty   1
 2   The Blonde Aura of Queen Margherita   33
 3   The Rise of Professional Beauty   58
 4   Fascism and the Allure of the Female Image   80
 5   Beauty and National Identity after the Second World War   107
 6   Catholics, Communists and Beauty Contests   125
 7   The Female Film Stars of the 1950s   142
 8   Mass Consumption and Ideals of Beauty   170
 9   Emancipation, Eroticism and Nostalgia   191
10   Beauty and Ethnicity in the Era of Globalisation   223
11   The Return of the 'Bella Italiana'   245

Conclusion   261
Notes   269
Index   292

ILLUSTRATIONS

		page
1	Domenichino, *The Sybil* (1616–17) (Galleria Borghese, Rome)	6
2	Francesco Gonin, 'Lucia Mondella' – from *I promessi sposi* (1840)	17
3	'Italia' – from Cesare Ripa, *Iconologia* (1603)	20
4	Francesco Hayez, *La ciociara* (1842) (Bergamo, private collection)	22
5	Francesco Hayez, *La meditazione* (1848–51) (Verona, Civica Galleria d'Arte Moderna)	23
6	Odoardo Borrani, *Il 26 aprile 1859* (1861) (private collection)	24
7	Carlo Stragliati, *Episodio delle Cinque Giornate Piazza Sant' Alessandro* (1848) (Milan, Museo del Risorgimento)	25
8	Regimental postcard of the 45th Infantry depicting 'Italia'	29
9	Regimental postcard of the 2nd Artillery depicting 'Italia'	29
10	John Singer Sargent, *Head of a Capri Girl* (1878) (private collection)	31
11	Rosa Vercellana, 'La bella Rosina', photograph	35
12	Queen Margherita of Savoy, *c.*1877, photograph	36
13	Queen Margherita of Savoy, popular postcard image	39
14	A young noblewoman of the late nineteenth century, photograph	41
15	Eleonora Duse, photograph	47
16	Peasant girl from the Abruzzo region, postcard illustration	50
17	*Illustrazione italiana,* cover, 11 January 1885	51
18	Sicilian peasant girl from Piana dei Greci, photograph	53
19	Lina Cavalieri, postcard image, Reutlinger, *c.*1900	63
20	Lina Cavalieri, postcard image, Reutlinger, *c.*1905	67
21	*Comoedia illustré,* cover: Lina Cavalieri, 15 November 1909	69
22	Poster for *La Nazione* newspaper, 1899	72
23	Poster for the National Exhibition of Rice Cultivation and Irrigation, 1912	74

24	Poster for Moriondo & Gariglio chocolates, 1900	77
25	Marcello Dudovich, *La signorina dalla veletta* (1919–20)	83
26	Mino Maccari, 'Cocktail', from *Il Selvaggio*, 15 June 1932	88
27	*Le Grandi Firme*, cover: illustration by Gino Boccasile, 25 August 1938	90
28	*Le Grandi Firme*, cover: illustration by Gino Boccasile, 22 September 1938	90
29	*Eva*, cover, 15 September 1934	93
30	Pasta advertisement with peasant girl illustration	95
31	*Gente Nostra*, cover, 8 September 1929	96
32	Eva, cover, 29 July 1933	97
33	Tipi No.2, from Carlo Scorza, *Tipi. . .Tipi. . .Tipi. . .* (Florence: Vallecchi, 1942)	100
34	Maria Denis, publicity photograph	104
35	Alida Valli, chocolate card	105
36	*Sette*, cover: illustration by Varga, 2 September 1945	111
37	*Sette*, cover, 30 September 1945	111
38	Fruit advertisement, illustration by Gino Boccasile	113
39	*Tempo*, cover, 15–22 June 1946	115
40	Rossana Martini in *Tempo* magazine, 21–28 September 1946	117
41	*Tempo*, cover: Silvana Pampanini, 21–28 September 1946	119
42	Miss Italia 1947 contest, photograph	120
43	Miss *Vie Nuove* competition Milan, photograph, *c.* 1953	132
44	Miss *Vie Nuove* jury, photograph, *c.*1954	136
45	Ivana and Ena Zanotti, photograph, *c.*1958	138
46	Ivana Zanotti wins Miss Moto B title, photograph, *c.*1960	139
47	*Riso amaro*, film poster 1949	144
48	*Lavoro*, cover, 18 May 1952	146
49	Gina Lollobrigida, studio photograph, *c.*1952	148
50	Gina Lollobrigida as 'La fornarina' by Raphael, *Epoca* magazine, 1 May 1960	150
51	Promotional booklet for the film *La donna più bella del mondo*, 1956	152
52	Sophia Loren by Philippe Halsman	153
53	Fruit advertisement, with girl resembling Sophia Loren, *c.*1955	155
54	Artists' images of their ideal woman, *Le Grandi Firme*, 16 June 1938	161
55	Giuseppe Tampieri, *Adriana* (1951)	164
56	Ampelio Tettamanti, *Portrait of a Rice Weeder* (1951)	164
57	Pietro Annigoni, *La bella italiana* (1951)	165
58	Still of Claudia Cardinale from Luchino Visconti, *Il gattopardo*, 1963	168
59	Fruit advertisement, with girl of urban appearance, *c.*1964	174
60	Stefania Sandrelli, publicity photograph	178
61	Giovanna Ralli, publicity photograph	182
62	Sophia Loren, publicity photograph	184
63	Still of Claudia Cardinale from Sergio Leone, *C'era una volta il West*, 1968	187
64	Ornella Muti, photograph	195

65 Still of Laura Antonelli from Salvatore Samperi, *Malizia*, 1973   202
66 Carmen Russo photo-spread, *Playmen*, 1 January 1982   204
67 Still of Serena Grandi from Tinto Brass, *Miranda*, 1985   208
68 Ilona Staller (Cicciolina), publicity photograph   213
69   Moana Pozzi, photograph   216
70 *Playboy* (Italian edition) cover: Alessandra Mussolini,
     August 1983   220
71 Denny Mendez, Miss Italia 1996, photograph   225
72 *Illustrazione italiana*, Spring 1993, photograph by Mimmo Cattarinich   230
73 *Sorrisi e canzoni tv*, cover: Valeria Marini and Alba Parietti,
     19–25 June 1994   236
74 *Il Venerdì di Repubblica*, 8 December 2000, photomontage   238
75 Lavazza calendar 1996, photograph of Maria Grazia Cucinotta by
     Ferdinando Scianna   241
76 Monica Bellucci, photograph   247
77 *Oggi*, cover: Sabrina Ferilli, 9 September 1998   254
78 Sabrina Ferilli, photograph   256
79 Gorgonzola advertisement (Manuela Arcuri)   258
80 Miss Italia 2006 calendar, photograph for September of Edelfa Chiara Masciott
     by Gianni Berengo Gardin   266
81 Miss Italia 2006 calendar, photograph for November of Edelfa Chiara Masciotta
     by Gianni Berengo Gardin   267

ACKNOWLEDGEMENTS

Very many people have provided me with help, advice, encouragement and criticism during the years that I have worked on this book. I hope that in these brief acknowledgements I can do justice to some of them and record by name others. I should first like to offer my thanks to Patrick McCarthy and Veronica Pye, and their daughter Kate, who offered me generous hospitality at their house in Normandy on a number of occasions in the mid-1990s. The idea for this book was in fact born there, in discussions about Italy and in some gentle teasing about the fact that I had been spotted in the library of the Gramsci Institute in Bologna leafing through old copies of the Communist illustrated weekly *Vie Nuove* and taking notes on beauty contests. In defending my decision to study such an apparently frivolous and minor subject, I began to reflect more broadly on the theme of feminine beauty in Italian history. This led me to many years of gathering material from newspapers and magazines, films, television, flea markets, second-hand bookshops and libraries. Whenever I found myself with an opportunity to visit a market such as Rome's Porta Portese or the Montagnola and Piazza Santa Stefano markets in Bologna, I seized on it in the hope of finding some old magazine, postcard or advertisement to place in my collection. The teasing never entirely stopped, but I remained convinced of the validity of the project. Patrick died after a long illness just as I received the proofs of this book. I would like to dedicate it to the memory of a friend who always knew how to combine scholarship with humanity.

Numerous friends and colleagues have been generous with their time in allowing me to float ideas in conversations or probe their perceptions of Italian female beauty. Paul Ginsborg has always given me the greatest encouragement in my work and on this occasion he was no less forthcoming with valuable guidance and advice. He and Ayse Saraçgil did not once object to my seeking their opinions or to being asked to comment on mine. In Florence, Barbara Corsi and Daniele Nannini were also happy to share their views with me, while in Bologna Ignazio Masulli and Serena Linea helpfully steered me towards certain judgements and away from others. As always, David Ellwood and Franco Minganti were forthright and good-humoured in their reactions. Katia Pizzi, Catherine Brice, David Forgacs, Martin Conway, Alberto Banti, Sandra Ponzanesi, Stefano Magistretti, Albertina Vittoria, Arabella Natalini, Fabrice d'Almeida, Penny Morris, Chiara Barbo, Paola Bernasconi, Rosalinda Dal Prà, Emanuela Poli, Philip Cooke, Luciano Cheles and Vanessa Roghi all provided me with insights that helped me develop aspects of the research. I have presented versions or parts of this project at a number of conferences and seminars. I wish especially to acknowledge the Oxford University Italian seminar, and its then organisers Martin McLaughlin, Peter Hainsworth and Robert Gordon, who provided me with my first platform in 1997. Marc Lazar gave me the opportunity to spend a period at the Institut d'Études Politiques in Paris in 2003 and Catherine Brice hosted my paper in her postgraduate seminar in the History department there. Both occasions provided very fruitful exchanges of ideas.

Among those who kindly gave or lent me material that has been employed in this project are Ena Zanotti, Filippo Ceccarelli, Anne Mullen, Erica Croce, Luciano Cheles and Piero Boragina. I should also like to thank the librarians of the National Libraries of Florence and Rome, the Gramsci Institute in Bologna, the British Library and the Getty Research Institute for their assistance while I worked in those locations.

In the Italian department at Royal Holloway, Giuliana Pieri helped me develop a better understanding of aspects of nineteenth-century Italian culture, and especially D'Annunzio, while Nina Rothenberg and Maddalena Spazzini's work on the contemporary Italian media was a genuine stimulus. Anne Mullen and Lia Buono-Hodgart also gave me their advice and encouragement. In preparing the chapters on the film stars of the 1950s and 1960s, I was grateful to Reka Buckley for kindly lending me her expertise. Her work on the stars inspired some of the treatment they are given here.

I am greatly indebted to Michela De Giorgio, whose work on Italian women's history has been a real inspiration to me. Her enthusiasm, passion for her subject and extra-ordinary knowledge were both an example and a challenge as I conducted the research. The chapter entitled 'La bella italiana' in her book *Le italiane dall'Unità a oggi* (Laterza, 1991) provided me with the initial framework for my project. Never once has she shown the slightest irritation that I have chosen to work in an area that she pioneered. On the contrary, she has been extremely generous with her advice and suggestions.

Special thanks are due to Lucy Riall who read and commented in detail on a draft manuscript. She engaged with the topic and provided me with just the sort of constructive criticism and advice that enabled me to strengthen my argument and iron out certain weaknesses, especially on the period – the nineteenth century – that she knows far better than me. In addition, my deep gratitude goes to Simona Storchi, who commented on parts of the manuscript and helped me to get certain chapters and sections 'right' when I was beginning to despair of ever doing so. Although the topic of this book is distant from her own academic interests, she has been generous with ideas and comments throughout the period that I spent writing up the research and has provided numerous insights that I have been more than happy to adopt. Her moral support has been invaluable.

The final text was mainly written during 2005, when I benefited from two terms of sabbatical leave from Royal Holloway, University of London and one term financed by the AHRC Research Leave Scheme. I offer my thanks to both.

London, 2006

INTRODUCTION

The cover of the February 1996 issue of the British edition of the men's magazine *GQ* (*Gentlemen's Quarterly*) featured a full-length photograph of the Italian actress Maria Grazia Cucinotta looking sultry and sexually alluring in a black slip. Fresh from playing a key supporting role in the hit Italian film *Il Postino* (The Postman) she was offered to the magazine's readers as an exotic, Mediterranean beauty, a dark-haired and olive-skinned alternative to the standard-issue Anglo-American cover girl. Posed by the photographer in such a way as to give British readers a sight of her generous bosom, her slip pulled up sufficiently to expose her long legs, Cucinotta was the very embodiment of concentrated sensuality. Accompanied by the exclamatory Italian title 'Bellissima!', this image evoked the seductive power of the rich, dark beauty she displayed in the film. The erotic nature of her appeal was confirmed when another British men's magazine, *Maxim*, placed her top in its 1997 'lingerie awards'. As the tabloid *Daily Star* put it, in a caption beneath a waist-up picture of the actress wearing just a black bra, which covered half of page one on 28 March 1997, 'Maria voted bust actress': 'The steamy star of the film *Il Postino* beat off swell supermodels like Claudia Schiffer and Caprice to scoop men's mag *Maxim*'s award for best-looking woman in her undies.'

It is not surprising that men's magazines should drool over a new starlet or that a British tabloid should leap at an opportunity to put a beautiful semi-naked woman on its front page. The phenomenon repeats itself at such regular intervals that it might almost be described as a routine practice. But it is quite unusual both for a continental European actress to receive such treatment on this scale and for her beauty to be under-lined by a superlative taken from her own language. The main reason why Cucinotta was taken up in this way was the special appeal of the pedigree that her dark and exquisitely Mediterranean image boasted. Italian female stars are often grouped and labelled in a collective way because of this. Another dark-haired, erotically-connoted Italian actress, Monica Bellucci, was given similar treatment a few years after Cucinotta. In publications ranging from *GQ* to the *Daily Telegraph* magazine, her dark charms were amply featured. She was hailed as the most beautiful actress in the world and reference was made to her 'bella figura' and to 'bella Bellucci'.[1]

Cucinotta may have been a star of the virtual age, with only a couple of small film roles and a web site to her name, and Bellucci best known for her largely cameo roles as a dark lady in French and American films, but they both evoked an idea of Italian female beauty that had previously been associated with the Italian movie bombshells of the 1950s. Stars like Sophia Loren, Gina Lollobrigida and Claudia Cardinale are remembered today for the dark and earthy contrast they provided in the post-war decades to the carefully-groomed Hollywood figures who dominated the big screen. The Italian stars of that era appeared as natural and spontaneous, not as the manufactured products of the studios. They came over as passionate, a little wild and quite traditional. They flirted and flounced but they were loyal to their men and fought tooth and nail to defend their families. They had a mystery and a fascination that was enhanced by their alternate moods, which were sweet and domesticated at one moment and strong and determined the next. Their curvaceous figures signalled a hyper-femininity that seemed appropriate for a hot country and which was expressed in an apparent unwillingness to dress at home in more than underwear. To movie audiences looking for something different that was more spicy and sexy than the standard American or British fare, they offered a taste of the sun, the sea, olive groves and of Mother Earth. Along the curves of their bodies were written the desires of at least one generation of men.

Following a long period in which this type of beauty and the image of womanhood that it implied found no place in fashion, advertising or film, it enjoyed a return in the second half of the 1990s. After two decades in which the dominant model of beauty in the western commercial media was light-skinned, fair-haired, flat-chested and androgynous, dark Caucasian women again began to find a place in fashion and beauty advertisements and in film. Aided by the rise of Italian fashion in world markets and a small resurgence in the fortunes of Italian cinema, Mediterranean womanhood once more won recognition and found representation as an erotic lure.

Cucinotta was the first of the new generation to attract attention. She was followed by the more urbane and middle-class Bellucci and by a series of other actresses, including Penelope Cruz and Salma Hayek, who were not Italian but whose Latin or Mediterranean origins meant that they were sometimes grouped together with their Italian cousins. In fact both the Mexican Hayek and the Spaniard Cruz were more personally successful in the United States than either of the two Italians. They could play the sort of fiery and sexually-connotated characters that Loren or Cardinale had played three or four decades previously. Yet they could not rely on the support of a heritage of representation and discussion of beauty that was available to the Italians. Only in Italy is there a culture of beauty that has its roots in the art and poetry of the medieval and Renaissance periods and which has given rise to numerous images in the modern age. It is Italian superlatives and not Spanish ones that are drawn on by tabloid sub-editors to communicate an idea of beautiful earthy Mediterranean femininity.

The international reaffirmation of a certain type of Latin beauty coincided with, and indeed was probably responsible for, its re-evaluation within Italy. For reasons connected to its comparatively recent unification and relatively late development, Italy only truly rejoices in many of its talents and achievements once foreign approval has been given. Within the country, *Il Postino* was at first seen mainly in relation to the performance of the much-loved comic actor Massimo Troisi, who died just after the end of filming. Only after it aroused interest abroad were its secondary attractions explored. Among these, indeed first among them, was Cucinotta, who played Beatrice, a sultry waitress with large breasts who provides the love interest. The film was set in the 1950s on the remote Mediterranean island of Lipari, a location that allowed for Cucinotta to be constructed as beautiful in an unsophisticated, 'natural' way, as one of the charms of the island's land-scape and habitat. Before long, her image was to be seen everywhere in Italy. She appeared on the cover of news and other magazines, a photo-shoot by leading glamour photographer Marco Glaviano became a special gift calendar sold with *Panorama*, she was dressed by Giorgio Armani, and information about her life and views was sought by illustrated family magazines. At a time of economic success for the country, she became an emblem, a brand image, whose marketing value was attached to a variety of products and to the export image of Italy as a whole.[2]

The interest aroused by Cucinotta helped create the premises for the rise to prominence within Italy of a series of actresses who, like her, embodied aspects of the consolidated image of the *bella italiana*, that is to say, who had regular, though not necessarily classically perfect, features, long, simply-styled dark hair and expressive eyes, who wore little make-up or jewellery, and were of a cheerful, easy-going disposition. Large breasts were an added but not essential attribute. Only Bellucci, whose connections to the fashion world gave her some advantages over others, as well as a slightly more aloof attitude, managed more than ephemeral success abroad. But at home the Roman Sabrina Ferilli emerged through cinema to become a popular television actress, presenter, best-selling calendar model and all-round celebrity. In the first few years of the new millennium, her path to recognition was imitated by Manuel Arcuri, a glamour model with a pin-up's physique, who became an actress and television presenter, working across several media and appealing to wide audiences. All three women deliberately situated themselves at least in part within the tradition of Italian female beauty. They used it as a platform while trying also to establish some distance from it and assert more individual identities.

For Italians, these women are not exotic and different; their appeal, although undoubtedly linked to sex, is profoundly traditional. The image of ordinariness and typicality they cultivate brings to mind the neo-realist films of the 1940s and the great heroine of the films of that era, Anna Magnani. Magnani's unkempt locks and exuberant personality are also reference points for women who want to be seen as women of the people. More forcefully though, they recall, for Italians no less than for foreigners, the sexy stars of the 1950s. In their homeland, Sophia Loren and Gina Lollobrigida were more than just sex symbols. They were bearers of an idea of Italy that was peace-loving yet determined and keen to succeed. Like many women of their generation, they were tough and enterprising, yet also in many ways deeply conventional in their attachment to family. In an Italy that was rapidly developing and about to exchange rural values and ways for urban ones, these women, in the melodramas and light rural comedies in which they made their names, offered an element of continuity, an illusion that the Italy of small villages and traditional communities was still there, unchanged, and that it was dynamic, spirited and sunny. Although Lollobrigida and Loren soon made international films and cultivated an off-screen image of quasi-regal glamour, their early films took audiences into a familiar world of rice weeders, peasants, fishwives and pizza girls. They were of the people and their characters often stayed close to their roots.

More recent personalities offer the same reassuring sense of continuity with place and tradition in a time of flux. Only in part is this a fabrication. Bellucci may be an international figure who spends more time in Paris and Los Angeles than in her own country, but 'in her eyes there is the Mediterranean and its perfumed land'.[3] Like their precursors, Cucinotta, Bellucci and Ferilli all hail from the south and the centre of Italy, the repository par excellence of the most enduring Italian imagery. The familiar and fundamentally maternal idea of womanhood that these women represent is confirmed by their traditional ideas: Ferilli speaks in the illustrated weekly *Oggi* about her love of cooking and her preference for Italian men,[4] Cucinotta wins approval from church spokesmen for refusing to undertake nude work,[5] and Bellucci waxes lyrical about her roots in the Umbria region.[6] Their full figures, dark hair and large eyes, golden skin and beautiful yet familiar faces are photogenic in a very modern way, yet what they provide is reassuring. They connect up with ideas about Italy and images of the country that are broadly shared. Both Ferilli and Cucinotta have made television advertisements for pasta. In her 1999 advert for the Cuore pasta brand, Cucinotta is situated in a context defined by the sky, the sea, the sun, tomatoes and basil. She makes her entrance, tall and splendid, into a piazza where the stalls of an open-air market are brimming over with the fruits of nature.

The aim of this book is to explore the relationship between feminine beauty and Italian identity. It considers why beauty occupies such a central place in public culture and investigates what lies behind it. I will assess the way in which a certain type of feminine beauty became identified with Italy and map the numerous disputes that took place over this. It is easy to dismiss these debates as trivial. The pseudo-scientific meditations of prominent nineteenth- and early twentieth-century men on the beauty of women read today like dubious generalisations forged in the course of male conservations in the café or the inn (which is what they may well originally have been). Yet the issue was one of great political relevance because it played a role in defining the bonds of belonging that Italians felt to their nation. Representations of women occupied a key place in the imagery of the nation and virtually every political force or movement that aspired to, or which actually exercised, national leadership sought in some way to appropriate or make use of them. In different ways, all the structures of power, including the state, the Church and the entertainment industry, were able to mould and condition beauty but each had different ideas and purposes, which sometimes coincided but which at other times clashed. Within each structure (especially the state and the entertainment industry) there was also a variety of requirements and views that at different times produced incompatible effects. Beauty was an appealing and in some respects necessary tool of persuasion, but not one that could easily be harnessed or turned unambiguously to specific ends. These failed attempts to harness it and the conflicts that occurred over different ideals reveal much about Italian social and political history, as well as the polyvalent appeal of beauty itself.

The issue of national identity emerged from the mid-1990s in Italy as a major area of historiographical inquiry. A series of books under the banner title of 'Italian identity' was published on themes ranging from pizza and pasta to historical figures such as Verdi and D'Annunzio – not to mention a male film star, a department store and a motorway. In addition, a three-volume collection of essays appeared that adapted the French historian Pierre Nora's notion of the *lieu de mémoire* to Italy. In none of these is the question of beauty considered.[7] Indeed, as a theme, it has been almost wholly ignored.[8]

This lacuna is striking, for one of the most enduring images of Italy is of a land of beauty, and of feminine beauty in particular. Poets from Dante and Petrarch developed a set of ideals which informed the values, both aesthetic and social, which the artists of the Renaissance sought to represent. Only a people with a deeply ingrained sense of the aesthetic, it was widely assumed, could give rise to such rich ideas and high artistic expressions, and then accord them such a central place in the common culture. This led to the conviction that the Italian people were possessed of an unusual physical harmony and beauty. In the nineteenth century the country was, both according to educated foreigners and to Italians, poor and, with respect to the industrial north of Europe, backward. But in compensation it was a land of great natural beauty, of striking landscapes, clear skies, fertile earth and endless sunshine. It was also a land of poetry and art, of creativity and genius. It was not only a land of beauty but a place where beauty was understood and appreciated. It is this background that distinguishes Italy from all other countries. While feminine beauty occupies some place in national identity in every country, the very long-standing high cultural tradition of preoccupation with it provides a bolster and a platform that are unique to the peninsula.

Because of the central importance of beauty of all types in Italian culture, it would be possible, in the Italian case, to discuss the issue in relation to either men or women.[9] Michelangelo's David is, after all, the defining image of male beauty in the western artistic tradition. However, as elsewhere, it was feminine beauty that came to enjoy a near monopoly of representational functions, symbolic purposes and popular manifestations. Beauty and femininity were so closely associated that the emphasis was almost natural, and the symbolic function of womanhood, or idealised images of it, played a role in this. Not only was the *Patria* feminine, but it was represented by female imagery. This occurred in part due to a long-standing tradition, dating back to classical antiquity, of allegorical female figures. But, more particularly, female images took on a role because of the way, in the eighteenth and nineteenth centuries, the rise of the bourgeoisie, the class that was mainly responsible for nationalism, heralded a radical hierarchical redefinition of the gender order. Within the nation men exercised full citizenship while women were confined to the domestic sphere. Given that it was difficult – perhaps even impossible – to bind men into patriotic devotion to an abstract entity, the nation was figured in womanly guise. It was at turns a protective mother, an erotic ideal, a fragile maiden and an amazon. Each of these grabbed at emotions and desires and encouraged men in a passionate attachment to the nation.[10]

Even after Italy was unified, it lacked a shared culture. It was deeply fragmented in its traditions, economy, language and attitude towards the state. A commonly-held national sense of identity was barely existent, and institutions and symbols were weak. For this reason special importance was attached to factors relating to the informal culture that Italians did share. If Italy was not yet fully a nation, it was certainly a country. 'The warm reasons, of feelings, of the heart, are those . . . that lead us to identify the country that lies behind our being a nation', Ruggiero Romano has written.[11] Among these, for Romano, were eating and drinking, religious and/or magic beliefs, language and dialects, behaviour patterns and games. To this list might be added a framework of aesthetic norms concerning masculine and feminine physical appearance. The issue of beauty was never at the very forefront of formal debates and discussions of Italian identity, but unlike food and games it was regularly caught up in intellectual reflections, public campaigns and debates. Language and literature were more central, but beauty was unique because it was both a reference point in the artistic and aesthetic tradition and something that was an aspect of life, a part of the lived experience of the country. It united intellectuals and the people; it was a sort of lingua franca and it was subject to change and, potentially, manipulation for ideological or symbolic purposes. For this reason, it was championed not only by the elite but by those who would have preferred the unified state to have come into being as a result of a democratic, republican revolution.

Within this general pattern, the pronounced Italian emphasis on the sexual desirability of iconic female images deserves a brief reflection. The coming of modern mass society and the diversification of the means of communication and reproduction of images meant that commercial eroticism played a part, but this was the case everywhere. Rather, the root lies in the particular sexual fixation of Italian men. To explain this, reference can be made to the writings of the historian and man of letters Guglielmo Ferrero, who first came to prominence as a collaborator of his father-in-law, the criminologist Cesare Lombroso. In the course of his career, Ferrrero produced several works of comparative psychology and sociology. In his view, Latin males (he included France and Spain in his discussion) reached puberty earlier than Northern Europeans. This fact had a series of psychological, social and cultural consequences which went from the rigid separation of the sexes in education and social life to a strong physical emphasis in all male discourses on love and beauty. 'Love for the man of the South is above all admiration for the physical beauty of a woman, and the desire to enjoy it', he observed, while the northern European conceived love as a more diffuse moral and affectionate bond with a woman in which the physical element was less dominant.[12] 'The pleasure . . . of love is always sought in a delight of the senses, of the eye, touch and hearing: in the sight of a beautiful face or beautiful locks, or in contact with a fine skin. The Englishman, by contrast, finds pleasure in images, ideas and emotions of various types that are associated with the idea or the sensation of the loved one.'[13] The sexual fixation of Italian men was fuelled by the difficulty of having any contact with women except prostitutes, a fact that in turn bred a male culture that was shot through with obscenity and lewdness. 'Between the ages of sixteen and at least thirty, the young men of southern countries are tormented by a real sexual obsession that very often explodes in orgiastic exhibitions unknown to northern men', Ferrero concluded.[14]

Embodiments of the nation in such a context were bound to take on explicitly sexual connotations. However, the way in which this occurred was not as overt as would be the case in the second half of the twentieth century. Although sexualised descriptions and evocations were routine in the nineteenth century, only with the First World War would commonplace images also become carnal. However, there was nonetheless a marked emphasis on the breasts. The voluptuous woman of the people was especially favoured on the left, which deployed female beauty as a symbol of the failed hopes of democratic renewal and of the promise of what could be. But the variety of meanings that could be attributed to breasts meant that virtually all sectors of opinion could somehow make them their own. In her history of the breast, Marilyn Yalom describes them as 'sexualised ornaments – the crown jewels of femininity'.[15] She also raises the important question of 'who owns the breast?':

> does it belong to the suckling child, whose life is dependent on a mother's milk or an effective substitute? Does it belong to the man or woman who fondles it? Does it belong to the artist who represents the female form, or the fashion arbiter who chooses small or large breasts according to the market's continual demand for a new style? . . . Does it belong to religious and moral judges who insist that breasts be chastely covered? . . . Or does it belong to the woman for whom breasts are parts of her own body?

The answer, of course, is that the breast belongs in different ways to all of these. For this reason, numerous tensions and conflicts involving individual women, women in general and public opinion have occurred around their public exposure and representation.

In the Italian national context, two factors which historically had often been separated, mixed and mingled in specific ways. These were the idea of the breast as a source of male delight, a notion that characterised the depiction of upper-class breasts in the Renaissance, and the idea of the lactating breast, which in the same period came to be associated with the lower-class women who often acted as wet-nurses for the children of their employers. The idea of the healthy, fertile female body played a role in nationalism because it provided a link to the reproduction of the population that could be counter-posed to the dissolute and in-bred aristocracy. In the course of the Risorgimento, great stress was placed on the role of mothers, and the sacrifice of the mothers of volunteer combatants was turned into a part of the narrative of national unification.[16] As mothers, women could both be drawn into the nationalist cause and confined to a conventional domestic space. In the period that followed, the mother became one of the strong symbols of the nation. A traditional idea of maternal femininity was woven into Italian identity and deployed to resist the influence of emancipated, foreign notions on young women.

How, then, does the notion of the mother, who was often depicted as a mature woman in mourning or as a strong, defiant figure, relate to the beautiful young woman? The young beauty was a mother-in-the-making. Because the breast is the key organ in the relationship between a mother and her child, large breasts are always evocations of a man's relationship with his mother or a substitute for it.[17] They are consolatory and re-assuring, as well as a symbol of the reproductive function of a woman. They are a marker of sexual difference that, when highlighted, confirm the specificity of the biological role of women. This does not preclude their role as a sexual lure or allusion, but it does link sex to reproduction. In Italy, national beauty has almost always been represented as large-breasted, despite the possible subjection of breast-size to pressures of fashion. This may be taken to be a result of a highly sex-differentiated culture and of the special relation-ship between mother and son that is seen as a national trait. As mentioned above, this is not a timeless feature of Italian society, although there may well be elements of a deep-rooted mentality. Rather, it is a relationship that was drawn into the construction of the nation in the nineteenth century and employed as a building block. Later in the century there were special reasons – connected to the development of the press and entertain-ment industries – which explain why images of women multiplied and became a cipher of modernity, but in Italy this merely had the effect of reinforcing the central importance of a certain type of imagery, which was already established. Both ideal images and real people formed part of a remarkably varied and continuously evolving collective, and sometimes official, discourse.

In his magisterial three-volume study of Marianne, the female symbol of the French Republic, Maurice Agulhon has explored the origins, manifestations and uses of a figure that was always an abstraction associated with precise political values, at least until the film stars Brigitte Bardot and Catherine Deneuve were recruited in the 1960s and 1970s to pose for the busts that are placed in many French town halls.[18] They humanised Marianne's image and helped her transformation from political symbol of the republic to generic symbol of France. Any attempt to replicate Agulhon's work by examining manifestations of the nearest equivalent of Marianne, the symbolic figure of Italia, would yield very meagre results. In part because Italy was a monarchy up until 1946, Italia was never developed fully into a potent symbol either of the country or of political values. A little like the British Britannia, her role has been a minor one, confined mainly to philately and coinage and given a general mobilising function only during the First World War. Not even after the creation of the republic was there any official or unofficial drive to expand her representational role. Thus the *bella italiana* is not, and cannot legitimately be considered to be, an equivalent figure to Marianne, although at times this construction has performed similar symbolic functions. However, the meanings attributed to her and the debates over her appearance have been no less polyvalent and contradictory. For these reasons, Agulhon's study is an important reference point for this book, but not the only one. I will cover some of the ground that he has staked out, while also considering other issues and sources more appropriate to the particular focus on national beauty that is a characteristic of Italy. In order to convey something of the totality of the topic, the materials employed are eclectic and diverse; they range from the writings of novelists, intellectuals, politicians and journalists to paintings, posters, illustrations, films, songs, television advertisements and calendars. Autobiographical writings and published interviews with some women of recognised beauty have also been employed.

More than a study of a particular figure, the present work is a diffuse cultural history that will take in many aspects of Italian history, values and customs. The task is to examine the origins and evolution of a very specific and remarkably durable stereotype of the Italian woman that has a long history, one that can be traced in literature, painting and the writings of foreign travellers for at least a century before it was represented on the cinema screen. The stereotype of the dark, passionate, instinctive, and bewitching Italian beauty is a crucial trope, which was shaped by politics and economics as well as culture. The chapters that follow will show that images of women served many purposes and were relatively uninfluenced by changes of regime. They could be taken over, shaped and used by political power but never totally; rarely if ever were any images discredited by association with a particular regime or political faction. Images of women served as bearers of patriotism, of national or racial vigour, of health and fecundity, and of moral purity (or its opposite). They could inspire loyalty, pride, honour, and also enthusiasm, passion and desire. Although the discourse on beauty often merged with nationalism, examples of it could and did emerge from a variety of sources. It was not just patriotic artists and famous women who forged or lent their images. In the age of photography and the popular illustrated press, emblematic female figures could emerge from anywhere and most especially from the field of commercial culture – that is, the applied arts, theatre and cinema. How women were chosen and deployed was often related to the specific forms that patriarchy took in different sectors and it is in relation to these that the responses of women to their collective and individual representation need to be plotted.

These considerations lead me to spell out explicitly how the concept of beauty will be defined in this book. In contrast to definitions which stress universal aesthetic qualities such as harmony and regularity of features, a narrower view will be employed here that is more appropriate to the specific requirements of the present analysis. Beauty will be treated as a gender-specific and culturally-validated summation of the ideal physical qualities of a specific ethnic group or population. Such qualities must be collectively approved and reinforced through the periodic proposition of new examples that will prevalently be drawn from the section of the population whose age falls between adolescence and maturity. The distinction between ethnic group and population is important because not all nations are based on ethnicity and, even where they are, immigration has in many instances led to a shift of emphasis to a more loosely-defined notion of the national community. The term 'feminine beauty' has been preferred to 'female beauty' in the title because it suggests more strongly the notion of an ongoing process of construction rather than a fixed and universal biological given. However, the terms are used interchangeably in the course of the text.

From the late nineteenth century, and especially from the years around the First World War, the nature of Italian beauty was always considered in relation to the foreign. Foreigners had always viewed it like this. Stendhal and Mme de Staël had compared Italy to their own countries and made it a receptacle of their desires. But wider travel and the development of photography and the press meant more general comparisons could be made by a wider range of people. Urban ideas of beauty, or ones deriving from the social elite, became more familiar to lower social classes as did foreign notions. Italian beauty became defined as an 'Other', a specific that was different from and defined against often more powerful, more standardised northern European or North American models. It was a cipher of change, but also a value to be preserved and safeguarded from alien modernity, a banner to employ in the battle against unwelcome changes. This idea of Italian beauty as somehow being antique and primitive, close to nature and uncivilised, continues to shape the presentation of Italian actresses and photographic models. It is one that has a certain appeal in Italy too, especially in the more developed regions, where nostalgia for a lost sense of organic culture finds various outlets.

Italian beauty is often seen in relation to a relatively unchanging stereotype. However, it has always been a stereotype in continuous evolution. Change and renewal have been as important as continuity. It has been a site in the battle between tradition and modernity, between religious and secular, or even pagan, values and also an issue in the relations between the different political factions and geographical parts of Italy. It is striking that, until the 1960s or 1970s, there was an absence of middle-class beauty ideals, a fact which reflected the peculiarities of Italian development. The extraordinary process of modernisation which occurred in the 1950s and 1960s led to new modern norms of foreign, and especially American, origin gaining a foothold in everyday life and in commercial culture, leading to new syntheses which took the place of the long absent bourgeois ideal. However, while strong elements of modernity were incorporated into the image of the *bella italiana* at this time, certain traditional features remained and indeed were often highlighted in such a way as to evoke feelings of nostalgia for a bygone rural order in which gender and class roles were clearly defined. For the Italians, who today look back on several decades of rapid and disruptive socio-economic change that have seen their country emerge as a leading industrial power, it is no exaggeration to say that the women who are the public embodiment of the *bella italiana* function as a repository of consolatory and reassuring ideas about the country and its identity. This role is not performed solely for men, but undoubtedly it is mainly performed for them. To contemporary Italian women, the idea of the *bella italiana* offers little beyond some limited career opportunities for a handful. Nevertheless, there are complex reasons why the stereotype has survived the cultural revolution of feminism, and not all of these are to do with that movement's limited impact in Italy.

The debates about Italian beauty that have taken place since the nineteenth century have at times been high-minded and aesthetic, in keeping with the country's artistic and cultural tradition. At other times, however, they have been more political or primitive and sexist in attitude, in tune with the hierarchical gender order which still prevails today. In all instances, the debates have been male-dominated, for to discuss female beauty in the abstract and the particular is to objectify women, to reduce them to their visual appearance and consign them to the realm of *being* (as opposed to *doing*, which in this context is regarded as masculine). Representation, as feminists and others have shown,[19] was the work of men and occurred within the workings of power. Women have of course contributed to debates, and many women discussed in this book have been powerful, influential and anything but purely passive receptacles of male desire. But it is necessary to recognise at the outset that this book does not cover a neutral terrain, but rather a deeply controversial and problematic one. My focus is a predominantly male discourse that has universal pretensions but which depends on the existence of an asymmetrical gender order.

Many of the women who are discussed in the course of this book were or are professional performers who have used and shaped for their own ends the canons of beauty to which the press and the public related them. They sometimes fought against restrictive expectations that diminished their individuality and sometimes stimulated changes in established ideas that provided a signal or an example for ordinary women. In some instances, they ignored or rejected the prevailing paradigm of beauty. The emphasis on beauty both took something from women (in so far as its deployment could be – and was – used against claims for legal equality and access to education) and gave them something, namely visibility and a central place in the construction of the national community.[20] The Italian case confirms that representation was a contradictory process, in which women made contributions and found some room for appropriation or subversion. Which women contributed and within what constraints will be drawn out at each step of the analysis.

Finally, I should say something about why I have chosen to write this book and also alert the reader to some of the difficulties that I have had in doing so. My aim has been to tackle a topic that seemed to me, as an outsider who has spent over twenty-five years studying Italy, to be so evident and unavoidable an aspect of Italian culture as to be crying out for analysis. In all media and in much of the collective discourse about the country that takes place in Italy, the issue of female beauty and the women who over time have been deemed to embody it are recurrent reference points. Today, the annual Miss Italia pageant, that was founded in 1946, is still a national event that mobilises the energies of tens of thousands of people, and engages many millions of magazine readers and television viewers. It is a central ritual in the perpetuation of the national community. Yet, at the same time, the question of female beauty is so primordial an aspect of Italian culture, so diffuse and embedded in the national psyche, that it scarcely occurs to many Italians that it is a distinctive feature of their culture, with a specific and highly controversial history. With the humility, therefore, that is proper to a foreigner who studies a culture that is not his own, I hope to bring to the surface a history that in some ways is well known but which in others is almost wholly hidden.

As a male scholar tackling matters of feminine beauty, I am aware that there are certain difficulties in selecting appropriate terms and expressions to describe my subject matter. The language that has been forged to describe the beauty of women, and which is still in constant use in the press in Italy and abroad, is neither neutral nor always appropriate to serious analysis. Rather, it encapsulates male desire and reflects the way that this sets the tone in the public realm. As such, it is indirectly drawn into the present study. In writing about male desire and the cultural and political uses of that impulse, my aim is to draw attention to the specificity of the discourse itself, the type of female selection it entails and also to the structures of power that underpin it. However, I would be naïve if I did not admit that at times I have found it difficult to avoid employing terms and descriptions that are redolent of some of the objectifying processes that I analyse. I hope that readers will understand this dilemma and appreciate the effort that has been made.

CHAPTER ONE

ITALY, THE LAND OF BEAUTY

In the course of the Italian Risorgimento, a variety of narratives and symbols were deployed by patriots in their efforts to mobilise the consciousness and energies of those who were deemed to belong to the nation. Nationalists drew on and promoted elements that Italians were deemed in one way or another to share. These included the artistic and cultural heritage, a sense of the natural environment, elements of a common language, hostility to foreign domination and a shared ethnicity. As in other countries, the nation was often symbolised in female form. Feminine symbols are a recurrent feature in nationalist movements because they act as banners of the health and fecundity of the nation and allude to the idea of it as a family. They also arouse the desires of men and harness them to the nation. In Italy, the national allegorical symbol was significant, but much more important was the wider phenomenon of identifying all sorts of young women with the nation by means of the mediation of literature or art. The beauty of women was one of the most striking and continuous themes in the formation of Italian national identity in the early and mid-nineteenth century. Not only was Italy seen through its young women and their representations in the arts, but their beauty was deemed to be one of the most significant manifestations of a general Italian superiority in matters of aesthetics.

In this chapter, the origins of this particular identification will be explored. Italy's long heritage of artistic and poetic creativity certainly bore on the processes whereby feminine beauty became a factor in the formation of the nation. After all, nations are fashioned from the resources that are available and the identification with art and beauty was one of Italy's hallmarks. But at least four additional factors need to be taken into account. First, the northern European custom of travelling to Italy, writing about it and depicting it created a repertoire of images and ideas about the country that were current in European culture. Among these was the idea of the country as a feminine land of art and imagination. During the ascendancy of Romanticism in the early nineteenth century, this idea became more insistent and programmatic. Foreign writers surveyed the women of Italy and discussed the qualities and potential of the country in relation to them. Second, Italian patriots employed female symbolism to win the attention of their fellow men and harness their emotions. By giving Italy an attractive face, writers and artists were able to express their belief in the nation's future while also manifesting sadness about its current state. Third, the Risorgimento brought ordinary people into the picture and the enthusiasm of young women for the nation became one of the ways in which the struggle for national unification was visualised. Finally, the lack of a genuine national revolution led radicals to seek to harness feminine beauty as a symbol of a deep Italy that had not been fully incorporated into the state.

In the course of this chapter, it will be shown that the employment of female imagery by no means always implied a commitment to female citizenship or a recognition of any actual female contribution to the nation. On the contrary, the whole period was marked by the consolidation of a sexual hierarchy. The importance attached to female beauty was a product of this, and the insistence on it showed a persistent subordination of women in the life of the nation. However, there were contradictory aspects to this, since the centrality accorded to female beauty granted women a visibility and gave them a purchase on the idea of the nation that were not without consequences.

Italy and the Grand Tour

Northern Europeans began visiting Italy systematically in the seventeenth century. Men and women from France, England, the German states and the Low Countries arrived in Italy in search of aesthetic and cultural enrichment. Imbued with at least a rudimentary classical education and some knowledge of history of art, they came with the intention of seeing for themselves some of the key locations of western culture. Visitors to Italy came to see the works of painters and sculptors in the context in which they had been made. Roman ruins, Renaissance palaces, and museums and galleries displaying the works of Italy's master painters were the highlights of every traveller's itinerary. The main itinerary focused on three cities that hosted many of the riches of the peninsula: Rome, Naples and Florence. Although Milan, Turin, Venice, Palermo and Milan had their champions, it was these three cities which became the main attractions. Each offered something unique to the traveller: Florence the treasures of the Renaissance, Rome the decayed glories of the ancient world, and Naples the marvels of landscape combined with the thrill of the exotic.

For some, Italy as an imaginative realm had more in common with the Orient than with the Europe of progress and reform. It delighted, entertained and stimulated the senses. Its warm climate was seen to favour effeminacy and sensuality, something that put the wary on their guard. At the same time, there was some admiration for the primitive, natural aspects of the people, especially those of the south, who were contrasted to the reserved English and the artificial French. Naples was associated with the picturesque, largely on account of Vesuvius, while Sicily was viewed as a semi-civilised outpost that was visited exclusively because of its numerous classical remains.

Among the cultural themes that were most identifiably Italian, and which drew travellers, was the preoccupation of Italian culture with beauty and its representation. Among foreigners, this reputation derived principally from Renaissance art. However, the imagery of Italian art was sustained by a discourse on feminine beauty that had older roots in medieval poetry. The feminine principle, always a major inspiration for poetry, exercised great influence in Italy.[1] Dante's Beatrice constituted one of the great iconic female figures of the western poetic tradition, while Petrarch, as the first author to idealise women, to treat the expression of love and to address the issue of the description of beauty, played a key part in fixing ideals of femininity. The approaches he pioneered not only permeated the literature of the time, but influenced many spheres of cultural life. They could be found in lyric poetry, in disquisitions on love and on the beauty of women, in writings on art and on behaviour and comportment.[2] In the aftermath of Petrarch and those, including Boccaccio, who followed him, a canon of female beauty took shape that was taken up and restated in the works of poets including Poliziano, Bembo, Ariosto and Boiardo. Petrarch was also seen as important because he anchored beauty to an idea of Italy. In 'Ad Italiam', he described Italy as a 'most holy land dear to God' that was 'more noble than any other and more fertile and more beautiful'.[3] This background was taken to have informed painters as diverse as Botticelli, Bronzino, Titian and Leonardo and provided them with a frame of reference for their numerous female portraits. This special interest dovetailed with a more general image of Italy as a wonderful stage set that had been created by God to inspire man's creative genius and aesthetic powers.

Travellers generally viewed the country through the prism of their own reading and experience. Arriving with their own servants, their own *forma mentis* and their own suspicions, they often reduced contacts with the natives to a minimum. It was expected that foreign travellers would always be on guard and should seek to return unspoiled. The English had a particular horror of the Catholicism of the Italians. Their aim was to sample Italian culture without being contaminated by the Italian milieu.[4] The discouragement of independent vision was further reinforced by the standardisation of routes and destinations as early as the first decades of the seventeenth century. Guide books pointed the distracted or fearful visitor to the main sights and provided him with ready-made responses to what he saw. Formulas were ascribed to cities, regions and the mores of the people living in them. Despite this, some foreigners were tempted to stray from these paths and explore more of the country.[5] Young men found Italy to be a land of pleasure in which warm weather, cheap wine, relaxed company and sex provided the main attractions. Prostitutes were readily available to them but there are also numerous accounts of brief liaisons with married women. Due to the widespread practices of marriage for interest and 'cicisbeiship' (according to which a married woman often had an official companion who might also be her lover), enterprising travellers found that women were relatively relaxed in their customs. As a consequence, Italian women acquired a reputation for being highly-sexed that would prove remarkably persistent.[6]

Italians were generally viewed with condescension. At the very best, they were treated patronisingly as amusingly musical, colourful and superstitious – in short, picturesque, like the environment they were fortunate enough to inhabit. At worst, they were indolent, apathetic, dirty and violent. However, because Italy was seen in terms of its past, the people were also seen as living descendants of the subjects that travellers saw in galleries. Italian women, especially, were commonly viewed in relation to an aesthetic of beauty that could be traced back at least to the fifteenth and sixteenth centuries. Appreciation of this sort was not universal. Some deplored the ugliness of the women of Genoa, who were deemed to have large heads and heavy features, and the bad complexions and unhealthy appearance of Neapolitans. Nevertheless, with few mediating mental processes or cultural adaptations, visitors compared living people to the paintings they encountered. The connection between the male and female figures in art and the people that visitors saw with their own eyes would soon become a commonplace observation. One early traveller, Kenelm Digby, endeavoured to find in Verona in 1790 'beauteous females' like the figures painted by Veronese, while another British visitor, Sacheverell Stevens, praised the unchanging beauty of Roman women.[7] For writers, this device was particularly convenient, since they could strike a chord of recognition with their readers by describing a character's appearance in relation to a work by Leonardo, Raphael or Giorgione.

Romanticism brought a new set of ideas to the engagement with Italy. From the late eighteenth century, Italy was counterposed simultaneously to aristocratic refinement and to the industrialism and alienation of northern Europe. Foreigners were drawn to the country because of its pastoral nature, a certain pagan undercurrent in its culture and its more humane rhythm of life. A specific Romantic contribution was the attention accorded to nature. C. P. Brand has observed that 'English visitors, with memories of "terror-novels"', such as Anne Radcliffe's *The Mysteries of Udolpho* and *The Italian*, 'which set many of their wildest episodes in Italy, went in search of "romantic" scenery, and spared no effort to discover it, wandering round the Coliseum by moonlight, or climbing Vesuvius during an eruption'.[8]

Romanticism also heralded a connection with politics. Among most early visitors, there was no interest in the political situation of Italy or the aspirations of its people. This changed in the early decades of the nineteenth century. The Francophone authors Madame de Staël, Stendhal and de Lamartine were among the key figures who began to take an interest in the destiny of the peninsula. They engaged with the Italian cause and to some extent took possession of it in order to express their personal concerns and desires. Yet, while there were some elements in common in their respective visions, their common stress on Italy's feminine identity concealed very different gender perspectives. It is these differences that need to be explored in order to identify the manner in which feminine beauty was drawn into Italian nationalism and conditioned the whole subsequent place of beauty in the representation of the country.

Madame de Staël and Corinne

The Swiss-born woman of letters Madame de Staël visited Italy for the first time at the end of 1804,[9] at a time of considerable disruption in the peninsula and in Europe. The Grand Tour in its established form came to an end with the French revolutionary wars.[10] Napoleon occupied the north of Italy after defeating the Austrians in 1796. He conquered the rest of the peninsula by 1799 but was then forced out due to the combined military efforts of the Austrians and the Russians. With his generals, he returned in 1800 and by 1808 had re-established his control over the country. He would retain control until 1814. De Staël had challenged Napoleon by organising in Paris a salon that was a forum for opposition. This led to her banishment from France. Her intention from the start was to write a novel about her journey to the peninsula. She had ideas about Italy that did not coincide with those of Napoleon and she planned to elaborate these in relation to what she observed.

Over the following months, she travelled to Milan and Turin, Bologna, Florence and Rome. She noted customs, habits and attitudes, but found little of abiding interest in them. Only when she reached Naples did she find the sensuousness of the countryside and the indolence of the people worthy of reflection. The peoples of the south, she sweepingly observed, prefer imagination to thought; they often pass suddenly from great excitement to complete repose.[11] Moreover, the poverty of the Neapolitan people, unlike that of the French, was picturesque and artistic. In this view, she was not alone. Naples and nearby areas had a special appeal for foreigners. They were seen as sensuous and voluptuous. They were well known for their archaeological remains and also as the historic location of pagan mother cults. Here, in ancient times, mother goddesses had symbolised ideas of fertility, abundance, consolation and protection. All this provided de Staël with the stimulus she had been seeking. She began writing her novel while she was still in Italy and wove many of her own experiences into it.

Published in 1807, *Corinne ou de l'Italie* is centred on the figure of a woman of beauty and talent named Corinne (Corinna in Italian) who is presented as the embodiment of Italy. The heroine's qualities are amply described and, indeed, are formally acknowledged in a ceremony. The reader first encounters her in Campidoglio in Rome as people gather to witness a ceremonial crowning, in which she will be honoured in the same way that, in their time, the poets Petrarch and Tasso were. She is introduced as 'the most famous woman in Italy . . . poetess, writer and improviser, and one of the most beautiful women in Rome'.[12] Along the route of the procession, the crowds shout 'Long live Corinne! Long live genius! Long live beauty!'. Once she is installed inside Campidoglio, she falls for the first time under the admiring gaze of Oswald Nelvil, the Scottish nobleman who will love and leave her. Employing the device of his gaze, the author describes her heroine as: 'dressed like Domenichino's Sibyl. An Indian turban was wound round her head, and intertwined with her beautiful black hair. Her dress was white with a blue stole fastened beneath her breast, but her attire, though very striking, did not differ so much from accepted styles as to appear affected . . .':

I *The Sibyl* by Domenichino, one of
the inspirations for Mme de Staël's
Corinne.

Her arms were dazzlingly beautiful; her tall, slightly plump figure, in the style of a Greek statue, gave a keen impression of youth and happiness; her eyes had something of an inspired look. In her way of greeting people and thanking them for the applause she was receiving, there was a kind of naturalness which enhanced the effect of her extraordinary situation. At one and the same time she gave the impression of a priestess of Apollo who approaches the sun-god's temple, and of a woman who is completely natural in the ordinary relationships of life. In short, all her movements had a charm which aroused interest and curiosity, wonder and affection.[13]

Apart from her poetic talent, Corinne displays a great knowledge of Italian literature and art. In the novel, she acts as Nelvil's guide to all things Italian. She introduces him to historical sites and buildings and explains them to him. She speaks of man and nature being in close communion in her country. In this way, she proves herself to be not only proud and patriotic, but also articulate. The two discuss – and write to each other – about Italian history and customs. When Nelvil advances criticisms of Italians and their ways, Corinne robustly counters them and defends her country.

The novel is a complex work that was informed by its author's desire to defend the opportunities that had arisen in the climate of change following the French Revolution to promote female influence. She objected to Napoleon's intense dislike of intellectual females and to his belief that women were of use only as machines for making babies. She took an idea of Italy that had been current for several decades, according to which it was a beautiful country, a feminine land of history, poetry and picturesque charm. She then tried to imagine what it would be like if these special Italian qualities were to be rendered active and personalised. According to Madelyn Gutwirth, Corinne is 'an embodiment of Italy's natural physical loveliness, of its uncontested primacy in the creation of the visually beautiful, and of the splendour of poetry'.[14] De Staël adopted a similar female-centred approach in her writings about France and Germany, but it is only in *Corinne* that the identification established between woman and country is so powerful. Corinne is not just a beautiful and cultured heroine who is the incarnation of her country, but also the promise of its future.

De Staël's conception would not have been possible without the French revolutionary custom of allegory and allusion. The revolution revived the classical tradition of using feminine images to embody ideals and principles such as justice, liberty and the republic. This gave a new stimulus to the practice of describing nations and peoples by reference to female figures who had some of the characteristics of goddesses. New images were necessary because, in the post-revolutionary era, the nation was no longer embodied by the person of a king. It was an abstract entity in which loyalty and belonging needed to be mobilised in new ways. In order to lure men into identification with the state and consolidate loyalty to the nation, female figures – often with a marked erotic appeal – were employed. Nations were 'imagined communities' of equals that needed to inspire passion and devotion.[15] By giving the nation a female identity, male citizens were encouraged to think of it in terms that equated to the emotional attachments that they had to their mothers, sisters, wives and lovers. The erotic did not always integrate easily with the maternal and family dimension, and in specific manifestations clearly escaped it, but the iconography of nations was never fully consistent. As a representational realm that was a patrimony in the making, to which many contributed and that was drawn from an eclectic mixture of old and new materials, it contained polyvalent messages.

In recent years, the issue of how the two sexes were hierarchically integrated into nations and the role of female imagery has become a significant area of inquiry.[16] It has been highlighted how the symbolic centrality of the feminine did not mean that women acquired greater influence in national communities.[17] Rather, symbolic prominence went hand in hand with an emphasis on female domesticity.[18] The proliferation of female images during and after the revolution occurred in a context in which women were being excluded from public affairs. The use of young female figures to represent the nation had a variety of motivations. There was the desire to promote the ideals of fecundity, health and purity against the dissolute mores and corruption of the aristocracy. To establish a common ethnic identity through physical traits was also important. There was also a need to turn men into warriors who were prepared to defend the nation as they would the women of their community. In his analysis of the symbol of the French

Republic, Richard Sennett says that the sheer robes and exposed body or breasts of this figure did not give 'the slightest hint of a lascivious woman revealing herself, in part because the breast appeared by the late Enlightenment as much a virtuous as an erogenous zone of the body'.[19] Her upright, heroic body stood in contrast to the pleasure-seeking bodies of the *ancien régime* and served 'as a political metaphor uniting society's vast variety of unlike human beings within her frame'.[20] In an alternative interpretation, Marina Warner points out that, in the nineteenth century, imaginary women who called to mind the ideals of liberty or the nation were 'often seen as sexual beings, driven by passion, not political considerations'.[21] Such figures could be depicted as wild and dishevelled, as well as stern and combative. This ambivalence suggests a connection with the pagan heritage. While goddesses were frequently virginal, they could also be promiscuous, as befitted their association with the fertility of both crops and human beings.[22] In whatever form, the yearning for femininity was emblematic of a whole, non-fragmented identity. There was a mythic plenitude about such women that consoled and embraced. The maternal body and the erotic body, often indistinguishable one from the other, became a homeland.[23]

De Staël took inspiration from the potential in this imagery in fashioning her heroine into a spokesperson for her conquered country and for women. One of the great original works of Romanticism, *Corinne* has been dubbed 'the worst great novel ever written' by the author's biographer, on account of its being 'ineptly plotted, hysterical, and romantic in a ludicrous sense'.[24] As a novel of ideas, with a strong autobiographical component, it may be imperfect, but it made a crucial contribution to nationalism. Certain aspects of the novel were based on, or incorporated, existing stereotypes about Italy. The country is seen in relation to its artistic heritage and the creativity of its people. Corinne was based on a mixture of sources, including Isabella Pellegrini, a poetic improviser who de Staël saw perform in Rome, and Domenichino's sixteenth-century portrait *The Sibyl*. Corinne is the expression of the natural and man-made beauty of Italy and is accepted as such by her fellow countrymen. 'Look at her, she is the image of our beautiful Italy,' says Nelvil's love rival, Prince Castel-Forte, in the novel: 'she is what we would be but for the ignorance, the envy, the discord, and the indolence to which our fate has condemned us'.[25] 'We would follow in her footsteps,' the prince declares, 'we would be men as she is a woman, if men could, like women, make a world for themselves in their own hearts, and if the fire of our genius, compelled to be dependent on social relationships and external circumstances, could be fully set alight by the torch of poetry alone'.[26]

Corinne justifies the relaxed mores of Italy and the freedom they afforded women in their relations with men. Unlike the restrictive hypocrisy of England, Italian morality is presented as transparent. There is no sex in the novel, but the heroine is clearly a woman who is imagined as sexual. Her passion for Nelvil is simple and without reservation. When she dances the tarantella, a Neapolitan folk dance that is supposed to mimic the effects on the body of a bite from a tarantula spider, her movements are described as having 'a graceful litheness, a modesty mingled with sensual delight'; everyone, including the musicians and spectators, is stimulated by this 'magical dance' and transported 'into an ideal existence which was out of this world'.[27] The sensuous scene is merely one of many that repel the reserved Nelvil.

As a dark-haired heroine, Corinne was highly unusual within literature. Since medieval times, fair heroines had been the rule. However, although fair hair was by no means unknown in Italy, foreigners generally preferred their Italians to be dark.[28] For Gutwirth, Corinne's dark hair links her to the fatal women described by Mario Praz in his famous study of romanticism.[29] Yet, while she is bewitching to the pale and northern Nelvil, she is no simple force of transgression. In a subversion of stereotype, she is a positive figure who is complex and possessed of considerable depth. She also has some of the reserve and timidity of a literary blonde. Nevertheless, in the end Nelvil opts to marry Corinne's meek and domesticated blonde half-sister. This abandonment, which leads to Corinne's eventual death, mirrored the author's own romantic disappointment.[30] More significantly, it also symbolised the defeat of the hopes for female emancipation that de Staël had nurtured.

De Staël sometimes caricatured Italians and in this way contributed to the process of stereotyping that would continue after her.[31] For example, in order to lend plausibility to Corinne's use of rational argument to explain Italy, she made her half-English. Although she embodies Italy, and has chosen Italy as her homeland, it is her element of Englishness, inherited from her noble English father, that enables her to act as the advocate for her silent and occupied land. For Italy, like all disunited, backward lands, was not able to represent itself or speak for itself.[32] In other respects, especially in her appearance and her spontaneous poetic gifts, she is more typically Italian. Through her feminine appeal and talent, she represents her country. In this way, she contradicts the belief of the English poet Robert Browning, who remarked that the Italians who '*are* poetry, don't and can't *make* poetry'.[33] Corinne is the synthesis of what the Italians were and what they might become.

Despite her recourse to stereotypes, de Staël brought a range of social and political sensibilities to her encounter with Italy. Unlike many earlier and later authors, she did not portray Italy's women as static or passive. She recognised a variety and a potential in the women of the peninsula that made them distinctive with respect to the more 'civilised' and less 'natural' women of the northern countries. 'Life is nothing more than a dream-filled sleep under a beautiful sky. But give these men an objective, and you will see them learn and understand everything', Corinne asserts. The women, too, who Nelvil sees 'as indolent as harem odalisques' are persistent and active like the men. Once their passions are aroused, they 'are suddenly capable of very devoted deeds'.[34] De Staël asserted the intellectual power of women and demanded a role for them. However, her appeal fell largely on deaf ears. *Corinne* remained popular through the nineteenth century and was enthusiastically read, especially by women travellers to Italy.[35] Echoes of the novel could be found in the writings of women such as Elizabeth Barrett Browning.[36] However, the issue of women's creativity was not one that caught the imagination of Mme de Staël's male successors in writing about Italy.

Stendhal

It has been said that de Staël's observations on Italy 'in some ways ... anticipated Stendhal'.[37] Yet the two authors who contributed most to the establishment of a modern connection between Italy and beauty held diametrically opposed political views: whereas Mme de Staël was fiercely anti-Napoleonic, Stendhal was a Napoleonic sympathiser. The fact that the identification of Italy with women crossed political alignments shows that the practice was a cultural one not motivated by a single design. However, there were marked differences in the way that women were depicted. Stendhal may have been 'deeply influenced by Staël',[38] but he elaborated a male point of view on Italy which stressed the beauty of its women while denying them any actual or potential creative role.

Because of the quantity and quality of his writings, Stendhal is the author who is most associated with the foreign passion for Italy. His relationship with the country was complex and motivated by a variety of personal, sexual, political, social and aesthetic concerns. As the leading theorist of 'Italy', as well as an analyst of sensations, he turned the myth of Italy into a sort of romantic religion. It has been said that his *Rome, Naples and Florence*, first published in 1826, is 'the portrait of an imaginary rather than a real Italy'.[39] Certainly, it is an idealised vision, the romanticised view of a man who saw Italy as the symbol of everything he aspired to in art, politics, social behaviour and love. Unlike many earlier authors, he paid systematic attention to the people, and in particular to Italian women.[40] There was a personal, erotic element here, given his passionate, but unfulfilled love for two real women, Angela Pietragrua and Mathilde Viscontini. But his observations go beyond the personal dimension. He saw Italy as the land of happiness and this was so at least in part because it possessed such an abundance of beauty, which was itself 'nothing but a *promise of happiness*'.[41]

Stendhal admired the naturalness of Italy, not merely the scenery but the lack of artfulness and artifice in social relations in comparison with his native France. Italian men, he found, were physically fine but generally dull. By contrast, 'the faces of the women time and again betrayed a passionate intelligence embodied in forms and features of the rarest beauty': 'Their hair and eyebrows tend to a deep magnificent auburn; their faces may at first seem sombre and reserved – yet wait a while, until some deep disturbance in the soul should rise up to breathe a sudden animation into the sleeping surface. . . . There were . . . instants when I, a foreigner, found something sombre, almost menacing, in the fine features of these Italian women'.[42] *Rome, Naples and Florence* is filled with references to women who are described as pretty, beautiful, still beautiful and uncommonly beautiful. Each city reveals new fair types for Stendhal to praise and evaluate. To the 'chilly perfection' of a leading French ballet dancer, he prefers the 'living, vivid *sensuality*' of her Italian counterpart.[43] The spontaneity of Italian women is lauded and the absence noted of 'those habitually sour-tempered females, such as I have met with in the North, in Geneva, for instance'. Repeatedly, he contrasts the sincere and disinterested attitude to love in Italy with the vanity of France and England.[44] There is little doubt that his point of view is marked by erotic interest. Whereas 'the English style of feminine beauty' harmonised most easily with 'the atmosphere of a ball-room', the Italian style was as wild and as unpredictable as the landscape.[45] Thanks to 'the fires that flash in Italian eyes', Stendhal was convinced that 'in Italy, even in the arms of the most venal of mistresses, no man need ever go in fear of boredom'. 'Caprice,' he observed, 'is ever on the watch, armed to affright the monster'.[46] Of his four categories of love, presented in his text De l'amour, one only was associated with Italy: physical love, a love that was brief and purely physical and that involved a male hunter and a female prey. 'Going hunting, meeting a fresh and beautiful peasant girl who runs off into the wood' was the manifestation of this type of love sketched by Stendhal.[47]

Stendhal was convinced that there was a close link between the achievements of Italy's artists and the beauty of its women. Unlike de Staël, however, he praised the women solely as the subjects without whose beauty and inspiration male artists could not have achieved so much.[48] As he saw it, artistic genius was a male quality that found inspiration in feminine beauty. On surveying the works assembled in the studio of a Milanese painter, the author launched into a singular panegyric:

Could there be anything more striking than the beltà folgorante of Signora R[uga], or the stirring loveliness of signora Marini, hinting as it does with unmistakable evidence of some sharp struggle between religion and sensibility? Could there be anything more fascinating than the beltà guidesca of signora Ghirlan[da], with its echoes of some Madonna by Guido Reni, and recalling, if less directly, certain heads of Niobe? All the purity of the various Madonnas by Sassoferrato is incarnate in the portrait of the pious signora A[nnoni]. And could there be anything more original than the portrait of signora N****, with its plain tale of youth and energy displayed in the service of a tempestuous and impassioned soul, as familiar with the machinations of intrigue as the Cardinal de Retz himself, who understood neither caution or restraint? This head, so fine yet bearing not a trace of the antique, seems to follow you to every corner of the painter's studio, with those vivacious, brilliant eyes which Homer bestows upon the goddess Minerva.[49]

Stendhal re-stated and elaborated the view that contemporary beauty contained within it echoes of the Renaissance masters Leonardo and Raphael. Here there was a double valorisation at work. On the one hand, the evaluation of the beauty of living women was ennobled and dignified by the establishment of a connection with the pictorial heritage. On the other, they were seen as the contemporary bearers of a heritage that was a vital aspect of the culture of Italy and not merely a closed experience belonging exclusively to the past. They were a promise and a resource for the future. It is significant that Stendhal made these connections without regard to class. Noble women and peasants alike fell under his gaze and drew flattering comment. Impressed, like some other travellers, by the relative lack of social hierarchy he found in Italy, he saw the country as a land of leisure where love was motivated by passion, 'where aristocratic *sensibility* and plebeian *energy* contrive by some miracle to exist side by side, neither quality sapping nor devouring the other'.[50]

Stendhal's masterpiece, *La Chartreuse de Parme*, developed many of the themes of his travel writings. Set in Italy during the Napoleonic conquest, it is a novel of love and war. Through the eyes of male characters, including the hero, Fabrice del Dongo, the reader is introduced to a variety of beautiful women. Most of these are aristocrats, and their beauty is evoked both by means of physical description and by association with the pictorial tradition of Renaissance art. The Marchesa del Dongo is described as being 'in the full bloom of her beauty . . . with those lovely eyes of an angelic sweetness, and the dusky gold of her hair which made such a perfect frame for the oval of that charming face'.[51] The French lieutenant, Robert, who is struck by her appearance, comments: 'I had in my room a *Herodias* by Leonardo da Vinci, which might have been her portrait'.

The Duchess Sanseverina is held up in the novel as the model of Italian beauty.[52] She is admired by Prince Ernesto, one of whose courtiers tells her that the Prince is dismayed to have no beauty to rival her at his court.[53] The prince notes, while she defiantly addresses him, that 'her face and figure attained at that moment to a sublime beauty'. Although she is making a firm political point to him, he is more influenced by her appearance, saying to himself, 'Great God! How beautiful she is! One ought to make some concessions to a woman who is so unique, when there probably is not another like her in the whole of Italy'.[54] However, in a subsequent passage, Stendhal suggests that she had 'a little too much of the *recognized* beauty of the ideal type, and her truly Lombard head recalled the voluptuous smile and tender melancholy of Leonardo's lovely paintings of Herodias'.[55] The Duchess sparkles with wit and irony and passionately engages with all the subjects of conversation that come up, but she adds nothing to the established canon of Italian beauty. This observation reveals the author's desire to identify a beauty possessed of a more present-day spirit.

In the course of the novel several comparisons are made between the Duchessa and Clelia, the daughter of General Fabio Conti. Clelia is described as charming and, although only an adolescent, 'the best-looking person in the States of the Prince' save for La Sanseverina.[56] She immediately strikes the hero Fabrice, although at first she lacks animation. Whereas the Duchess offers an earthly beauty, Clelia's is a 'heavenly beauty' that enraptures Fabrice when he casually meets her for the second time. It is noteworthy that her beauty is not quite of the classical type:

Clelia Conti was a young girl still a trifle too slim, who might be compared to the beautiful models of Guido Reni. We make no attempt to conceal the fact that, according to Greek ideas of beauty, the objections might have been made that her head had certain features a trifle too strongly marked; the lips, for instance, though full of the most touching charm, were a little too substantial. The admirable peculiarity of this face in which shone the artless graces and heavenly imprint of the most noble soul was that, albeit of the rarest and most singular beauty, it did not in any way resemble the heads of Greek sculpture.[57]

In contrast to the Duchess's passion, Clelia is aloof and possessed of 'that manner as though of a person superior to everything'. She shows herself 'calm and slow to move, whether from contempt for her natural surroundings or from regret for some unfulfilled dream'. Unlike the worldly Duchess, she shows no interest in going to balls and is thought to be destined for the religious life. Stendhal makes the comment that in England and France, 'lands of vanity' as he calls them, the beauty and attitude of Clelia would be valued above the qualities of the Duchess. But, in his own view, in a striking authorial intervention, he states that precisely the aloofness and self-possession of the younger woman 'weighed down the balance in her rival's favour'.[58] However, the reader is led to believe that there is a potential passion in Clelia's soul. Her father, General Conti, is of the view that his daughter's eyes are finer than the Duchess's and that they are occasionally animated by passion and life. This never occurs, he regrets, in a drawing-room, but only when they are out driving alone and some injustice or suffering comes to her attention. Otherwise, she seems to prefer her 'beloved solitude' and 'secret thoughts' to society.

It is the knowledge that Fabrice, her admirer, who has since taken up religious orders, has been arrested that transforms her. At this point she believes him to be the lover of the Duchess, but, despite this, the unacknowledged feeling developing in her soul for him gives her a new radiance. At a party given by the Minister of the Interior at which, on account of her father's position, she learns of the arrest, Clelia's beauty is deemed, unusually, to outshine that of the Duchess. 'The beautiful eyes of the girl wore an expression so singular and so profound as to be almost indiscreet'. As 'the two reigning beauties' converse, 'the girl's eyes showed more fire, and indeed, if one may use the term, more passion, than those of the beautiful Duchessa'.[59] For the first time, her charms emerge fully and the cause, immediately suspected by the Duchess, is a burgeoning love in her heart.

From the point of view of Stendhal's treatment of Italian beauty, these passages are of great interest. Clelia is a classical romantic heroine, virginal, composed, inward-looking. There is little or nothing about her that conveys the sort of 'Italian' qualities that the author praised in his travel writings. Her hair is described as being 'of an ashen fairness', which stands out against 'cheeks that were delicately tinted but, as a rule, rather too pale'.[60] Like Corinne's conventional half-sister Lucile, she is an innocent and demure young woman who lacks the earthy sensuality of the Duchess. Not by chance, she is compared to the aloof models of Reni rather than the darker, more terrestrial beauties of Leonardo. It is clear that Stendhal's own preferences broadly lie with the Duchess, who has the qualities of caprice and animation he admired. It is the literary transfer of some of the qualities of the latter to Clelia that bring her to life and turn her into a more developed, and more 'Italian' figure. In the final stages of the novel, she becomes a worthy heroine, her beauty and her soul brought to life by passion. When she visits Fabrice in prison, believing him about to die from poisoning, she impulsively gives herself to him. 'She was so beautiful, half unclad and in this state of intense passion, that Fabrice could not resist an almost unconscious impulse. No resistance was offered him', Stendhal writes.

The transformation of Clelia from contemplative, romantic heroine into a beautiful, active, sexual woman brought her more in line with the author's own preferences. It was also an allegory for the transformation that he augured for Italy. Published in 1839, long after the Napoleonic era had given way to the Restoration, the novel is set in the period before 1815. As Italians once more appeared resigned under the yoke of repression, Stendhal offered them clues as to how to mobilise their spirit and passion to take hold of their destiny. However, Clelia's passion, unlike that of de Staël's Corinne, was clearly the fruit of a male imagination.

De Lamartine

The Stendhalian perspective on Italian beauty developed in tandem with the progressive eclipse of de Staël and her work.[61] Over the nineteenth century, her standing declined as the hierarchical gender order of bourgeois society became normative. The most comprehensive dismissal was supplied by the French writer, poet and politician Alphonse de Lamartine. An ardent admirer of de Staël during his youth, he argued in a late essay that creative genius was incompatible with feminine delicacy. By becoming a prominent figure in the world of letters early in her adult life, de Staël had, he claimed, lost 'the charming modesty appropriate to her sex and her age' and that 'modesty of soul' that was the essence of femininity.[62] She would, in other words, have been better off leaving writing to men and cultivating her feminine qualities. De Lamartine's attitude sheds light on his own literary depiction of an Italian woman.

Of all the works produced by foreign writers during the Risorgimento, few enjoyed more success than the 1852 novel *Graziella*. Ostensibly, there was no connection at all between its content and the political situation in the peninsula. Yet the author's sympathy for Italy's national aspirations was well known and was woven into *Graziella*. In keeping with the author's democratic beliefs, the novel's heroine is not an aristocrat but the humble daughter of a fisherman of Procida in the Bay of Naples. De Lamartine had made many visits to Italy and was an attaché at the French embassy in Rome from 1825 to 1829. By employing the picturesque setting of the Bay of Naples, he ensured that the allure of Italy's established aesthetic appeal was used to communicate the political message. By comparison with the more subtle appeals of other cities, Naples was obvious; its fascination derived from an unusually spectacular combination of sea, light, mountains, landscape and volcano. By setting his tale in deepest Italy, de Lamartine showed a commitment to the aspiration for an Italy in which all parts of the country would be incorporated. As the region that was most remote from modern civilisation, southern Italy was seen as containing people and places that were close to both classical antiquity and nature, terms which broadly coincided in the Romantic intellectual outlook.[63]

Graziella lacks the grace and refinement of de Staël's intellectual heroine Corinne. She is not associated with an artistic and cultural tradition which, in de Lamartine's view, rested on the work of male creators, but rather is closely identified with natural beauty. It is not Italy's cultivation she represents but its population and sensual habitat, although it is also worth noting that, even though she is not in any way noble, she possesses the same type of statuesque, dignified beauty as Corinne. Moreover, she is compared favourably to the women of other countries, in particular to those of 'our countries' of the north. Graziella is dark and attractive, and a dancer of the tarantella. Wild yet reserved, she is a creature of drama and passion. It is these various qualities that make her the object of the rapt attention of a young foreigner of noble extraction who finds her sexually irresistible. As with de Staël, it is de Lamartine's first description of Graziella that sets out most fully and explicitly his vision of his heroine. Walking at night, the male protagonist and a friend hear a sleepy voice and a window opening, through which they catch sight of 'the silhouette of a ravishing young woman through the shutters'.[64] The dark-haired girl is partly undressed:

The nightshirt, fastened around the neck, permitted a glimpse of a tall and slim figure whose soft youthful curves were barely outlined by the material. Her large eyes were of that colour that is situated uncertainly between deep black and sea blue, whose splendour, softened by a tearful expression, contains in equal proportions in a woman's eyes tenderness of spirit and force of passion; celestial tint that the eyes of the women of Asia and of Italy steal from the burning light of the day and the calm blue of their skies, of their sea and their nights. Her cheeks were full and rounded, firm in outline and of a colour that lay between the slightly pale and the lightly bronzed by the air, not the sickly pallour of the North, rather the healthy white of the South that is similar to the shade of marble that has been exposed for centuries to the air and the water. Her mouth, with lips that were more open and generous than those of the women of our countries, expressed candour and goodness. Her teeth, small but flashing, caught the reflex of our torch like splinters of mother of pearl under the glistening surface of the sun-beaten sea.

Graziella is explicitly described in relation to the sea, the sun and the sky that form her natural frame. She is a creature of her environment who can be perfectly understood and explained in relation to that natural context.

It is significant that the figure of Graziella was not entirely fictional. De Lamartine's posthumously-published memoirs revealed that his novel had been based on a true encounter that took place in 1812.[65] Like other travellers, he had gone to Italy with the intention of improving his mind and instead found himself struck by the sexual opportunities that were available to him.[66] It was by drawing on his own memories of a youthful seduction that he was able to render Graziella both individual and iconic. She is an erotic object but, long after departure, the author's hero is unable to forget her. Attilio Brilli argues that her description was relatively unstereotypical, because the 'imaginary undressing of Graziella . . . hints at a body underneath the clothes, a physical reality beneath the Oriental finery, a person beneath the folklore and the stereotype'.[67] In fact, it was the focus on the body that situated Graziella in the realm of the masculine conception of a woman without culture or autonomy. This also lent her some of the allegorical qualities of a symbolic woman.

Graziella was the first fully-articulated expression of the stereotype of the vital and passionate southern Italian peasant girl. Whereas Stendhal's female figures had been varied, de Lamartine proposed just one. The novel was an immediate success in France and was widely read abroad. It had a considerable effect on the visual arts. In contrast to the empty landscapes, southern peasant girls now provided the code through which Italy was most commonly visualised and interpreted. They had already been present but now they assumed an unprecedented prominence. Like other stereotypes, this one offered a general, and therefore at least partially false, summary of real traits or features. Stereotypes are always based on superficial impressions and a firm conviction that those impressions will always be renewed and reinforced. They define phenomena in such a way that their essence can apparently be captured by simplification.[68] The cultural and physical distance that separated travellers from the native Italian population had already given rise to a range of sometimes contradictory, but generally interlocking, stereotypes that proved to be remarkably durable. The simplifications inherent in them confirmed some negative images of Italians as primitive and violent, dishonest and ignorant. However, de Lamartine's synthesis confirmed that stereotypes could also be pleasurable and emblematic.[69] His creation synthesised in a single portrait the main traits that foreigners associated with the peninsula.

Manzoni's Lucia

Foreigners continued to create images of Italy, but increasingly Italians also sought to define the imagined contours of their country. Writers and artists contributed to the national awakening that would develop fully in the Risorgimento. The narratives of many nations were shaped in the early nineteenth century by historical novels that traced the original characteristics of a community. In the wake of Walter Scott, whose works enjoyed great popularity throughout Europe and beyond, authors wove tales of chivalry, heroism, love and sacrifice and, in doing so, fuelled a largely mythical sense of their own country's past.[70] In Italy as elsewhere, the novels always featured canonical heroes and heroines, evil oppressors and a vast cast of minor characters. Writers including Guerrazzi, d'Azeglio and others used medieval or other remote settings to develop narratives that were really about the present.

The theme of foreign occupation and tyrannical political authority was central to
I promessi sposi (The Betrothed), the great historical novel published by Alessandro Manzoni
in 1827. An admirer of Scott's works, Manzoni set about writing a novel that was no less stirring and adventurous. *I promessi sposi* is set in 1628 to 1630 in Lombardy during the period
of Spanish domination. It depicts the Milan of the Thirty Years War and features oppression,
bread riots and the plague. Manzoni undertook considerable historical research for the novel
but it is clear that he was no less keen to ensure that it breathed the contemporary air of the
Viennese occupation of the Restoration period. The novel is full of signs that the author
wanted it to be a contribution to national literature. The language is rich and indeed it was
rewritten by Manzoni in Tuscan Italian for a new edition in 1840. Especially in this second
edition, the novel bolstered nationalist aspirations. The characters are varied and fascinating
and, crucially, the heroes are not nobles, as was the convention in historical novels, but two
simple peasants, Renzo Tramaglino and Lucia Mondella. This was a highly significant departure from custom that demonstrated a democratic commitment to the nation as a phenomenon based on brotherhood and equality.

Writers and artists sought in various ways to define a place for young Italian
women as symbolic bearers of national aspirations and characteristics. Lucia, the most
famous literary *italiana* of the nineteenth century, has two features in common with
the sort of young Italian women that foreigners depicted: she is a peasant and, like
Corinne, she is dark-haired rather than blonde in the usual manner of a literary

2 Manzoni's heroine 'Lucia
Mondella', in the officially-approved
illustration by Francesco Gonin.

heroine. This choice, according to Verina Jones, 'implied a flagrant break with the literary canon'.[71] In all literature from medieval and Renaissance times, blonde had signified beauty and dark hair some form of evil. Much more conventional was the darkness of the anti-heroine of *I promessi sposi*, Gertrude, the aristocratic and sinful nun of Monza. She is a standard dark lady, arrogant and aloof, menacing and the possessor of a 'disorderly beauty'. So strong was this tradition that de Staël's inversion had barely dented it.

Lucia is also sweet, modest, timid, pure and reserved. Far from being a wild, sexually available temptress, she is devout and virginal. This reflected Manzoni's own Catholicism, which permeates the entire novel. Much has been written about the influence of Catholic thought on Manzoni's work.[72] Certainly, Lucia embodies goodness and godliness. Her innocence also explains her dignity and refusal when faced with the lecherous Don Rodrigo, who is determined to block her marriage to Renzo and make her his mistress. This refusal to bend to the will of a powerful outsider and her determination, in the face of obstacles, to make her own life, was an allegory for the path that Italian patriots were seeking to tread. For Manzoni, her virginity was a better metaphor for national independence than the sexual passion of Stendhal's Clelia.[73]

Lucia is not particularly beautiful. In fact, while an earlier draft of the text referred to her 'uncommon beauty', the final one describes only her 'modest beauty'. The picture of her by Francesco Gonin that was approved by Manzoni for the 1840 illustrated edition of his novel confirms this.[74] She is, according to Jones, typical of the woman who is 'angel of the hearth, not very exciting but down-to-earth and good-natured'.[75] In other words, she is blonde, in the manner of a fictional heroine, in all respects except her hair colour. She is brown-haired precisely because this would have been typical of Lombard peasant women. In successive drafts of the novel, Lucia gradually loses charm and individuality and becomes more typical. In other words, she is removed from the realm of literary references and placed in relation to a real context. Indeed, at the end of the novel, when Renzo and Lucia, now married, settle in Bergamo, their neighbours are disappointed to find that she does not have the aspect of a heroine 'with hair that is truly golden' but is rather 'a peasant girl just like many others'.[76] In this perspective, Lucia becomes an emblem of the ordinary Italian girl who is reclaimed from the foreign authors who had represented her.

Some were not convinced that Lucia was suitable as a symbol. The literary historian and politician Francesco De Sanctis observed that she was 'a first version of an ideal and rather passive' who did not really have 'enough substance to be worthy of representing a poetic ideal'. She seemed too abstract and too remote, too saintly, as though she were a Madonna.[77] For others, it was this abstraction that permitted her to assume a universal status. It might be added that there are two ways in which Lucia remained beautiful. First, she clearly has sufficient allure to attract the attentions of a predatory nobleman who sets about thwarting her marriage plans. Second, she has an inner beauty that stems from her virtue. For Manzoni, if not for secular artists, this was the key feature, a quality that made her truly beautiful.[78] Manzoni pulled back from using feminine physical beauty as a central myth of the patriotic cause because it was secular or pagan. Ultimately, he preferred to bring other elements, such as language, to the fore. However, the emphasis he placed on virtue and female honour, and the gap that he established between a moral peasantry and the corrupt mores of aristocracy, ensured that his heroine became an emblematic figure in the literature of the new nation.

Art and the Risorgimento

The aim of those who believed in the nationalist cause was to free the peninsula of foreign domination, overcome internal divisions and assert Italy's rightful influence in the world. To achieve this, myths and symbols were required that could arouse emotions and provoke feelings of loyalty. There were obvious difficulties with this process, since the nationalist cause was a subversive one. But much cultural work could be undertaken without engaging directly in political activity. Italian nationalists sometimes shared with foreigners a dim view of the vices of their fellow countrymen.[79] But they also attached importance to the task of identifying and promoting awareness of the 'natural' elements that Italians shared.[80] These included geographical location, elements of a common language, the artistic and cultural heritage, and a sense of belonging to the same racial group.

The origins of the symbolic representation of Italy, a figure bearing a turreted headwear who was known as 'Italia', have not been investigated as thoroughly as those of the French 'Marianne', the British figure 'Britannia' or the American 'Columbia'. Images of Italia first entered general circulation in the early 1700s and were informed by the celebrated text by Cesare Ripa and published in 1618 entitled *Iconologia*.[81] This handbook of representations offered an unusual compendium of female incarnations of cities, moods and attitudes. Despite this, the allegorical figure of Italia was given what has been called a 'weak elaboration' in the iconography of the first half of the nineteenth century.[82] Compared to the extraordinary quantity of French symbolic images, as well as the allegorical images of other nations, female representations of Italy were few. In part, of course, this can be explained by the repressive political situation in parts of the peninsula.[83] Precisely because the struggle for independence faced obstacles and repression, approaches to the topic were sometimes oblique and indirect.

With French influence, symbolic figures were occasionally employed in the Napoleonic period. Of particular note is the figure carved by Antonio Canova between 1806 and 1810 for the tomb of the poet Vittorio Alfieri. According to Fernando Mazzocca, this statue, which is located in the Church of Santa Croce in Florence, follows exactly the canons set out by Ripa. She is solemn and wears a head-dress of towers; her attitude is that of a mother who cries for one of her most illustrious sons. The statue attracted wide attention on account of its beauty and the significance of its location in the main pantheon of Italy's artistic greats. The young Massimo d'Azeglio even commented that, with this sculpture, Canova 'gave the first breath to national life'.[84] Patriots were united in drawing inspiration from the beauty and nobility of an

3 'Italia' from Cesare Ripa's
compendium of allegorical
representations *Iconologia* (1603).

embodiment that somehow represented a synthesis of the talents of two great artists: Alfieri and Canova. When the poet Ugo Foscolo saw it, he exclaimed, 'Italia is really beautiful! Beautiful!'[85] The statue became a propaganda weapon for those who wanted to give a political expression to a national spirit that could not be trampled on by the foreigners who were occupying parts of the peninsula. Ultimately, the tears of Italy were an expression of unhappiness for those who faced sacrifice or exile because of the lack of an Italian state. The Romantic poet Giacomo Leopardi expressed a similar frustration with the prevailing circumstances in his 1818 poem 'All'Italia', in which he symbolically identified the country as a 'formosissima donna' (woman most fair):

> Io chiedo al cielo
> E al mondo dite dite:
> chi la ridusse a tale? E questo e' peggio,
> che di catene ha carche ambe le braccia;
> siche sparte le chiome e senza velo
> siede in terra negletta e sconsolata,
> nascondendo la faccia
> tra le ginocchia, e piange.
>
> (To heaven I cry
> And to the world declare:

Who reduced her to this? And worst of all,
Bound both her arms with chains;
So now, dishevelled and unveiled
She sits on barren and unhappy land,
Hiding her face between
Her knees, crying.)

As a civil painter with a strong sense of the power of allegory, Francesco Hayez often used themes and subjects to convey nationalist messages to those who wished to read them. Produced in several versions between 1848 and 1851, his paintings *Melancholia* and *La meditazione* depict a dark-haired and pale-skinned young woman whose breast, in two versions, is exposed. A precise link has been established between this emblematic young beauty and the historical moment of the production of the paintings. Her melancholic attitude is explicitly connected to the failed hopes of 1848 and the Cinque Giornate in Milan. Indeed, it has been shown that the original title of the painting *La meditazione* was *Italia nel 1848*.[86] In the first version, the woman is of higher social class; in later ones her elaborate gown is exchanged for a simple, loose-fitting white dress that may even be an undergarment. This removes the connotations of class and turns her into an allegorical Italian female figure embodying a collective sentiment. Her beauty is a sign of health and harmony, while her exposed breast connects her with an emerging pictorial code for nationhood.[87] Hayez's paintings of women generally avoid the martial or sacrificial bearing of depictions of Italia. They were intended to be 'a novel depiction of the image of Italy, the land where the allure of the ancient still combined with the beauty of a blessed Nature. But the sadness that shadowed her face alluded to a political situation that was not equally propitious and which was destined to worsen still further after the bitter disappointment of 1848'.[88] The loss the following year of any remaining hopes of a national revolution was a major setback for patriots.

Melancholy was by no means Hayez's only mood, but it was a recurrent one. His 1842 painting *La ciociara* (woman of Ciociaria) shows a beautiful peasant woman seated against a background of a magnificent landscape. Her isolation, while emblematic, does not suggest any Stendhalian happiness. As a painter of the Risorgimento, Hayez is best known for his paintings entitled *Il bacio* (The Kiss), produced in two versions in 1857 and 1867, based on his earlier *Romeo e Giulietta* (Romeo and Juliet) of 1823. The painting depicts a soldier kissing a woman goodbye. Although the costumes and setting suggest the fourteenth century, it was read as the image of a Garibaldian volunteer in the act of kissing his beloved farewell. The interruption of intimacy it depicts was entirely in keeping with the idea of patriotic duty as a matter for men alone.[89] The soldier puts his personal sentiments below the higher love he feels for his country.

Hayez's preference for allusion and historical allegories was not shared by the mainly Tuscan 'Macchiaioli'. These painters adopted an iconoclastic approach to art that owed something to French impressionism. They rejected the formal rhetoric and exaggerated

4 *La ciociara* by Francesco Hayez, one of many emblematic paintings of peasant girls.

imagery of some nationalism and championed a more immediate and overt engagement with the national cause.[90] Several of them fought with Garibaldi. Although none of the Macchiaioli paintings show urban working-class women or carry any suggestion of the political consciousness of peasant and working women,[91] their many depictions of women in a variety of situations and attitudes showed a desire to draw them into the nation in ways that did not reduce them to allegorical symbols. Some, indeed, even show women as readers and painters, surrounded by books and artistic paraphernalia. However, they do not escape the gendered pattern of power that was specific to bourgeois society. This sexual division took shape in the work of thinkers like Rousseau and constituted a key presupposition of the formation of the modern nation.[92] Pictorial realism therefore bore witness to female subordination. Some of the best-known patriotic paintings by the Macchiaioli depict women providing support for male combatants and sewing national flags. Odoardo Borrani's *Il 26 aprile 1859* shows a young woman at home in Florence intently sewing a tricolour flag, a small open window offering the only link to the wider world. The date was the eve of the peaceful revolution that would see the Austrians ousted from the city and the Italian flag raised above the Fortezza da Basso. With such imagery, the painters accorded women a place in the struggle for independence and national unification while also confirming the division between male and female spheres.

5 *La meditazione* by Francesco Hayez, also known as 'Italy in 1848'.

This is true even of the boldest painting associating women with the tricolour flag, Carlo Stragliati's *Episodio delle Cinque Giornate* (Episode from the Five Days), which refers to one of the most glorious episodes of the Risorgimento, when a popular revolt in Milan in March 1848 succeeded in briefly wresting control of the city from the Austrians. The painting shows two joyful young women, one of whom is dressed in patriotic red, white and green, waving a large Italian flag on a pole from an open window. Below them, crowds are gathered in the Milan streets also waving patriotic flags, while to their side a seated old woman appears to be smiling at them. The contrast between the humble older woman, who is clutching a rosary and has at her feet a sewing basket, and the vivacious enthusiasm of the girls, signals a generational break. However, the impact of this is tempered by the fact that the women of all generations are in the home. Only men occupy the street below, the spectator must assume.[93] For all the presence of realistic women in the work of the artists, their role in the final analysis is a supporting one that is most significant on the symbolic plane.

One foreign author who timidly brought a female character to the forefront in his account of the process of unification was the English writer George Meredith. Best known today for his novel *The Egoist*, he brought the theme of national unification into two of his earlier works. In both *Emilia in England* (later re-titled *Sandra Belloni*) and

6 *Il 26 aprile 1859* by Odoardo
Borrani illustrates a young woman
sewing a flag that will be waved the
following day during the peaceful
revolution that outsted the Austrians
from Florence.

Vittoria, Italy is personified by a young woman. Like de Staël's Corinne, Meredith's
heroine, Emilia, is half-English. She is not a genius or educated, and in this respect she is
a lesser figure than Corinne, but she is simple, natural and passionate and she is devoted
to music and to the cause of Italian freedom. She has dark eyes, 'particular charms of
feature' and 'possessed an incomprehensible attractiveness'.[94] Her problems with her
indecisive lover Wilfred Pole recall Corinne's with Oswald Nelvil. Compared to the cold
and reserved English women – the sisters of Wilfred – who populate the novel, Emilia is
a warm, passionate woman who speaks without reservation of her feelings for Wilfred,
whom she openly describes as her lover.

In *Vittoria*, a novel originally conceived as a sequel to *Emilia in England*, the heroine is
no longer named Emilia, but Vittoria, although the two women have much in common.
Reputedly, the character was inspired by Jessie White, an English woman who was influenced by Mazzini and spent much time with Garibaldi. A great propagandist for the
Italian cause, she married a Venetian exile, Alberto Mario, who she met while in prison
in Piedmont in 1857. The novel's convoluted plot sets a variety of personal stories against
the backdrop of the struggle for Italian unification. For Meredith, a passionate supporter
of the Italian cause, it depicted the development of individuals through experience and
the pressure on them of social forces. Whereas Emilia had held back from travelling to

7 *Episodio delle Cinque Giornate* by Carlo Stragliati shows the patriotic fervour of two young women who nonetheless remain confined within the domestic space.

Italy to participate in the insurrection because she felt herself to be immature, in her new guise she is given the task of triggering the revolt by singing a patriotic song at the end of an allegorical opera which has somehow won the approval of the Austrian censors. At the end of the novel, she is left holding the lifeless body of her patriot husband, Carlo, who has been killed in an ambush.

Meredith makes Vittoria's mourning coincide with the struggle for freedom and situates her life and her talent at the centre of a ceremony of national foundation. In the final passages of the novel, he has her intervene at a grand event to give thanks for liberty. At this ceremony, 'when an Emperor and a King stood beneath the vault of the grand Duomo, and an organ and a peal of voices rendered thanks to heaven for liberty, [she] could show the fruit of her devotion in the dark-eyed boy', that is her son. 'And then once more, but for once', writes Meredith, 'her voice was heard in Milan'.[95] The real event alluded to here is the visit of Kaiser Wilhem I to Milan in October 1875, an occasion that was marked by numerous musical and other festivities. Within this official frame, the woman who has not only lent her beauty and her talent to her country, but who has also produced a son, takes her final bow before returning to anonymity. The symbolic affirmation of the rule of men signals not just the end of the story but the end of any extraordinary role for women.

The foreigner's gaze on unified Italy

The dramatic events that led to Italy's unification in 1861 aroused great sympathy among foreign observers and supporters of the national cause. However, they did not fundamentally shift the way Italy or the Italians were viewed. The creation of the Italian state was a political innovation that brought relatively few cultural changes. This especially applied to the custom of appreciation of Italian women. Old stereotypes persisted, even if they were more likely to be tempered by some sensitivity to the people, their individuality and their evolving situation. Sometimes they were accompanied by judgements about the progress that had occurred or the lack of it. The Goncourt brothers, for example, brought to their travels the same inquisitive and flaneurial eye that they cast over the Paris of their time. They travelled to the peninsula in 1855 to 1856 and then again in 1867, bringing with them two grids of interpretation: on the one hand, the pictorial heritage and, on the other, contemporary Paris.[96] Influenced by Stendhal, like many before and after them, the brothers found Italy to be a land where everything was beautiful: 'Everything is beautiful here: women, the sky, flowers are crudely, brutally, materially beautiful. The beauty of a woman is the beauty of an animal. The horizon is uninterrupted, the landscape is devoid of atmosphere and imagination. The cloudy mystification of everything in the North does not exist here'.[97] On the street, they were struck by the wild hair of girls, which was so black that it seemed blue. Darkness was still the feature that, in the eyes of foreigners, most readily distinguished the Italian woman. In Rome, which would not become the capital until 1870, the brothers found little of the flame of nationalism and instead noted the persistence of a historic indolence. 'The beauty of the features of the women of the people in Rome has something of the beauty that one sees on the faces of the dead,' they observed. Apart from their burning eyes, they found their movements slow and sleepy, 'with that slightly scary inhuman quality of waxworks'. What marked them out was 'the static quality of a fatalistic sadness, which is probably inherited from an ancient Etruscan sense of gravity'.[98]

The ambiguity of these attitudes was apparent in the fact that foreigners would never cease to prefer their Italians to be instinctive and 'natural'. Moreover, the beauty of women still provided one of the main terrains on which the Italians were judged, with the pictorial frame remaining popular. Frequently, women were described in relation to specific cities and regions. Théophile Gautier, for example, observed of Venice that 'one still finds there in reality the models of Jean Bellin, Giorgione, Titian and Veronese'.[99] Even though 'the brown southern type is very rare in Venice among the women', there was still a marked difference with respect to northern countries, where the anxieties of civilisation spoiled the countenance of the women:

> Their noses are more pure, strong and more bony than northern noses, and are always full of the unexpected and caprice. Their eyes also have a brilliant placidness that is

unknown in our country and that recalls the clarity of expression of an animal. They are often black despite the fair colouring of the hair. Their mouths have this grimace that is a sort of smile but full of the haughtiness and charm which endows the heads of the Italian old masters with such character.[100]

He concluded that, 'After a walk in the public gardens, one is no longer surprised by the golden splendour of the Venetian school. That which was assumed to be a dream of artists is nothing other than the translation of a reality that is sometimes superior'.[101]

The expansion of organised tourism reinforced and rendered more widespread among foreigners some of the more picturesque qualities of Italy. Writers no longer embarked on an adventure but sought to supply a market, the same market that eagerly bought pictures and prints of Italian subjects. This attitude was matched by a desire to construct an inventory, to identify sights, facts and events that could sum up Italy. Published in 1865, the two volumes of the historian Hyppolyte Taine's *Voyage en Italie*, a highly pedagogical guide to the artistic treasures of the peninsula, were an influential example of the sort of mixture of aesthetic and social commentary readers expected. The book went through more than fifteen editions and was still in print after the First World War. Interestingly, Taine felt that the specificity of Italian customs, especially naturalness and love as passion, those qualities praised by Stendhal, were in decline. He found parts of Italy, in Tuscany and Umbria especially, that were very similar to the France of the Midi. The small towns and villages were a sort of 'backward France, a younger sister who is growing up and beginning to resemble her older sibling'.[102] As Italy took shape as a nation, it was modelling itself on its neighbours, and particularly on France 'the foremost Latin nation'. But he still was able to highlight the lack of cynicism and vanity in the Italian attitude to love. In Bologna, he observed four handsome women walking one morning with a proud and confident air: 'one cannot imagine a more naturally triumphant physical presence, a similar attitude of the *prima donna* on the street. With such character, such spirit and the fantasy of men, they must be mistresses'.[103] The faces of young people in Florence were notable for their air of being in love, their gracious smiles and tender and spontaneous expressions – the opposite of the dry, mocking attitude to be found in France.[104] In his view, the strong, expressive heads of Florentine women, their striking dark hair and sweet airs gave them a nobility that was exactly as depicted by artists and painters. 'One finds among them', Taine noted, 'the same character as goddesses and allegorical goddesses, their heads are small, round, crudely merry and sensual.'[105] Taine observed the girls taking the air on their balconies in Rome and commented on the difference between the decayed housing and the beauty and vigour of the youth that lived in them. Like many earlier visitors, his eye was taken with their 'vigorous, expressive heads', 'lustrous black hair', 'flashing eyes' and fresh clothes.[106]

Garibaldi's female figures

After unification, the female figure of Italia was one of the symbols that was attached to officialdom. The process of rooting the monarchy and building support around it, however, was a long and difficult one that involved the forging of social alliances, changes to topography, the building of statues and the mobilisation of symbols and sentiments. The female representation of the nation was employed in Garibaldi's declarations of 1861 and on numerous calendars, and was embroidered on to the throne that was created for King Vittorio Emanuele II in Florence in 1866.[107] Italia also appeared on coins and postage stamps, as well as regimental insignia. Like her counterparts in other countries, she served certain purposes since such national figures allowed an individual empathy with public events or campaigns that went beyond official or political symbols.[108] On a par with Marianne, Italia was not of aristocratic extraction but rather a generic woman of the people endowed with some of the attributes of a goddess. She was not refined and composed but a near savage, a creature of instinct and passion who was meant to evoke blind loyalty to the nation. She served certain purposes since 'the personalization of the nation established a language of psychological connection to the country that ran deeply beneath religious or political obligations'.[109] Generally, she was represented as a generously built, statuesque figure with a full bosom and dark, flowing hair. She appeared as a figure of abundance and of pleasure, willing to give herself in any useful way to the nation or to those who would sacrifice themselves for it. Italia was never depicted by great artists, but rather by popular illustrators who took full account of common tastes and expectations. It even became commonplace at the end of musical stage shows for a woman to appear in the guise of Italia, waving the national flag. The presence of such a figure showed the power of political will and its capacity to encompass all, at least symbolically. 'Every state will define its own "wild" differently and then try to annex it', Marina Warner has observed.[110] Thus the dark mane and full figure of Italia, her carnality and instinct, symbolised the lower classes and the turbulent and fragmented history of the peninsula.

In the Italian context, the pagan and classical heritage of goddesses and allegorical figures was balanced by a strong Catholic influence in culture and society. As the case of Manzoni illustrates, female beauty was considered less by Catholics in relation to physical appearances than to moral qualities. From this point of view, in Italy the nineteenth century was a 'century of hagiographical female virtues'. For Michela De Giorgio, beauty was represented 'much more with the signs of the spirit than with the signs of the body'.[111] In a context marked by a substantial 'decorporisation', the physical manifestations of feminine beauty, that had been accorded such high value in earlier centuries, were given little status. The patriotic drive shifted this, but only modestly. After Hayez, nudity was virtually unknown. Thus the literary creation that came to symbolise most clearly the aspirations of the Italians for independence and freedom was not a vivacious and primitive peasant girl but the pious and demure peasant bride-to-be Lucia, whose morality was more evident than her beauty.

8 and 9 Regimental postcards. Both cards employ images of a strong and shapely 'Italia' to celebrate the vitality of the new country.

Nevertheless, the 1860s witnessed a proliferation of images, some of which were novel. In general, the ideal of the dark-haired peasant beauty that had taken shape during the Risorgimento was more associated with radicals and democrats than with the political or cultural elite. It stood for the deep Italy that had not been fully drawn into the process of unification and that was excluded from power. In this connection, the novels written by Giuseppe Garibaldi during his years of semi-exile on Caprera are of great interest. Although they are of scant literary value, they sought to provide an account, using the form of the historical novel, of the various events that had led up to unification and the subsequent conquest of Rome. They also offered a critique of some perceived Italian vices and some beacons for the future. The latter took the form of human examples of beauty, courage, patriotism and self-sacrifice.

It is Garibaldi's female characters who mostly bear the burden of his hopes. Although he wrote one novel which remained unpublished in his lifetime and for many years afterwards, that was dedicated to a male hero, to whom he gave the name of his own son, Manlio,[112] it is his women who figure most prominently. His outlook was shaped by his Brazilian-born wife, Anita, who fought alongside him and had died in 1849 after the fall of the Roman Republic. He also knew Jessie White well, as well as the American journalist Margaret Fuller, who, like White, married an Italian patriot.

Clelia ovvero il governo dei preti (Clelia, or the government of priests), is set in the time of the Roman Republic and recounts the story of three women of very different backgrounds who join together to serve the cause of national unity. One of these, Giulia, is a wealthy English woman, who is a friend of Italy. The other two are Roman: Irene, the aristocratic daughter of a prince, and Clelia, a young woman of the people, who is the true heroine of the novel. All three are said to be 'of rare beauty'.[113] Giulia is described as 'the very beautiful daughter of Albion', while Irene is said to be a Roman type and to have 'an angelic smile', 'very beautiful cheeks' and black eyes and hair.[114] Her standing is reflected in an 'enchanting and majestic deportment'. However, it is the beauty of Clelia, 'the pearl of Trastevere', that is most radiant. She had 'brown, thick plaits', and remarkable eyes:

> Their flash struck like lightning whoever dared to stare at her. At sixteen, her deportment was as dignified as that of a matron of ancient times. Oh! Raphael would have found in Clelia all the graces of his ideal girl combined with the robust virility of her ancient Roman namesake who threw herself into the Tiber in order to escape Porsenna's Etruscan prison camp. . . . It was said that Clelia had the angelic traits of her mother and the robust, majestic dignity of her father.[115]

There are male patriots in the novel, but one of them expresses the view that only the women will be able to cleanse Italy of its shameful subordination to the foreigners and the clergy. Similar views are expressed by the hero of another novel, *Cantoni il volontario* (Cantoni the volunteer), who exclaims that 'the women should lead the human family'.[116] Cantoni, in fact, is only fifteen years old when he volunteers to join the patriotic forces, but he is handsome and heroic enough to attract the keen attention of a fourteen-year old, Ida, 'the most beautiful of the daughters of Felsina', when he marches through Bologna with the volunteers. She runs away from home to be with him, leading her parents to place an appeal for help in a newspaper. This describes her as 'a young girl of around fourteen years – of average height – black eyes and hair – a most regular face – with a slim and strong physique and a rather rare beauty'.[117] Cantoni is so taken with the patriotic war that he only notices the beauty of his devoted admirer when she faints from exhaustion. On picking her up and loosening her red shirt, 'he uncovered the ivory spheres that nature had sculpted with a skilled hand; that neck, that delicate flesh, those shoulders that, for all their slight virility nonetheless had all the exquisiteness of the most beautiful of the daughters of Eve'.[118] In an instant, he has fallen in love with her. Alberto Banti argues that the love between the two is of a virile and predominantly chaste character. When she joins the soldiers, Ida in fact is dressed in men's clothing. But the argument that all they enjoy is the standard de-sexualised bond that is the norm within national narratives is at least partially contradicted by the strong physical attraction manifested in the above passage.[119]

It was entirely conventional for the heroes and heroines of historical novels to be beautiful and good, but the particular emphasis that Garibaldi gave to characters takes on programmatic connotations. Not only did his novels feature real people alongside the idealised characters (himself as 'il solitario' in *Clelia*, the patriotic aristocrat Cristina di Belgioioso in *Cantoni*), but there was a critique of the cowardice and timidity of those who had ruled Italy and an attack on the effects of papal rule. 'I believe that before the existence of the papacy and its allies in Italy, the Italian race was better looking, stronger and more intelligent', he asserted.[120] The emphasis on the dark-haired beauty and nobility of ordinary young men and, especially, women who joined the patriots served not merely to highlight the heroism and justice of the cause but to assert the moral and physical virtues of the common Italian people against the country's present rulers.

10 *Head of a Capri Girl* by John Singer Sargent offers an alternative to the artist's better-known portraits of the Anglo-American Edwardian elite.

Intellectuals highlighted Italy's importance by asserting that the country had, like a mother, given birth to beauty. Fifty years after unification, in 1911, the Turin newspaper *La Stampa*, wrote that, 'With our revolution we have not only reconstituted the organism of the nation but also increased the beauty of the world; we have reconsecrated the nobility of life in so far as it is the exercise of duty, the victory of action and the domination of intelligence'.[121] In the same year, the nationalist Scipio Sighele referred to 'the grandiose outlines of that divine work of art that is Italy', urging the need to 'continue and perfect an architectonic order'.[122] This did not mean that the country was seen as feminine. The building of a national political system and civil society was seen as a task that involved the assertion of a rational, masculine Italy.[123] As part of this project, a generic, all-purpose portmanteau concept of beauty evolved that served a variety of rhetorical functions. However, the imagery and culture of the new nation took shape on the basis of complex mediations between inherited traditions, present-day concerns and political aspirations. Within this, feminine beauty occupied a place that reflected the way that it had been drawn into the process of creation of the nation. It was a complex construct that was the product both of a specific gender ideology and an aesthetic sensibility. It encapsulated the spirit of the nation, its physical existence and the qualities of its people. This gave it an unrivalled communicative power that could never be entirely controlled by officialdom. It at once met the need for attractive unifying symbols and stood for the unfulfilled promise of Italy's national revolution.

CHAPTER TWO

THE BLONDE AURA OF QUEEN MARGHERITA

Broadly speaking, two distinct currents of feminine beauty were deployed in the struggle to shape the late nineteenth-century political order. The first of these was a regal one centred on the figure of Princess – and from 1878 Queen – Margherita. Margherita was a fair-haired, blue-eyed young woman of a certain charisma, who was widely held to be beautiful. She was often compared to Renaissance paintings and all aspects of her appearance attracted comment. The second current was lower class and predominantly rural. A significant number of images of peasant and working women appeared in the press. Engravings of paintings, illustrations and photographs presented the readers of illustrated weeklies with a picturesque selection of smiling flower girls, cheery shepherdesses and seed-sowers. Invariably, the region of origin of these unnamed subjects was mentioned to show the picturesque diversity of the peninsula. There was a strong nostalgic strain to such visual enticements. They offered to the mainly northern, urban readership a profoundly sanitised image of rural life as a natural, healthy existence in which the fecundity of the land was equated to the genuine values of the peasantry. This current rested on a rustic ideal that had been elaborated earlier in the century. The primitive but enchanting girl of the people was identified with the mass of the population, and especially the southern peasantry.

Such a dual pattern of popular and elite representation was not in itself unusual, but in other countries the place of each typology within an established hegemonic system was clear. In Italy, the duality reflected the instabilities that were inherent in the attempt to create such a system rather than its successful achievement. They were an indication of the gulf that separated north and south. In the period following unification, the south of the country was a source of continuous instability. As such, it came to be seen as remote and different by northern Italians whose views of it were often coloured by the perceptions of foreigners. On the one hand they feared its backwardness, but on the other they looked on it with feelings of nostalgia for a way of life that was fast disappearing.

There was also a political dimension to this dichotomous representation. For republicans and radicals, images of earthy dark beauty were not a picturesque appendage to a given pattern of rule. Rather, they evoked the democratic revolution that they had urged but which had not occurred. Nevertheless, there was much slippage between fair and dark models of beauty and the latter was not solely embraced by the left. Even Margherita acknowledged that at an emotional level the Italians more readily appreciated dark-haired, dark-eyed beauty. The poet and right-wing politician Gabriele D'Annunzio, who was a keen observer and tireless seducer of the high-society beauties of his age, as well as a strong supporter of the monarchy and an admirer of the queen, also played a crucial part in championing the dark, olive-skinned beauty ideal. By the end of the century this was generally accepted as typically Italian. It was therefore drawn into a series of discourses and policy discussions about race, health and fertility.

Regal beauty

The primary institution of the new state created by the proclamation of Italian unification in 1861 was the monarchy. However, the female presence in the public projection of royalty was weak. King Vittorio Emanuele II's queen consort Maria Adelaide had died in 1855. The sole figure who was associated with royalty was the king's mistress, and subsequently morganatic wife. Rosa Vercellana, who bore the king two illegitimate children, was a stocky woman of peasant extraction. Born to a soldier in the Napoleonic army, she was a robust and healthy woman of the people. 'La bella Rosina' offered a simple, natural womanliness that seemed to match the dominant taste of a predominantly peasant country. 'May was resplendent in all its multi-coloured glory when, in a field of wheat in which poppies were aflame and cornflowers were smiling', the king is reputed to have said of his first meeting with her, 'a true fresh, perfumed rose appeared before me'.[1] Although photographs reveal little of the appeal she exercised for the king over a thirty year period, she was widely thought of as an example of unrefined beauty. Contemporaries admired her personality and commented favourably on her beauty, although her anomalous status exposed her to some personal hostility. Through Rosina, the king established more contact with the people of his country than he might otherwise have done.

After his death, Rosina – who by now was the Countess of Mirafiori – expected to continue to enjoy a certain prominence. However, along with many royal retainers, she was quickly marginalised by Umberto, Vittorio Emanuele II's first son and heir. She was also eclipsed in public affections by another figure, who would enjoy lasting influence. Born in 1851 to Duke Ferdinando of Genoa and Maria Elisabeth of Saxony, Margherita of Savoy would be the only woman of some Italian parentage to become queen consort in the history of the monarchy. She married Prince Umberto in 1868 and became queen when Umberto succeeded his father in 1878. Margherita played an important part in popularising the monarchy after the capital was moved to Rome and in making it a physical presence in the life of the nation. After the death of Vittorio Emanuele II, she fulfilled

11 Rosa Vercellana, dubbed 'La bella Rosina', mistress and, later, morganatic wife of King Vittorio Emanuele II.

a role which her clumsy and retiring husband could not, attracting admiration and enthusiasm wherever she and Umberto travelled.

Virtually from the moment she appeared on the public stage, Margherita became the subject of a discourse about her beauty. As a young woman endowed with blue eyes and blonde hair, she attracted much comment. Remarking on her appearance at a ball at the Quirinale palace, Alessandro Guiccioli wrote: 'the Queen is resplendent with beauty and diamonds. I find her one of the most gracious women ever dreamed of. Her complexion and her hair are stupendously beautiful'.[2] During a royal visit to Vienna in 1881, a journalist observed that she 'looked as though she had stepped down from a painting by Titian or Paolo Veronese', while Gabriele D'Annunzio, catching sight of her at the theatre, defined her 'a real triumph of beauty'; 'the queen . . . seemed very beautiful. . . . Looking at her, I felt as never before the magical allure of the eternal regal feminine'.[3] It is well-known that Giosuè Carducci, the most prominent Italian poet and a one-time republican whose conversion to the monarchy caused much amazement, was especially alert to the beauty of the young Margherita. Although it is probably a legend that it was her beauty alone that caused his change of mind, his ode entitled 'Eterno femminino regale' strongly suggested that his new stance was not entirely separable from his admiration for the queen.[4] Edmondo De Amicis, the author of the popular patriotic novel *Cuore*, a socialist and an admirer of the monarchy, wrote to his publisher Treves in 1878: 'I have seen Queen Margherita, what a beautiful creature! It was a dream'.[5] The focus on the regal beauty of Margherita allowed writers to connect a poetic tradition to the nation. It also served to mask the fact that the House of Savoy, which ill-advisedly had fostered in-breeding, had not produced any examples of male beauty.

Naturally, the blonde and regal Margherita did not win approval from republicans. Most of those who had campaigned and fought for Italian unification believed in Mazzini's ideal of a revolution from below. They wanted to see Italians take charge of their destiny in a democratic republic. They opposed the monarchy politically and resented the idealisation of Margherita. The emphasis on her blondeness and fair skin as regarded as an extension of the northern domination of the new state and the undemocratic monarchical system of government that prevailed. However, Margherita had presence and she proved to be a great asset to the House of Savoy when the royal couple undertook numerous journeys after their wedding and in the years that followed.[6] Advised by Countess Irene della Rocca to become 'a Garibaldi of the peace', she aimed to become a figure who mixed elements of reality and fantasy in the minds of Italians. The couple undertook important visits to Naples and Sicily, where the Savoy house was regarded as an alien imposition, and to republican Romagna, where opposition to the monarch was a

12 Queen Margherita of Savoy,
c.1877. Her beauty was much praised
by Italian writers and poets.

part of broader social unrest. Her popularity was such that she was the real star of monarchical politics, while her husband was a sideshow.[7] As the consort, she enjoyed a greater liberty than Umberto. In addition, as a woman, she brought into the public realm a quality that was otherwise largely confined to marginal and private spaces. Margherita was greeted as a great hope for Italy when she first emerged and she did not disappoint. The monarchist De Meiss's demand that a king should be tall and handsome, strong and courageous, gallant, sensual and magnificent, but also religious, was met in large part by Margherita.[8] Margherita had little time for Parliament and developed an acute sense of the need to develop the symbolic and cultural role of monarchy. She gathered intellectuals and artists around her and turned the royal court into a pole of social attraction that began to rival the papal one.

She was known for her ample greetings, her smiles, and her elegant clothes and strings of pearls. She invited cultural figures to court and organised numerous balls. She had charm in abundance. But at the same time, she was religious and made a great display of her devotion. Although the Church did not recognise the Italian state, Margherita did not attract any personal opposition. She never wore make-up, in keeping with the nineteenth-century view that sincerity and naturalness were to be shown through the face. Because nature never lied, an unadorned face was taken to be an honest one.

The Italian cult of Margherita turned her into a latter-day Corinne, an embodiment of all the Italian virtues of poetry, culture, beauty, charm, elegance and natural nobility. Although she was fair, not dark like her fictional counterpart, she too was half foreign. Her mother tongue was German but she had made Italy her home and was passionately attached to it. According to V. De Napoli, author in 1894 of a volume devoted to *L'eterna bellezza della Regina Margherita di Savoja* (The eternal beauty of Queen Margherita of Savoy), she was the perfect woman 'who inspires in one a devotion similar to that occasioned by the sight of Titian's Madonna in Palazzo Pitti'.[9] 'This sort of woman and queen, who represents . . . the religious and popular poetry of Italy, is embellished by eternal goodness and beauty. . . . It seems as if Canova has returned to life and brought to life his paintings of Venus and Flora, both brimming with . . . colours and flowers'.[10] Comparing her to Dante's Beatrice and Petrarch's Laura, De Napoli wrote that:

> she is a ray of divine light, such that it seems as if the heavens are smiling down on the Italians. . . . She has a correct, slim, fetching appearance, blonde hair that underlines her white, gently coloured cheeks; her eyes, that are of the most beautiful shade, scintillate with marvellous sweetness. In such a beautiful and gracious body, the virtues of invention and art are most powerfully apparent when she is seated to play the piano or the mandolin or when she makes an appearance in an art gallery or industrial exhibition.[11]

These views were echoed by Benedetto Croce, who wrote that she 'joined sweet compassion and a natural smile to the love of art and poetry; it seemed that she was herself a poetic creature who had come to embody in the most perfect way the idea of a queen of Italy, of the land of the arts and of everything beautiful'.[12]

The stress placed on Margherita's blondeness was entirely conventional. In Dante and Petrarch, it is never specified that the hair colour of the idealised woman is blonde; rather, reference is made to light and aura. But in ancient Greece and Rome, it had been customary to envisage the gods as blonde.[13] In consequence, it was unsurprising that lightness was turned by Boccaccio into blondeness and became consolidated in the broader poetic tradition that influenced painting and customs. A relatively rare feature in Italy that was found more commonly among the aristocracy than in other classes, fair hair was taken without question over several centuries as an ideal of beauty. Examples could be found in the north, but also in Sicily, where the Norman influence could still be seen many centuries after the invasion. Titled Sicilians could sometimes trace a direct line back to the Normans.[14] It attracted attention and distinguished the bearer from the darker colourings that were more commonly found in Italy. Blondeness, in short, was prized because it was rare. Botticelli's favourite model, Simonetta Vespucci, who posed for his *Birth of Venus* and *Spring*, was fair. So too were other celebrated Renaissance beauties, including Isabella d'Este, Giulia Farnese and even Lucrezia Borgia, who was magnificently painted by Pinturicchio, and was known to wash gold into her hair. However, the iconic status of fair-haired and fair-skinned beauty was largely created and perpetuated by the poetic and artistic tradition.

The cult of Margherita's beauty has been explained in relation to the gratitude that intellectuals felt for the attention that she paid them.[15] However, poets, intellectuals and monarchists needed her to be beautiful. The chorus of adulation and praise to which her beauty gave rise bore witness that it was something which the country required 'to console itself or to delude itself'.[16] This sentiment was felt even more widely. 'In the popular imagination she went from being pleasant, which is what she was, to very beautiful', comments Gigliozzi.[17] There were several reasons for this. Her appearance had political importance because it helped win support in all social classes and even in marginal regions of the country for an institution that would otherwise have been remote. By becoming the queen of the Italians as well as of Italy, and even winning the admiration of some republicans, she broadened support for the country's fragile institutions.[18] Intellectuals who identified Italy as the land of beauty ardently desired the queen to be beautiful. They could scarcely conceive of the opposite.

Despite this, her beauty also had its detractors. Harsh observers at home found her legs to be short and thought that at best she was 'almost a beauty'.[19] Even at the time of her wedding, when she was seventeen, some found her to be 'beautiful certainly, but not very beautiful' with even her fair hair seeming anaemic. 'Nature had favoured her only up to a point and had endowed her with a very beautiful face, expression and arms, but a body that was not entirely pleasing due to the unharmonious lack of proportion between the upper body and the lower limbs', according to one account.[20] Some said her beauty was best appreciated from a distance and that she was at her best when seated, in a carriage or in a box at the theatre. In subsequent years, it was said that she was 'beautiful, but above all gracious'.[21] Her talent was for seeming beautiful and giving the impression of being elegant in the eyes of non-specialists. But the dominant view in Italy was that she was a great beauty. In 1883, *L'Illustrazione italiana* spoke of the 'blonde and diaphanous figure of the queen' and expressed the view that 'she has now arrived at the fullest maturity of feminine beauty'.[22]

Margherita understood perfectly what was required of a queen and acted her role with conviction. She deliberately offered herself to the public as a slightly theatrical personage, somewhat over the top, in order to meet popular expectations, to provoke appreciation and thereby increase her personal popularity and that of the monarchy. Margherita was regal and refined, while offering an image of kindness and apparent accessibility. She developed a repertoire of gestures bordering on the seductive, which she deployed in public appearances. At the same time she made sure that she remained an ideal figure, for example by never being seen eating in public. Margherita used her charm and, as one contemporary observer noted, 'she knew how to appear more beautiful than she really was'.[23]

Margherita was held up as an example and was praised as a model of beauty, elegance, morality and even hygiene. 'Margherita of Savoy, even if she was not Queen, would still represent the sublime of the fair sex, the undefinable, a woman ideally pious, ideally

13 A popular postcard image of Queen Margherita of Savoy.

good, ideally intelligent, the most aristocratic in Italy due to the ancient nobility that she boasts', proclaimed De Napoli.[24] This valiant author underlined the pedagogical role of the queen's person. 'This eternal beauty and goodness should be imitated by all Italian women so that, for the good of the fatherland, there will be a single type of female'.[25]

Fashionable beauty

The queen was careful to strike the right balance between showiness and aloofness, accessibility and restraint. She refused to be painted, for example, by the celebrated Paris-based portrait painter Giovanni Boldini, who specialised in sexed-up paintings of the wives of the wealthy elite. Boldini's reputation for real-life lechery and pictorial sex appeal was sufficient to deter her.[26] Yet not everyone found the queen to be elegant or tasteful. She was frequently adorned with great quantities of pearls and diamonds, given to her by her husband, and multiple pearl necklaces became her trademark. Foreign experts commented that her jewellery was excessive and that her *toilettes*, in bright and inappropriate colours, were in bad taste. 'Her dream, if she had not been queen of Italy, would have been to be *une grande mondaine* [a great courtesan]', was the telling remark of the French man of letters Ernest Tissot.[27] A similar observation was made by the famous beauty Empress Elisabetta during a royal visit to Vienna in 1881. Margherita was not as beautiful or as elegant as the famous Sissi, who found her to be both too regal and too showy in her way of dressing.[28]

It was customary that female royalty should attract comment and provoke discussion in this way. Yet the many comments on the queen's dresses, jewels and appearance show how Margherita's visual appearance was related to fashion and commerce. The attention she received was to some extent fuelled by a growing commercial sphere. Women looked to her for inspiration and were keen to have details of her gowns. With little or no active intervention on her part, the queen became a fashion icon in Italy, if not abroad. The social elite in the capital took her as a point of reference and, in the 1880s and 1890s, thousands read the upmarket fashion magazine *Margherita*, that was named after her. Founded by the writer Cordelia, it was the first Italian periodical to present a discourse on fashion, beauty and appearance to upper- and upper-middle-class Italian women. The magazine was a luxury production that featured the queen's head on its title. This was not the only tribute Margherita was paid. Theatres and cafés were named after her, girls were baptised with her name and in Naples a patriotic tricolour pizza was dedicated to her. Margherita brought a feminine presence to public life and a variety of innovations were attributed to her in the realm of health, hygiene and diet. She symbolised on the one hand elegance and class and on the other simplicity, naturalness and conventional feminine concerns.

Margherita was a natural blonde, but the same could not be said for all the fair high-society women in this period. Her ascent to the throne coincided with, and reinforced, among the aristocracy at least, a strong fashionable emphasis on models of female

14 A young noblewoman of the late
nineteenth century.

appearance that either derived from old aristocratic associations or from northern
Europe. D'Annunzio noted in his *Breviario mondano* (fashion notes) that 'around thirty
years ago all the women were brown-haired . . . now, by contrast, a woman who is not
blonde is not a woman'. There was a view in the elegant world, he noted, that since Eve
was blonde and Venus was also blonde, and since Queen Margherita was also blonde,
every woman should have blonde hair. As a result of a sort of 'great decree', 'nowadays
in Rome you only see blonde women, women of every sort of blondeness'.[29] As an
arbiter of fashion and style, D'Annunzio observed this trend, but he also emphasised its
significance. He delighted in the refinement and wealth of Roman high society and
conveyed his sensations of it to his readers with great enthusiasm.

Margherita's reputation was fundamentally that of a pure woman, a mother and a
perfect consort. But the fashion sphere, especially in Rome, was sexy and daring. In a city
where the influence of the Pope was still strong, new fashions and influences from
abroad had a certain transgressive quality. D'Annunzio did not only report on beauty, he
also contributed, through his writings, to the formation of fashionable canons of appearance. He was a mediator who was one of the creators of what the critic Mario Praz
termed 'Medusan beauty'.[30] That is to say, he concentrated on qualities that were not

conventionally beautiful, such as deathly pallor, animalesque features, enigmatic smiles and vampirism. Feminine beauty, for him, was not an autonomous value. Rather, it was intimately linked to sexuality and in particular to the stimulation of male desire. By weaving sexy images around aristocratic personalities, he flattered them and made them think of themselves as irresistibly alluring. D'Annunzio's first novel, *Il Piacere* (pleasure), contains numerous references to pale-skinned, fair-haired women and indeed the novel features several English women. While foreigners expressed admiration for Italian beauty, he developed an ideal of feminine beauty that was informed more by English poetry and painting. The image of the pale, fragile maiden in the poet's early works owed much to the influence on D'Annunzio of the pre-Raphaelite painter Dante Gabriel Rossetti. The influence of Tennyson and of the painter Alma-Tadema on his literary output has also been traced. According to Giuliana Pieri, 'D'Annunzio's descriptions of women of Roman High Society are explicitly based on the beauties in the pictures exhibited by Alma-Tadema in Rome in 1883'.[31] She goes on to suggest that in *Il Piacere*, the author was 'creating a world in the style of Alma-Tadema, but with no specific relation to any painting'.[32] It was difficult to present a specifically Italian idea of female beauty at this time because Italy was not itself a fashion centre. As in other spheres, the country found itself confined to an inferior position with respect to the great powers that also dictated norms and ideals in terms of the appearance of women. Among other things, the triumph of fashionable blondeness showed the failure to elaborate a strong middle-class ideal of a darker Italian model of beauty.

D'Annunzio took a type of representation that was already stereotyped and embraced it as such. Diaphanous beauty, a beauty that was deprived of fullness and strength, was for D'Annunzio a transitional enthusiasm that was an important step in a process that would lead him to develop his own type of *femme fatale*. In *Il Piacere*, he elaborated a model of sensual beauty that preserved Renaissance painting as a crucial reference point. His mysterious heroine Elena Muti is said to recall Correggio's Danae, with her extremities being described as 'a little in the style of Correggio'.[33] Her feet and hands are small and delicate as with statues of Daphne. Donna Bianca Dolcebuono is described as 'the ideal-type of Florentine beauty, as rendered by Ghirlandajo in his portrait of Giovanna Tornabuoni that is now in the Church of Santa Maria Novella': 'She had a pale oval face, a high, white, open forehead, a timid mouth, a slightly upturned nose, and eyes of that dark weathered colour praised by Fiorenzuola'.[34] Donna Maria, who becomes the protagonist's object of seduction, is seen by him as having a concealed sex appeal. He sees 'inside the spiritual woman, the pure Siennese Madonna, the worldly woman'.[35] When she appears in all her splendour at an evening function, her hair is arranged 'in that style that Verrocchio preferred for his busts'.[36]

Within this traditional frame of reference, that would have been recognised outside and inside Italy as conventional, D'Annunzio brought to bear more contemporary fashionable influences. Rossetti is explicitly mentioned at one point, and the presence of a young English lady, Liliana Theed, whose complexion is a combination of 'light, roses and milk' establishes a foreign reference point for the emphasis on the fashionable pale skin of the Italian women. The ideal of white skin, blonde hair and whiteness is clearly established.[37] One Italian woman, who is deemed 'very beautiful' is mistaken for an English rose on account of her colouring. Sometimes pictorial references served as a high cultural justification for explicit eroticism. By comparing the seductress Elena Muti to Danae, the writer leads his readers to picture her naked. Donna Maria's beauty attracts Andrea Sperelli only as a lure. He is sure that, once he has had her, he will be freed from the enchantment.[38] His descriptions of Elena and Donna Maria stress, singly and separately, hands, mouth, shoulders, arms and skin. For example, Elena's hands, 'white and very pure had, in their movements, the lightness almost of butterflies'. 'Those incomparable hands, soft and white', he continued, 'were marked by a web of barely visible veins.'[39]

A similar fetishisation of the single parts of the female body is evident in his second novel, *Il trionfo della morte* (The triumph of death). Hands, arms and shoulders acquire a particular significance in a culture in which women were most of the time fully covered. Apart from the face, the hands were the only part of the body that was visible, and even they were often covered in gloves. They were also an expressive part of the body, denoting femininity and class as well as suggesting touch and physical contact. The novel's heroine, Ippolita Sanzio, is once again pallid, and her pallidness is linked to a fashionable unhealthiness. She is 'afflicted, ill'.[40] Her skin is described as being alabaster. Her beauty is 'almost deathly'; she seems bloodless. The narrator, her lover Giorgio Aurispa, thinks that 'when she is dead she will reach the supreme expression of her beauty'.[41] Her form is 'slim and long, perhaps excessively long but full of serpentine elegance'.[42] She is not maternal but rather a sterile beauty incapable of reproduction. Her beauty is fragmentary. She is described as having 'three divine elements of beauty: the forehead, the eyes, the mouth: all three divine'.[43] The air of decadence is rendered explicit in a phrase in which her skin is described under a warm light as being amber and like 'a slightly wilted rose'.

Ippolita is an instrument of pleasure for the protagonist: 'the woman of delight, the strong and delicate instrument of pleasure, the lustful and magnificent animal who is destined to adorn a table, cheer up a bed and arouse the ambiguous fantasies of aesthetic lust. She was a splendid example of an animal: happy, restless, flexible, soft and cruel'.[44] The male gaze is explicit. As Aurispa looks at Ippolita resting, he reflects on her as a construct of his imagination: '"How many guises does she have before my eyes! Her form is designed by my desires, her shadows are produced by my thoughts. Whenever she appears before me, it is purely as an effect of my continuous internal creativity. She does not exist except through me. Her appearance is as changeable as dreams"'.[45] She is defective. He sees her feet as 'deformed in the toes, they are plebean, utterly lacking refinement . . . they have the mark of the lowly bred'.[46] But this does nothing to diminish her appeal: 'the most vulgar traits exercised for him an irritating attraction'.[47] This was the proof, 'the proudest sign of the great carnal obsession that one human creature can exercise over another'.[48] This physical fragmentation was typical of a certain late nineteenth-century cultural current evidenced, for example, in the giant hands and feet of du Maurier's character Trilby and the striking hands of Rossetti's pictorial subjects.

D'Annunzio also stressed the material. There are insistent fashionable references in descriptions of the clothing and *toilettes* of the women. Jewels and gloves are given erotic connotations in the novel in keeping with a contemporary tendency, that derived from Paris, to shift sex appeal from the physical body to the world of objects. In this he was not alone. Paolo Mantegazza, who will be discussed later in this chapter, declared that 'the splendour of silk, the luxurious softness of velvet, the hundred and one beauties of feathers, of furs, of lace add enchantments to enchantments and the frame sets off the "picture"'.[49] Women were often associated with greyhounds, which D'Annunzio himself kept, as if to allude simultaneously to their elegance and their primitive qualities. Yet D'Annunzio's female characters are not purely passive. They have desires and are real to an extent, but they are also compelling and dangerous in the eyes of the male protagonists. Their overt sensuality is often a destructive force. By turning them through fiction into powerful *femmes fatales*, the writer offered Roman aristocratic women a highly fashionable picture of themselves. In his novels, they were fashionable, highly sensual and uncaring of convention. Elena Muti, for example, is undisturbed by 'malicious gossip'. Her illicit sexual activity is glossed by her beauty, her luxury and her great name.[50] Such glamorous portraits were also tantalising for D'Annunzio's numerous middle-class readers.

Race and aesthetics

In the late nineteenth century, the country's elite took an interest in all parts of the unified peninsula. Politicians and intellectuals from the north and centre viewed the less developed region of the south with a mixture of attitudes, some of which were derived from foreign observers. It was a problematic area, a source of instability, that was cut off from the experience of modernity and was fundamentally different. Nonetheless, a cultural shift occurred. The fear and ignorance that once marked northern attitudes gave way to a more active engagement. The south was not only a source of picturesque Italian images. It was a part of Italy to be treated by public policies and understood in relation to a wider concept of national development. This shift was complex and involved a variety of intellectual contributions. D'Annunzio was also crucial here. Over the years, he modified the refined and aloof attitude of his early fictional work to a more open engagement with the nation and the destiny of its people. As a right-wing nationalist and an anti-democrat, he took to political involvement, first as a Member of Parliament and then as a military propagandist and agitator. In the years between the 1880s and the First World War, he also strengthened his convictions concerning the supremacy of the Latin race. At a time when race theory was enjoying considerable popularity, he merged a patriotic commitment to national development and influence with a morale-boosting emphasis on the special qualities of the Italian people.[51]

The poet may have been a dandy and a socialite but he hailed from the Abruzzo region and his early poetry celebrates instinct, force, wildness and the primitive. He was thus well-placed to harness these qualities to the national project. These themes are also present in his second novel. In *Il trionfo della morte*, the protagonist goes in search of energy and renewal amid the peasants and participates in their religious fervour. He encounters Favretta, a peasant girl who is 'as brown as an olive'. She was short 'but she had robust features, a wide and generous bosom. . . . She had curly hair, thick eyebrows, a Roman nose and a wild personality'.[52] Her outdoor location, physical robustness and darkness distinguished her from Aurispa's lover Ippolita, the sick, pallid beauty. Favretta was part of a natural scene that inspired the hero. Aurispa needs to get in touch with his roots and feel a sense of belonging; he seeks 'that tenacious internal bestiality that forms the basis of the female being'.[53] He felt drawn to primitive people and wanted to feel 'a material connection with the lowest stratum of his race, with that deep, permanent stratum in which the traces of the primitive perhaps remained intact'.[54] But, as he mixes with the ugly and deformed who seek divine grace, he recoils, realising that he hates the masses and feels extraneous to them. His experiment a failure, he turns to Ippolita, who has taken note of his preferences and is taking the sun: '"I want to become truly like you say: *like an olive*". "Will you like me?"', she asks him.[55] Woman, earth and the elements blend in a form of implicit pantheism.

Many intellectuals and artists regarded beauty, not just the beauty of women but beauty in all its forms, as their special preserve. It was a value that only a select few could comprehend. The concept was not just deployed against the lower classes however, but against the new bourgeoisie born of industry and trade and the values that it promoted.[56] Unlike Carducci, D'Annunzio saw the peasantry as a possible ally in his battle against the bourgeoisie and its modernity of industry and commerce. His observations on Italy as the mother of beauty and the qualities of the Latin race multiplied in the years that led up to the First World War. This emphasis on race was an attempt to resist the rise of anonymous mass society. The horrors of the latter could be avoided by making the grace, strength and beauty of the people the hallmark of the nation.[57] In his third novel, *Le vergini delle rocce* (The virgins of the rocks), D'Annunzio elaborated a vision of the Latin superman, who was to be the product of a dignified, high concept of the nation. There is an emphasis on the perfect integrity of the Latin human type and one of the tasks that the hero, Claudio Cantelmo, must achieve is to have a son who will be a perfect product of the stock, and who will have the task of restoring Rome to its ancient glory.[58] To have this son, Cantelmo seeks an ideal mother among the three beautiful virgin daughters of the noble Montagna family. These are the graceful Massimiliana, who is about to become a nun and who represents the beauty of the soul, Anatolia, who stands for fertile femininity, and Violante, the sterile embodiment of lust and sensual indulgence. For the author, these were the three principal types of female beauty and his protagonist would ideally have married all three. In the end, Cantelmo makes a choice between the women, but the reader is not informed which of them he has selected to conceive and give birth to the superman.

D'Annunzio's militancy was motivated by a desire to 'save something beautiful and ideal from the sinister wave of vulgarity that by now has covered the privileged land where Leonardo created his imperious women and Michelangelo his indomitable heroes'. Beauty was a discourse of elitism to be deployed against the banality of post-Risorgimento Italy. This was not of course principally feminine beauty, but this discourse was connected to it. As Carlo Salinari observed, the poet had 'a conception of the nation and the fatherland that was almost physical and naturalistic'.[59] He found the source of national renewal in a naturalistic concept of the Italian 'based on blood and on race and other physical elements, both of the nation and of the superman who was destined to embody it and lead it'.[60] The fate of Italy was seen to be bound up with the state of beauty. D'Annunzio gloried in his Latin blood and held out a vision of masculine assertion and national conquest. Women had a subordinate and ornamental role that was nonetheless given much attention by the poet. He reflected a widespread nineteenth-century belief that women had a sacred mission to beautify the world. In the end, erotic beauty and reproduction of the nation were linked.

Curiously, Margherita also took a keen interest in matters of reproduction. Like her father-in-law, who was conscious of his red whiskers and regularly dyed his moustaches with black boot polish 'out of vanity and so as to resemble more closely his brown-haired subjects',[61] she was concerned with physical appearances. She had no time for flatterers who attempted to please her by saying that the dark-skinned Italians were inferior racially to the peoples of the north.[62] She believed that the royal family should share the ethnic characteristics of the people. It was with this thought in mind that she took a hand in choosing a bride for her son, Vittorio Emanuele, fearing that, if left to his own devices, he might opt for a less than beautiful woman. 'A year ago at the races, he swooned over a lady who was short, ugly and fat, a real gnome' she allegedly lamented in 1893.[63] Elena of Montenegro, who the young prince met in 1895 and to whom he became engaged in 1896, was a young woman whose dark hair and skin promised the sort of renewal that Margherita felt the House of Savoy needed. In this, she took her cue from former Prime Minister Francesco Crispi, who had previously suggested an alliance with the royal family of Montenegro. Crispi himself told a fellow politician, 'We need a woman who is beautiful, dark and strong, to reinvigorate the line – and the Montenegran race is right'.[64]

Elena was faintly praised by D'Annunzio, who pronounced her 'truly beautiful and embellished with delicate graces that are not evident at first glance but which are revealed one by one as they take light like candles in a candelabra of many branches until finally they are all aflicker'.[65] Others commented on her thick hair, her dark eyes and her smile. Her physique and expression, it was said, amounted to something attractive rather than beauty as such. She lacked the elegance and class of her future mother-in-law. However, her arrival signified a transition. 'Margherita's is a blonde smile, while Elena's is a brown smile', commented the senator Luigi Cremona.[66]

The shift from fairness to brownness also took place in the theatre. D'Annunzio's collaboration with the leading Italian actress of the day, the dark-haired Eleonora Duse,

won him a new platform. It was one that led him to become a leading representative of
an aesthetic current in Italian life that would increasingly be matched to nationalism and
an aesthetic form of racial supremacism. The couple first met in 1894 and began a
passionate liaison soon afterwards. La Duse was a world-renowned actress who always
performed in Italian, but she was not a recognised beauty of the classic type. 'Je suis belle
quand je veux', the Venetian actress used to say, implying that as a performer she could
mould herself any way she liked. However, some felt that her beauty was simply more
complex than the usual. 'I want to proclaim loud and clear the beauty of her smile', wrote
the popular novelist Neera.[67] Like her rival Sarah Bernhardt, Duse played several *femme
fatale* roles, including *La dame aux camélias*, Cleopatra and Sardou's Theodora and
Odette. D'Annunzio was one of several young writers whose work she championed. She
differed from Bernhardt in her understatement and her naturalism and taste for playing
tormented women. Her refusal to wear make-up, a trait she shared with Queen
Margherita, also marked her out as highly individual within the context of the theatre. It
was a sign of honesty or eccentricity. When she played pretty or young women, she relied
on movement and nuance to create an illusion of beauty. For example, she could not only
cry but also blush at will.[68] This 'naturalness' was her distinguishing feature, unlike the
highly rouged Bernhardt. She was also a very modern figure, who was one of the first to
champion Ibsen's problematic heroines on the European stage. Her performances were

15 The great actress Eleonora Duse,
who was widely seen as a modern Mona
Lisa.

spare and measured, even though her own personality often dwarfed the character she was playing.

La Duse attracted D'Annunzio because, more than a great beauty, she was an aesthetic presence. She was a striking figure who influenced fashion. She had her own repertoire of gestures and used her hands extensively in her highly mobile performances. Although she was far more famous and influential than him, he believed that he could subordinate her to his creative genius.[69] In his play *La Gioconda*, which he dedicated to 'Eleonora Duse of the beautiful hands', D'Annunzio operated one of his habitual fragmentations of the female body. He severed the hands of the character played by Duse, a sculptor's wife, and forced her to conceal her arms for most of the play. This was a sadistic act towards the actress rather than a real dramatic requirement, but Duse rose to the challenge and extended her reputation for bold and innovative interpretations. His most destructive act regarding her reputation as an alluring performer able to give realistic life to young, beautiful women was his novel *Il fuoco* (The flame). Published in 1900, the novel offered a thinly disguised account of his own affair with Duse. In it he deliberately contrasted the two protagonists to flatter himself. Although D'Annunzio was in fact only four years younger than the actress, his alter ego is a vigorous, young, handsome poet of unlimited talent and energy while hers is a famous actress in her early forties who is ageing and desperate. Based on the 1895 to 1900 period, although set in 1883, a device that allowed Wagner to make an appearance, the novel offers a sad and pathetic picture of La Foscarina (Duse), who is portrayed at turns as tyrannical, pathetically submissive and jealous.

Nevertheless, the poet's association of Duse with the 'Gioconda' (the Italian title of the painting universally known as the *Mona Lisa*) was not casual. It coincided with foreign perceptions of the actress as the ultimate woman and a modern, mobile Mona Lisa. The critic Arthur Symons believed that her great range as a performer derived from the fact that she contained all the emotions of the past and present. Just as Walter Pater, the originator of the modern cult of the *Mona Lisa*, saw Leonardo's subject as an exquisite self-contained beauty, so Symons, echoing Pater's reflection, regarded Duse as spiritual and enigmatic.[70] In 1898 Edward Garnett suggested that a typical spectator at the theatre was drawn to what felt like a whole, unbroken experience of life: 'he feels that, for example when he watches the Duse at her best, or when he stands before Leonardo da Vinci's "Joconda" in the Louvre and is absorbed by it'.[71] For Neera, 'only the brush of Leonardo could have depicted the unsettling expression of a beauty that is all light and mystery, dark like the canals of her lagoon and like them dotted with golden rays'.[72]

Italy's dark heart

In the first decade after unification, the ideal of the dark-haired, peasant beauty that had taken shape during the Risorgimento was more associated with radicals and democrats than with the political or cultural elite. It stood for the deep Italy that had not been fully drawn into the process of unification and that was excluded from power. The emphasis that Garibaldi placed in his novels on the dark-haired beauty and nobility of ordinary young men and, especially, women who joined the patriots served not merely to highlight the heroism and justice of the cause but to assert the moral and physical virtues of the common Italian people against Italy's present rulers. However, this was not the sole way in which it was employed, especially later in the century. Although the Church did not formally recognise the Italian state, Catholics were nonetheless active in every sphere of social and cultural life. They were especially involved with defining female roles and matters concerning the family. Even well before unification, Catholic writers had sought to embrace the religious and domestic virtues of Italian women. In an 1833 text entitled *Le donne italiane* (Italian women), Niccolò Tommaseo argued that Catholic women represented the spirit of the nation.[73] In a series of pedagogical writings, he contrasted the vanity and frivolity of high-society women with the ordinary women who were the true expression of the majority of the population. Poor peasant women were more virtuous and admirable than 'the wives of the rich', who had been contaminated by vice and fashion. They were the guardians of traditional domestic life. The critique of upper-class morality was accompanied by an elevation of the ideal of the true Italian mother. There was no place for physical beauty in these considerations, but Tommaseo did suggest that peasant women were healthier, more physically robust and, ultimately, more Italian.

In unified Italy, a variety of symbolic strategies were deployed to incorporate the lower classes visually into the nation. While Piedmont imposed its ruling class, its monarchy and its economic and military power, the south, by contrast, provided domesticated picturesque images of Italians cast in terms of violence, passion, folklore, popular music and laziness, so long as these were domesticated through the picturesque. Neapolitan songs and Sicilian puppets were the acceptable face of an internal source of potential instability. In a magazine like *Illustrazione italiana*, founded in 1875, which served as a sort of establishment house journal, there was a strong tendency to pictorialise those elements of the nation which lay outside the realm of the official and the acceptable, yet which were nonetheless objects of a patriotic discourse.[74] In the context of a dominant aesthetic that valued sentimental effects, the different and the backward could be seen as curious, exotic and amusing. Influential Italians had less leeway than foreigners in describing elements which they did not accept as representative of the nation as a whole, but rather sought to ascribe solely to the south. Nonetheless, even for them, the amusingly picturesque also carried implications of danger and instability. Neapolitan songs and quaint poverty, together with the natural scenery, were welcome but corruption and banditry were not.

Illustrazione italiana presented on its covers a range of stock visual types, including the king, heroes and achievers, exotic scenes from distant lands, significant events and so on. A significant minority of covers featured young women, invariably of peasant extraction. They were never named but instead were described as the example of a type: the fisher

16 Postcard image of a young peasant girl
from the Abruzzo region.

girl, the flower-seller, the woman from Ciociaria, the shepherdess, the gypsy and so on.[75] The women are almost always dark-haired and sometimes smiling. Very often the pictures are reproductions of paintings and drawings that feature a beautiful young woman as their subject. They provide evidence of a continuing belief that female beauty was part of the landscape, a natural feature of the peninsula. None of the images, it is worth noting, were of middle or upper-class women.

In a close analysis of the magazine, Nelson Moe found that its evolving imagery signalled a progressive depreciation of the cultural traditions of the south accompanied by a valorisation of those of the centre-north.[76] This found expression in the interest that the middle classes expressed for the natural and rural features of the south. The landscape was especially important since it formed the perfect frame for pictures of beautiful peasants and popular costumes. Rural poverty and disease were never shown; instead there was a 'folklorisation' of the south which tended to 'freeze' representations of it in accordance with established stereotypes. The purpose of this was to provide 'pleasant emotions', and images drawn from the southern countryside and provincial villages amply met this need.[77] The pictures of a traditional, picturesque world served several additional purposes. They established the superiority of the centre-north and the back-wardness of the south. The latter was marked by certain visual clichés such as a lack of

17 A typical cover of the establishment weekly *Illustrazione italiana*, featuring a peasant girl from Urbino.

shoes. Moe identifies bare feet as one of the landmarks along which *Illustrazione italiana* drew the north-south axis.[78] They also provided reassurance that, at a time of industrial growth and change in the north, Italy still kept faith with its roots. The south, Moe notes, 'was figured as a reservoir of customs and traditions that the modernizing nation was gradually eliminating and for which the middle classes often felt a certain nostalgia'.[79]

This aestheticisation of southerners was a process in which foreigners had been engaged for some time. It continued apace in the later decades of the century and beyond. The expansion of the illustrated press produced more comparison than before, as well as a demand for imagery that was pleasing and different. Because Italy had long been a destination for tourists, there was a heritage of representation and a keen sense of why images of Italians appealed. 'The brunette complexion . . . suggests to the mind the idea of *stored-up sunshine*' and in consequence it was healthy, noted Henry Finck.[80] 'A brown eye is commonly more lustrous than a light eye', he added, since 'the light eye or gray eye appears shallow. All its beauty seems to be on the surface, whereas the "soul-deep eyes of the darkest night" appear unfathomable through their bewitching glamour'.[81] Finck had an explanation for the particular aesthetic appeal of Italian peasants. 'Italian Beauty' was more prevalent among them because they 'are free to choose their own mates'.[82] Physical attraction rather than material interest was the sole basis of marriage in this social group.

In particular, the girls of Capri contributed to this iconography because the island came to be inhabited by numerous foreign artists. A destination favoured by poets and musicians from the late 1700s, artists came following the opening of the first hotel and the establishment of regular ferries to the mainland in the 1860s. They found their models among the local peasant girls who spent their days carrying water, stones and vegetables. Among them was Rosina Ferrara, the lithe and beautiful seventeen-year old who captivated the Italian-born painter John Singer Sargent and also posed for Frank Hyde and others. Sargent was accustomed to painting the pale white women of British and American high society. His portraits conferred on them a patrician air of composure that concealed what in many instances were the relatively recent origins of their wealth. However, although these portraits made him a rich man, he always hankered after more spontaneous subject matter. Rosina made a special impact on him. Fascinated by her unkempt jet-black hair, her mellow brown skin and the suggestive curves of her body, Sargent painted her repeatedly in academic pose, dancing the tarantella, walking, and draped over a small tree. According to the painter's biographer, 'she was a highly compliant subject, responsive and able to convey spontaneity, fierce energy and unself-conscious grace. She was sufficiently malleable to fit into a scene without dominating it'.[83] 'But, most important', he adds, 'Rosina was part of Capri; she belonged to the terrain. The combination of her appearance and the sharp brilliance of Capri was electric'. For Sargent, Rosina was the epitome of a type of beauty that he eagerly explored as an alternative to the gilded whiteness of the Anglo-American subjects of his paid commissions.

18 A late nineteenth-century photograph of a Sicilian peasant girl from Piana dei Greci.

The energy and barbaric vitality of the southern people was something that northerners preferred to keep at a safe distance. The idea of primitive earthy humanity could rapidly turn into something frightening. The Sicilian writer Verga was not averse to embracing this stereotype and contrasting it to civilised life. In his short story 'The She-Wolf', he offered a memorable portrait of a wild, instinctive woman who voraciously desires a man and repeatedly seduces him even after he has married her daughter. In the end she is killed by the man, who is tormented at having fallen prey to her lure. Yet barbarism was also a national resource that some commentators celebrated. Angelo Mosso and Mario Morasso, for example, were two reformers who shared a vision of the special qualities of the Italians and their capacity for overcoming the inferiority to which they were presently confined. As they saw it, such an improvement would derive from economic and social progress, education and good institutions. But it could draw strength from the particular qualities of the people. 'Barbarism and civilization are mixed in Italian blood in the just measure that forms the characteristic and the strength of the Italian people', argued Mosso, in a statement that at once acknowledged and tried to make a virtue of Italian backwardness. Not intelligence but 'strength of will' was the main resource of the Italian people, he asserted.[84] Morasso took the view that the climate and the environment, the fertile earth, rich sun and ample seas of the Mediterranean, combined with the 'virtue of good popular blood' and the 'most noble supremacy of the race that is elect and expert in refinement' made conditions perfect for a national resurgence.[85] In contrast to northern peoples, whose inhospitable climate drove them to excesses and illnesses, Italians were better placed to develop modern ways in harmony with nature and good health. In the period that followed, this sort of approach would be institutionalised, along with more systematic interventionist measures from the state.

It was just this primitive wildness that was harnessed to the nation in the national female emblem of Italia. After 1900, the year of the assassination of King Umberto, this figure was more widely employed in popular imagery. The prominence of the young Margherita had limited the space that was available to such a figure. The fact that her successor as queen was not Italian by birth contributed to the wider diffusion of images of Italia in the early twentieth century. But images and emblems were no substitute for living symbols. The alluring presence of Margherita in preceding years had accustomed Italians to a personalisation of female beauty that no allegorical representation of the country could satisfy. By the end of the century, the demand for living embodiments of Italian beauty had turned away from royalty and towards the entertainment world. Before looking at this in the next chapter, some developments in the study of beauty must be mentioned.

Beauty and science

The question of beauty was one that emerged on the margins of a variety of scientific and pseudo-scientific disciplines in the late nineteenth century. Anthropology, criminology and racial science were all in the process of being constituted as fields of enquiry and they shared some concerns. The scientific discourse of positivism saw the importation into Italy of misogynistic assumptions that were commonplace in the medical and academic community of the period. There was also a growing preoccupation with hygiene, physical fitness and diet. The frenzy of publications and commentary in these areas needs to be seen in relation to a desire to construct the nation in both gendered and racial terms. Within this, there was a widespread denigration of women as inferior. They were seen as bodies, creatures of instinct rather than reason, who were the object of a variety of discourses shaped wholly by men. In the later part of the century a whole science of anthropometry grew up that measured, assessed and judged bodies, especially female ones. Hygiene and health were two factors that bore on this, but also present was a desire for national definition and quantification. Industrialisation was seen as having negative effects on the population's health and the quality of what was referred to as the stock. At the same time, the criminologist Cesare Lombroso argued that ugliness was indicative of deviance.[86] The very qualities that had once been seen as typical of Italian women – wildness, large feline eyes, a volatile temperament – were now said to show criminal tendencies. These were virile traits that needed to be marginalised and cast out of the community. It was an example of the curious complicities of the time that such positions, and their association with the south, should have been embraced and perpetuated by Lombroso's Sicilian pupil, Alfredo Niceforo.[87]

The considerations that practitioners of scientific disciplines advanced were often informed by casual observation, personal preference and a certain literary verve. Loosely dressed up as science were disquisitions that derived more from the masculine conversations of the café or the club than from fieldwork, the laboratory or the library. In the cases of men like Niceforo and Lombroso's son-in-law Guglielmo Ferrero, beauty was an issue that they addressed in the context of broader reflections on the cultural differences between different peoples.[88] It was more central in the work of Paolo Mantegazza, a public intellectual and prolific author who held the first Chair of Anthropology at the University of Florence and who established the city's anthropological and ethnographic museum.

Mantegazza was a qualified doctor who travelled widely over several continents before emerging as a prominent academic. He was also a Member of Parliament from 1865, first as a deputy and then a senator. Something of a Renaissance man, he practised vivisection, experimented with cocaine (conducting trials on himself) and wrote novels, including a work of science fiction entitled *L'anno 3000* (The year 3000),[89] in addition to producing a variety of texts of an academic and quasi-academic nature. A staunch liberal, he defended Darwinian ideas at a time when the influence of the Catholic Church over official science and culture was strong. His treatments of matters of love, gender and sex brought him into conflict with Catholic opinion, whose representatives accused him of producing immoral works.[90] Feminine beauty was addressed by Mantegazza in his book *Fisiologia della donna* (Physiology of woman), published in 1893, when he was 62.[91] He returned to the theme in a series of short stories published under the title *Le donne del mio tempo* (The women of my time) in 1905.[92] By this time, the professor was a mature man whose moustache and goatee beard lent him more than a passing resemblance to Buffalo Bill. The first work contained reflections on the women of all European nations and many extra-European peoples. He justified this attention on the grounds that 'the woman in every race displays more clearly the ethnic characteristics of the stock that she belongs to and preserves them with greater determination'.[93] Thus the study of peoples could be advanced by paying close attention to women. Mantegazza made no pretence that his analysis was gender-neutral. 'Contemplating the body of a beautiful woman, we caress with our eyes that whole marvellous concert of curved lines that marks hills and opens valleys', he confessed; 'and over those treasures desire extends a tight net of possession that envelops them and holds them prisoner'.[94] However, he did acknowledge that the focus on feminine beauty was a consequence of the patriarchal order of society. He foresaw that 'civil progress will lead us gradually to demand other virtues from the daughters of Eve', but was swift to add that, 'as long as man walks the surface of the planet, the primary virtue of woman as far as he is concerned will be that of being beautiful'.[95]

Mantegazza's comparative analyses were extensive. In Europe only Russian women were unknown to him. The French woman was deemed to be 'feminine three times over and delightful three times over. . . . The little impertinent nose, the fine features, and the beautiful mouth render her adorable, tasty and seductive';[96] the Spanish woman was 'regally and magnificently beautiful. She has tiny hands and feet and great big eyes that seem like open windows in a marble palace, a marble that has been darkened by the eastern sun'. For her part, the English woman was 'within the blonde type, the opposite of the Spanish woman, but she is not inferior to her. She is just beautiful in a different way'.[97] Indeed, for the professor, the English woman was 'in a word, the perfect woman'. Like Ferrero, who reached similar anglophile conclusions, he found that, 'When she is solid in shape, as she often is, she combines all the most contradictory virtues, of quantity and of refinement, of the grand and the gentle, of the princely and the rural. She is beauty itself in all its attitudes and in all its omnipotence'.[98] Her only defects were big hands and feet.

Curiously, the celebrated anthropologist did not hold the beauty of Italian women in high regard. Indeed, he took the view that in Italy men were better looking than women. He announced that there were two basic types of beauty, the virile and the feminine; when the characteristics of a race were more like the latter, then the women were more attractive. However, where a virile trait dominated, such as the strong nose that was a feature of the Latin race, men were the more beautiful sex.[99] Mantegazza was of the opinion that no national type of Italian woman existed; there were only regional varieties. However, he did not pass up the opportunity to attempt a generalisation that included and celebrated this variety. Of the Italian woman, he pronounced as follows:

If she is brown-haired, she is physically beautiful; she is very beautiful indeed if, in addition to dark eyes, a sun-kissed skin and blossoming lips, she has fair hair. She comes in different types, as many as the waves of humanity that have rolled up on the shores of her twin seas.

Chubby, flexible and sensually soft, with a little Celtic nose, if she is found in Lombardy, possessed of Titianesque blondeness and marble skin in Venice, of divine and sculpted forms in Bologna, almost Latin but more mobile than the Roman type if in Tuscany, statuesque and imperial in Rome, terribly Greek in Naples and Palermo; the Italian woman offers us almost all the beauties of the European Eve.

Besides, she is artistic, passionate, ignorant, modest and less faithful than many of Europe's women, because she has almost always been married off without ever having been in love. Often she is unhappy because she does not have the safeguard of divorce.

She is adored by the men of the North who find in her the qualities that they seek in vain in their own women.[100]

The dark-haired woman was more passionate, ardent and energetic, he argued: 'She is warm, passionate, provocative. Rather than long, soft caresses, she seems to offer an invitation to the supreme ardours of love, to red hot kisses, to blood-drawing bites. Her psychological temperature is always hot or boiling. From her tresses spring electric shocks, from her eyes lightning flashes, from her skin deep blushes'.[101] 'The brown woman, to be beautiful, must have not only black hair, but black eyelashes, eyebrows and pupils; everything black', he continued; 'she must have a skin that is golden brown. She can be thin so long as she is not wanting where woman sings most loudly the hymn of sex'.

It was not clear if he was referring to the 'men of the North' or to himself when he observed that travellers generally 'find beautiful the women of the countries they have visited, or at least they are more indulgent with them'.[102] His personal preferences were not absolutely clear. He liked darker women and he quoted with approval a French artist, Charles Rochet, who had concluded that blondes lacked individuality and all seemed alike.[103] However, he was also drawn to the 'blonde woman' who was 'sweet, good-natured, pliable, tender and, one supposes, good'.[104] 'There were saints with black hair and eyes but our ideal would be this: that a lover was always dark and a wife always fair, or that, without committing any sin, the dark wife, on becoming a mother, turned into a blonde', he concluded.[105]

The professor believed that in future (and the author of *L'anno 3000* clearly cared about the future) there would be a European woman who would most likely look like a French woman since France constituted a sort of average European nation for its language, tastes and geographical position. In contrast to the racial theorists of his day who deplored the degeneration that had allegedly resulted from the mixing of different races, Mantegazza believed that the ideal woman would have a mixture of Andalusian and English features. The height and size of an English woman combined with the small hands and feet of the Spaniard would unite 'the two most excellent forms of life, the two splendid creatures of the human universe'.[106] The outcome, he enthused, would be 'heaven on earth'.

Paolo Mantegazza was an energetic polymath who enjoyed the pleasures of life. He was a friend of his near contemporary Pellegrino Artusi (who cited him in his pioneering work *La scienza in cucina e l'arte di mangiare bene* [Science in the kitchen and the art of eating well]),[107] and it is easy to see him as a lover of fine food, foreign travel and beautiful women. If his writings were merely the musings of an ageing Casanova, one could read them with a certain amusement. What makes them serious is the cloak of science, albeit of the popular variety, that surrounded them. For the dominant culture of the time, women were not intelligent beings who could participate in civil life and pursue an education. While many lower-class women worked in the cities and the countryside, bourgeois women were confined to the domestic sphere and were seen purely in relation to their roles in the family. They were there to complement men and to please them. The discourse of beauty was already a product of this state of affairs. The addition of secular scientific authority by one of the leading intellectuals of the day gave it a new foundation in the bourgeois nation. Only in the field of entertainment did some women achieve a wide measure of autonomy. However, it will be shown in the next chapter that their freedom and visibility made them liable to more individual scrutiny from men who aimed to reinforce and extend the connection between feminine beauty and Italian identity.

CHAPTER THREE

THE RISE OF
PROFESSIONAL BEAUTY

Of all the women who have been deemed to represent Italian feminine beauty in the modern era, none more than Lina Cavalieri won plaudits in equal measure at home and abroad. A flower-seller from Trastevere who performed at the Folies Bergère and became a leading star of the New York Metropolitan Opera before winning further praise for her performances on film, she forged a unique synthesis of popular and regal beauty. Hailed by D'Annunzio as 'the highest expression of Venus on earth', she combined the natural qualities that were seen to distinguish Italian beauty with the elegance and refinement that characterised the belle époque. There are recordings of some of her operatic performances, but she is remembered today mainly due to the 1955 film based on her life, *The Most Beautiful Woman in the World*, directed by Robert Z. Leonard, in which she was played by Gina Lollobrigida.[1] Greta Garbo also played a character inspired by her, the Italian opera diva Rita Cavallini, in *Romance*, a Clarence Brown film taken from a stage comedy of the same title by Edward Sheldon. Cavalieri was painted by Giovanni Boldini, Vittorio Corcos and Francesco Paolo Michetti, but above all it is postcards and photographs that bear witness to a beauty that bewitched an age that was especially sensitive to feminine allure.

Cavalieri's career began in a Roman *café chantant* (cabaret) in 1890, when she was fourteen. It ended when she finally withdrew from public life in the early 1930s, after she ceded to her brother control of a chain of beauty parlours she had founded. Over this period, she worked in five separate spheres: *cafés chantants*, variety theatres, opera, cinema, and the nascent beauty industry. She was as great a celebrity in Russia and won lasting fame in America and France as well as Italy. She married four times, first to a Russian prince and then, in succession, to an American millionaire, a French tenor and an Italian racing driver. Her lovers probably included W. K.Vanderbilt and the Sicilian entrepreneur Ignazio Florio. She was regularly featured in the press on account of her art and her private life, and her image was sufficiently well known for it to be often reproduced, sometimes in caricature.

Cavalieri was recognised as a great beauty, to the extent that her appearance always eclipsed her singing voice. The designer Erté, who saw her in St Petersburg, described her in his memoirs as 'my idol'. 'Over the years, hundreds of journalists have asked me whom I regarded as the most beautiful woman in the world,' he wrote:

> Invariably I replied: 'Lina Cavalieri'. Why? She was tall and extremely slender – a rarity among turn-of-the-century prima donnas. Her classically pure features were enhanced by dark hair and eyes, and a long swan-like neck. Yet her beauty was not cold. Her expression was full of animation and she moved with grace and authority. Cavalieri's most dominant quality, however, was her extraordinary charm. What is charm? I would define it as a quality of mind and soul which finds expression in a person's physical appearance and behaviour. Cavalieri possessed it to a superb degree.[2]

Cavalieri enjoyed renown at a time when an extraordinary series of technical, social and cultural changes were taking place. As one of the very first multi-media international stars, she occupied a place at the intersection of these innovations. The discourse about her beauty was underpinned by the rise of the actress and performer at the expense of the royal or aristocratic figures who had dominated society up until that point. As the theatre became a store window, actresses and performers gained respectability and above all visibility. They conveyed to people of all ranks the sense of elegance, beauty, charm and manners that could be imitated and adopted. 'Actresses and Society "beauties" were coming to represent a new kind of femininity that was closely tied to the mass production of images', Erika Diane Rappaport observes, adding that 'the late Victorian actress was thus strongly identified with fashion and consumption'.[3]

Cavalieri was certainly a commercial or professional beauty but she was also a performer who invested considerable effort in building a personality and a career. In her time, she wrote in her memoirs, the great women were distinctive; 'each one had a personal and distinctive beauty'. Later, the cultivation of beauty became more widespread and standardised.[4] But Cavalieri was also known for her generalities: her elegance, her deportment and her Italianness. For the British fashion photographer and illustrator Cecil Beaton, she was 'supposed to be possessed of the perfect Roman face'.[5] In a period in which women carried a special burden of representation and were, to use Nira Yuval-Davis's phrase, 'constructed as the symbolic bearers of the collectivity's identity and honour, both personally and collectively',[6] a celebrated woman took on a special role. As an Italian known for her beauty in Paris, St Petersburg and New York, and as an exponent of an art that was especially identified with Italy, Cavalieri came in some way to symbolise Italy. Her humble origins and passionate temperament fixed her in foreigners' minds as a being in continuity with the Romantic ideal of the *bella italiana*. But her classical looks and refinement situated her more in the aristocratic tradition. To Italians, she combined certain traditional, even specifically Roman features, with an international allure and style. She brought Parisian elegance to Italian beauty.

Beauty between the fin-de-siècle and the belle époque

Female imagery was widely employed throughout the period between the late nineteenth and the early twentieth centuries for a variety of aesthetic purposes in art, design, interior decoration, illustration, and advertising.[7] This was not the same sort of appropriation that had occurred earlier during the phase of nation-building, although it too stemmed from the exclusion of most women from public roles and responsibilities. Rather it was related to the rise of a modern notion of femininity that was associated with urban living and consumption. This was principally associated with Paris, the capital of fashion and style since the time of Louis XIV. The *Parisienne* was an expensive, high-maintenance woman possessed of a certain spirit, and artfully fashioned. Parisian beauty was admired by artists because it was distant from the natural essence of woman. For Balzac, the elegant, coquettish *Parisienne* was infinitely preferable to the Venus de Milo.[8] Her beauty was geared more to pleasure than to duty and did not suggest either reproduction or unrepeatable perfection. While being imitable and widespread, it was also complex and stylised; it required, to sustain it, some sort of external stimulus or example. Actresses and courtesans were the most fashionable people in Paris, figures of chic whose beauty and elegance was legendary. The Spanish dancer La Belle Otero and her rival Liane de Pougy were women of humble origins who, by determination and erotic appeal, rose to the top of a hierarchy that began with the common prostitute and finished with the grand courtesan. 'Paris had been supreme in women's fashion for decades and, as the year 1900 drew nearer, the *Parisienne* became the world's great sex-symbol,' observed Raymond Rudorff.[9] 'She was extolled and made legendary in books, plays, posters and magazines. The eroticism of the *belle époque* was at its height. Paris was the international capital of Woman.'

Parisian beauty was not exclusively French. Indeed, as cultural critic Octave Uzanne noted, many Parisian women were not Parisian or even French by origin. It was the city and its special atmosphere that refined and moulded women so that their femininity was enhanced.[10] In his view, it was perfectly possible to be 'Parisian' anywhere, provided one adopted a certain lightness of spirit, playfulness, and an openness to erotic experience. Also important was a sense of the feminine as a construction involving the deployment of consumer goods including fashion, perfume and cosmetics. In Italy, the supremacy of Paris was confirmed by fashion periodicals that were entirely in thrall to the dictates of couturiers including Worth, Doucet and Paquin. Moreover, the great courtesan performers regularly toured the peninsula, appearing in theatres in Milan, Rome, Naples and Palermo.

The degree of artificiality in the Parisian woman led to some hostile reactions. The Paris-based commentator Paul Adam, for example, deplored the fact that most women preferred fashion to beauty and were happy to wear anything, no matter how hideous, so long as they were persuaded it was 'chic'.[11] Ugly and strange fashions, which looked even worse when copied by the lower classes, had resulted in an aesthetic impoverishment of the nation. In Italy too, there were strong cultural resistances to the wholesale absorption of the Parisian model. For the writer Neera, 'It has been said that the Milanese woman is the Parisian of Italy, but this comparison only works from the physical point of view. A huge difference undermines the comparison because, while the Parisian is frivolous, the Milanese loves her home and is a good housekeeper'.[12] 'Provincials who see a well-groomed Milanese woman, with a fashionable hairstyle, think that she does nothing all day but look at herself in the mirror', she continued. However, in reality, while she might be well-groomed, she also cooked, made her own clothes and cared for her family.

While Paris was admired, advice manuals from the turn of the century found Italian qualities in simplicity, naturalness and dedication to family. Even Matilde Serao, who wrote a short book in praise of feminine grooming sponsored by a cosmetics company, rejected 'artifice' and praised 'general simplicity'.[13] Writing in 1900, Mara Antelling urged educators to combat the uncritical acceptance of modern influences and foreign fads. Italian girls were urged to 'show themselves as they are, without fakery or embellishments'. While they were 'daughters of progress', 'they will always be sweet and gentle in that they add education to natural genius and goodness'.[14] She warned against 'the new trend' that 'renders them artificial' and 'making them artificial, gives them a strange, irresistible glamour'.[15] 'I have known many brunettes with that golden shade of brown that is so soft, so caressable when it frames a fresh little face, and then I have seen them again as blondes or redheads. The blonde is brash like gold, the red is hard and metallic with iridescent streaks . . .', she lamented. Against this deleterious practice, Antelling pointed to the example of the actress Eleonora Duse who 'never uses make-up, or dyes and whose face has the supreme suggestion of her very spirit, of her genius'.[16]

The idea of fashionable beauty, that was inspired by foreign examples, and was associated with elegance and artifice, was current in large cities as well as in the theatre. But Italian beauty was still informed by more established ideals. There was the classical Italian tradition of pictorial beauty that had been conferred on Queen Margherita and which was also applied to other very prominent beauties with fair hair and pale complexions. This pictorial frame of reference enjoyed great prestige throughout the civilised world. Proust's hero Swann, for example, frequently employs it to describe his beloved Odette de Crecy.[17] In addition, there was a darker, more physical ideal of beauty that was associated especially with younger women and that was seen as most typical of the new Italy. For example, Paul Adam thought of Italian women as having 'heavy breasts, a rounded figure, black hair under a scarf, strong thighs and long legs'. He believed that the Mediterranean climate had produced 'brown, large-breasted women with passionate faces'.[18] One prominent example of this sort of beauty was Donna Franca Florio, the beautiful dark-haired and olive-skinned wife of Ignazio Florio, who was widely regarded as the 'queen of Palermo'. She was described in 1896 in *Il Torneo*, the Palermo high society magazine, as 'tall and slender with a laugh that recalls the virgins of Guidi, with eyes full of goodness and poetry, like a new Beatrice, she passes among people provoking everywhere admiration and respect'.[19] The absence of any comment on her dark colouring illustrates both the dominance of the blonde and pale ideal of beauty among the upper classes,[20] and the common association of darkness with lower-class women, who were deemed most representative of it. The natural ideal of beauty that was widely held in Italy drew succour from the rustic ideal of the unspoilt peasant woman, whose flashing eyes, fiery temperament and long dark hair bore witness to her spirit. On the whole, this type of beauty was identified with Rome, Naples and Sicily. It had already come to public attention through literature and art but found wider approval. Serao, for example, praised Franca Florio, describing her as 'the very beautiful woman, whose loveliness, defined by a physique that is so exquisitely ours and by a bewitching blooming quality, is so frankly Italian'.[21] In the early twentieth century, beauty contests would allow for the selection of human examples from the wider populace. The significance of Lina Cavalieri lay in the fact that in some way she combined the models of beauty and contributed to the unification of the various conflicting discourses on beauty that had arisen in the wake of the first decades of the Italian state.

From Trastevere to St Petersburg

Cavalieri's key appeal lay in that she was a dark-haired beauty of lower-class origin who had a regal deportment and who acquired a reputation for elegance. A 'girl of the people' who conquered Paris, St Petersburg, London and New York, she was often praised for the instinctive grace of her performances. She was born Lina (Natalina) Cavalieri in the Trastevere district of Rome in December 1875. From a young age, she sold flowers in Rome's Piazza Navona and earned extra money folding newspapers. According to her not always reliable memoirs, she enjoyed singing while she worked and received her first rudimentary voice training from a music teacher who worked as a coach to promising beginners in the city's *cafés-concerts*.[22] She made her public singing debut at the age of fourteen in a theatre in Piazza Navona and progressed through various cabarets in the capital. At the age of sixteen she gave birth to a son whose father, it has recently been established,[23] was her music teacher. To compensate the Cavalieri family for this seduction, and to avoid prosecution, this man agreed to contribute to the family budget until Lina was able to support herself. She soon resumed work and began to appear at the higher-class *cafés-chantants* of Porta Pinciana and the Via Salaria before winning a place on the bill first at the prestigious Esedra *café-chantant*, where she made her debut in 1893, and later at the Grande Orfeo theatre.[24]

It is likely that her rapid progress was assisted by a wealthy male sponsor. In Italy, as elsewhere, female stage performers were public women who were widely regarded as being sexually available, especially to men of means. Cavalieri's transfer from the Italian stage to the considerably more prestigious Parisian one was rumoured to have been promoted by a leading Italian *viveur*, Carlo di Rudini. It is he who is credited by some authors with having refined her and turned her into a high-class courtesan,[25] a role Cavalieri denied ever having played. She had some traits in common with the great

19 The variety performer and opera singer Lina Cavalieri in one of the many postcard images of her distributed by the Reutlinger Studio, Paris, c.1900.

courtesan-performers of the age, such as physical beauty, an instinct for publicity, a love of expensive jewellery and a certain cynicism in her choice of lovers. She was different to them, however, because she took her art seriously and possessed a significant talent. This gave her an advantage, since the 1890s were exactly the period that witnessed the development of the popular entertainment industry. New theatres opened at a great rate, old ones were reinvented, and the press sustained mass interest in performers. Moreover, after the First World War, changes to the social and political order eliminated the role of the courtesan and left the field free for the professional performer.

The main factor in Cavalieri's rise was her increasing popularity. This led to an invitation to perform at one of Italy's leading theatres, the Salone Margherita in Naples, which had opened in 1890 and had been named after the queen. Theatres required regular new performers, who for the first time were separated from the audience and situated on an elevated stage. Impresarios knew that female beauty was a highly commercial quality and were always happy to have a beautiful singer in the programme. Cavalieri appeared on the scene at the right time to take advantage of the opportunities offered by an industry that was increasingly international and which could confer or consolidate fame. The Salone Margherita provided the scene of her first consecration. She remained there for several months in 1895 and became a local celebrity. She added Neapolitan songs to her repertoire and blossomed as a stage performer. Accompanied by a band of mandolin players, she sang traditional and satirical songs and danced the tarantella. Her engagement at the Salone Margherita placed her in the company of international artistes like La Belle Otero and Eugenie Fougère who also performed there. The theatre's stars were largely international and it was said to have a Parisian flavour. It was natural therefore that Cavalieri's success should lead to offers from the French capital.

In her memoirs, Cavalieri made much of her success in Paris, 'the great tempter of provincial spirits, the huge international metropolis, the oasis of all loves'.[26] At the legendary Folies Bergère, she became a more modern type of celebrity whose fame extended beyond the theatre to the city at large. The press turned her into an icon of femininity for the public at large, for whom she became 'the Italian'. Her image was spread far and wide through posters, photographs and postcards, many of which bore the signature of the famous Reutlinger studio. The twenty-year-old singer revelled in her celebrity. 'I loved being idolised by anonymous masses', she later wrote.[27] Naturally, her earnings increased dramatically over this period and she added considerably to a stage wardrobe that already included peasant costumes and several sumptuous gowns.

Because it was such an international crossroads, success in Paris led directly to offers to perform in other capitals. In the second half of the 1890s, Cavalieri was an international star who was performing in leading theatres in Paris, Vienna, Berlin and London. Her fame reached the same level as Liane de Pougy and even the fiery Otero, to whom she bore a passing resemblance and with whom she entertained a publicity-driven rivalry. She first performed in St Petersburg in 1897 and she returned several times to that city and to Moscow in the following two years. During these sojourns, she made the acquaintance of Prince Alexander Bariatinsky, the man who, she claimed, became the first of her four husbands.[28] After meeting him, she left the theatre and exchanged showbusiness for the stage of society. During her period of retirement from the variety stage, Cavalieri frequented artistic circles and held a salon in her magnificent apartment, to which figures from the arts were welcomed. It was here, during private performances, that the desire for an artistic career that was more noble than that offered by the variety theatre flourished. Hearing her voice, the tenor Francesco Marconi and the soprano Luisa Tetrazzini urged her to consider the step towards opera. 'Petersburg', she later wrote, 'was for me the final arrival point of my variety career, the official entry into smart society, the first manifestation of my dream of becoming an opera singer.'

Cavalieri began her operatic career with the consent of Bariatinsky, although it would soon lead to their separation. Trained by the retired soprano Maddalena Mariani-Masi, her first public performance was in the role of Nedda in *I Pagliacci* in Lisbon in January 1900. The debut was a disaster, according to Cavalieri because two young hecklers forced her to abandon the stage temperamentally in mid-performance. In fact, the failure resulted from a poorly-prepared and premature debut that exposed the smallness of Cavalieri's voice. The first night's performance was tolerated, the second drowned in protests.[29] The lack of proper training contributed throughout Cavalieri's operatic career to some critical dissatisfaction. But she improved considerably and was not discouraged by this early setback. Having cast off her prince, she proceeded with her operatic ambition. She appeared in the role of Mimi in *La Bohème* at the San Carlo theatre in Naples, the city that had first sanctioned her success in the world of variety. Her debut, on 7 April 1900, was seen as a big test of the validity or otherwise of her aspiration to the status of serious artist. As *Il Mattino* wrote that very day, it was a matter either of 'clipping the wings of an audacious illusion' or 'encouraging a sincere vocation and a great and noble fervour for art'.

In the following day's edition, the paper's music critic decreed that Cavalieri had been vindicated. Any reservations were swept away amid unanimous applause for her determination, the improvement in a voice that had once been thought rather slight, and for the skill with which she occupied the stage, infusing the role of Mimi with unusual expressiveness. In the course of the performance her initial nervousness disappeared and she won over her audience, receiving at the end four curtain calls. This positive outcome meant that 'Lina Cavalieri [had] every right to take the risk and aspire to the positive judgement of the Neapolitan audience which, by its verdict, has sanctioned the felicitous start of her journey on the road of art towards ever greater successes'.[30] Some criticised her phrasing, but no-one denied her ability to dominate the scene or her courage. As the city of song and the site of the two most important triumphs of her career, Naples occupied a special place in the affections of Cavalieri to the extent that she always thought of herself as being in equal measure Roman and Neapolitan.

Between 1900 and 1905, she added to a growing repertoire with leading roles in *Manon Lescaut*, *La Traviata*, *Fedora*, *Faust* and, her favourite, *Thaïs* (winning special praise from its composer, Massenet) in many cities including Warsaw, Monte Carlo, London, Paris, St Petersburg and Moscow, as well as Genoa, Milan, Florence and Palermo. The singer confirmed herself as one of the leading operatic performers of her day, even though she never completely won over the critics. Throughout her operatic career, Cavalieri encountered reservations and criticism from those who resented or disapproved of her brusque crossover from the world of popular entertainment, or who regarded her successes as being based largely on her physical beauty. Nevertheless, her fame was such that in 1906 she was invited to sing in Philadelphia and at the Metropolitan Opera in New York.

Cavalieri's attitude to her new career was determined and commercial. She was not averse to using publicity stunts to arouse controversy and win attention, especially in the United States, the home of ballyhoo. The most famous of these occurred on 5 December 1906, when, instead of simply embracing him, she kissed Enrico Caruso full on the mouth on stage at the New York Metropolitan theatre (long enough for photographers to capture the episode) at the conclusion of a duet in Giordano's *Fedora*. Her intention was to raise the interest of the audience after the first act had been received rather unenthusiastically. Although the gesture was not entirely new – Eleonora Duse once shocked Parisian audiences by kissing her leading man at length on the mouth in a performance of *La Dame aux camélias* – it led to sixteen curtain calls and attracted huge press coverage, with Cavalieri being dubbed 'the kissing prima donna'.[31] Designed in part to eclipse her Metropolitan rival, Geraldine Farrar, it did nothing for her artistic reputation but everything for her legend.

Publicity filled theatres but it did not quell all doubts about Cavalieri's ability. Her appearance in the title role of Puccini's *Manon Lescaut* at Covent Garden in June 1908 produced reviews that were positive, if not ecstatic. The *Illustrated London News* noted that she was better known for her jewels and her beauty than for her voice. Given this premise, her singing was 'an agreeable surprise': 'Mme Cavalieri has certainly become an artist to be reckoned with, though it is clear that her gifts are the outcome of studious effort rather than the expression of a natural talent. Her voice has no very even quality, but is good where it is best, and at times she contrives to express the dramatic significance of a moment happily.'[32] The singer was warmly received, even though it was not yet clear that she would rank among leading prima donnas.

Cavalieri continued to appear on stage until 1920, although rarely after 1913. At that time she was still a big star, with large followings above all in New York and St Petersburg. Her presence in various cities still gave rise to displays of excitement not usually associated with opera. She was followed by 'tireless admirers, journalists anxious to gather up her every word, her every movement, all possible indiscretions'.[33] It was said that a fireman accompanied her everywhere, on account of the fires that her presence could provoke. Every public appearance was an event that 'provoked excitement as if she was a true phenomenon'.[34] If anything, her star quality increased further in 1912 when she married a fellow artist, the French tenor Lucien Muratore. The couple performed

20 Lina Cavalieri displays her elegance and refinement, as well as her beauty, in another Reutlinger image, c.1905.

together and they also made a joint move in 1914 into the new, but fast-developing, sphere of cinema.

Cavalieri made eight feature films between 1914 and 1920 – five in the United States, two in Italy and one in France. It was a phase in which film producers were inducing with tempting contracts already famous actors and singers to try their hand at the new medium. Although the voices of celebrated sopranos would not be heard by film audiences in the pre-sound era, the fame and beauty of a singer like Cavalieri made her an attraction. Only a few fragments of these films have survived to the present day, but contemporary accounts show that her first American film, *Manon Lescaut*, was an epic production that was highly publicised. Emphasis was placed on the lavish treatment of the subject and the reputation of its star: 'The Incomparable Cavalieri, the World's Most

Famous Beauty – and Lucien Muratore, the Great French Tenor and Lyric Actor – in a Superb Production … 300 scenes, 300 people, 6 acts'.[35] The success of the film was such that Paramount Pictures distributed her two Italian pictures, *Sposa della morte* and *La rosa di Granata*, both luxurious, melodramatic productions, which had been directed by the actor-director Emilio Ghione. Following the critical and box-office success of these films, the star was contracted to Famous Players-Lasky. The most interesting of the films she made for this company, *A Woman of Impulse*, revealed her to be developing as a dramatic actress. The plot contained autobiographical elements, featuring a poor Italian girl who cannot afford singing lessons until she is adopted by an American couple. It also featured Cavalieri in several stage roles that were adapted for inclusion in the narrative of the film. Her last American film, *The Two Brides*, released in 1919, however, was a poor film with a weak plot and it was not well received. Although she made one more film, in France, Cavalieri's career in the movies was at an end. She was now forty-four years old and the lack of a producer willing to guide her strategically in the careful selection of material meant that she could not capitalise on her early successes.

Staging beauty

Cavalieri's beauty was always central to her appeal and reputation. Part of this was straightforwardly physical. In contrast to the complex beauties of the Parisian demi-monde, whose elaborate costumes and mastery of a specifically Parisian language of eroticism and seduction constituted the core of their appeal, she was evidently a natural beauty. Her dark hair and eyes signalled that she was Italian in a way that keyed in with the observations of the writers of the first half of the nineteenth century. She had a sweet, small face and a figure that was both lean in a modern way and sufficiently shapely to attract the attention of men of all classes. Unusually for the time, her beauty was widely appreciated and understood across countries, classes and media. Matilde Serao described Cavalieri as an embodiment of beauty, referring to her 'little face like that of an apocryphal Madonna' which had 'a line of purity and of adorable grace', while her bust had 'the blossoming of a stalk and her eyes a languour halfway between sadness and delight'.[36]

The one-time flower girl who rose to become an international star was someone with whom everyone could identify. Like Marta and Maria-Luisa, the mother and daughter protagonists of Carolina Invernizio's novel *La regina del mercato* (*The Queen of the Market*), she was a beauty who appeared to be candid and regal.[37] In the *cafés-concerts*, female stars were usually classified by national type. The French were small-featured and haughty, while the Spanish were proud and curvaceous. However, before Cavalieri, the Italians were rarely beautiful and often had 'the air of a clumsy country girl got up for a celebration'.[38] Cavalieri's Italian-ness contrasted with the international appearance of many popular artists, that was highly standardised. Most performers, especially those that attracted a higher class of audience, were foreigners, and foreign fashions and influences were strong. One Italian observer in 1907 noted this in deploring the rise of the artificial blonde.[39] Cavalieri was said to have had dark, flashing eyes, a trait that recalled early traveller portraits of Italian peasant girls. 'One of my most vivid and cherished memories is of the marvellous sparkling eyes of Lina Cavalieri', wrote Ulderico Tegani in his memoirs: 'tender and calm eyes, naughty eyes, dreaming eyes, seductive eyes . . .'[40]

Despite being of humble background, Cavalieri possessed the grace and style of a lady. This quality was noted by Erté and was further underlined by Beaton, who called her 'a woman of innate distinction'.[41] 'Physically, she was hardly a woman of heroic proportions, being of medium height and slender build', he observed. 'But Cavalieri was undeniably a great beauty in the classic mould. Her features were of a blunt, Roman cast, a magnolia complexion that complemented the black wavy hair, which was parted in the middle like that of a Spanish dancer and gathered in a bun at the nape of the long neck.'[42]

Like many beauties of the nineteenth century, Cavalieri was deemed to be statuesque. That is to say, she had poise and presence. For Beaton, she had the gestures, bearing and grace of a woman in her prime even when she was young: 'Her Italianate aura of sad perfection was dominated by large eyes, compassionate and sombre, set beneath eyebrows raised not in question but in inner sorrow. Her equally sombre but sensuous mouth completed features that seemed to have derived from a painting by Murillo.'[43]

21 A portrait of the diva Lina Cavalieri on the cover of French theatre magazine *Comoedia illustré*, November 1909.

For foreigners, Cavalieri's beauty and temperament, as well as the instinctive, natural-istic style of stage acting she adopted, singled her out as a specifically Italian beauty. In her early career, she was seen as the embodiment of angelic, ingenuous beauty, even as she sang suggestive songs. Wherever she went, she could be sure that the press and public would comment on her beauty and its evolution. Wealthy admirers appreciated her majesty and commented that, unlike her competitors, 'her fame was based on classic beauty rather than novelty'.[44] However, while her 'Madonna face' may have inspired noble sentiments, her 'serpentine, sinuous figure' was highly suggestive.[45] This duality was underscored by her preference for roles, such as the dying courtesan Violetta in *La traviata*, in which beauty was mixed with forbearance and happiness was spoiled by fate.[46] As an opera singer, she remained a Latin performer. Her repertoire was limited to romantic heroines such as Manon, Fedora and Tosca.

Even several years after her death, she was referred to as a stereotypical Italian beauty who aroused much interest among foreigners. 'The southern and Mediterranean beauty of La Cavalieri could not but touch the mystical, dreaming Russian spirit' wrote *La Settimana Incom* in 1950, referring to her first marriage and her triumphs in Russia. Her eyes of fire could not but melt snow and ice. However, she had no shortage of admirers in her home country. When she appeared in *La traviata* in Florence in October 1901, the critic for *Il Marzocco* expressed satisfaction that at last a singer who did not look like an elephant or a whale had been cast in the role of Violetta. The stage had been occupied 'at long last by a singer whose pure beauty evokes the agile grace and the sober perfection of the best sculptures of the Fifth century'.[47] The Florentine audience 'expressed . . . with a certain noisy ingenuousness its admiration and, for the gratification of the eyes, it willingly sacrificed in certain moments the enjoyment of the other senses'. Cavalieri 'if nothing else, has the great merit of not obscuring with her voice the splen-dour of her beauty'. However, although the critic was happy to sing the praises of 'the exquisite grace of a person who is as flexible as a reed', he found that as an actress she was 'on occasion a little embarrassed and hesitant'. Nonetheless, 'the eye demands its fair share' and it was to be welcomed that audiences were no longer to be expected to engage in improbable 'gymnastics of the imagination'. 'To hear that a woman is called fascinating and irresistible on stage and then see her and find that in reality it would be more natural to reject her than run after her is a thorny contradiction that easily leads to exhaustion and disgust,' he added.

Contemporary witnesses were full of praise for Cavalieri. 'La Cavalieri is well known in two hemispheres for her grace and her truly triumphant beauty', wrote the critic G. Piccini; 'everyone knows the legend, or better the legends, that surround her: judging and speaking of her, it is impossible to separate the woman from the artist, her glamour from her intelligence . . . She has a splendid figure, her head is fine, delicate and pure, and she has a sparkling smile; she is slim and majestic; her wardrobe is costly and in exquis-ite taste'.[48] Her Violetta in *La traviata* was deemed the most seductive and eye-catching of interpretations. 'The audiences, when they have seen her in the dress that exposes her shoulders and arms (one might say that she has gathered up those lost by the Venus of Milo) and all the rest, are dumbfounded by the lack of artifice. "She is so beautiful" – one man assured me – "that even if she went to a desert island she would find a thousand admirers."'[49]

Cavalieri met D'Annunzio, on a number of occasions. In September 1900, after meeting her in Viareggio, he gave her a copy of *Il Piacere*, with the following dedication: 'To Lina Cavalieri, to the highest expression of Venus on earth, this book that sings the praises of her power.'[50] This flattery failed to turn the head of the girl from Trastevere and perhaps because his efforts at seduction failed, the poet turned to banter. Many years later, in 1933, he received a card from the now retired singer, a fact which led him to recall in his *Libro segreto* (Secret book) that he had once said to Cavalieri during a dance, 'Your legs are well-designed but it would be better if they were eight or nine centimetres longer!' At the time, he remembered, Cavalieri had replied: 'You are mistaken: they serve me well just as they are and indeed they could not be better!'[51]

There can be no doubt that Cavalieri was a passionate and strong-willed woman. She became more sure of her beauty and the power it gave her as her fame grew. The competitive efforts of Russian noblemen and army officers to court her especially boosted her confidence.[52] Her memoirs, co-written with her then lover, Arnaldo Pavoni who employed the pen name of Paulo D'Arvanni, play up to the myth of the femme fatale. At least two prominent men, Bariatinsky and a rich American, Robert W. Chanler (who was married to her for a week in 1910), compromised themselves on her account, while other men, including Pavoni, sacrificed their marriages for her. Yet she was also an artist who was never happy to be regarded solely as a beauty, even if observers on both sides of the Atlantic covered her with compliments and dubbed her 'the most beautiful woman in the world'. In 1908 she was asked how it felt to be a beautiful woman. 'I am not very interested in it', she replied; 'I am more satisfied if people speak well of me as an artist.'[53] At repeated intervals, she voiced the opinion that the obsession with her looks was impeding appreciation of her talents as a serious artist.

Beauty and publicity

In 2004 two important biographies of Cavalieri were published, one in Italian and one in English. Both offer significant insights into her life and career but neither considers in any depth how the focus on her beauty tied in with a more general interest in the selection and presentation of female beauty. In fact her fame and notoriety as a beauty provided an impulse to a variety of uses of her image. For example, Cavalieri was one of the celebrity favourites of the short-lived but influential boulevard newspaper *Verde e azzurro*. Founded in 1903 by an inventive publicist, Umberto Notari, as an Italian equivalent of Paris papers like *Gil Blas*, it made feminine beauty one of its chief calling cards. Notari was a patriot who often dedicated space to 'our home-grown stars' and who championed the cause of Italian beauty in all its varieties. Cavalieri appeared on the cover several times and was also featured in caricature. Notari organised what became the first Italian beauty contest by inviting photographers to send in pictures of women they deemed to be representative of the beauty of their regions. He appointed a jury of writers and journalists including F. T. Marinetti, Enrico Corradini and Roberto Bracco. Such an initiative could not but give rise to the disapproval of moralists, and strong reservations from women who feared the consequences of public exposure but, despite this, some 1,257 photographs reached the paper in the first few weeks, more than the number that had been received in analagous foreign contests by the Parisian *Le Figaro* and the London *Daily News*, a fact which led Notari to claim that 'this proves, naturally, that there are many more beautiful women in Italy than in France and England'.[54] Among the pictures sent were those of high society women and peasant girls. Some were artistic, others folkloric, some elegant, others spiritual, yet others naïve. Some smiled, others did not. It was lamented that few professional artists submitted photographs, but one amateur photographer in Rome sent in a photograph of Cavalieri, indicating her as a Roman type of beauty.

The competition was interesting because, although it shied from seeking to identify one embodiment of a national beauty ideal, it nonetheless considered beauty to be an autonomous quality detached from social class or category. Italian beauty was conceived

22　Poster for the Florence newspaper *La Nazione* illustrating the contribution of women, most of whom appear to be peasants, to the life of the nation, 1899.

as varied within the country but unified when placed in comparison with that of other nations. The competition aimed to be 'a consecration and a revelation of the supremacy of the beauty of the Italian woman, whatever she may be, whether a woman of the people or a great dame, a theatre performer or a society debutante. The cult that we promote of feminine beauty is so supremely developed that for us all social distinctions disappear. What does the social background of a woman matter to us if that woman is beautiful?'[55] At the end of the day, 32,741 voted for the ten most beautiful women in Italy. Cavalieri won the Roman category, while actresses and high society women dominated most of the other regional categories.[56]

There were strong cultural and religious objections to the public exhibition of women who were not actresses or performers, but the growing interest of the foreign press in female beauty acted as a stimulus to Italian journalists to defend their country's reputation in the field. In 1908, the women's magazine *La Donna* responded to an invitation issued by *The Chicago Tribune* to find 'the photograph of the most beautiful woman or girl in Italy' by running its own contest. The magazine recognised that it was challenging widespread reservations but nonetheless felt the initiative worthwhile to assert 'that effective primacy in the typology of female beauty that is universally accorded to our femininity'.[57] Many photographs were sent in by women of all types and, with the assistance of a jury of artists and a photographer, three were selected to be submitted to the popular vote. The women were known only by floral nicknames that they were given by *La Donna*: Rosa, Verbena and Fior di campo. Rosa was a tall girl of about twenty from Lazio who had a job in a large northern city. She had an urban appearance and a slightly flirtatious manner. Verbena was an elegant aristocratic woman from near Turin with an aloof attitude. For her part, Fior di campo was 'a typical rural beauty' who had been spotted by a photographer in the remote countryside. The photograph showed a rigid, unrefined girl who was held up as an 'example of typical beauty'.[58]

In November 1908, the magazine announced that Rosa had withdrawn and that the recipient of the most votes was Fior di campo, who was revealed to be Zelinda Vittoria Moscoloni, 'the daughter of a modest businessman from Fermo. . . . She is from a humble background and is devoted to work in the house and the fields'.[59] She was aged twenty, was 1.66 metres tall and had 'dark chestnut wavy hair and dark eyes'. There was satisfaction that the winner was 'a type of popular beauty that is characteristic of central Italy', the region that had submitted most entries, but concern that the quality of the winner's photographs was not equal to international standards. It was therefore decided not to forward them to the American newspaper as representative of Italian beauty.

This outcome demonstrated three things: first, that in a context where there was a popular vote, the dark ideal of popular beauty would triumph; second, that the selection of Italian beauties was becoming a matter of national pride; and, third, that Rome and Lazio were proving better than other regions at offering symbols of national beauty. In addition, it showed that, while the ideal of the peasant girl might have satisfied internal ideological requirements, it had little currency in a commercialised international context.

23 A 1912 poster for the National Exhibition of Rice Cultivation and Irrigation, featuring a rice weeder in the foreground.

The celebrations for the fiftieth anniversary of the creation of the Italian state in 1911 provided an opportunity for cities to elect beauty queens. The contest in Rome was particularly well-organised, with each of the eighteen districts selecting a princess and handmaidens. The chosen women paraded in horse-drawn carriages through the avenues of the Exposition and were greeted by district presidents and officers all dressed in seventeenth-century uniforms that had originally been made for an historic tournament. Each woman was presented by an orator and the degree of her success was gauged by the warmth of the applause. In the ballot that followed, Palmira Ceccani of Trastevere, the birthplace of Cavalieri, secured the largest number of votes and was proclaimed the winner. *La Tribuna Illustrata* declared that the winner was 'a blossoming beauty with perfect, harmonious features, a gentle smile, a healthy colouring and long brown hair'.[60]

Despite the popular success of this contest, there was widespread coyness about it and a conviction that it only had a rationale as a complement to the ethnographic exhibition that was part of the Exposition, 'as a celebration of one of the ethnic and natural features of Rome'. This sort of resistance to a phenomenon that was developing quickly abroad revealed that there was a huge gap between those, like members of royalty and actresses, who were expected to be professionals of self-presentation, and the mass of ordinary women, for whom exposure of any sort was likely to be condemned. This placed a woman like Cavalieri in a special position and concentrated the focus on her physical being.

Like other amply robed and highly visible professional beauties of the belle époque, Cavalieri inspired masculine fantasies about what was never seen: her naked body. Several of the photographs of her taken by the Reutlinger studio and turned into post-cards featured revealing stage costumes that left exposed her shoulders, arms and neck. At least three legends bear witness to the way interest in her rested on this unrequited desire. Enzo Biagi reports the story – which has all the flavour of a legend – that Cavalieri was rumoured to have disrobed in the Louvre so that she could be compared to the Venus of Milo.[61] Rumours also circulated that she had posed for one of the painter Giovanni Boldini's unidentified nudes. A more elaborate story was recounted by the critic Piccini. He relates that in St Petersburg, a young admirer wagered that he could penetrate the strict security that surrounded the theatre where Cavalieri was performing, enter her dressing room and photograph her without her costume. He took the place of a fashion house delivery boy to carry a gown to her. As she prepared to try it on, he whipped out a camera and snapped her in a state of undress. According to Piccini, even the Tsar heard about the prank and was shown the resulting photograph.[62]

Journalists played on these fantasies, giving voice to the voyeuristic aspirations of their readers. When Notari waited outside a Milan hotel room to interview Cavalieri, he over-heard 'a rapid rustling of silk around the body of an elegant woman who was dressing or undressing'.[63] 'I allowed my mind to muse on the positions of that body during the delicious stages of a feminine toilette and I thought that only a thin, perhaps indiscreet hotel door was separating me from that mysterious intimacy,' he continued. He related how his eyes drank in the beauty of Cavalieri, as he described her neck, eyes, hair and 53-centimetre waist. 'As an expert in palmistry', he accorded particular attention to her hand, a part of the body whose expressiveness was extensively explored by D'Annunzio. 'Her hand, that I saw just for a moment', Notari wrote, 'is fresh, the skin is translucent, the fingers are short but tapered. It is the hand of a woman who is very proud, imperious and submissive all at the same time. She refused to tell me how many gloves she owns and the size of her shoes even though her feet are small and arched.'[64] Although she was no longer so young when she began her film career, Cavalieri's beauty carried over effectively on to the screen. No one was more favourably impressed than her Italian director Ghione. 'She is not just beautiful; she is perfect', he wrote in his memoirs. 'Lina seems as though she has been formed by a poetic sculptor.'[65]

Elegance and style

Female performers were expected to offer a spectacle of fashion and elegance. Theatres were like shop windows and part of the show that audiences savoured was a display of colours, materials, accessories and jewellery. Actresses and entertainers offered inspiration to women and communicated the fashions of the day to their audiences. The Italian publication *Il café-chantant*, that was required reading for artistes and theatre managements, contained many advertisements in the early years of the twentieth century for singers which stressed their fashion appeal. For example, announcements appeared for 'the beautiful Paolini Giorgi, the super elegant Italian starlet'; Armida Marini 'the very elegant Italian singer: youth, chic, beauty, elegance, grace, repertoire, success'; and Cleo Diamante, who promised 'excellent repertoire, elegant costumes'. There was even a certain 'Contessa Vera di Pavignon' promising 'original dances and transformations: exclusive, very luxurious wardrobe'.

At the start of her variety career, it was said that, while Cavalieri was certainly beautiful, she had an unfortunate 'air of a country bumpkin'.[66] This was soon corrected as her first earnings were spent on improving her wardrobe. Costumes provided her with a special appeal from early on. She was aware that extravagant, eye-catching stage dresses were necessary to the construction of a public personality. But she also had an ability to use understatement to highlight her beauty and grace. It was an article of faith at this time in Italy that regal qualities of the type exemplified by the queen could also be found at lower levels of society. The royal family provided the focal point of national unity and the example of behaviour that all women were expected to aspire to. The humorous magazine *Il Travaso delle idee della domenica* described the contestants in the Roman beauty pageant of 1911 as girls 'who boast no noble titles beyond a regal deportment, a face of majestic beauty and a moral standing that not even an anarchist bomb could destroy'.[67] In the contemporary world, in which women were no longer confined to the kitchen and the drawing room, wrote *La Tribuna Illustrata*, elegance could not be the privilege of 'a few [who had been] touched by good fortune' but needed to be taken as a collective quality.[68]

Cavalieri was seen as a beautiful woman of the people who had a natural instinct for elegance. When she first appeared in variety shows in St Petersburg, a reporter for a local newspaper wrote that: 'she is very elegant, graceful and dressed with rare taste. I have travelled much across Italy, but I have never seen so refined an Italian woman as Cavalieri. She is an Italian of Paris, who is able to combine the Italian simplicity and the French stylishness'.[69] In performance, she alternated folk costume with superb gowns that became richer and more strewn with gems as she entered into competition with Carolina Otero. Such was her popularity that one impresario groomed an imitator, who performed Italian songs under the name of 'Maria Cavalieri'.

Diamonds and jewellery were the sign of the well-born lady but also the mark of the *demi-mondaine*. Lovers bestowed costly gifts on courtesans, who exhibited them in public as proof of the value accorded to their beauty. They were a sign of status for respectable women and a mark of success as seductresses and as performers for others. Cavalieri was known for her jewellery collection and she often performed bedecked in pieces from it. Her pearls, diamond necklaces, tiaras, and her unique collection of emeralds, were said to rival those of royalty. Cavalieri received her first serious gifts of diamonds from Bariatinsky and did not hesitate to wear them in public. After announcing her retirement in November 1899, she appeared at the opening of a restaurant wearing such dazzling jewellery that a St Petersburg newspaper dubbed her 'the

24 The beauty of its young female workers is employed by a Turin chocolate factory to promote its wares, 1900.

queen of diamonds'. As Paul Fryer and Olga Usova comment: 'Whether princess or commoner, on stage or off, Cavalieri retained the same overwhelming fascination both for journalists and for those who eagerly consumed their popular society columns'.[70]

When she embarked on her operatic career, audiences were not interested only in the musical aspect or even in her beauty; they also came to evaluate Cavalieri's costumes and diamonds. While some expressed reservations about her voice, no-one was ever disappointed by her physical beauty or the luxurious and elegant costumes that she wore during her performances. The day after her debut at the San Carlo theatre in Naples, Matilde Serao wrote a detailed article for *Il Mattino* describing the costume and accessories that Cavalieri had worn for each act.[71] She concluded that 'a true instinct for elegance dominates and complements her pulchritude'.[72] Cavalieri's rich costumes and abundant jewellery were legendary. Much later, and even though she had been warned of possible negative consequences, she insisted on wearing her jewellery in abundance when she went on tour in Russia at the time of the revolution. 'Certain evenings, depending on the opera that she is playing in, she takes the scene resplendent in very precious jewels', noted Piccini.[73]

Cavalieri was received in high society in many, if not all, of the countries she visited. Only in her native Italy was she reputedly shunned by some aristocrats. In particular, Princess Vittoria Colonna di Sermoneta was rumoured to have turned her back on Cavalieri, although the noblewoman said in her memoirs that in fact she never had occasion to meet her.[74] The singer acquired a Parisian dimension that distinguished her from

Italian women of almost all classes and regions. She was recognised as an elegant woman, even an arbiter of taste. In Russia, girls imitated her style and combed their hair 'à la Cavalieri'. She launched at least two fashions, that for ostrich feather boas and that for tassled shawls. In 1909, the magazine *La Donna* praised her, observing that 'of the true beauty, she has not only the purest form of the face, together with raven hair and big thoughtful eyes, but also an instinctive elegance of movement, the flexible elasticity of a perfect body and a fine, full grasp of the arts of grooming that she employs to underline these rare qualities'.[75]

Erté commented on her elegance and so did Beaton. Her 'lady-like bearing', the latter noted, 'gave her the appearance of a czarina or an empress. She possessed the cool impassivity of a statue. The line of her back merged with the nape of her neck to create a noble column. Whatever the origin of her instinctive physical perfection, it lent authority and even grandeur to all bodily movements. She used her Italian opulence with a wonderful and probably unconscious distinction, a Mediterranean Valkyrie on a small and graceful scale'.[76] According to Beaton, the Duchess of Rutland advised her children that, if they wished to comport themselves in the most graceful and dignified manner possible, then they could not do better than 'study every detail and gesture of Lina Cavalieri'.[77]

She was the subject of portraits by several leading Italian painters, including Boldini and Michetti. The latter's portrait captures her beauty and dignity while the painting by Boldini goes against type. The painter was famous for his sexy, fashionable portraits of society ladies but, when faced with Cavalieri, he opted for a sober, even reserved, portrait in which the singer is depicted from the waist up, wearing a dress that covers her shoulders and neck. Around her neck are two strings of pearls.

She was patriotic, indeed 'an ardent chauvinist', according to Notari, who witnessed her send away the representative of a German postcard company that wanted her to pose for a picture that would be adorned with a signature.[78] 'Italian by birth, by temperament and by beauty, she will not bend before anything that might damage the name or reputation of her country', he reported. However, in fashion terms, she remained Parisian. When she went to America, she reputedly took with her the largest wardrobe an opera star had ever taken across the Atlantic. She patronised Doucet, the couturier of the seductive woman, whose clients included de Pougy, La Belle Otero and the great actress Rejane. Another designer, Paquin, made the sumptuous costumes she wore in the film *La sposa della morte* in 1915.[79]

For many in Italy, Parisian luxury was artificial and unnatural. It was not simple and direct, like conventional beauty, but complex, refined and alien to true womanliness. 'A magnificent *mannequin*, that is what today's beautiful woman is happy to be', wrote a commentator in a women's magazine; 'not as nature wanted her, holy and very pure, a model to which the whole of humanity would render a homage of faith and love, for the health of its body and its spirit'.[80] No one ever condemned Cavalieri, however, since her achievements and the lustre she brought to her country placed her beyond criticism of this sort.

After Cavalieri's film career drew to a close, she dedicated herself to the beauty business. In 1909 she opened a perfumary and cosmetics shop in New York that she later handed over to her brother Oreste. The cosmetics were said to be made according to a recipe of Caterina de' Medici that Cavalieri herself had found in an antique volume. In 1911, she opened another shop in Paris and began to write a beauty column for the magazine *Femina*. Like many performers, Cavalieri was a professional beauty who was regarded as an authority on matters of health, appearance, cosmetics and seduction. In her capacity as 'the world's most famous living beauty', she wrote a series of articles for Hearst newspapers that were gathered together in a book in 1914.[81] In these, she advocated close control of diet and regular facial massages and offered over fifty recipes for lotions and creams. In the 1920s, she consolidated this activity by opening a beauty salon and launching a perfume bearing the name Eau de Jouvence.[82]

Cavalieri's personal life continued to win her considerable publicity.[83] Relations between the singer and her husband deteriorated and this led to divorce in 1927. Soon after, she married the Italian motor racing champion Giuseppe Campari, but separation followed in a matter of months and the marriage was not even mentioned in her memoirs.[84] In 1930 she returned to Italy, where she lived between apartments in Rome and Florence and villas in Rome and near Rieti. It was in the latter residence that she wrote her memoirs in 1936 with the assistance of Arnaldo Pavoni.

To describe Cavalieri as a professional beauty may seem reductive, given the range of her talents and activities. But beauty was always central to her appeal in each of the fields into which she ventured. She displayed an acute awareness of herself as an erotic commodity who was available not merely for consumption by wealthy sponsors but by a wider public. The stage-setting of the person and the suggestive self-promotion in which she engaged enhanced her fame. Although she was immersed in fashion and consumption, and spent most of her time abroad after 1895, she was always identified as Italian. More than any other woman of her time, she was hailed as the embodiment of Italian beauty.

CHAPTER FOUR

FASCISM AND THE ALLURE OF THE FEMALE IMAGE

Given that the heightening of sexual difference was central to Fascism, it is not surprising that cultural battles around questions of beauty and fashion were repeatedly waged in the inter-war years.[1] Many commentators and even senior figures took an interest in the appearance of Italian women and had strong views about what was acceptable and what was not. One problem that came up repeatedly was that of foreign influence. Throughout the period, the mass media – principally cinema and the press – presented ideals of beauty that were either directly American or French or were imitations and adaptations of these. The vast numbers of secretaries, typists, shopgirls and students who populated the cities of the north and centre of Italy took their cue from these media and were at the forefront of a process of modernisation of female roles that affected not only exterior appearance, economic status and leisure habits but more fundamental attitudes and aspirations. The phenomenon of the flapper or the *garçonne* found a relatively limited echo in Italy in the form of the *maschietta* (tomboy) and the *ragazza Novecento* (twentieth-century girl), but it was widely recognised that the growth of cities, service industries and modern entertainment was leading women towards ideals of self-fashioning and independence that conflicted with their conventional confinement to the domestic sphere. Modern notions of womanhood which were geared to the public sphere and involved the consumption of goods like cosmetics, clothes, magazines and cinema were sustained by advertising agencies, big stores, magazines, novels and entertainments. All of these offered attractive pictures of modern women, often in explicit contrast to the traditionalist preferences of the Fascists and official Catholic opinion.

The figures who most widely embodied an ideal of feminine beauty in this period were to be found in advertising and the press. Often they were purely fictional, graphic ideals that were the products of the imaginations of their male creators. The dynamic silhouettes of fashionable women that the poster artist Dudovich drew to accompany motor cars and cruise ships, or to feature in store advertisements, set the tone for commercial modernity in the 1920s. The short-lived, but widely-admired Signorina *Grandi Firme*, who was drawn by Gino Boccasile for the covers of Pittigrilli's magazine of the same name, was the most prominent figure of the following decade. Her striking long legs and especially her small waist were not officially approved, but her pin-up qualities made her an idealised version of the secretaries and shopgirls who could be found on Italian streets. Such images were a source of conflict in the complex rearguard battle that was fought against imported ideals of beauty. In this battle, the tradition of Italian feminine beauty was repeatedly evoked and mobilised in all its forms in defence of a conservatively-defined national ideal of woman. This ideal was the product of a certain male hostility to the modern woman and of the authoritarian policies that underpinned Fascism's campaign to increase the birth rate. At a visual level, it never found an appealing form, even under a regime that was obsessively concerned with matters relating to race, physical health, ideal-types and gender.

The rise of the modern woman

The years after the First World War witnessed a significant change in female styles everywhere in the industrial world. In countries that had been involved in the war, women had worked in factories, enjoyed an unusual measure of independence and been drawn into the public sphere. Partly in consequence, demands for female suffrage increased dramatically in this period. Due to the growth of the consumer economy in the 1920s, many women worked and enjoyed leisure in the cities, even in a relatively undeveloped country like Italy. Almost everywhere there was a moral panic over the behaviour of young women who seemed to reject all the restraints and expectations to which they had previously been subjected. They cut their hair, drank and smoked cigarettes, disdained convention and wore practical clothes suited to the faster movement and mechanised transport of the time. Such young women seemed to some to be rejecting femininity itself, at a time when a range of forces preferred to take consolation in conventional images of the wife and mother. Flappers and *garçonnes* (or *maschiettes*) were few and far between in Italy, but nonetheless there was considerable controversy over the implications of the *ragazza Novecento*. The era was marked by the appearance of peasant girls in city shoes, factory workers in silk stockings and office workers with permanent waves and fashionable outfits.[2]

Developments in the press and advertising ensured that in the 1920s, for the first time, a modern urban idea of femininity entered general circulation and offered something to young women from all but the poorest sections of society. Cosmetics, fashion, public entertainments and sport came to some extent within the reach of most urban classes. Cinema and the press were powerful influences and also sources of the negotiation of new models of appearance and behaviour. The role of the Parisian designers Poiret and Chanel in defining freer, more practical clothing for modern women was fundamental. Due to them, corsets were abandoned, dress and skirt hemlines rose and mobility became a key consideration. But in many other instances, it was the great new industrial power, the United States, that became the source of new ideas and models of behaviour. This led to an ongoing cultural conflict in which anti-Americanism served as a filter through which modernity itself was evaluated and absorbed. At a time of change, Mary Louise Roberts has remarked of France, the modern woman served as a symbol of rapid change and cultural crisis.[3]

Beauty was not at all a secondary issue in the 1920s. The influence of fashion and the widespread use of cosmetics – previously the prerogative of actresses and prostitutes – served as visual markers of generational as well as gender difference. They signalled the rise of an artificial beauty in which appearances were deracinated from milieu and morality. Family, church and community pressure were no longer the sole forces shaping the way most women presented themselves to the outside world. Other systematic and seductive influences were to be found in the mass media. The work of Marcello Dudovich was highly influential. His posters and advertisements, which were influenced by Jugendstil and Art Deco, elevated the decisive, dynamic woman into a symbol of modernity. The women he drew were healthy and physically strong, although a strong erotic element carried over from the work he undertook in the pre-war period.[4]

The fashionable female provoked negative responses from male commentators. The writer Alfredo Panzini wrote an article in which he attacked a fashionable femme fatale figure painted by Dudovich in 1919 to 1920 and given the title *La signorina dalla veletta* (The girl in the hat-veil). He accused the artist of composing a hymn to the virago, the woman who regards man as an enemy and who seeks power by rejecting all convention.[5] Such comments were not isolated. Returning soldiers did not find waiting for them the acquiescent women of their dreams. Women had taken part in the war effort, had emerged from the four walls of their homes and were eager to take part in the opportunities that cities offered. The Futurists were the first to produce a misogynistic reaction to these developments. Hostile to the family and to Parliament, they were ostensibly favourable to female political and social emancipation. Indeed, they roundly condemned traditional morality; Italo Tavolato authored in 1913 two eloquently-titled works: *Elogio della prostituzione* (In praise of prostitution) and *Contro la morale sessuale* (Against sexual morality). But in the writings of the movement's founder Marinetti and others, even taking account of contradictions and inconsistencies, there emerged a contempt for perceived female qualities, such as sentimentalism and comfort, and a marked view of women as sexual objects (notorious, in this regard, is Marinetti's pamphlet *Come si seducono le donne* (How to seduce women)). Behind a widely-debated article by Emilio Settimelli ('Disprezzo della donna' – 'Contempt for women', published in *Roma futurista* in September 1918), lay an ostensible desire to destroy conventional conceptions of woman and replace them with an idea of her role in the development of the race. Marinetti penned a sharp denunciation of feminine luxury in which he deplored the emphasis on fashion and perfumes which produced a standardised material femininity. In such circumstances, he argued, 'the male loses little by little the powerful sense of

25 *La signorina dalla veletta* (1919–20) by Marcello Dudovich, was attacked as a hymn to the virago who seeks power and regards man as her enemy.

female flesh and replaces it with a vague, ambiguous and artificial sensibility that responds only to silk, jewels and furs'.[6] He urged beautiful women to exalt the beauty of the flesh and leave luxury to the ugly ones. He proclaimed that he spoke 'in the name of the race, that requires hot-blooded men and inseminated women'.[7]

The biggest single factor in the spread of what critics saw as a standardised artificial femininity was cinema. During the war, Italian cinema had given rise to a series of new stars who were highly influential. Lyda Borelli, Pina Menichelli and Francesca Bertini all performed roles of femme fatales; they played heroines of a D'Annunzian stamp, histrionic, passionate women who revelled in luxury and who drove men to distraction. In the brief period of Italian cinema's ascendancy, young women imitated the languid poses and affected speech of Borelli, just as in an earlier era they had taken their cue from the mannerisms of Duse.[8] The influence of fashion and cosmetics was dramatically magnified by the new medium, a fact which did not diminish as Italian cinema went into decline. From the mid-1920s, Hollywood exercised a strong fascination that was not related to established domestic tastes. Screen icons like Greta Garbo and Joan Crawford became great idols. Referring to the 1932 film *Grand Hôtel*, a film also starring Garbo in which Crawford played the part of a socially aspirant typist courted by the wealthy visitors to the hotel where she worked, Irene Brin wrote that the 'Crawford mouth' ('with the upper lip in the form of a liver sausage and the lower one like a slice of water melon') was much imitated.[9] 'The secretarial staff left their offices in the evening', she added, 'certain that they resembled her and that, like her, they deserved a villa in California with a swimming pool'.

The ideal consumer of the Hollywood film, the sort of person producers had in mind, was a young, single secretary or shop assistant. In Italy as elsewhere, young women responded with enthusiasm. Hollywood movie stars offered an ideal of femininity that was glittering and alluring as well as emancipated. Many young women were tempted to appropriate the look of the star by altering their hair, make-up, attitude and dress. The trend steadily increased and probably reached a peak with the rise of Jean Harlow, the platinum blonde, who was dubbed 'the most beautiful woman in Hollywood' by the women's magazine *Eva* in 1935.[10] Her almost translucent wavy tresses contributed to a fashion for bleached hair and for the spread of permanent waves.

The American star system was promoted in Italy by local agencies of the US majors, by the film press that they supplied with photographs and material, by posters and by related minor parallel media ('signed' photographs for fans, *figurine*, etc.). There was also a range of techniques that were employed to enhance the identification of young people with stars and the star culture. Competitions of one sort or another linked to particular films were commonplace, as were beauty and lookalike contests. These began after the death of Rudolph Valentino in 1926. Convinced that Italy was the breeding ground of beauty and talent, the majors indulged in periodic searches. In 1932, MGM held a Greta Garbo lookalike competition for promotional purposes (it was won by Romilda Villani, later the mother of Sophia Loren, who did indeed bear a striking resemblance to the great actress). More commonplace than these exceptional, much-publicised initiatives, however, were the lookalike competitions and the 'photogenic' contests that the film magazines ran. These were held constantly and often each one ran for months on end, with a regular page being devoted each week or month to news, comments and photographs.

Very often the competitions were launched to the accompaniment of photographs of current starlets to give people an idea of the sort of look that was desirable and in fashion. One in *Cinema Illustrazione* in October 1930, for example, featured the starlets Leila Hyams, Mary Philbin and Alice White. The pictures sent in by readers are a remarkable testimony of the penetration of the star culture into everyday life. There was a lot of attention to hair, pose and expression. Permed hair (sometimes bleached), plucked eyebrows, make-up and careful dress were common among women, although there were also photographs of simple girls who used little or no artifice to improve on their natural appearance. Most of the photographs were of face only or of head and shoulders, but there were also a few full-length portraits of subjects wearing swimming costumes. This was a reflection of the image of the Hollywood life conveyed by the magazines as being one of leisure, sport, healthy outdoor pursuits, and the cult of the body and the body beautiful.

As Italian cinema struggled in the early sound era to recover from the decline of the 1920s, it produced films that were heavily influenced by foreign models. Successful foreign films were remade using Italian casts, while environments, scenes and human types were imported and overtly imitated. Many actors also seemed to be modelled on Americans in physical appearance and personality. As a result, Italian cinema acquired, for sophisticated domestic audiences, an unfortunate second-rate reputation. This provoked negative comment, especially from observers who noticed the social influence that the medium exercised. As the art critic Raffaele Calzini wrote in 1934, Italian cinema was failing to contribute to the growth of national pride:

> Not content with making frequent recourse to foreign directors, using foreign scipts and imitating as much as possible the style of foreign cinema, it has populated its 'visions' with Italians who are camouflaged in their gestures, clothes and hairstyles as Americans. Competent actresses and excellent extras or lazy typists, once they have reached the screen, have immediately falsified their birth certificates not only as far as age is concerned but also to change face, personal data and customs. We have seen examples of more or less successful aping of the Anglo-Saxon Gretas, Brigittes and Marlenes. In their wake, there have been minor counterfeits that populate the streets, hotels and stages of Italy at this time of national affirmation. One almost feels nostalgic about La Bertini who, with her floreal poses and movements, at least had the seal of the beautiful, harmonious and gentle Neapolitan.[11]

It is clear from all this that the whole idea of beauty and of attractiveness was being redefined in a way that tended to displace traditional ideas. Emphasis was placed on a glossy exterior appearance and new, international standards were being introduced. Critics complained of standardisation and conformity, but cinema was also offering women a new capacity to alter and shape their appearance to some degree, to choose an image and to make the best of themselves.[12] Nonetheless, the direction in which this process went was the one mapped out by the new standard and producer of beauty: Hollywood. Confirmation that centuries-old standards were tending to be displaced by new, cosmopolitan ones was offered by the publication *Cinema Illustrazione* in 1931, in the form of an image of the Mona Lisa on whose features those of Marlene Dietrich had been superimposed.[13]

Whereas the Italian stars of the silent era were mostly remote, fantastic creatures, although recognisably familiar as physical types, the American stars of the 1930s were realistic, if highly-polished. Harlow, Carole Lombard, Myrna Loy and others conformed to types and were manufactured by a remarkable industrially-organised studio system in which every aspect of the process of star recruitment, grooming, launch and utilisation was meticulous and scientific. Although few films were being produced in Italy in the late 1920s and early 1930s, it is still striking just how few pictures and articles relating to Italians appeared in *Cinema Illustrazione*. There were occasional pictures of the actress Dria Paola (who took the lead role in the first Italian sound film, the 1930 film *Canzone d'amore* (Love Song)), sometimes wearing a swimsuit. The vivacious Elsa Merlini was also featured. The star of Goffredo Alessandrini's 1932 success *La segretaria privata* (private secretary), a remake of a German film about a woman rejoicing in the independence and social possibilities that her work as a secretary brought her, she became an idol for working girls and for those who aspired to be such. Chirpy and spirited, her springy step, manner and hairstyle with a fringe were much imitated. But these were only occasional presences in a universe that was dominated by the Americans.

The discourse on female beauty

Male authors and critics commented repeatedly on the appearance of women in the inter-war years. They observed a variety of new female types who were present in the cities: the typist, the shopgirl, the seamstress, the shopper, and the film fan. But the broad thrust of commentary was geared towards preserving the conventional attractions of Italian women. The established opposition between, on the one hand, a cosmopolitan, fashionable and artificial beauty and, on the other, an unadorned, more nationally-specific beauty that was shaped by ethnic, moral and cultural factors formed the basic template for most contributions. No one defended the former, which was the repeated object of polemics, often misogynistic in tone, against novelty, commercialisation and foreign influences. For example, in 1919 *Il Primato artistico italiano* deplored 'the gigantic emigration of girls towards the martyrdom of the typewriter. The war has favoured the acceleration of this youthful mass that teeters on illogical heels and is composed of flesh diminished by past poverty or present-day lechery, of idiotic but attractive little faces, of scrawny but indestructible little bodies'.[14] Instead, the magazine held up the example of the beauty of Sicilian peasant girls, whose nobility and purity of appearance were deemed to have survived the 'shipwreck of beauty'.

Few female voices intervened to correct or balance this male obsession with the negative appearance of modern women. The women who did engage with these themes tended to be even more hostile to the innovations of the post-war years than the men. Very often it was a case of older women expressing their disapproval of the young. In her book *Femminilità contemporanea* (Contemporary femininity), Daria Banfi Malaguzzi railed against cosmetics, perfumes and fashion.[15] Young women should be forcibly kept away from movie theatres, dance halls and some popular literature, she argued, to preserve their innocence from spiritual corruption. 'The young woman, as she is today, is ugly, wilted, rude, unloveable and restless' she insisted: 'she emits an excitable and frustrated animal quality and is on the look out for any sort of satisfaction'.[16] She urged a moral rebellion against the spread of fashions such as the *garçonne* hairstyle, smoking, mascara and tiny hats.[17] Girls needed to be educated as to their sacred duty of motherhood. 'The sweet and delicate beauty of the young woman,' she urged, 'must remain so sweet and delicate in order to please the man who will give her, in exchange for her love, the protection that she needs.'[18]

In the writings of male authors of the inter-war years there is a recurrent fantasy of women as passive, available, maternal, uncontaminated in any way by modernity. Such women never speak, never challenge men, never betray expectations and are always surveyed by men. Such fantasies tended not to be idealisations of individual imagined women, but rather, generic images often of groups or categories of women. One example of this sort of escapism is a short story by Emilio Cecchi, published in 1924. *La giornata delle belle donne* (The Day of Beautiful Women) describes a festival of women that takes place in an unnamed city at the end of a summer. Cecchi writes like the foreign travellers of the nineteenth century, who surveyed the peasant women who passed before them, except that what results is an erotic dream rather than an evaluation. The women, he writes, are 'all beautiful, even the ugly ones, especially the ugly ones'. Many of them are market women, since 'lower class beauty triumphs in noisy gatherings'. Most are shapely, as the narrator observes that 'the blouses of the women who passed by me seemed on the point of splitting under the pressure of their breasts'. 'Among the many fleeting apparitions' one young woman is memorable, 'with her wide straw hat like a nun's, her impetuous body moving against the rustling silk of her dress': 'the lovely contradiction of her aristocratic face on top of a solid peasant trunk! Her fine, crystalline nose, her lips opening in the form of a shell-like violet, lent her face a composite and anxious air. But in the mystery of her eyebrows and lashes an ingenuous laugh that was all gold and coffee confirmed her completely carnal intimate nature'. The overall impression is of a bucolic dream of timeless rustic femininity.

The debate on beauty sometimes functioned as a platform for male opinion. For example, *Galleria,* the monthly cultural supplement of the *Corriere italiano,* ran a regular feature entitled 'Opinions on beautiful women' in which intellectuals offered their reflections on beauty. The painter Armando Spadini declared that he preferred shapely women whose skin had not been exposed to the sun. He concluded that, 'The most beautiful women are to be found in Italy and probably in Lazio. I am convinced that beauty is concentrated in Rome'.[19] Cecchi, for his part, proved undogmatic. Every type of beauty was acceptable, he argued and writers would do well to 'avoid being too precise and not close the door to any variety of God's grace'.[20]

The regime's basic position on the place of women in the new Italy was articulated clearly from Mussolini's Ascension Day speech of May 1927, which saw the launch of Fascism's demographic campaign. In pursuit of this, professional women were excluded from the workplace and women workers were encouraged to leave their jobs to make way for unemployed men. This campaign encountered the approval of the Church, although conflicts arose when the regime, which was not without contradictions, tried to combine its stress on 'exemplary wives and mothers' with forms of female organisation, including sport and exercise. But there was substantial agreement on hostility towards several of the defining features of modern women, including cosmetics, fashion, short hair and skirts, intellectual activity, and political activism. This position resulted in problematic efforts to define an idea of the modern woman that was in harmony with official directives. However, as autarky took hold in the 1930s and the idea of a predominantly rural Italy became a dogma, the apparently timeless image of the young peasant woman emerged once more as a cultural idol. However, in the inter-war years she was represented more by photography than by painting.

The regime attributed great importance to images. It promoted its own model of the subservient but patriotic woman through posters and the official press. It also sought to combat manifestations of the type of modern femininity of which it disapproved. This was encapsulated in the cliché of the '*donna-crisi*' (crisis woman). Influenced by Paris and Hollywood, thin and well-groomed, unencumbered by children, cosmopolitan, often blonde, remote and vaguely androgynous, the crisis woman was to be found in films, fashion magazines, and the novels of daring popular authors such as Pittigrilli and Guido Da Verona.[21] This model of woman was deemed to have no interest in having a family and was often depicted holding a small dog. A cross between the femme fatale or temptress, and the flapper, she was portrayed in *Il Selvaggio* sitting on a bar stool sipping a cocktail, with a long cigarette holder in her hand. The campaign against the fashionable

26   The crisis woman (1932) (originally entitled 'Cocktail') by Mino Maccari, a celebrated satirical image of the fashionable female.

woman was an international phenomenon. In Britain, fashionable women were deplored as 'vulgar, absurd, improper, fast, over-sexed, abominable, shaming, humiliating' and as 'sexless, bosomless, hipless, thighless creatures'.[22] Everywhere, they were attacked as painted travesties of womanhood who bore no resemblance to the women of old.

In the *Enciclopedia Italiana*, compiled under the direction of the philosopher Giovanni Gentile, the 'crisis woman' was condemned since 'renouncing her shapeliness, she abandons her natural vocation for motherhood without, what's more, gaining anything from an aesthetic point of view'.[23] When Mussolini's son-in-law Galeazzo Ciano took over as director of the government press office in 1933, he instructed editors that 'the Fascist woman must be physically healthy in order to become the mother of healthy children according to the "rules of life" formulated by the Duce. Therefore drawings of female figures that are artificially thin or masculine, or that represent a type of sterile woman typical of decadent western society must be eliminated'.[24] The instructions (*veline*) that were issued by the Ministry of Popular Culture from the early 1930s on matters of women and fashion forbade the depiction of thin women and encouraged authors and cartoonists to ridicule them.[25] The commentary reached the most minute levels: 'The *Corriere della sera* on the fashion page has reproduced female figures that are too much of the crisis type in the bust while being very generous in the posterior parts. It would be more opportune to have regular figures, that should not however be too crisis-style . . ..'[26]

Even the Signorina *Grandi Firme* fell foul of dispositions of this sort. This illustrated figure, one of the most popular depictions of the young urban Italian woman of the 1930s, was the creation of Gino Boccasile. Invented by the artist for the cover of a magazine edited by the scandalous writer Pittigrilli, she was depicted from 1935 in a variety of guises: running for the tram, and as an admirer of film stars, reader of magazines, sports fan, potential actress, cyclist, secretary etc. Almost always, she was outdoors, with her skirts billowing in the wind. Her style was dynamic, cheerful and tantalisingly erotic. She was well-dressed and groomed in a modern style, with lipstick and high heels, her tight-fitting clothes suggesting a carnal shapeliness that was balanced by an innocent facial expression. Boccasile's Signorina *Grandi Firme* was precisely the sort of working girl represented by Elsa Merlini's character in *La segretaria privata*, except that she was more a focus of male fantasy than of female aspiration. In a way, the Signorina *Grandi Firme* was every fetishist's ideal. Each of her body parts was highlighted separately. While D'Annunzio had been the first to eroticise female body parts in Italian literature, in particular through his attention to the hands and, to a lesser extent, feet, Boccasile made much of arms, the bust, and above all, legs. Overall, the figure had a certain sculptured solidity to her. His Signorina was similar to the illustrations of women that featured in the advertising for luxury products, except that she had a more realistic, populist, girl-next-door appeal to her. Clearly influenced by the women of Hollywood cinema, Boccasile tried to give her aspects that were both international and modern, and familiar and reassuring.

Enrico Sturani suggests that the Signorina was a product of the male imagination of the time: 'For these repressed men, who were in a state of permanent mental arousal, caught between fantasies of the school, the barracks and the brothel', he argues, 'the woman, more than a person, was a collection of attributes. Each one of these was translated by repressed desires and unconscious needs into an image. They took shape with the powerful realism that is typical of a hallucination'.[27] Boccasile catered exactly to these desires by creating a female figure who was neither the modern androgynous *garçonne* nor the rural housewife. His models were not neo-classical Venuses, Sturani observes, but idealised extensions of real-life types such as secretaries, cashiers and shopgirls who were attractive but not necessarily great beauties.

According to Antonio Faeti, the long, firm legs of the Signorina *Grandi Firme* were phallic.[28] He saw her as having masculine qualities that fitted with the virile emphasis of the regime. Yet, while it is true that the legs, and consequently the movement, of the Signorina suggested a certain purposefulness and dynamism, there was nothing in her activities that fitted with Fascist propaganda. Indeed, the emphasis on the legs was more likely to be seen as American. The French scholar Michel Beynet asks perceptively if it was not precisely the fact that American beauty was seen to reside in the legs rather than

27 and 28 Commercial artist Gino Boccasile's cover-girl illustrations for *Le Grandi Firme* in 1937/38 which captured the spirit of the modern young woman.

the face that made it less expressive, more uniform.[29] The beauty of the leg was not classical, but it corresponded to a modern taste and was appreciated by all the women who wanted to assert a certain liberty of movement and behaviour.

These interpretations of the figure of the Signorina relate her solely to a male imaginary world. In fact, she needs to be seen in relation to the project of the magazine. *Le Grandi Firme* was largely aimed at young women, among whom adolescents, students and secretaries figured prominently. One notable series of articles, written tongue-in-cheek by Pittigrilli was entitled 'Accelerated course in 5 lessons on how to become a classy woman'. In some ways, women seemed to 'write' the features since so much space was given over to brief vox pop interviews and instant enquiries (among the questions asked were: 'Why are you in a hurry?' 'Where are you going?' 'How did you and your fiancé meet?'). Boccasile himself claimed that 'I find my models in the street'.[30] The periodical was very modern and dynamic and the stress on the lower limbs, while it reflected the illustrator's self-definition as a 'leg man' ('the feature that I tend to appreciate the most in a woman is, after the spirit, the leg'), also bore witness to modernity and movement. The women who read it were on the move. The magazine's great curiosity for, and spectacularisation of, daily life captured this. It was published on Saturday mornings but had nothing of the regime-inspired 'Fascist Saturday' about it. Indeed, Fascism is totally absent from its pages and its spirit, as though it were peripheral or irrelevant. Boccasile's Signorina may be a slightly comical figure who inadvertently provokes havoc when men are repeatedly distracted by her beauty, but she is a free spirit who goes where she wants and engages in the most varied activities. Her world is one of leisure, shopping, cinema and tourism. In this sense, the emphasis in the drawings on her legs and buttocks signals movement and freedom, qualities which in that context implied a rejection of reproductive sexuality. Her supposed 'virility' is contrasted with maternal, breast-oriented femininity.

Despite her ubiquity and modernity, the Signorina occasionally found herself faced with stern authority. On one cover she appears in the guise of a typist wearing a plain black dress, her head bowed as the severe office manager reproves her for having written a letter to her fiancé in company time.[31] These glimpses into what the real experiences of young women at work must have been like are highly revealing, precisely because they occur in a context where realism was minimal. Mostly though, she was depicted as carefree and optimistic, an idealised example of the young women of her generation. Not by chance the popular song 'Signorina *Grandi Firme*', composed by Alfredo Bracchi and Giovanni D'Anzi, was in Swing style. Its lyrics hailed her as an 'original little type' and 'the "star" of the moment', announcing that 'Now this type of girl. You see her in every square/ in the meeting places – in the cafés'.[32] Only at the end of the second verse was there a hint of the disapproval that modern girls attracted: 'They wear tight clothing/ They want to be seductive/ And they have a bit of a sexy style/ But this great mania/ Is really crazy/ Who know if this woman really exists . . ?'

After Cesare Zavattini took over the position of editor, the attention to female beauty increased. The magazine even launched a competition in 1938 to find a girl who embodied the cover illustration. 'Female readers! We are looking for a star', it proclaimed, promising the winner a movie contract for a year.[33] 'We are looking for a young woman endowed with a fresh beauty. She does not have to resemble in every way the Signorina *Grandi Firme*. That would be impossible. She should resemble her in general terms, in her healthy and youthful beauty'.[34] In one issue a sculptor was invited to draw inspiration for a model posed like the Signorina, in another a selection of male artists were invited to sketch their ideal woman. The results all presented the face of a dark-haired woman of a recognisably Italian appearance with full lips and a small nose.[35] Although this illustrated figure was not at all a *donna-crisi*, but rather 'a transformation of the official model into a model of a popular type', the popular element was 'a bit too marked' for official tastes.[36] Mussolini himself ordered the closure of the magazine after he saw an issue containing a short story by Paola Masino entitled *Fame* (hunger) and featuring a cover design by Boccasile in which the waist of the Signorina, at approximately 50 centimetres, was deemed too small.[37]

Female beauty in the Fascist era

In pursuing their campaign, the Fascists sought to elaborate an alternative model of women. For the new Fascist woman physical health and exercise were the best basis for beauty. In Calzini's opinion,

> the modern Venus, although she resembles the ancient one, is more lively, more aware and more dynamic. In this way female aesthetics today fuels the cult of the physical, not in terms of brute force but in the exquisite rhythm of nerves and muscles, in the submission of all movements to the measure and control of the intelligence, in the triumph of resistance, of the agility and energy of the spirit. . . . Thus lipstick, face powder, mascara, hairdyes, corsets, bustiers and elastic stockings will soon no longer exist in Italy except as a ridiculous exception.[38]

'Motherhood does not diminish female beauty', Mussolini declared in a celebrated phrase and various articles in the press sought to persuade women that beauty and maternity were perfectly compatible. If women sought to prolong their beauty by having only one child, 'in order to please and be as attractive at forty as at twenty, at fifty as at thirty' then they reduced themselves to being purely objects of male pleasure, wrote one commentator in *Illustrazione italiana*. Instead it should be recognised that, once the fresh beauty of a woman's twenty years has faded, 'another spiritual beauty can take its place: the aura of motherhood'.[39]

Perhaps the single biggest problem with the elaboration of this model was in making it visually appealing. The very basic, and even faceless, graphic images of mothers that

29 Women's magazine *Eva* often featured Hollywood-style images of women on its cover.

featured in the Fascist press and propaganda illustrated perfectly, if unwittingly, the difficulty of simultaneously honouring and rendering appealing a figure who was the product of repressive policies.[40] Even the Catholics, in their magazines, offered an image of 'maternity composed more of mystical abstractions than of concrete reality'.[41] Nonetheless, in support of its campaign, the regime drew on two resources. The first of these was rural women. The fecundity of the earth and prolific peasant families were held up as two features of the battle against corrupt and sterile foreign and metropolitan influences. Fascism saw rural Italy as the repository of true national virtues, and throughout the regime there was an emphasis on the honesty and simplicity of country people. Mussolini posed as 'the first peasant of Italy' and the Battle of Wheat, which began as early as 1926, was an important part of the struggle for autarky. It also served to remind city dwellers of the importance of the rural economy to national prosperity. Demonstrations of threshing took place in the piazzas of major cities, while officially-approved trucks took fertiliser and seed to country districts. Italian bread was used as a symbol of the country's independence from foreign products, and images of young peasant women were used to bolster the idea of a people whose beauty resided in their spirit and energy.

The image of the florid peasant woman was widely deployed in the periodical press and in popular song. In contrast to the fashionable and often film-related images of women that continued throughout the 1930s to appear on the covers of best-selling popular women's magazines like *Eva* and *Gioia*, *Gente Nostra*, the weekly of the Fascist

After-Work Organisation, consistently featured peasant girls from the regions of Italy. So, too, did all the publications geared to peasant readers or related in some way to the regime's campaigns concerning agriculture. The unnamed girls were often identified as being typical of their regions, a fact that was underlined by their traditional costumes. Some of them were clearly unfamiliar with the camera, and are unlikely to have been aware of their role as Fascist cover girls. Pictures of the rural world had been a staple of the bourgeois weekly *Illustrazione italiana* since the nineteenth century, and the images of the 1930s were no less likely to have found their main audience in the cities. Articles, cover pictures and songs all underlined the attractions of the Italian regions. The most popular song of this type was 'Reginella campagnola' (Country queen), which sang the praises of a peasant beauty of the Abruzzo region. Composed in Milan by Eldo Di Lazzaro, who was originally from Molise, and made into a hit by Carlo Buti, it was enjoyed by urban dwellers who listened to, or owned, radio sets or record players. 'O beautiful country girl, you are the little queen/ In your eyes there is the sun, there is the colour of the violets of the valleys in blossom' went the words, but the country girl of the title was not immune to the appeal of the city. In a later verse, she rides to town on an ass and returns in the evening: 'She is so happy to tell/ what she has seen in the city'.

In her study of the Massaie Rurali (Rural housewives) organisation, Perry Willson points out that peasant women were often called upon to perform an ornamental function at Fascist events.[42] With their traditional costumes – some of which were in fact not traditional at all, but invented from nothing – they added a welcome touch of folklore and visual variety to rallies and assemblies. Groups of them were engaged to promote produce and add an aura of genuineness to foodstuffs. However, the organisation brought little benefit to its three million members. It was 'demagogic, populist' and 'designed by an urban elite for the peasant masses'.[43] Far from improving the conditions of women and families, it 'patronizingly romanticised the harsh lives of the rural poor'. Yet the effect of its activities was not always the desired one. The events the organisation arranged, including visits to fairs, training courses, photographic sessions and so on had an unsettling effect. They gave rural women glimpses of the attractions of the urban life style and brought them into a new relationship with the state and the nation.[44]

The simple peasant beauty bolstered a conviction that Italy and its people were at the forefront of a new civilisation in the making. Such was the confidence in this model, or at least the conviction that it could be mobilised for propaganda purposes, that it was even held up as a positive contrast to the artifice of the stars at the Venice film festival of 1934. According to Raffaele Calzini, 'The blonde and brown-haired Venetian girls from the vegetable and fish markets, devoid of make-up, nail varnish and bleached hair, healthy and florid like the Venetian women of the time of Titian, Paolo Veronese and Tintoretto did not pale by comparison with the global stars gathered there'. International sanctions imposed after Italy's invasion of Ethiopia in 1935 provided a further reason for patriotic pride in unadorned beauty. However, attitudes sometimes appeared to be more contingent than permanent. 'A parsimonious, hard-working family-based sense of virtue

30 Peasant girls were often featured in illustrated form in advertising, in this case for a pasta company.

resists intact and postpones to the year 2000 silk stockings, radiators, radios, holidays, and cosmetics in order to build up bit by bit hard-earned savings' boasted a *Gente Nostra* contributor:

There has been some infiltration of exotic weirdnesses even among us, but compared to the few thousand wretches who go crazy for the dresses of Patou and Lanvin, for the perfumes of Coty, for the textiles of London, for the cars with foreign names, there are twenty million of our women who adorn and satisfy themselves with next to nothing, certain as they are in the conviction that Italian beauty and grace has no need of laces and fancies to bring out the fullness of their allure.[45]

However, *Gente Nostra* could not ignore the fact that many of its readers were urban dwellers who were familiar with cinema and consumer lifestyles. Indeed, it regularly printed photographs of film stars and advertisements (for example, for Palmolive soap – in which blonde models assured readers that 'beauty is not only that of the face. The body too must be attractive'). 'It must be recognised that the type of womanly beauty that is in vogue in the whole world today belongs to the category, continually renewed and ever-fresh, of American film stars or at any rate of stars launched in Hollywood', noted one writer in the magazine:

Even among the least aristocratic classes of our country the irresistible vamps or stars, that everyone by now is accustomed to worship by calling them with the name

31 Rustic peasant beauties were often featured on the cover of *Gente Nostra*, magazine of the Fascist After-Work Organisation.

'stars', find imitators of their deportment, their hairstyles and their physiognomic prerogatives. As a logical result, the natural blossoming and expansion of the Italic womanly type, in all her innumerable and seductive varieties and shades, that reflect the changing and ever picturesque physical face of our common fatherland, is compromised.[46]

In keeping with the allotted role of the magazine, it engaged in a cultural battle to shatter the dreams associated with these stars and to promote an idea of the person more geared to political priorities. But, by definition, this was a rearguard campaign. This is reflected in some of the extraordinary hybrids of modern and rural beauty that appeared on the covers of commercial magazines in the late 1930s and early 1940s. Under pressure from the authorities, magazines made concessions to ruralism and featured smiling peasant women from time to time, although the gulf between the polished cover girl of convention and the working peasant woman could hardly have been greater. On occasion, attempts were made to fuse the two models directly. For example, *Eva* featured some models, of obviously urban extraction and wearing make-up, disguised as peasant girls. Such images illustrate just how difficult it was to translate the dictates of the regime into pictures that might be found attractive by urban dwellers.

The second resource that the regime sought to mobilise was the Italian artistic and poetic tradition. Against foreign influences, it was proudly asserted that Italy was the true seat of western ideals of feminine beauty. One of the most impressive manifestations of

Spighe d'oro e giovinezza in fiore!

32 A hybrid image combining the qualities of the peasant beauty with those of the starlet.

this polemical use of the tradition was a handsome volume, entitled *La bella italiana: da Botticelli a Tiepolo* (The beautiful Italian woman: from Botticelli to Tiepolo), that was published as a supplement to the December issue of the design review *Domus* in 1934. Compiled by Raffaele Calzini, the album of pictorial reproductions was preceded by an introduction in which the critic asserted that he had gathered images of the beauties of three centuries in order to demonstrate the continuity, originality and supremacy of their beauty. Dismissing the recent claims of Paris and Hollywood, he argued that the most beautiful women were still to be found in Italy:

Anyone who travels knows, anyone who explores the roads of Italy sees it. Even today in the countryside of the Abruzzo or Siena or Romagna, alongside the lowgrade cinemas where the shameless American advertising displays in the form of photographs the sterilised and standardised type of Venus born from the froth of Hollywood, authentic, beautiful Italian women walk tall with bread baskets on their heads or solemnly carry children in their arms, like queens in exile. While on the beach of the Lido, the cinematic gathering exhibited a few months ago the world's 'stars', moulded by beauty contests, by a labyrinthine and gossip-ridden press and brought suddenly by scandal or a crime of passion to the forefront of attention, you could see (in the vegetable and fish markets) without make-up or varnished fingers strong and free creatures of the people, just like Titian used to paint them.[47]

Calzini's aim was to oppose Hollywood and 'the international female type' and seek out 'the noble titles and the special patents of our race, that is the best and immortal in this field too'. The volume 'sincerely hopes that, by taking inspiration from the past, the living examples of feminine beauty that the next generation, freed from zenophilia, will once again offer to the world, will become mothers to the strongest athletes and the best soldiers'.[48]

One problem with the deployment of the Renaissance pictorial tradition was that most of the paintings that comprised it depicted aristocratic women or models with fair skin and blonde hair. By reaching into the countryside and the south for its ideals of beauty, the regime privileged a popular ideal that saw darkness as an essential quality.[49] For Calzini, this pictorial blondeness was the painterly equivalent of a photogenic quality that did not fundamentally affect the substance of the discourse on beauty. With respect to the past, some refinements were added to this. For example, the existence of several varieties of Italian beauty was highlighted: 'the types are at least three and they are, roughly speaking, those of northern Italy, central Italy and southern Italy. Although the art of the three great centuries accords pride of place to those of Tuscany, Venice and Umbria, the regional richness of Italy, in this field, is such that any number of schools can present a type and every region of Italy could boast a living masterpiece'. [50] This was still valid even if the spread of modernity made it difficult to identify the original typologies in large cities like Milan or Turin. However, even if immigration had not been without effects, 'even in these large cities we are far from seeing the monotonous and grey equality of women without sex or beauty that crowd the underground passage-ways of Paris, London and New York'. 'In Italy', he argued, 'even if the variety of regions that are different in terms of their history, diet, climate and water, creates diverse examples of female beauty and marks them indelibly directly from birth, they are still united by an ideal bond and by a blood relationship that clearly exists. Thus the language of art that describes them and the pictorial medium that depicts them identify and exalt their intimate unity.'

Beauty, race and autarky

A key component of Fascism's campaign to instil a new spirit in the Italians was an emphasis on racial pride. The invasion of Ethiopia in 1935 was seen as finally putting Italy on an equal footing with France and Britain. Colonialism served its main purpose politically by establishing a terrain on which Italian superiority could be affirmed. The same techniques of picturesque annexation that had once characterised relations with

the troublesome south were now employed to incorporate acceptable images of domesticated Ethiopians into the national imagination. In keeping with the universal practice
of characterising colonised peoples as feminine, particular emphasis was placed on
photographic images of Ethiopian women, whose proud nakedness was offered up to
satisfy a new taste for the exotic. Immortalised in the popular song, *Faccetta nera* (Little
black face), the 'bella abissina' (Beautiful Abyssinian) was seen as a harmless ornamental appendage to the glories of the Italian state.[51] The 'beautiful appearance and
noble bearing' of Ethiopian women became a trophy of Italian colonialism.[52] However,
there were constant fears that Italians might become confused with the native population. Fears of blood contamination were such that great efforts were made to maintain
racial boundaries. Since the 'renowned beauty of the local women, seen as black venuses'
had 'created the inevitable racial-sexual encounter called "madamismo"',[53] interracial
social contacts were regulated and miscegenation became a criminal offence for all
Italians from 1937. Ruth Ben-Ghiat highlights a significant difference with French colonialism in that the Italian colonial authorities rejected assimilationism in favour of 'a
politics of difference that would continually remind Africans of their inferior status'.[54]
One might add that such a politics was also intended to remind Italians of their superiority. This mentality also informed the ban on jazz music in the 1940s. Anxieties over
how difference could best be established and maintained led to a series of dispositions
designed to ensure that Italian colonists' behaviour was at all times in keeping with the
superior status they were claiming. The very qualities that Italians had sometimes been
seen to share with blacks – earthiness, sensuality, emotional expressiveness, a lack of
embarrassment about the body – were to be banished.[55]

During the 1930s, racist social science developed in Italy to accompany the colonial
endeavour and inform public policy on demographic and racial issues. This developed
further in 1938 when race laws established legal differences of status between Italians and
Jews, Albanians, Slavs and Ethiopians. Although modelled on German legislation, these
laws conformed to the long-range desire to eliminate any doubts about Italian racial
status and integrity. Debates about the primacy or existence of the Mediterranean race,
and the connected question of racial divisions between northern and southern Italians,
were subsumed into a more general assertion of the Aryan status of all Italians.[56]
Although there were disagreements among race specialists, the homogeneity of the
Italian race became a dogma. While biological issues were not stressed in the way they
were in Germany, a belief in cultural-racial purity was widely affirmed. According to
Fascism, an Italian race had existed for a thousand years and it was now reasserting itself
through a proud sense of identification. 'The Italian race exists, it is alive, robust, pure',
asserted Carlo Cecchelli; 'the Italian race has a mission to achieve in the world and it will
achieve it'.[57] To some extent, what was being expressed was national pride but a battery
of legislation and discrimination gave Italian identity politics a very sharp racist edge.

The racial emphasis that was given to all debates about population, demography
and health in the late 1930s and 1940s led to much boasting about past and present

accomplishments. At the centre of this current was Umberto Notari, a polemicist who had already made his name as a journalist, writer and publicist. According to Marinetti, Notari had 'a religious passion for Italy that [tended] to become worship of every one of its qualities and every one of its defects'.[58] Among the Italian qualities especially appreciated by Notari, who had earlier been an admirer of Cavalieri, was female beauty.

Notari's books ostensibly conformed to the official policy of criticising foreign fashion and beauty influences, metropolitan types of femininity, and the relative disinterest of the modern woman in procreation. However, they won attention also because of their attractive visual presentation of modern women and the slogans and catchphrases Notari coined to designate them. His commentaries on the modern female condition were informed by a grasp of contemporary dilemmas and anxieties. *Signora '900'* (Mrs 20th Century), *La donna 'tipo tre'* (Women of the 'third type'), *Basìa ovvero le ragazze allarmanti* (Scary girls) were among his first titles. The 'voluntary infecundity' of well-off or economically independent women was repeatedly denounced in these works. In

33 The modern young woman, contrasted unfavourably to the traditional women in the background, in a 1942 pamphlet by Carlo Scorza.

particular, Notari identified and commented on the impact of what he called the 'third type' of woman. This was the woman who worked and who enjoyed a measure of autonomy, as opposed to the first type – the mother, wife or daughter, who was subject to male authority, and the second type – the woman of pleasure who existed solely to satisfy male needs. The exterior behaviour and appearance of this woman of the 'third type', who travelled unaccompanied by tram or car, who wore short hair and skirts of a length that facilitated movement, followed from a transformation of attitude. According to Notari, maternity required a 'superhuman act of abnegation' from the woman of the third type. To stop her influence spreading among women of the first type, he suggested radical measures, such as banning women from offices and factories.[59]

Notari's essays always ended on an optimistic note. He did not only criticise Italian women; he also flattered them and highlighted their qualities. He returned on numerous occasions to their beauty. In a 1933 volume entitled *Dichiarazioni alle più belle donne del mondo* (Declarations to the most beautiful women in the world), he claimed not only that 'Italian women are the most beautiful women in the world' but that 'feminine beauty is increasing markedly, both in "quality" and in "quantity"'.[60] In contrast to the French, whose beauty was distorted by fashion, and the Americans, whose beauty appeared to be 'manufactured in series' and impersonal (to the extent that 'the most beautiful American women are beautiful roses without perfume'), the Italians conserved a spontaneous beauty: 'The sensitivity of the Italians to feminine beauty is visible even on public streets, where many unknown beautiful women can be seen promenading', Notari observed. Italy may have been a poor country but it had two great natural resources in its artistic sensibility and its abundance of beautiful women.

Notari called for the formation of a 'revolutionary committee for the aesthetic independence of Italian women' to combat foreign influences.[61] In true Fascist style, he urged action squads to undertake punitive missions to reduce the use of foreign beauty products. He claimed that Italian women should not wear jewellery since no precious stones were found naturally in Italy. Neither Dante's Beatrice nor Petrarch's Laura had worn jewels and 'no halo of jewels can add nobility, seduction or allure to the quality of feminine beauty; neither can it add intensity to an expression, sweetness to a smile, grace to a silhouette, or smoothness to skin'.[62] This was a more flattering way of putting a point that Marinetti had made in the manifesto 'Contro il lusso femminile'. To combat luxury, he had argued, 'soon we shall have recourse to that hygienic measure taken by a Venetian doge who required the beautiful Venetian women to expose their naked breasts at the window, between two candles, in order to lead males back to the straight and narrow'.[63]

Due to Notari's energy and his eye for a publishing opportunity, the campaign against the modern distortion of beauty reached a mass audience composed largely of women. Between 1929 and 1939, he authored a large number of popular essays, all published by his own publishing house. They appealed widely to average readers and sold in hundreds of thousands through news kiosks, at stations and in bookshops.[64] Notari argued that beautiful women should lead the revolt against foreign tastes, ways, customs and products

34 Cinecittà's girl-next-door, Maria
Denis.

that she liked fast cars but, since petrol rationing was introduced, 'she takes the bus just like any woman of the people'.

However, not all were satisfied. There were complaints that, like the Americans, even the young actresses of Cinecittà all resembled each other. There was also some disquiet about the fact that several prominent actresses, including Assia Noris, Vivi Gioi and Irasema Dillian were of foreign origin or had non-Italian sounding names. 'But, really, do all these blessed girls of the cinema have to be so smooth and beautiful, smooth and beautiful like porcelain dolls? And do they have to choose strange names that do not seem to belong anywhere?' wrote one critic.[75]

Many actresses did not conform to Italian standards of beauty at all, although they adopted a model of feminine modesty and submissiveness that was favoured under Fascism. At a time when the Northern European type of looks associated with Garbo, Harlow and Dietrich was current, the 'platinum blonde, plucked eyebrow' look was also the norm in Italian cinema. Several Italian actresses were exotic-looking and as such served a purpose by being well-suited to the unreal atmosphere of the escapist, so-called 'white telephone' films which tended to be set in Budapest or other cosmopolitan environments. There were some darker, more Mediterranean types (although some of these, like Luisa Ferida and Duranti, had a distinctly Eastern or gypsy appearance). The success of Maria Denis in the 1936 to 1942 period is probably due to the fact that she, although no great beauty, was a recognisable Italian type, a lively, dark-haired girl-next-door who was regarded as an ideal daughter or sister.

In the early 1940s, the role of prima donna of Italian cinema was taken by Alida Valli. A former student of the Experimental Film School from Pola (Istria) whose real name was Lidia von Altenburger, Valli won her pre-eminent position as a result of her performances in lightweight comedies (such as *Mille lire al mese* – One thousand lire per month and *Ore 9 lezione di chimica* – Nine o'clock chemistry lesson), costume films (*Piccolo mondo antico* – Little old world) and the dramatic *Noi vivi-Addio Kira* (We the living – Goodbye Kira). Valli's appearance fell within the broad frame of beauty defined by the Italian cinema of the period. Oval-faced and green-eyed, with 'the eyebrows of a surprised cat' (as an American journalist would later describe her), she was exotic with respect to Italian norms. She was a classic, refined, European type, and of obviously bourgeois origin. Her dark hair and natural looks completed an appearance that was at once austere and good-natured. Valli was photographed in a more realistic way than other actresses, the use of light and shade adding character and removing some of the aura of idealisation and perfection with which some other actresses were always surrounded. Thus she reflected in her face a more complex inner life than most of her colleagues.

35 A chocolate card image of Alida Valli, the most popular Italian screen actress of the early 1940s.

Valli was the highest point of originality that Italian cinema reached in the Fascist period. Yet no one ever described her as a typical beauty, or even as a representative of the Italian tradition of feminine beauty. Although American stars were remote, and indeed were absent from Italian screens after 1938, they introduced a set of codes, rituals and genetic traces that determined what people understood by stardom. Hollywood cinema did not merely offer an extraordinary range of female types and assert itself as the primary producer of influential ideals of beauty, it also provided indications of how its models could be imitated and applied by ordinary young women. In her prime, Valli was an adaptation of this model, albeit an original one.

Fascism ultimately failed to give rise to any model of Italian beauty that was widely appreciated either inside or outside the country. The battle to reassert the Italian tradition and connect it to everyday life with reference to a restricted idea of femininity encountered serious, and ultimately insurmountable, obstacles. Although the regime employed many policy tools and methods of persuasion to orient women towards what were seen as their natural domestic and reproductive duties, it could do little about the fundamental trends of industrialisation and urbanisation that had led to the decline of the birthrate.[76] Commercial culture proved a vital pole of attraction to younger women who found in it opportunities, suggestions and models that in many respects ran counter to the aims of the regime. The idea of a type of modern Italian feminine beauty would take shape more readily in the more open conditions of the post-war years. Although the male domination of the public discourse on beauty would continue, the abandonment of the autarkic mentality, the removal of legal restrictions on women and the democratic atmosphere allowed for tradition and modernity to combine in more spontaneous ways and with more input from women themselves.

CHAPTER FIVE

BEAUTY AND NATIONAL IDENTITY AFTER THE SECOND WORLD WAR

After the fall of Fascism and the experience of civil war and foreign occupation, Italians struggled to found a new collective identity. The division of the country, the abolition of the monarchy, and the influence exercised by the Allies over Italy's destiny all left their mark. Nevertheless, the return of democratic politics and the extension of the vote to women in 1946 were important factors in determining the bases on which collective life was re-established. Other factors that bore on the issue were the economic state of the country, the desire of ordinary people to improve their circumstances, the presence of appealing American examples of progress and prosperity, and the greater role of the press and other media in making Italian society visible to itself. In this context, the tradition of feminine beauty was once more called upon to play a role in providing the country with a source of cultural reference.

There were, however, important differences with respect to the past. In the first place, women were more prominent than had been the case previously. They had taken on new roles during the war years and were drawn into the economic and political life of the nation more fully than before. At the same time, the breakdown of social order during the final stages of the war and the explosion of prostitution produced a more open emphasis on sexuality and its indirect, as well as direct, commercialisation. The new desire for leisure and amusement brought by the end of war fuelled a huge development of both spontaneous and commercially-organised entertainment. In addition, the controls that had existed over foreign influences and public images of women now fell by the wayside. All this meant that the discourse on feminine beauty ceased to be abstract and general, concerning 'types' such as the sterile 'crisis woman' (*donna crisi*), the curvaceous Signorina *Grandi Firme*, the fertile rural housewife, or Italian women as a whole, and instead became related to specific flesh and blood individuals, and the women of the lower classes in general.

This is not to say that the accent fell entirely on novelty. At a time of national collapse and rebirth, there was a re-assertion of conventional ideals of beauty, which helped to bolster a sense of national identity. Faced with a far-reaching challenge from Hollywood, the traditional criteria of Italian beauty were at first strenuously defended against examples that appeared to be artificial and immodest. The conventional focus on the face was held up as preferable to the exposed body of the American pin-up or starlet. However, this defence occurred in a context in which conventional ideals were first undermined and then modified and commercialised. Beauty contests proved to be a vital vehicle in this transition, since they acted both as a forum for the reassertion of national ideals of beauty and as a focus for the rebirth of Italian identity on new lines. Banned in 1938 by the Fascists, beauty contests turned the issue of female beauty into a permanent national discourse that was at least partially democratised. Moreover, they provided a vehicle for the displacement of old ideas centred on the face with a new concept based on the eroticised body. For several years, during the reconstruction of Italy and after, the material benefits that were on offer to the victors of beauty contests acted as a major draw that far outweighed any reservations about the morality of subjecting oneself or one's daughter to the public gaze.

The press and cinema were among the first commercial institutions to seek to adapt to the democratic climate. Some publications and films gave ordinary people unusual prominence, while others merely exploited the opportunity to pander to individual desires for upward social mobility or escapism. Illustrated magazines tried to provide both continuity and innovation in the experience of the Italians. A magazine like *La Domenica del Corriere*, that had existed since the 1890s, offered the least innovation. It provided a reluctant mirror for new trends and developments – such as the prevalence of pin-up pictures and the arrival of notions like 'sex appeal' – that were recognised and broadly deplored. More modern illustrated weeklies, like *Tempo*, or the newly-established *Oggi*, were more open and even, in the case of the former, took an active part in framing a post-war beauty ideal by sponsoring the nascent Miss Italia pageant. They helped foster a new prototype of Italian womanhood: the beauty contest winner and film actress, whose humble social extraction was not concealed, but rather was the first guarantee of her special appeal to the very public from which she had recently sprung. The sexualised and manufactured beauty that was the hallmark of the United States thus found a form of adaptation in Italy. In such a context, there were significant cultural battles between Catholics, bourgeois traditionalists, commercial forces and the left over the nature and meaning of such exposure and its relation to the collective identity of the Italians. These battles would carry on well into the 1950s.

The return of Hollywood

The Allied presence on Italian soil, from the landing in Sicily in July 1943 to the liberation of the northern cities in April 1945 and beyond, brought many Italians into direct contact for the first time with a variety of modern ideas, ways and conveniences. The impact was most marked in the south and rural areas. Tinned foods, medicines and clothing, as well as the robust and healthy appearance of the American soldiers, all confirmed the impression of America as the country of abundance. The Americans also brought their culture. In the cities of central and north Italy, American films and cartoons had been popular in the 1930s, but between 1943 and 1945 Italians could see for the first time how American civilisation found expression in such unfamiliar yet attractive things as boogie woogie, chewing gum, chocolate bars, nylon stockings and pin-ups.

The Americans had a clear idea of the role of cinema in the re-education of the Italians. Initially, a package of twenty films selected from the catalogues of the major studios was distributed in Italy by the Psychological Warfare Branch of the Allied Command. These included titles such as Chaplin's *The Great Dictator* and Frank Capra's *Why We Fight* documentaries. Following the abolition in November 1945 of all controls imposed by Fascism, American companies freely imported commercial films once more. According to the film historian Gian Piero Brunetta, the first American films to be shown since the embargo of 1938 were greeted with the joy reserved for the first drops of rain following a drought.[1] However, the initial drops turned into a flood. No fewer than 800 American films were imported by the end of 1948.[2]

What this meant was that Hollywood cinema was an integral part of the experience of the transition from war to peace and recovery for many Italians. America positioned itself as a new democratic model but also as a model of modernity, in part through the rich corpus of seductive attractions that Hollywood offered. In terms of both political struggle and social development, this was important. Alongside cinema, or bound up with it, was a series of alluring and attractive features that pointed the way forward, not just to recovery but to modernisation. These included magazines, personalities, products, advertising, fashions and lifestyles.[3]

Two of the most popular American stars of the period were Betty Grable and Rita Hayworth. For no less than ten consecutive years, between 1941 and 1951, Grable was among the top ten money-making stars. In a sequence of extraordinarily popular Technicolor musicals for Twentieth Century Fox, including *Down Argentine Way* and *Coney Island*, she presented an unambiguously wholesome, girl-next-door image. Hayworth took on various roles in musicals, comedies and dramatic films. Labelled 'The Goddess of Love of the Twentieth Century' by *Life* in 1941, she established herself as an international star in the part of Dona Sol in *Blood and Sand* in 1941 before appearing, in her most memorable role, as *Gilda* in 1946 and in *The Lady From Shanghai* in 1948. Whereas Grable always played 'dewy-eyed ingenues',[4] Hayworth was less predictable. 'Subsequent to appearing in *Blood and Sand*,' writes Gene Ringgold, she 'commanded the attention of screen audiences with an ambiguous sexuality that also had flash and flair. The audience was aware that we could never be quite certain how she would use her beauty and aura of sexual desire – for good or for evil – by always keeping us guessing whether her endowments were to be a means to self-gratification or whether they were to be offered to the man whose heart she captured.'[5] Hayworth's signature auburn hair, which tumbled down to her shoulders, added a lustrous crown to a seductive screen persona that made her appear physically available while remaining psychologically reserved. The leading lady of Harry Cohn's Columbia Pictures, she was in fact half-Mexican by birth and upbringing, and had been turned into an all-American glamour girl by the studio alchemists of star quality. She was the ultimate constructed star, who presented an unusual mixture of hyperbolic, manufactured beauty, perfect fashioning, healthy physicality, vampish behaviour and innocence of spirit.

As an image, an image to be consumed, Hayworth offered Italians a powerful taste of the capacity for manufacture of America's film industry. At the level of image, she filled the demand in post-war Italy for a dream of abundance and freedom. With her perfect figure and the costumes of Jean Louis, she entranced a generation and her films were even referred to in other works of art. Posters of the film *Gilda* are being affixed around Rome by the protagonist of *Ladri di biciclette* (*The Bicycle Thieves*), for example, and Pasolini wrote a memorable account of the film's impact, which then appeared in reworked form in his novella *Amado mio*. Gilda's easy sexuality 'was like a cry of joy, a sweet cataclysm that brought down the whole cinema in Caorle', Pasolini wrote.[6] 'Gilda speaks a universal language that crosses all frontiers and enters into direct communication with the spectator by means of that very special channel which is called *sex appeal*', wrote Gion Guida in *Cinemoda*.[7] This 'very special channel' reflected the fact that American 'mass' culture was shot through with a particular vision of feminine beauty. In publicity material, posters, film magazines, and advertising, Italians were presented with innumerable polished images of physically flawless, smiling young women often dressed simply in swimsuits or bikinis. For men overseas in the armed services, pin-ups were a morale booster and a reminder of what they were fighting for. The implications for the American star system were far-reaching. As Greta Garbo's biographer puts it, 'Wartime audiences needed Betty Grable's great legs more than they needed Greta Garbo's great art'.[8]

Pin-ups were not an entirely new phenomenon in the early 1940s, but never before had they performed such a prominent role. To conform to the rules of the genre, the image had to be 'inviting but not seducing, affectionate but not passionate, revealing by suggestion while concealing in fact'. The 'pin-up girl' was typically 'the healthy, American, cheerleader type – button-nosed, wide-eyed, long-legged, ample hips and breasts, and above all with the open, friendly smile that discloses perfect, even, white teeth'.[9] That the pin-up was a type rather than a person was borne out by the fact that she was often drawn, by illustrators like Varga and Gil Elvgren; even in photographic form the elimination of all physical details and peculiarities of the model meant that the pin-up was 'a man-made object disguised as a girl'.[10] The body was made to fit a format and deprived of logical scale. It could therefore be blown up in size for a billboard poster or reduced for a calendar or a magazine advertisement. Boccasile's Signorina *Grandi Firme* had been a similar figure, but without the explicit erotic appeal of the American model (for example, she never looked directly at the spectator or offered a 'come hither' expression).

Once part of a male subculture, the American calendar girl permeated many aspects of life in the 1940s, setting a new standard of youthful feminine beauty. The sociologist C. Wright Mills argued that the 'All-American Girl' really existed in the form of debutantes, fashion models and professional entertainers who set the images of appearance and conduct that were 'imitated down the national hierarchy of glamour, to the girls carefully trained for the commercial display of erotic promise, as well as to the young housewife in the kitchen'.[11] But she was essentially a fantasy figure who found her only living form in celebrities like Grable and Hayworth who inhabited the realm of magazines and film screens. In fact, Grable is best remembered today for her role as the poster model whose rear view 'swimsuit plus high heels' image (with a smile cast over her shoulder) decorated millions of wallets, walls and lockers during the war. Her 'million dollar legs' figured prominently in a pin-up that was printed in *Time*'s overseas edition as well as *Yank*, the official G.I. magazine. Requests for copies allegedly ran as high as 20,000 per week.[12] Hayworth, too, combined pin-ups and film work. Much to the chagrin of the actress, one of the former was reportedly stuck on to the atom bomb dropped on Hiroshima.

36 The 'American Signora *Sette*' by *Esquire* illustrator Varga.

37 The Italian Signorina *Sette*, a brief postwar re-edition of the Signorina *Grandi Firme*, prepares to go out.

On a larger scale than ever before, the United States introduced into post-war Italy ideas of sex appeal, such as female sexuality employed for commercial ends, and the ordinary girl as an ideal. A vast range of pictures of American starlets and pin-ups, provided by the newly-established agencies of American film companies, appeared in new Italian film magazines like *Star* and *Hollywood*, as well as in established magazines and newspapers. The short-lived magazine *Sette*, which was both born and closed in 1945, was the only one to seek to adapt the Signorina *Grandi Firme* in the light of pin-up culture. The Signorina *Sette* was less innocent and carefree than her predecessor; cover images of her fleeing from an American soldier or preparing to go out showed that she was more aware of her sexuality and the risks it could entail.

The reaction to *Gilda* in Italy and the influence it had on the collective memory shows that Italians were ready to receive new ideas and images, even if they were incomprehensible to some and represented a precursor of social and economic developments rather than an integrated part of the development of a new industrialised imagination. The star and the pin-up were symbols of leisure, prosperity and of consumption, all of which were intensely desired in a country marked by war damage, unemployment, homelessness and hunger. For women, the artificial femininity of Hollywood may have been bemusing but it was also liberating, in the sense that it implied a degree of feminine assertiveness and self-confidence and offered opportunities – to a few at least – for social mobility.

Responses to sex appeal

The extraordinary projection of a new idea of beauty as a standardised product of industrial civilisation provoked a variety of reactions. Although most people in 1945 to 1946 were primarily concerned with more pressing matters, among conservatives and some intellectuals there was a fear that the American cultural presence was resulting in a brusque displacement of Italian traditions. These fears were not new. However, in contrast to the 1930s, it was rarely possible to articulate such sentiments in an overtly anti-American way since the Allies exercised considerable control over communications and an attitude of gratitude to them prevailed. One example of this was the second edition of *La bella italiana*, a handsome, large format collection of Renaissance portraits first issued by the design magazine *Domus* as a contribution to the assertion of an Italian tradition in 1934, which was re-published in 1945. The original preface, by art critic Raffaele Calzini, asserted that: 'This blessed land of ours that is modelled in its landscape of mountains, seas and woods as the most superb matrix of creation, is wrapped in a climate of perennial love and fecundity. . . . Over the centuries it has produced the most beautiful women in the world. Their true sky, their surest home, their most fruitful alcove, is here'.[13] However, a significant passage from the preface to the first edition was missing in the reprint. This is indicated between the parentheses in the quotation that follows: 'Still today, in the countryside of the Abruzzo, near Siena or in Romagna, [alongside the low-grade cinemas where the brazen American publicity-mania pours out photographs of the sterilised and standardised type of Venus born from the froth of Hollywood,] beautiful women, authentic Italians, walk upright with jugs and bread-baskets on their heads, or solemnly with a child in their arms, like exiled queens'.[14]

Nevertheless, in publications such as the hugely popular *La Domenica del Corriere*, a family weekly founded as the Sunday supplement of the *Corriere della sera*, veiled criticisms did combine with national pride. In November 1945 beneath the title 'Where is beauty?' (which itself appeared beneath a head-and-shoulders photograph of an elegantly-dressed woman) there was the following comment:

Italy is full of legs: news-kiosks are covered with them, certain theatres bustle with them. But we don't want to believe that feminine beauty has finished up in the extremities: it shines above all in the face, and we provide here a persuasive proof, and are ready to give others if we receive worthy examples. It is not the precise and standardised beauty of the North or the other side of the Atlantic; it may be less exemplary, we can admit as much, but it is full of the flame of life. It is a tonic not a drug.[15]

Through 1945 and 1946 the magazine insisted that 'beauty belongs in the face' and rejected the new emphasis on legs.[16] It regularly published photographs of the faces of

38 After illustrating mainly urban girls in the 1930s, Boccasile concentrated on peasant beauties after 1945.

young women submitted by readers. Although the minor polemic against swimsuits and legs – and the standardisation and anonymity they implied – continued, it is worth noting that the 'genuine' beauties, 'without frills and distillations, without ambiguous mischievousness',[17] that it published were never named, although city of origin was occasionally mentioned. In other words, they too were not seen as individuals but rather as representatives of an alternative model of beauty. Italian beauty was seen as residing in a graceful face whose 'gentle composure' and 'thoughtful tranquillity of expression' did not require 'make-up, swimsuits or ambiguous and studied little smiles accompanied by jazz'.[18] The seductive quality of the Italian female face sprang from the 'sense of intimate goodness' of the woman it belonged to, not from the 'super-modern "perverse glamour"' of the cover girl.[19]

Other publications adopted similar strategies. The newspaper *Corriere Lombardo* published a picture of a young woman photographed in the Vittorio Emanuele gallery in Milan and invited readers to identify her. Announcing that similar images of pretty girls captured in shops, the library or the street would appear in the next few days ('From today, 18 December, a respectful persecution of pretty Italian girls gets underway . . .'), the paper claimed it wished to 'show that magnificent-looking girls are to be found not only in Palm Beach, Santa Monica and Miami but also among us. They can be such without a Max Factor *maquillage*, a dress by Adrian, a publicity launch of the type they specialise in over there and that desperate optimism which often is the fruit of clever, rigorous staging'.[20] Character and spontaneous elegance were the qualities valued most highly.

The American authorities believed that Italian women were imprisoned in a backward social order. In some instances, it was thought, they were living little better than animals and had minimal social status and recognition. This perception was widespread. In English-language novels written a little later but set in Italy during the war and liberation periods, Italian women are depicted in a way that is highly reminiscent of the accounts provided by nineteenth-century travellers. In *Catch 22*, Joseph Heller describes his character Luciana as passionate and instinctive. She is earthy and exuberant, buxom and dark.[21] For his part, John Burns sketches in *The Gallery* the dark eyes and skin of young Neapolitan women. They seemed to him to encapsulate something fundamentally feminine and maternal.[22] Despite some resistance, the American authorities were keen to promote the emancipation of Italian women. While soldiers during the occupation period may have been the main clients for the state-licensed brothels that were a key symbol of the sexual division of power, the Psychological Warfare Branch saw the improvement of women's conditions as a vital condition for the consolidation of democracy. It therefore provided opportunities for Italian women to reflect on their own situation and begin challenging some of the circumstances that reinforced their backwardness. For example, a new radio programme *Parole di una donna* (Words of a Woman), was established, which was presented by the journalist Anna Garofalo and which addressed all aspects of the female condition in a free and unprecedentedly frank manner.[23] This was a major break with the past that the Church and conservatives disliked.

Reformers like Garofalo believed that the liberation struggle and the return of democracy would lead 'immediately also to the installation in our country of more modern customs', as well as legal advances and changes in 'family relations and relations between the sexes'.[24] This was because women took part in the Resistance in significant numbers and for the first time participated in the process of democratic renewal that occurred as the parties re-emerged and established an organisational presence. By acquiring the vote for the first time in 1946, women had the potential to assert their influence more strongly in public life than ever before.[25]

Appropriately, the republic itself was often represented by the face of a woman. *Tempo* magazine, for example, bypassed the allegorical figure of the old national symbol, Italia, in favour of the open, hopeful face of a smiling young woman. This symbolic elevation of the ordinary girl became a commonplace feature of the post-war period. On 14 September 1950, *Epoca* featured an ordinary girl on the cover of its first issue with the caption 'Liliana, Italian girl'. A notice on an inside page read: 'We chose Liliana, on a September Saturday, at the lake, because her day of freedom belongs to everyday life; *this is the magazine which tells your story, looks for you in the crowd, frees your image and*

39 *Tempo* magazine chose a bright young female face to symbolise the birth of the Italian republic.

brings it to our attention; in short makes you a leader in today's world'.[26] In Italy, as Wright Mills noted for the United States, the everyday girl was queen. Yet, while typicality and ordinariness were in tune with the democratic spirit of the post-war years, they were an insufficient basis for the commercial uses to which women's bodies would be put as the economy recovered.

For Garofalo, the proliferation of sports competitions, dances, beauty contests, public bathing, travel and so on were positive because they provided women with opportunities. However, she soon came to realise that immediate change was a vain hope. The war had shaken old certainties and produced many more possibilities for women to seek economic independence and participate in habits and leisure activities in ways of their own choosing. It also induced some to question patterns of authority within the family. Yet, despite this, there was strong conservative pressure at all levels of society. This created tensions and contradictions that were reflected in the way cultural industries sought to exploit the female market. Garofalo commented negatively on the women's magazines that treated 'female readers like children, like toys or like slaves' and that regaled them with highly traditional images of elegant upper-class women and family-oriented lower-class women.[27] She also opposed what she called 'the dictatorship of beauty', by which she meant the habit of judging the worth of girls, even from the earliest years, according to their physical appearance. 'A big improvement in moral values will be achieved in this age of collapses when women come to believe that one seeks in them not only physical beauty but also personality, the gifts of the brain and the heart, and a new capacity of expression and behaviour', she asserted. This was so not least because 'beauty easily leads to compromises and it often comes hand-in-hand with stupidity'.[28] In fact, this 'dictatorship' would find a new expression in the phenomenon of beauty contests.

Miss Italia

Already in the pre-war years, the cosmetics company GVM had combined with the weekly *Tempo* and the women's magazine *Grazia* to sponsor a photographic competition based on natural faces and smiles.[29] One of the most successful advertising promotions of the period, the 'L.5,000 for a smile' competition ran for three editions before war forced its closure. When it was revived in 1946, with the same sponsors and the same organiser, the advertising pioneer Dino Villani, it took on many of the structures of the modern beauty contest. Unlike the pre-war version, participants were restricted to young, single women, who, at the national final, paraded in evening dress. Initially entitled 'La Bella Italiana', it became widely known as the Miss Italia competition. At first, its aims were strictly commercial. It was supposed to facilitate a transition from the allegorical and abstract representations of women of the past to the selection of emblematic real-life individuals who could stand for the newly-enfranchised masses. This was a significant shift, one that Zavattini had tried to make in his effort to find a real girl who corresponded to the Signorina *Grandi Firme*, although conditions had then been less

than propitious. The contest's historic importance was underlined by the journalist Orio Vergani:

> For Villani, Miss Italia is nothing other than a sort of 'living poster', a sort of marvellous three-dimensional *affiche*, brought to life by a flashing smile. In short, a young woman is chosen by means of a competition to compete with the thousands of beautiful young women that we have seen on posters in half a century of commercial art. If, in the world of the *affiche*, beautiful women have for thirty years been signed by the Cappiellos, Cherets, Dudovichs, Metlicovitzs and Boccasiles, I would like to say that the beautiful living and smiling women selected from the ranks of aspirants for the title of Miss Italia, to become, as some of them have become, the living emblem of Italian beauty, carry the signature of Dino Villani. He did not paint them, but discovered them and, in a certain sense, 'invented' them, directing on to their faces the projector of an advertising slogan.[30]

Because the artistic poster was part of an Italian, and European, advertising tradition that had come under threat from a more practical American model, this project of modernisation was rather a bold one.[31] It was all the more so because Villani's intention was to learn from and domesticate the American example. 'This event, it is true, was based on the American contests that we saw were taking place in magazines and newspapers', he noted, 'but here it had to take on a tone of our own that continued the atmosphere of courtesy and gentility that had surrounded the awarding of prizes to beautiful smiles'.[32]

To ward off criticism, Villani took steps to make sure the event was not sleazy. Jurors were advised not to evaluate beauty as such (or, still less, sex appeal) but to choose the ideal fiancée for their son. 'The juries of the competition have always refused to let Miss Italia or La Bella Italiana be impersonated by types whose physical attributes were displayed with too much evidence', he asserted, in an explicit rejection of the full-figured pin-up.[33] As Vergani put it, 'Villani's dream is of a "family-oriented" beauty, a sweet support assisting familial happiness'.[34] In this way, he ensured that traditional ideas of Italian femininity were perpetuated and that the way was paved for the competition to become a national institution, even though there would still be opposition to it. Clashes nonetheless occurred between different camps over the type of woman who should represent Italy.

The first post-war contest, held in Stresa in September 1946, ended in a controversial dead heat between a confident, well-groomed young Roman woman with a shapely figure, Silvana Pampanini, whose beauty was described by Villani as 'explosive and exuberant', and a Florentine 'girl-next-door', Rossana Martini. Although the public present on the occasion backed the extrovert Pampanini by a large majority, the jury (which included the pioneers of Italian neo-realist cinema Luchino Visconti, Vittorio De Sica and Cesare Zavattini) was deadlocked. Eventually a decision was reached in favour of Martini because she corresponded to 'the type of Italian woman that the greatest artists of our country chose as a model and for which they won a worldwide audience through their masterpieces'.[35] The winner, *Tempo* wrote, 'is a Florentine with brown hair and a virtuous look in her eye. Timid and emotional, when the great announcement was made, she covered her face'.[36] For one female observer, she had a 'gentle grace'; her 'Madonna beauty' was such that she 'represents in her own way an exquisitely Italian type of fourth-century beauty'.[37] Her photograph was published in *Tempo* surrounded by several sixteenth-century portraits. However, the prizes she received were very modern; among them were Lit.100,000, a fur coat, some high fashion garments, silk stockings, a radiogram, a manicure set and a suitcase, as well as the promise of a screen test.

Martini would enjoy a certain fame, but Pampanini's curvaceous figure and professional manner made her into a national pin-up. In contrast to Elli Parvo, a full-figured actress from the war years who was still dubbed 'the number one pin-up of Italian screens' in 1947,[38] she was the first new face (and body) of the democratic era. The magazines loved her and *Tempo* put her on its cover instead of the official winner Martini. What she symbolised above all was an escape from practical pressures. Her open smile, curvaceous figure and absence of melancholy or introspection made her especially appealing to returning soldiers, and also to Americans.[39] For the poet Vincenzo Cardarelli, 'Her beauty is of that exuberant, generous, florid type that is typically Italian

41 The runner-up in 1946 Miss Italia contest, Silvana Pampanini, secured the cover of *Tempo* on account of her star quality.

and which banishes from the minds of spectators any type of reflection and militates against any form of critical activity of the spirit or reasoning; but it is a beauty that entirely satisfies the vision of it by proclaiming itself to be . . . utterly relaxing'.[40] Her beauty matched a male idea of desirability that had little to do with art and aesthetics or moral qualities. As Villani would later complain, in the regions 'too frequently "buxomness" was confused with beauty'. Even before she took to cinema, Pampanini was described as an 'American beauty' or a '"glamour" beauty'.[41]

In 1947 the contest took on a more explicitly American feel, with the introduction of a swimsuit section and the comparison of vital statistics. While the contestants were expected to conform to tradition in the modesty of their declared aspirations and their demure manner, a decisive shift occurred from a type of beauty modelled on the face to a more commercially-oriented one focused on the body. Although the values of modesty were never overthrown in the contest itself, the contestants who would go on to greatest success were those women whose beauty was displayed most ostentatiously. The second contest would prove to be the most influential in the whole history of the pageant, since a large number of finalists and entrants were recruited by cinema and other branches of showbusiness. These included Gina Lollobrigida, Lucia Bosé, Gianna Maria Canale and Eleonora Rossi Drago. Each had a different background: Bosé, the daughter of a printer, worked in a cake shop in the centre of Milan; Rossi Drago was a single mother;

Lollobrigida hailed from a village in Lazio but had been to drama school. None of them was seen at the time as representative of the mainstream of traditional Italian feminine beauty. While they were dark-haired and mainly of humble origins, they were knowing and ambitious.

The contest was won by Bosé, the future protagonist of several films by Antonioni, including *La signora senza camelie* (The lady without camelias), a bitter treatment of a beauty contest winner who becomes a film star. Although she was only sixteen at the time of her victory, Bosé was immediately hailed for her modern looks and sexy demeanour. The beauty of this 'Milanese brunette' was referred to as 'provocative', in contrast to the 'warm romanticism' of Martini.[42] Bosé was in some respects atypical: she was an ordinary girl who had the fine features and grace of an upper-class woman. The daughter of workers, who had suffered hunger and poverty in the post-war years, she was initially spotted at her workplace by Visconti, who allegedly predicted her future cinema career. She was entered unawares for the photographic section of the Miss Italia competition. Her victory brought her instant success: 'I was amazed by everything that happened to me: one hundred thousand Lire for me alone, enough furniture to fill a huge house, gifts, clothes, invitations, screen tests'. She saw the whole experience as an adventure and decided to embraced it fully, 'even at the risk of finding the devil at the end of the road'.[43]

The risks of being exposed to public judgement were made immediately apparent. Bosé appeared on the cover of *Tempo* in a daring two-piece swimsuit and was tricked by

42 Contestants parade in bathing costumes at Miss Italia 1947. The winner, Lucia Bosé, is first on the left in a two-piece costume.

photographers the morning after her triumph into posing in bed with a cigarette dangling from her mouth. The photograph was reproduced in the *Corriere della sera*, where the sleazy connotations of the image caused the first genuine scandal in the competition.[44] The importance of respectability and modesty in prevailing conceptions of Italian femininity was underlined by a letter supposedly from a reader (but in fact, as was customary at the time, invented by the editorial staff) that complained that Bosé had been posed 'semi-naked and worse than naked, got up in the manner of a prostitute, lips shamelessly painted; and from her lip dangles a Lucky Strike while she holds a lighter in her hand, the fortunate child with the big wide-open eyes'.[45] The letter concluded by inviting the intervention of the Society for the Protection of Minors or the public morals squad.

In order to safeguard his contest, Villani raised the minimum age of participants the following year, discouraged two-piece costumes and restated his belief that winners should be modest, girl-next-door types. Fears about respectability would, however, always be present to one degree or another. In 1948, the contest for the first time became a focus for patriotism. The winner, Fulvia Franco, a gymnast and keen sportswoman who was a school student, hailed from Trieste, a city that was still under international jurisdiction following its removal from Italy at the end of the war. 'The beautiful, sporty, dynamic and delightful Fulvia Franco' enchanted the jury 'with that blossoming freshness of a 17-year-old, composed of subtle grace and impish self-confidence, with those brilliant and lively glances' wrote the *Giornale di Trieste*.[46] When she returned home after her victory, she was accompanied through the city streets by a parade of motor vehicles (hers bore the legend 'La bella italiana'). In a patriotic gesture, she donated her prize money to an association formed by those who had forcibly been made to abandon territory that now belonged to Yugoslavia. Along with other contestants that year, she appeared in the film *Totò al Giro d'Italia* (Totò at the Tour of Italy) with the great cycling champions of the period, Fausto Coppi and Gino Bartali. A member of the jury, the Neapolitan comic actor Totò was simultaneously shooting a film that would remain a unique record of the 1948 contest.

Beauty on the radio

The developments of this period occurred in a context in which women's organisations were keen to take part in collective debates and influence the shape of post-war democracy. While material problems were uppermost in many women's minds, the women's sections of the political parties, the cross-party Union of Italian Women (UDI) and other associations were working to ensure that the voices of women were heard. The election of the first women to the Constituent Assembly in 1946 and then to the Italian Parliament constituted a significant break with the past. At first, the press made light of this innovation by evaluating the beauty of new Members of Parliament, dubbing the Communist Laura Diaz 'Miss Parlamento' and remarking on the generous figure of her party colleague, Nilde Jotti. The process whereby women entered the public realm not just as bodies but as individuals with the power of speech was a complex one. At precisely the moment when Miss Italia and the press were framing the terms of a new democratic beauty for Italy's reconstruction, the radio hosted a series of talks by male writers and intellectuals on the theme of women. In their approach, the broadcasts were conservative in at least two ways. The male discourse on femininity was re-proposed in the same way as had been the case in the inter-war years. The writers were mostly former contributors to magazines like *La Ronda* and *Solaria* who had been occasionally writing and commenting on women for over twenty years. Furthermore, each speaker was invited to comment on the women of his city. This decision reflected a conventional view of Italy as a mosaic of regions and traditions, but it also bore witness to an unreflective localism that belied the national impulse of the period. Nevertheless, the talks offered a snapshot of sorts of intellectual perceptions of an issue that was undergoing redefinition.

Each writer offered some considerations on the beauty of the women of his own place of origin. In some cases, this was simply a matter of restating familiar qualities. Thus the Bolognese author of *Il Mulino del Po* (The mill on the Po), Riccardo Bacchelli, asserted that, by common consent, 'properly Bolognese would be a type of woman with a soft and generous body and an attitude to match, with a full and pleasingly rounded figure, a woman of a genial, pleasant disposition and beauty, all love and erotically aware'.[47] The Neapolitan Giuseppe Marotta argued that 'perhaps nowhere is woman genuine and natural as in Naples'.[48] In Rome, Antonio Baldini identified the conventional type of beauty as 'a bit papal and on the abundant side'.[49] With reference to Florence, Bruno Sanminiatelli traced a continuity from the women of the *dolce stil nuovo* poets through Botticelli and Leonardo da Vinci to the present day. 'Today no less than in the past', he said, 'the women of Florence are distinguished by a simple and reserved grace that is familiar and full of modesty'.[50]

Other writers chose to stress innovation. They particularly noticed that lower-class women were getting thinner as fashion filtered down the social scale. Moreover, women generally were less isolated and fearful of social contact. In his contribution on Venice, Diego Valeri was keen to point out that the image of the Venetian woman created by Titian did not correspond to reality. In the contemporary period, the beauty of the Venetian women 'is marked more by sweetness than strength, its attitude is elegant rather than impressive and it relies on an agile freedom that is distant from old-fashioned ideas of sublime stillness'.[51] Modern women moved freely, they rode bicycles, displayed curiosity in the world around them and adopted the habits of city dwellers. The modern Milanesi were no longer the 'florid and opulent beauties' of the past. Rather they were 'slimmer and more nervous figures, with less flesh on them and more paint on the face, while inside they burn with a desire to love and to please, to suffer and to enjoy life'.[52] The expectations of the women of the people had been changed by the war: 'workers, secretaries, and dancers at La Scala read photoromances and go out to have an aperitif on Sundays'.[53]

One or two writers seized the opportunity to promote the neglected women of their regions. Giovanni Titta Rosa argued that the women of the Abruzzi had not found a poet or painter of the authority of a Botticelli, Manzoni or Bacchelli. The region's greatest poet, D'Annunzio, had chosen instead to write about Roman and Venetian women. Yet, he said, 'the brown-haired and light-skinned women of Aquila, with their fine features shadowed by long eyelashes, the full-figured and thoughtful women of Teramo, the lively and often blonde women of Chieti and Pescara, who speak with a sing-song dialect, have sufficient gifts to rival the other girls of Italy'.[54] Gianni Stuparich found that the lack of an artistic heritage meant that 'making an appearance on the contested stage of feminine beauty without particular baggage or traditional obligations was undoubtedly an advantage for the Triestine woman. Her spontaneity was not weighed down, for example, by the smile of a Mona Lisa or the abundance of Titian's Flora or the sexual grace of the Madonna of Correggio'.[55] The *triestina* was natural, sporty and lively. She did not model herself on the classic model of serene, measured beauty or the wilder image of romantic beauty, Stuparich asserted. Rather 'she intelligently fulfils the modern instinct of women in an age in which they are about to free themselves from all pre-existing superstructures and assert their independence. Without being "American" in a standardised sense, the woman of Trieste is the "American of Italy" or, better, she is a new element in the canon of Italian beauty'.[56] In making these points, Stuparich knew that his listeners would have in mind the example of Fulvia Franco.

However, underlying the observations of all the writers in their radio broadcasts was a single dogma: that Italy was 'the classic country of feminine beauty' and that 'all Italian girls are beautiful'.[57] What was striking is that this was less and less asserted in relation to an old poetic and pictorial tradition and more in relation to the real women who were Italian citizens and not merely the country's symbols.

At first neither cinema nor the photoromance industry that blossomed at this time was interested in contributing to the construction of new national typologies of feminine beauty. Both were more interested in the exotic and the unusual, as well as in the commercial exploitation of recently-acquired fame. Pampanini made a series of musical films, low-budget comedies and historical films, as did Martini and Franco. For their part, the leading realist film makers of the post-war years were concerned to break with the forms of representation of the Fascist period and to promote a type of cinema that was closer to the people. Although actors were not disdained completely, many non-professionals were cast in the parts of workers, housewives and ordinary citizens. The American idea of the star, that had been emulated in the 1930s and early 1940s, was rejected. The one actress who more than any other embodied the moment was Anna Magnani, a variety singer and minor film actress who pioneered a new type of passionate and fiercely maternal woman of the people in her first dramatic role as the tragic Pina in *Roma città aperta* (*Rome Open City*). No-one more than her conveyed the resilience and spirit of ordinary Romans during the German occupation and the reconstruction. After her role in that film, Magnani trademarked the type of the passionate, authentic, maternal lower-class woman in a series of topical dramas and social comedies.

Although several directors took part in juries of contests, the neo-realists in general were wary of the artificial glamour and American air of some winners. Far from being representatives of the people, such women were ambitious and keen to escape their humble milieux. Despite this, it was widely recognised that new faces were needed and that these should be young and beautiful. Magnani became the symbol of the new Italy of the rebirth, but she was neither of these. While her warmth and passion shone through in her cinematic renditions of women of the people, she was 'too plebeian and insufficiently statuesque' to be the bearer of Italian beauty.[58] In the mean time, the popular commercial cinema that Magnani had abandoned to become 'the godmother of neo-realism' was not slow to capitalise on the new young beauties who were coming to the fore through the pageants. This fact would soon force leading directors to give them more consideration. Lollobrigida, Canale and Rossi Drago began in photoromances and started to make their mark in second-rate films, as did many others, including Miss Rome 1947, Silvana Mangano, and Sofia Scicolone (future Loren), who won the title of Miss Eleganza in the 1950 Miss Italia contest. Soon they would be demanding more attention from directors who were engaged in the struggle to reshape Italian culture.

The relationship between starlets on the one hand, and producers and directors on the other, was not an equal one. While the former had beauty, public appeal and sometimes talent, the latter held the power to select them and make their careers. Since they controlled the financing, making and distribution of films, producers and directors had a decisive influence over who was proposed to the public and how. Only when they achieved a measure of fame did actresses acquire a power of their own, and even then, it was always dependent on the male-dominated structures of the film industry. While democracy brought new freedoms and rights for women, it did not significantly change the structures of power in society.

CHAPTER SIX

CATHOLICS, COMMUNISTS AND BEAUTY CONTESTS

The prominence that beauty issues and beauty contests acquired in the post-war years meant that they were inevitably drawn into the broader political and cultural disputes that were dividing the country. Although commercial culture exercised a powerful influence at this time and indeed, constituted an ever-growing source of attraction and interest, many people could barely afford to take advantage of it. Even in the north and centre of the country, poorer people encountered illustrated magazines, the cinema, leisure pursuits and sport mainly through the activities of voluntary associations such as parties, trade unions and the Church. After the war, all political parties and newly-legalised associations struggled to establish a foothold in community life and then to consolidate and expand their support. At a national level, they established associations for women, children, pensioners, former partisans and peasants, held festivals and published a range of newspapers and magazines. At a local level, the parties themselves and the branches of these associations sought to rival the Church in offering activities for families, young people and children. At the outset, many of the associations were unitary, that is to say they crossed party lines as various forces collaborated to restore some sort of civil society just as the parties were cooperating in governing the country. However, they soon ceased to be unitary as the divisions of the Cold War made themselves felt in the domestic arena. As the political parties split on pro-western and anti-western lines, and prepared for the watershed election of April 1948, so civil society, especially in the centre, the north-east and the large cities of the centre and north, witnessed the formation of two blocs. One of these took its cue from the Catholic Church and was organised around the Christian Democrats, Catholic associations and parish activities. The other was left-wing and looked to the parties of the left, the Communists and the Socialists, for leadership. The issue of female beauty became caught up with a wide-ranging battle to capture for one part or the other the imagery of the nation and shape the direction of development.

The Catholics did not approve either of the immodest display of the bodies of young women or of the evaluation of beauty in terms of exterior appearance. As a result, they adopted a hostile approach to the proliferating contests. However, the Christian Democrats were more pragmatic. After their election victory, they were able to employ the instruments of state power in pursuit of their goals. Some of them at least understood that, while the Church remained attached to a traditional image of Italy as a mainly rural country whose values (the work ethic, simplicity and honesty of life style, respect for authority, and patriotism) sprang from man's relationship with nature, the Italians had voted for the Christian Democrats because of the promise of American-style prosperity that had been held out to them. Traditionalism appealed to some but change and modernisation offered the possibility of establishing a much wider and more durable basis of support. Thus they embraced the escapist commercial rituals of the period, recognising the role that they could play in lowering the political temperature and creating a new pattern of unitary interests that went beyond political and social divisions. The Miss Italia pageant offered an acceptable mixture of the conventional and the modern, of reassuring continuities and enticing novelties. Christian Democrat ministers were happy to endorse a competition which in some way functioned as a sign of the rebirth of the nation and of the health and enterprise of its young women. At once American and Italian, Miss Italia combined modernisation and patriotism.

For the Communists, by contrast, the task was to retain and expand a foothold in popular culture while seeking to combat the development of commercial entertainment and its effects on the lower classes. They were also keen to prevent the manipulation of these by the Christian Democrats. The Communists had the advantage that, because of religious opposition, neither the Christian Democrats nor the Church could ever organise, even indirectly, their own contests. They could only rely on the alignment of the Miss Italia contest with conventional values. But this did not mean that their own efforts were not fraught with contradictions.

Beauty and ideology

In the post-war years, the primary concern of the Church was to oversee a return to normality. It saw itself as the anchor of the nation, the one force that constituted a rock in troubled times and that had the authority and the resources to reconstruct civil society. Pope Pius XII had a clear view of the need for a return to conventional religious values after a period of great turbulence, that had witnessed, in some major cities, a total collapse of conventional morality. The family was the key institution in the return to normality and the Church acted as its main defender and promoter. As part of this process, it strenuously opposed the expansion of left-wing parties and the spread of their atheist ideology, even to the point of heavily backing the Christian Democrats in the 1948 election and formally excommunicating Communists in 1949. It also opposed commercial influences that were deemed to be undesirable or corrupting.

Catholics had always considered beauty in terms of spirit rather than body; goodness and virtue were its hallmarks. 'The most precious beauty lies in the quality of the spirit rather than the forms of the body' wrote the moralist Molino Colombino in 1860.[1] According to De Giorgio, Catholic influence consistently promoted 'a punitive down-grading of the body and practices aimed at cultivating it'.[2] With the development of modern fashion, the massive use of feminine imagery in advertising and the availability of cosmetics, Catholics came to adopt a systematically critical attitude towards what they regarded as deleterious modern trends. These attitudes informed their responses to Americanism in the post-1945 period. In Catholic magazines and publications, not only were modesty and spirituality praised but anything involving exposure and display of the female body was deplored. Dances were condemned because they offered opportunities for the 'low sexual element' to emerge, causing rationality, that was taken to be the core of man's nobility, to slide into 'expressions of an animalesque instinct'.[3] To offer a positive example of the value of purity and modesty to young people, the Pope ordered the beatification in 1947 of Maria Goretti.[4] A poor girl from near Rome who had died in the early years of the century defending her purity against a potential rapist, Goretti was held up as a modern Christian martyr.

Beauty contests were a prime target for criticism because of the systematic immodesty they cultivated. After the massive victory of the Christian Democrats over the left, the battle to restore Catholic moral values gathered pace. Thus the Church maintained a campaigning stance through the 1950s, promoting a significant development of grass roots organisations and parish activities.[5] In a pastoral letter published in October 1950, the bishops of Piacenza and Fidenza attacked the organisers of pageants including Miss Italia for holding rituals that 'exposed girls to the loss of their virginal reserve'. To take part in or organise such contests was deemed a 'grave sin'.[6] They were seen as 'a paganism that goes back to the cult of the flesh and of the passions'.[7] According to the Catholic illustrated weekly *Famiglia cristiana*, the bishops' letter:

> presented the serious, well-founded and understandable reasons for which the clamorous exaltation of young women and the display of their physical assets, without regard to any sense of delicacy and subjected to the unhealthy 'study' of a fatuous audience, is truly offensive to Christian sentiment, an irreparable degradation of the gentlemanly tribute to woman that should be considered part of the deepest values of her moral personality; and finally a deviation of the entire public mentality and customs, deviation that could have and indeed has a progressive deleterious influence by demolishing all the postulates of individual and social ethics.[8]

The bishops and their supporters called for the civil and political authorities to intervene to restrict such contests, even though they recognised that this was unlikely to happen in a multi-party context. Catholic militants denounced as offensive the measuring of women's vital statistics and deplored the role of illustrated magazines and other commercial interests including fragrance and cosmetics producers in promoting contests. They attacked what they saw as the 'ridiculous copying of American weirdnesses'.[9]

Catholics were divided over what caused the mass participation of young women in beauty contests. For some, the root cause was the alleged psychological disposition of women towards the display of their bodily forms. Others, including the Christian Democratic Member of Parliament Pia Colini Lombardi believed that it was the 'extreme over-evaluation' of the attributes of physical beauty that led women to prize them above all else. All were agreed, though, that the overthrow of reserve implied by the display and measurement of bodies 'almost in birthday suits or wearing beach clothing' was a bad thing.[10] Catholics disliked the general growth of showbusiness and mass culture which together levelled and homogenised values and induced an exhibitionism incompatible with decorum. They objected to the substitution of a moral evaluation of the beauty of a woman by a new commercial evaluation that considered her only 'for her exterior charm, her gracious ways, her enchanting voice, eyes or hair'.[11] For Lombardi, 'The sideshow of the manifestations that accompany this type of competition, from indiscreet advertising to the prospects of cinema stardom that are immediately opened or held out, accentuates the sensual atmosphere – as well as the commercial one – in which the young candidates find themselves immersed'. 'Physical beauty publicises moral beauty', she added. 'Therefore more beautiful than all other women, and praised as such even higher than the stars themselves, is the Madonna.'[12]

When it was not 'protected by modesty' physical beauty was seen as 'a terrible provoker of the least noble instincts and appetites' and a block to the development of the moral qualities of the person blessed with it. A novella published in instalments by the *Famiglia cristiana* entitled 'Roses and Thorns of Youth' included one chapter entitled 'Parade of . . . Misses' that described a typical beauty contestant as 'atheist, anarchist, presumptuous, who only obeyed and worshipped herself'.[13] According to Padre Atanasio, the priest who ran the problem page in *Famiglia cristiana* in the 1950s, exterior beauty was not a positive quality at all. 'Perhaps average beauty is the best gift for everyone', he observed. 'It does not dazzle the possessor, it does not disturb the observer, it leaves the field free for qualities of the spirit and provides room to act properly and do good without getting in the way.'[14]

Famiglia cristiana often featured on its covers well-made-up models in the Hollywood mould and family groups with a distinctly American air, but in its articles it revealed a wariness about the impact of urban styles of life. 'Modern cities have become dangerous sirens for country people, enormous octopuses that, with their tentacles, capture and ruin so many incautious young people that realize too late what is happening. Life in the fields is commonly recognized as more healthy physically and morally.'[15] The values of simplicity, hard work, sobriety and respect for older generations, that were seen as typical of rural communities were ones the Church aimed to defend. It railed against dances and the risks to decency of beachwear. *Famiglia cristiana* denounced the advertising and press that 'insists on teaching young people especially that women only count for their exterior allure, for their gracious ways and for the enchanting qualities of their voices, eyes and hair'.[16] It continued:

> True beauty cannot be bought at the market, young ladies! It is not manufactured in beauty parlours or before the mirror, through the more or less skilful use of creams, powders, lipsticks and perfumes! Everything that is artificial, and therefore that is the negation of naturalness and true grace, serves only to create the 'woman as type' – a mask without features, a face adorned in series like those of dolls, with the same eyebrows, the same way of moving the eyes, and the same empty, artificial laugh on lips artificially modelled on a little heart or a cherry with application of *crayon rouge*.[17]

Yet every week there were advertisements for 'Velluto di Hollywood' (Hollywood Velvet), a face powder produced by the Paglieri company that used highly glamorised faces to promote its products. By 1960, the attitude had softened somewhat and the magazine was informing its readers that 'it is not immoral to paint one's lips, colour one's cheeks, apply face powder or "touch up the façade" etc. when there is no malicious intention deliberately to cause arousal in another'.[18]

Although there were numerous local incidents involving police intervention to ban or halt beauty contests, there was never any high level intervention, for example to outlaw Miss Italia or restrict the proliferation of contests, as had occurred under Fascism. The initiative promoted in 1954 by thirteen Christian Democrat Members of Parliament to call for the abolition of all beauty contests by law as examples of 'astute and uncontrolled paganism' led to nothing.[19] While there were many examples of religious and moral bigotry in the Italy of the 1950s, the Christian Democrats on the whole adopted a more pragmatic approach than the Church. They saw the advantages that followed from a phenomenon that dovetailed with many other innovations of the period and which ostensibly did not work in favour of the left. The only significant effect of the campaign against beauty contests was the disappearance, after the contests of the post-war years, of the bikini. Two-piece costumes had been seen at the Venice film festival during the war years and had reappeared after the conflict. In the 1947 Miss Italia contest several contestants wore them. But throughout the 1950s, only one-piece costumes were employed in the contest and the emphasis fell squarely on the elegant evening gowns that the contestants wore in the final parade.

For the Communists, who became the largest opposition party in 1948, beauty had no ideological significance. It only became a matter of practical interest because beauty contests were so popular. The party was concerned to maximise its influence in the fields of high culture and popular leisure and it latched on to anything that attracted people. The idea of a woman being selected for masculine appreciation on the basis of her appearance did not pose any particular problem for those who regarded the involvement of large numbers of people in party activities as the only valid goal. For most senior Communists in the 1940s and 1950s, 'popular culture' was synonymous with popular education. In keeping with a tradition begun by nineteenth-century socialists, they believed that workers and young people should be encouraged to shake off their ignorance and acquire the attributes of a future ruling class by means of political instruction and education. But in building the mass party that the Communist leader Togliatti saw as a necessary precondition for the establishment of widespread Communist influence, the Communist party did not limit itself to reproposing old schemes or to denouncing the negative influence of commercial culture. It did both of these things, but it was also flexible and innovative in the way it approached leisure. Its festivals and press, its workers' recreational circles and the left-wing sports association all responded not only to political dictates but to the demand for relaxation and distraction that boomed after the war and which were a hallmark of the emerging industrial society.[20]

The Communists knew that the Catholics disapproved of dancing and beauty contests and decided to exploit the opportunities that arose from this by organising their own. In the immediate aftermath of the Liberation, local left-wing festivals quite commonly elected a *stellina* (starlet) or *stellina dell' Unità*, named after the Communist party's daily newspaper. Such events formed part of a long tradition of popular festivals that derived from the election of May or carnival queens. They were simply a custom accompanying and adding attraction to a particular moment of leisure. Local Communist festivals, generally held every September in support of the party newspapers, held fashion shows and beauty contests throughout the 1950s and, in some instances, for many years beyond that.[21] In Bologna in 1950, for example, a *stellina* was elected in each of the 60 section festivals. These then participated in a grand final which concluded with the election of the *Stellina provinciale dell' Unità*.[22] In deciding on winners, sometimes the political and moral qualities of the women were taken into account, but more frequently, the winner tended to be simply 'the candidate who in the opinion of the jury is the most beautiful and has the most suitable characteristics to participate in the making of a film', to quote directly from the rules presented for approval to the Communist party directorate.[23]

What caused disquiet was the way the beauty pageant phenomenon became so diffuse and so commercial from the late 1940s. The Communists understood that, in a climate of poverty and deprivation, young women of necessity grasped at any opportunity to improve their situation. Some also realised that the distorted feminine protagonism the contests offered constituted a modernising influence of sorts. But, in general, the Communists did not like the way they reflected an American influence on Italian customs and in particular the impact of Hollywood ideas of femininity. Nor did they approve of the way commercial interests exploited and manipulated the looks and aspirations of young women. Finally, the consecration of Miss Italia as one of the defining rites of post-war Italy alerted them to the way the Christian Democrats could draw indirect support from the most unexpected sources.

In the Communist press, the differences were always highlighted between down-to-earth *stelline* and the participants in other contests. 'Our *stelline* do not have excessive expectations', wrote *La Lotta*, weekly of the Bolognese Communists; 'they are not the provocative "misses" of the beauty contests but healthy and well-developed lasses of our province who on Sundays put on their best dress, that they themselves will have made, in order to spend a pleasant evening with their workplace comrades'.[24] Participants in these contests did not wear swimsuits or elegant clothes but presented themselves simply in their modest leisure wear. The competitions offered no route into showbusiness, even if the above rule suggests that some movie influence was present. For Communists, it was a great attraction to be able to offer the public the chance to see a parade of the most beautiful girls of 'our province'. But because their concept of the body was largely functional, not an object of narcissistic cultivation in a consumerised sense of self so much as a tool of labour, there was no real distinction drawn between this and a parallel competition for 'the bonniest baby of the province'. In essence, they were a primitive marketing ploy which enabled the Communist party to make itself part of local identity. The specificity of the appeal of beauty was recognised but largely left unspoken in Communist practice, although a cartoon about fund-raising published in the activists' guide, *Quaderno dell'attivista*, suggested that festival organisers wishing to maximise donations should place 'a table and a beautiful girl at the entrance to a dance floor'.[25]

Such competitions were accepted even by the politicised young women who were trying to undertake consciousness-raising work among girls who sometimes had little experience of life beyond the confines of their own village or quarter. These women – many of whom had taken part in the partisan struggle – sometimes shared a severe, rigid conception of political commitment that derived from their ideological training. Some regarded even dancing as frivolous and inappropriate for a Communist. Modest elegance and some use of cosmetics was acceptable, but only within strict limits. However, they embraced Togliatti's policy of reaching out to women and finding new ways of involving them.[26] They knew that the party could not expect women to give up their traditional roles and interests if it wanted to draw them in. As a result, militants found themselves organising sewing circles, typing courses and even being the first to step forward to take part in a *stellina* competition, so as to induce others to overcome their reservations. With hindsight, the leader of the young women Communists, Marisa Musu, who was also a Resistance heroine, described this practice as 'absurdly manipulative', but claimed that it did enable the Communist party to make contact with the real lives of women.[27] What concerned her was that any wider use of such contests would not only convey the wrong ideas but also be divisive. If, instead of uniting young women around campaign issues, it was setting the beautiful against the less beautiful, then it was engaging in a self-defeating exercise.

Miss Vie Nuove

The risks of such a problem arising greatly increased when the left-wing weekly *Vie Nuove* decided to organise its own national beauty competition. Founded in 1946 as a 'weekly of orientation and political struggle', the magazine gradually evolved into an illustrated publication similar in many respects to the established Sunday supplement of the *Corriere della sera*, *La Domenica del corriere*, and then to new illustrated weeklies like *Epoca* and *L'Europeo*.[28] Between approximately 1948 and 1956, *Vie Nuove* was one of the most popular of all Communist publications. Although it was not generally sold through news kiosks but only by volunteers and in party sections, and as such was a genuinely subcultural phenomenon, the weekly print run touched 350,000 copies in 1952.[29] The magazine used a number of techniques to increase revenues and sales: it put famous actors and actresses on the cover, it employed well-known writers to cover the Giro d'Italia cycle race, it featured advertising copy and, from 1949, it ran a beauty pageant of its own. Whereas *L'Unità* was conceived by the party as 'a workplace comrade' (*un compagno di lavoro*), *Vie Nuove* was the 'weekend friend' (*l'amico della domenica*) in whose company one might spend some pleasurable free time.[30] The magazine ran features on domestic and international politics, but it also provided articles about new films, fashion, sport, family matters, crosswords and puzzles, as well as scientific and technical novelties, particularly where these were of Soviet origin. In order better to counter the 'spreading tide of the

43 A local Miss *Vie Nuove* competition in Milan, c.1953.

reactionary and fascist press', *Vie Nuove* was obliged to dedicate space to light themes and popular pastimes, even where these were out of line with party ideology and Communist morality. It supported Italian cinema wherever possible, but it never rejected Hollywood *en bloc*, even though the Communist party was actively engaged in a campaign against what was seen as a politically-motivated 'American invasion' of films.[31]

Although it never displaced Miss Italia from the central place it had won in popular culture, the Miss *Vie Nuove* pageant gave rise to considerable enthusiasm in the cities and provinces of the north and centre, not least because of the prizes that were offered and the promise that the winners would receive a screen test. Although it came about in part because writers and directors identified with the left were excluded from the juries of Miss Italia from the late 1940s,[32] the event was presented from the beginning as being different from other contests. First of all, it was repeatedly underlined that the competition was not commercial. It had no sponsors and it was not concerned with the promotion of anything other than the magazine itself. Second, it was never officially described as a beauty contest. Rather, it was presented as an annual search for 'a new face for the cinema'. The Communists supported Italian cinema against American cinema and they approved of the new school of gritty, neo-realist films that emerged in the post-war years. At a time when the Christian Democrat party was seen as conspiring with the Americans to crush the realistic impulse in Italian cinema, the Communist party tried to sustain it. It thus constructed alliances with directors, critics and actors.

For Cesare Zavattini, scriptwriter of *Ladri di biciclette* and an ardent supporter of cinematic naturalism, the *Vie Nuove* competition was not about beauty as such but about the need for new faces. It would have been better, he said after judging the 1954 edition, 'if . . . we had known all about the girl who won, about the environment she lives in, we could have had a much more accurate and, we could say, human picture of her personality. It's not abstract beauty that we are interested in'.[33] As he saw it, beauty contests killed the spirit of cinema by promoting 'stardom, a cinema of beautiful women and beauty understood in a conventional way, outside of any deeper values'. Such competitions 'encouraged the audience in an idea that cinema is made up exclusively of beautiful women and handsome men, as has happened in Hollywood, where a great effort has been invested in producing women like Marilyn Monroe, who have become the very symbol of the United States'.

Despite its organisers' determination that *Vie Nuove*'s search for new faces should be different, the competition was nevertheless perceived by almost everyone involved as a beauty contest.[34] The only contestants who could aspire to the title of Miss *Vie Nuove* were young women aged between approximately 17 and 23. To underline the competition's alternative character to Miss Italia, local winners were often labelled simply as, for example, Miss Liguria or Miss Bologna. Moreover, many of the structures and procedures were those of a modern beauty contest. Swimsuits were not worn either at local heats, of which there were a large number, or at the final; but many of the photographic entries that were published in the magazine featured young women in two-piece costumes. Moreover, neither provincial finals nor the grand final were held in the open air but in cinemas or hotels. At the latter, candidates wore evening gowns and were judged by juries which included writers such as Alberto Moravia and Elsa Morante, film directors like Visconti, Blasetti and De Santis, and the actors Massimo Girotti and Fosco Giachetti, as well as Yves Montand and Simone Signoret. If local winners could expect to be fêted for an evening and to receive perhaps a subscription to the magazine as a prize, national winners were rewarded with sewing machines and radios in addition to being offered a screen test.

The Communists never pretended that Miss Italia did not exist. Rather they kept an eye on the contest while claiming the superiority of their own. When it turned out that Miss Italia 1950, Anna Maria Bulgari, was the daughter of a former Resistance leader, she was given ample coverage in both *Noi Donne* and *Vie Nuove*. As the latter commented, 'Anna Maria also deserves the title of "Miss reader of *Vie Nuove*", a title that would honour her beauty, which is of a serious type lacking standardized flirtatiousness, like that of all the participants with the best chances in our competition'.[35] Nevertheless, there were numerous objections to the contest. First of all, the few women Communists who retained influential positions after 1948 were less than enthusiastic about the event. It is noteworthy that the left-wing women's weekly *Noi Donne* did not cover it at all, even though it dedicated numerous articles to Hollywood films and even featured American stars on its cover from time to time.

In October 1950, *Vie Nuove* published a letter from Marisa Musu. 'You are lucky to produce a paper that has a print run of 300,000', she wrote:

> therefore your views and news reach many families, you educate hundreds of thousands of people and, undoubtedly, among these, thousands upon thousands of girls. In other words, *Vie Nuove* spreads our morality and our ideals, it clears the way of bourgeois conceptions of life. And we expect of you, editorial staff of *Vie Nuove*, continuous, intelligent, effective assistance. So, by all means run your competition for Misses. It draws to the paper many pretty girls and that is certainly a welcome and notable achievement. Try to make sure that these fine starlets do not get it into their heads that all girls must expect, as an ideal, to receive a letter from a film producer. If such a letter arrives, good, it is a stroke of luck, but in the mean time they should not dismiss from their dreams the mechanic from across the street and the milkman's mate. Above all, while they are waiting for the letter, they should carry on struggling for better wages, against redundancies and for peace. What is more, they should all struggle together, in a united way, starlets and non starlets.[36]

'We agree with Marisa Musu and indeed the results of the contest demonstrate that our fine girls are not motivated by "escapist myths"', was the complacent editorial response.[37]

Some senior figures in the Communist Party considered the Miss *Vie Nuove* contest to be little short of a disgrace and certainly unworthy of the party. Hard-line senior officials like Pietro Secchia, Edoardo D'Onofrio, Mauro Scoccimarro and Gian Carlo Pajetta signalled their dissent by never attending the gala finals at the Palazzo Brancaccio. Togliatti himself, it seems, was never invited.[38] According to the first editor of *Vie Nuove*, Michele Pellicani, who invented the competition, there were regular grumblings and complaints about the magazine and the competition at meetings of the directorate and the central committee. The term 'Miss', with its connotations of America and of bourgeois refinement, was particularly controversial. The hard-liner Paolo Robotti, Pellicani affirmed, 'literally shook' with rage at the use of cover girls and beauty contests.[39] At a time when there was strong pressure from the Soviet Union in the Cominform era to close ranks and turn the party and its press into an effective and uncompromising campaigning force for peace, the Miss *Vie Nuove* contest appears at the very least to have been an anomaly, saved only by the fact that the magazine itself was not regarded as having any particular ideological role. Yet the general editor was no less a figure than the deputy party leader Luigi Longo.[40] Moreover, Togliatti himself regularly made known his views about aspects of the magazine's appearance and content. So, it must be acknowledged that, while the contest can hardly be regarded as having been a central aspect of Communist cultural policy, it played a role that was recognised and that had considerable advantages for the party. It gave it a toe-hold in a burgeoning entertainment culture, allowed it to benefit in a direct way from the popularity of cinema, brought it kudos with youth and enabled it to provide some outlet for the aspirations of young women for self-expression and greater freedom. In this sense it reinforced the subculture by providing a channel for desires and hopes that might otherwise have had a corrosive influence. Moreover, the contest proved a powerful marketing device for a publication whose sales were so great that the profits subsidised a range of other editorial initiatives including the founding of the Communist publishing house Editori Riuniti. As Pellicani put it: 'There were murmurings and objections but it never went beyond this. The fact is that the paper was popular, it was widely-read and it generated millions of lira for the party. It enabled the party to organise activities, print books and so on. What more could you want from a party paper?'[41]

Miss *Vie Nuove* also had the side benefit of exploding the myth – widely propagated in the right-wing and satirical press – that all Communist women were ugly.[42] By aligning youth and feminine beauty with the left, the contest helped in some small way to render the face of the party more relaxed and humane. 'We must fight the common idea that everything in our Communist world is boredom, heaviness and long-faces. It is not our job to cultivate frivolous clownery but to cultivate smiles, yes', proclaimed Concetto Marchesi, the distinguished former rector of Padua University, in his address to the 1956 Communist Party congress. 'Someone who knows this well is Comrade Longo, who has opened the columns of *Vie Nuove* to pretty girls. Mere frivolousness? So what, for this is the propaganda that enters every door, that of the rich man as well as the poor man; it is listened to by all ears, contemplated by all eyes and applauded by all hands.'[43]

Yet, inevitably, there were contradictions. The initiative may have begun cautiously, but it was a huge success that exceeded the expectations of its promoters. For around six

months of the year the magazine provided regular weekly reports on the Miss *Vie Nuove* competition, with news of heats and photographs of entrants. In particular, the connection with cinema brought the competition a modern edge that enhanced its appeal in rural areas. Even the smallest festivals asked if an actor could be persuaded to attend the election of a Miss. In the larger events, producers and actors attended as a matter of course. Massimo Girotti, star of Visconti's *Ossessione* (obsession) and many other films, was a regular, as was Zavattini and Lamberto Maggiorani, the Brera factory worker who played the part of the unemployed man whose bicycle is stolen in De Sica's *Ladri di biciclette*. *Vie Nuove* profited from the extraordinary appeal which cinema exercised at the time. In 1952 it was reported that the Ponti-De Laurentiis production company had offered a screen test to the finalists representing Piedmont, Lombardy, Calabria and Emilia. Women taking part in the final were featured in the magazine in the company of writers and artists including Mario Soldati, Carlo Levi and Carlo Bernari, the directors Antonioni and Blasetti, among others. They were photographed, elegantly dressed, having breakfast in their hotel, travelling on a tram and visiting the Cinecittà studios. The gala final was a glamorous occasion, with the finalists in evening dress, mixing with actors and actresses. Moreover, correspondents representing magazines including *Oggi*, *Epoca* and *Settimo Giorno* covered the final, which also featured in a Settimana Incom newsreel shown in cinemas.

Beauty and the left

The Communists never claimed to have a model of beauty of their own. Rather it may be suggested that they embraced a certain aesthetic that was embraced and articulated more by some than others, which drew on feelings of class difference, a rejection of the Hollywood stereotypes that were reinforced in certain quarters of the Italian press, and moralistic prejudices. Like the Catholics, they preferred 'natural' to 'manufactured' beauty and disliked the commercialism of the latter, although it was its associations with bourgeois beauty to which they objected. There was a widespread belief that the healthy good looks of male and female workers symbolised the civilisation of the future and that the artifice of cosmetics and fashion belonged to a corrupt and decadent bourgeois order. In a largely unconscious appropriation of the position of Garibaldi, under whose name the left had fought the 1948 election campaign, it saw the beauty of the ordinary 'girl of the people' as a potential repository of hopes for a progressive national order that for the moment had stalled. Just as they rejected bourgeois lifestyles in other areas, Communists objected to bourgeois beauty and defended a model that occasionally had a distinctly rustic flavour. At the final of the Milanese heat of Miss *Vie Nuove* in 1950, the journalist Ugo Casiraghi announced that what was sought was 'a healthy and robust girl of the people, typically Italian' and not 'an American-style cover girl'.[44] When the winner was declared, it was judged proudly that 'her beauty, not at all derivative of Hollywood models, is truly typically Italian'.[45] By organising local pageants, the promoters of the left-wing competitions believed that they were assisting the development of a new popular idea of beauty by bringing working-class girls into the public eye.

Leonida Repaci, an intellectual who often took part in judging beauty contests – although he saw them as 'a madness of our time' – was one of the few who tried to theorise the idea of the beauty of the woman of the people. He saw it as an expression of pride in belonging to a young and dynamic class that was destined to play a historical role. The 'vanity' that rendered the woman of the people enchanting was of a simple type, he argued: it was rooted in the desire for a white wedding dress or the wish to see her child dressed and shod.[46] But it was not easy to either establish or implement an idea of popular beauty. The right-wing popular writer Giovanni Guareschi had fun in a fictional short story entitled 'Festival', describing how the daughter of a countess comes to be accidentally selected as a *stellina dell'Unità*. Only the last-minute intervention of her mother prevents the girl being photographed for *Vie Nuove*.[47]

Vie Nuove itself at this time regularly featured actors and actresses who were photographed reading the magazine. These included many of the most popular names of Italian cinema at the time. By 1954, the contrast between the supposedly anti-star ethos of the competition and the general atmosphere that actually surrounded it had become very marked. The winner and the contestant placed second that year were featured on the magazine's cover in the company of Italy's leading male film star, Amedeo Nazzari.[48] The following year the statement proclaiming the sixth year of the

45 Sisters Ivana and Ena Zanotti smile for the camera at a folk festival in the Marche region, c.1958.

contest asserted that, 'The girls we will choose should only look like themselves: only if they fulfill this condition will they be able to say something new. *Vie Nuove* has no intention of creating "stars", but it hopes to open the way to success for many honest and simple girls representing the intelligence and grace of today's Italian young people'. The contest's 'godmother' that year (whose autographed photograph was positioned directly above these words) was a rising young actress, Sophia Loren, who was just becoming widely known. To compound the increasing emphasis on photogenic qualities, *Vie Nuove* announced that it would be sending photographers to scour the country looking for girls with the looks, character and temperament that might help them to find a place in Italian cinema.

The engagement with cinema did much to arouse interest in the contest, but the ideological distinctions between mainstream and left-wing beauty pageants inevitably diminished as both became more established. In these circumstances, the risk of fuelling the dreams of vulnerable young girls at the expense of their involvement in political action was great. This mattered little to the organisers, who, despite their party affiliation, were only concerned to increase the sales of their paper. But it was felt strongly by Musu and others like her. They only went along with such contests if they prevented them from being left in the hands of reactionaries. To this end, the political merits of winners were sometimes underlined. For example, Miss Bologna 1951, eighteen-year-old Lucia Bertocchi, was proudly presented to readers of *La Lotta* under the title 'Miss Bologna does not like *Grand Hôtel*', in a reference to a highly popular photoromance magazine which the party regarded as reactionary. Although she now worked as a model, the article said, she had been raised in a working-class family and was modest. She read books rather than commercial magazines and watched Hollywood films 'so long as they are not too stupid' ('she has not had much luck in recent years' added an editorial note).[49] Musu feared from the beginning that a contest like Miss *Vie Nuove*, which was not restricted to the context of a political festival, would not stand any chance of combatting passivity or raising consciousness.

In the 1950s, few Communists in Italy, or anywhere else, had any sense that the escapism of cinema allowed the masses, as Walter Benjamin had suggested, to experience a utopian dimension which might have political value. 'Communists had to be concrete and pragmatic', Musu said; 'dreams were not allowed.' Thus there was a strenuous battle

46 Ivana Zanotti is elected Miss Moto B, one of many local commercial beauty contests that took place from the 1950s.

against photoromances, comics, football pools, lotteries and the like. According to Musu 'Grand Hôtel was seen as even more of an enemy than the propaganda of the Catholic Church. It was viewed as a huge tool of corruption. Politicized girls had to reject utterly this dream dimension'.[50] The problem was that this phenomenon was part of a texture of mass culture that was spreading across the country as a result of commercial enterprise. Largely as a result of the enthusiasm of the editorial staff, *Vie Nuove* was itself part of the phenomenon. In accordance with a key hallmark of consumer culture, the magazine increasingly featured feminine faces on its cover. Many of them were actresses, including Marilyn Monroe, who occupied the cover with a typically seductive pose on 21 June 1956. It also gave ample coverage to Hollywood films and it featured advertisements for cosmetics and beauty products. One product which was advertised repeatedly, usually on the very page which reported news about the progress of the search for new faces, was the face powder 'Velluto di Hollywood'.[51]

Communists like Pellicani and the film critic Casiraghi generally took the view that if something was popular it could not be wrong. 'At the time the use of film stars on the cover did not seem at all scandalous', Casiraghi later affirmed. 'After all we are talking about a "mass" party. At the time we regarded the American or British comrades we happened to meet as very schematic and hard-line. We were closer to the French. As for "lightweight" preferences, at the end of the day we *never* blamed people. Rather we took account of living conditions, level of education, possibility (or non-possibility) of choice.' When asked why his magazine condemned Hollywood stardom in general, but spoke favourably of Rita Hayworth, Pellicani simply said, 'Well, she was popular'. Although these views, and the practices that followed from them, caused consternation among old Stalinists and some young Turks, they were broadly in line with the change of perspective that Togliatti introduced after the war, when he decided that the Communist party should become a mass party and work to extend its influence ever wider in society.

A further contradiction was that it was impossible to avoid the sort of objectification of women that occurred in commercial competitions. A description of the election of Miss *Vie Nuove* Marche in September 1951 rendered something of the climate of these events. The girls were described as coming on to the platform with a certain reluctance, despite the whistles of encouragement from the largely male audience. As they stood awkwardly, the members of the jury examined them, evaluating their physical qualities: 'The face of this one is more graceful but the legs are less straight; that one has a beautiful body but the nose is too big; the bust of one is excessive, while the bust of another is lacking'. [52] Even more than the audience, the reporter wrote, the jury was divided in its judgement. In the end, the attention fell on two participants, a blonde and a brunette:

> the trouble was that, contrary to the custom of any beauty contest, you could not see anything more than their calves. So the jury drew close around the two contenders and, after much insisting, it succeeded in persuading them to raise their skirts a little, up to the knees and no more. 'A little more only if the men leave', one of the lasses kept saying; but the men did not want to leave. So, having seen the knees as well as the pretty face, the brunette won. [53]

According to Casiraghi, the search for new faces had been predicated on the supposition that, if Italian cinema was to recover, it would be on the basis of cooperative productions and the efforts of small producers. [54] In fact, this hypothesis did not come to pass and the neo-realist current had dried up by 1954, to be replaced by a long series of inoffensive popular comedies that left-wing critics attacked for avoiding topical issues or problems. Assisted by protectionist laws which gave the government ample direct and indirect powers, Italian cinema developed and entered its most florid and successful phase. As a consequence, the demand for new faces was largely satisfied by the time the *Vie Nuove* contest began. One or two finalists did enjoy minor careers, like Scilla Gabel, who became a theatre and television actress after making a number of films, and Edy Campagnoli, who became an assistant on one of the first television quiz shows. Most, however, returned to their lives in the cities and provinces, where their dreams of material success were reduced to a normal scale.

The rise of an integrated system of mass culture, still mediated in Italy by the presence of politico-religious subcultures, meant that the Communist party could no longer appropriate elements and codes derived from commercial culture and turn them to its own purposes. The smile of a young woman, which Marchesi had praised as a welcome relief from the tedious deliberateness of East European life, was perhaps already in the 1940s, and certainly would become by the mid 1950s, the distinguishing sign of commercialised escapism.[55] This meant that the ever more regular use of cover girls by *Vie Nuove* was not a mark of effective propaganda but rather of subordination to the cultural codes of the mainstream press.

The magazine's search for new faces came to an end in 1957, two years after Gambetti, Pellicani's successor as editor, left *Vie Nuove* and was substituted by the former editor of *Noi Donne*, Maria Antonietta Macciocchi.[56] Macciocchi tried to render the magazine more modern and cultural by recruiting the writers Curzio Malaparte and Pier Paolo Pasolini as columnists. But she was accused of making it less popular and of losing readers. The suppression of an event which had never enjoyed favour with Communist women was an inevitable consequence of her appointment. But, in any case, the circumstances which had given rise to it no longer existed. The beauty that was identified with Italy in the post-war years was one that bore strong traces of Italy's lower classes but it was oriented towards material progress rather than collective redemption.

CHAPTER SEVEN

THE FEMALE FILM STARS OF THE 1950s

For foreign film-goers between the 1940s and 1960s, Italian female stars were exotic, fiery, passionate, beautiful and adult. Whatever connotations they might have had for Italians, for English and American audiences they were anything but familiar girls-next-door and nor were they the sort of artificial product that the major Hollywood studios had been turning out for decades. Before all else, Italian stars appeared to be natural; they offered not the constructed sex appeal of the glamorised star, but a certain raw earthiness that seemed natural and unspoilt. To outsiders, Italy possessed the eternal appeal of an old civilisation and the fresh vibrancy of a country that, for all its problems, seemed basically dynamic and optimistic. Silvana Mangano, Gina Lollobrigida, Sophia Loren and others encapsulated the best of the qualities that had conventionally been associated with the country and the new spirit that was perceived to pervade it. The stars were taken as representatives of a lifestyle that rested on clearly-defined gender roles, a dramatic, emotional mode of personal interaction, and some vaguely-defined idea of the good life in which leisure, food, personal appearance and sex all had a special place. They were also an important component of the fashionable image that Italy enjoyed in those years. Together with Vespa scooters, coffee machines, sports cars and postcard images of the beauty spots of Rome, Naples and Venice, the stars represented a country that had put the bellicosity of the Fascist period behind it and once again was presenting a cordial face to the world.

The significance of attractive exportable images should not be underestimated at a time when the Italian economy was not only recovering but laying the ground for what would be the most sustained period of growth in the country's history. However, it is important also to explore the meaning of female stars for national identity. The connection between stars and identity was not automatic, rather it came about due to the type of roles the actresses played. Almost all the women who emerged in the early 1950s did so due to films that situated them in rural locations and disguised them as peasants or agricultural workers. None of the actresses was really from a rural background, although many had experienced poverty and deprivation. But in this way a connection was established between young women and the landscape that endowed the former with symbolic resonance. They could simultaneously appear to be products of the Italian heartland, like the lower-class girls who had enchanted the travellers and artists of the nineteenth century, and modern-day pin-ups. Their shapely figures did not stand as an advertisement for the prosperity of rural Italy so much as for the resourcefulness and ambition of young people who were already urbanised in their aspirations. However, by no means all their films were contemporary in their settings. A significant number were costume films that engaged, sometimes directly, with issues of Italian identity. These works were important in ensuring that the new stars were not rooted merely in the natural environment but also in historical moments and locations that were redolent of the national tradition. In making this connection, the actresses and their personal experiences were vital, but behind the scenes producers and directors kept tight control of the processes of representation.

The case of *Riso amaro*

The first film that produced a new icon of Italian beauty in the post-war years, *Riso amaro* (Bitter rice) is a melodrama set among the rice weeders of Vercelli. The key part is that of a young rice worker called Silvana Melega who dances the boogie woogie, chews gum, reads the photoromances, and eventually betrays her class. The director, the Communist Giuseppe De Santis, considered many candidates and conducted numerous auditions. Among those he rejected for the role was Lucia Bosé, the 1947 Miss Italia, who allegedly refused to comply with his suggestion that she should dye her hair blonde. He also initially passed over Silvana Mangano, to whom he would later award the role. Although her candidature had been supported by close colleagues, she made no impression on him when she first presented herself in his office, well-dressed and made-up. De Santis later said that he persisted in his view of her unsuitability,

> until the day I was walking up the Via Veneto to go somewhere I do not recall and I saw her appear before me under the rain, dressed in a worn light-coloured raincoat and her face pallid with cold. She had a flower in her hand and soaking-wet hair. It was like a bolt of lightning to see her again like that, beautiful and unassuming, authentic in her true state of a not well-off young woman, because when she had presented herself the first time she had obviously got on her Sunday best and she had dolled herself up, losing genuineness in the process. I did the screen test again, that turned out magnificently, and I signed her up for the role.[1]

Stripped of her finery, Mangano perfectly fitted the type the director had in mind, that is 'a character who was meant to resemble a Rita Hayworth of the Italian periphery'.[2] In the film, Mangano plays a girl who has America in her head, even though she is simply a

47 Poster for *Riso amaro*, with
illustration of Silvana Mangano in the
foreground.

worker. She knows she is beautiful and uses her beauty to conceive of an individual
escape from poverty and drudgery. Like Mangano herself, she might have been drawn to
cinema simply because of 'the need to earn a living' rather than through any artistic
interest.[3] Her special qualities with respect to the other women are emphasised in a scene
in the film that depicts her election as Miss Mondina (Miss Rice-weeder). Mangano had
only shone at local level in beauty contests, but her natural beauty and extraordinary
photogenic qualities were widely appreciated by the journalists and commentators who
visited the set, as well as those who worked on the film. All of them noticed something
special. Italo Calvino, at the time a 26-year-old journalist on the Communist daily
L'Unità, visited the set and saw the actress at work. 'Silvana Mangano . . . is, on my
honour, the most beautiful girl I have ever seen', he enthused:

Silvana Mangano will be one of the great advantages of the film. She is Roman, she is
18-years-old, and she has the face and hair of Botticelli's Venus but an expression that
is at once proud and remissive, with dark eyes and fair hair, a clear and . . . complexion
that lacks both shadows and light. Her shoulders open out on to a décolletage worthy
of a cameo and her upper body is harmoniously triumphant and shapely. Her waist is

like a slim stem amid an amazing rhythm of full curves and long limbs. In other words, in brief, Silvana Mangano made a big impression on me and no photograph can ever do full justice to her.[4]

Spanish Civil War photographer Robert Capa also visited the set and took some photographs of Mangano in her sexy rice worker outfit. The rustic images of the eighteen-year-old actress, standing thigh-deep in water dressed in a tight blouse and shorts, were reproduced by the international press. This raised interest in the film prior to its release. Her image was perceived throughout the world as a new Italian take on American sex appeal. The significance of the representation of Silvana in this film was stressed by Carlo Lizzani, who collaborated on the screenplay but who felt that the actual form the film took went beyond the original intentions. Mangano's magical presence suggested 'a relationship between nature and the human body that was not present in the screenplay, or that was barely hinted at', he later observed.[5] In this relationship, 'Nature is seen as a great container not only of water, rice, grasses, sky or trees, but also of human beings, of bodies'. The actress was, in such a context, 'offered up to view as a natural prodigy, a beautiful animal or a beautiful tree'.

This connection established in post-war cinema between the female body and the landscape was crucial insofar as it formed a basis for the 'rebirth' that was so frequently invoked in the period of reconstruction and neo-realism. Any discussion of 'cultural autonomy' or the 'Italian model' ran a risk of being confused with the earlier Fascist discourses of a superficially similar nature. To avoid this, the stress was placed on female-centred stories of rebirth.[6] To rebuild, it was necessary to begin again, to 'build for the first time while simultaneously going to one's own roots almost in a ritual gesture that, by seeking the origin cannot but dig into the earth that contains it. The earth, that is the landscape in its widest meaning. The origin, that is the place of a mother or more in general of the feminine'.[7] For Giovanna Grignaffini, the phenomenon of the 'body-landscape' thus became a key feature of post-war cinema. Specifically, she notes, the body emphasis derived from two sources. On the one hand, neo-realism absorbed the tradition of corporeal recitation that was a feature of popular theatre. On the other, many leading neo-realists took part in the juries of Miss Italia and found there the faces and bodies that would populate Italian films in the years that followed. Post-war Italian cinema was full of female roles and images because the female body was the 'imaginary place of its re-birth', just as it was of the country itself.[8]

In this perspective, *Riso amaro* was a key film. Its melodramatic plot was structured around the beauty of Mangano. She was presented as a creature of the earth, an archetype whose generous figure, overt sensuality and instinctive simplicity lent her a primitive, primeval quality. But, at the same time, she was a complex figure who derived something from recent female stereotypes: the pin-up, the Hollywood vamp, the variety showgirl, the heroine of photoromances, the beauty queen, even the Signorina *Grandi Firme*. It is the reciprocal contamination of these models, the appropriation of something from each of them, that made Mangano a unique figure. She represented a landscape into which new elements from outside were introduced.[9]

It is significant that, when the film was released in 1949, labour movement representatives did not accept that the film offered a realistic picture of the world of the rice weeders. The production company's publicity in any case drew attention to conventional filmic appeals. *Riso amaro* was 'a dramatic story warmed by sensuality, flashing with contrasts and shot through with intrigue', while Mangano was introduced as 'the marvellous new provocative Italian beauty'. The left-wing press hosted a variety of criticisms of the film from workers and intellectuals who rejected the plausibility of the melodramatic storyline and the presence of American dances and chewing gum.[10] The ideological hybridity of the film led them to see it as politically damaging. The left was puritanical and hostile to sex appeal as a product of mass culture. But in fact, De Santis's eroticism was not at all of the manufactured, American type. Indeed the American film industry reacted very strongly against the explicit sexual themes of the film. While the *New York Times*' reviewer hailed Mangano as 'Anna Magnani minus fifteen years, Ingrid Bergman with a Latin disposition and Rita Hayworth plus twenty-five pounds',[11] Joseph Breen of the Motion Picture Code Association of America was horrified by the film's flagrant indecency. 'This association, in the first instance', he exclaimed, 'was started with the purpose – among other things – to put an end to the exhibition in this country of pictures of this type.'[12] Although the film passed censorship in Italy, it was firmly

48 After *Riso amaro* even the trade-union magazine *Lavoro* featured sexy rice weeders on its cover.

opposed by Catholic opinion. It was deemed unsuitable for all spectators by the Catholic Cinema Commission, which objected to the explicit reliance on sex appeal. De Santis believed that his particular erotic sensibility derived from his origins in Fondi, in rural Lazio, where he grew up in close contact with peasant culture.[13] The attitude towards sex and eroticism in this culture was, he claimed, quite different to what it was in cities. Moreover, he felt a particular mission to address feminine themes in a way that was emancipatory and respectful. This steered him away from more conventional, studied forms of female appeal.

Although Mangano would remain a highly significant figure in Italian cinema, the fact that she became pregnant meant that she missed out on the director's next film, another rural melodrama entitled *Non c'è pace tra gli ulivi* (No peace among the olive trees). This was no less political in its implications than *Riso amaro*, but Mangano's presence would have added new layers of meaning to the film. Instead, the part went to Lucia Bosé. The film did not do as well in consequence, not least because Bosé did not fit so apparently naturally into the rural context. Her fine features and grace exemplified the rise of the working classes in a quite different way. With her performances in two films to which she was better suited, Antonioni's *Cronaca di un'amore* (Chronicle of a love affair), in which she played a bored and unfaithful wife, and the morality tale about film stardom, *La signora senza camelie* (Lady without camelias), she illustrated how a physically beautiful working-class woman could assume the characteristics of poise, elegance and restraint that were normally associated with women of higher classes. This made her into an iconic figure but not one with a special connection to national identity.

Other actresses would make the connection with landscape more effectively. Over time, the rural film role became a paradigm that was not limited to, or specifically associated with, one actress. It became the way that all actresses were related to a national cultural matrix.[14] Moreover, the specific sector of the rice workers acquired a special appeal that was even confirmed in the photographic representations of them that appeared in the left-wing press (the trade-union magazine *Lavoro* showed that, after *Riso amaro*, Mangano's screen costume of cut-off shorts, that had been criticised as unrealistic, was widely adopted).[15] The ordinary girl as potential star became as much a basic belief in post-war Italy as it had been in America. But, due both to the historical experience of war and Resistance, and the human representation of them established by Anna Magnan, the physical appearance of the young Italian actresses was very different from the polished glamour of the American stars.

Peasant girls and stars

The second actress to win special attention through her identification with the countryside was the runner-up in the 1947 Miss Italia pageant, Gina Lollobrigida. Born in Subiaco, 70 kilometres from Rome, the city to which her father, the owner of a carpentry business, moved in 1944, she was of lower-middle-class extraction and had attended

drama school. She appeared in a number of small films following her participation in the competition, but it was not until she played the parts of young peasant women that critics and the public noticed her. Some of the films were historical, a fact which served to fix Lollobrigida as a type with a pedigree in the national imagination. Others were contemporary and made her the idol of lower-class girls whose only advantage was their looks. By moving backwards in time and then coming forwards, without ever engaging with the genuine conflicts of the rural world, the actress became a convenient symbol of continuity at a time of social and economic change.

Lollobrigida's career is of interest because, unlike most of her contemporaries, she was not married to, or romantically engaged with, a producer. In some of her roles, especially the early ones, she was heavily moulded by a director. However, broadly speaking, she chose her films herself and managed her career alone, with some assistance from her doctor husband, Milko Skofic, who she married in 1949. The gradual process whereby she established an identification between her image and that of Italy was one in which she had more input than other actresses. She was able to respond to her audience, modifying her image carefully, by progressively adding layers through a mixture of historical and contemporary roles, Italian and foreign productions and publicity about her family life.

Lollobrigida's first rural role proved to be an iconic one because it marked the origin of the term by which the shapely stars of the 1950s were collectively designated: *maggiorate fisiche* (physically developed woman). This was first employed in a historical film, *Altri tempi* (olden times), in which the veteran director Blasetti offered an affectionate portrait of the customs of nineteenth-century Italy. The film's final episode 'Il processo di Frine' (The trial of Frine) was based on a novella written in 1884 by Edoardo Scarfoglio, a writer born in the Abruzzo region. The title contained a reference to the trial in ancient Greece of a woman named Frine who was acquitted of a crime purely on account of her beauty. Scarfoglio transferred the tale to the Italy of his time and turned Frine into Mariantonia Desideri, a beautiful and flagrantly unfaithful peasant woman from Chieti who repeatedly dupes her simpleton husband. When her mother-in-law threatens to expose her dishonesty, she kills her.

Scarfoglio describes Mariantonia as 'a stupendous creature', 'her large and florid person, not yet spoiled by excess weight . . . seemed as though it had been shaped from clay by a sculptor sensitive to the sensuous'.[16] 'Her round face . . . had in the harmonious purity of its outline a beautiful perfection that was new for the citizens of Chieti' he added. She is covered in gold necklaces, brooches and rings. At her trial, the prosecuting counsel describes her as 'a monster to whom capricious Nature had chosen to give a beautiful face'.[17] However, as the case proceeds, Mariantonia acquires a romantic aura and seems to emanate patience and goodness. Her lawyer, Don Pietro Saraceni, a man of artistic temperament, captures the mood of the public gallery and cites the example of Frine as a precedent for acquittal. He argues that a woman of perfect beauty could not be intrinsically bad. The motive for her deed therefore had to have been external to her person. It is suggested that her sexual appetite is determined by a typically peasant greed. She is, Saraceni asserts, like a beautiful beast who, unconstrained by morality, cannot control her appetites. In the end, she receives a short jail sentence of three years.

The film contained certain notable differences with respect to the text. In the first place, Lollobrigida, as Mariantonia, wore a cutaway costume that highlighted the form of her breasts, but no jewellery. Her lawyer, played by De Sica, does not offer the reasoned defence of his client that is set out in the novella. Rather, he delivers an impassioned speech in which he urges the jurors to think what foreigners would say if the court were to lock up a woman who deserved to be considered, along with the sea, the sun, the mountains and the rest of the landscape, one of the beauties of Italy. This, combined with the removal of all references to Chieti, gives the case a national rather than local flavour. In a final rousing appeal, that is also the last scene of the film, he appeals to the jury to acquit Mariantonia, the *maggiorata fisica*, as if she were a mentally handicapped person. The term *maggiorata fiscia*, an invention of the screenplay, is shouted with great emphasis. Pandemonium breaks out when a not guilty verdict is delivered.

In the film, Lollobrigida gave a recognisable contemporary face to a character who says little and offers merely a seductive appearance. In many of her early films, including *Miss Italia*, a 1950 fiction film that explored the world of the pageant, she played the 'good girl',

50 Gina Lollobrigida as 'La fornarina' by Raphael, one of several Roman beauties of the past that the actress interpreted for *Epoca* magazine, 1960.

the dutiful, quiet, family-oriented young woman with a demure smile and a respectful manner. In other words, she offered a traditional image of modesty. Only after she was referred to as a *maggiorata fisica* was this image combined definitively with sex. In her subsequent films, she added various additional facets to her emerging persona as a shapely peasant beauty. Three of these were especially significant. The first was a French film also released in 1952, *Fanfan la tulipe*, an eighteenth-century romp in which she starred alongside the great *jeune premier* of French cinema, Gérard Philippe. The second two were part of a series that would also have a third and final instalment in which Lollobrigida was replaced by Sophia Loren. *Pane, amore e fantasia* (Bread, love and dreams) and *Pane, amore e gelosia* (Bread, love and jealousy), respectively from 1953 and 1954,[18] were the actress's most memorable films, the ones that fixed her definitively in the Italian mind as a national type. In them, she played a spirited peasant girl, nicknamed *la bersagliera* (or 'Frisky' in the English version), from a village in the Abruzzo region. Although she is dirt poor and alone in the world, she is cheerful, exuberant and brimming with vitality. For one magazine, she was the ideal type of the proud, restless, argumentative country girl who, ready to risk being the subject of gossip, is basically good. The revealing ragged dresses that Lollobrigida wore for this part further concentrated attention on her breasts.

After this, the actress diversified. One of her most successful urban roles was as Alberto Moravia's Roman prostitute Adriana in the screen adaptation of *La romana* (woman of Rome). As with Scarfoglio's character, Adriana is a woman of instinct and appetite who practises a sort of joyous freelance prostitution that bears little resemblance to the reality of prostitution in the Fascist period, in which it is set. The idea of an instinctive, easy-going female sexuality was a recurrent product of a male imagination. Like Mariantonia, Adriana is a woman of the people (who, as it happens, resembles 'a certain film-star') with a beautiful face, a bust that is 'well-developed but firm and resilient . . . firm, straight legs, a long back, a narrow waist and broad shoulders'.[19] However, the film version was clearly shaped by the influence of Catholic opinion and fear of censorship. It has a strongly moralistic tone in keeping with many films of the period. Lollobrigida's character is driven into prostitution and is anything but happy. When she falls pregnant, it is not, as in the novel, by the boxer with whom she has had a liaison, but by Mino, her idealistic lover who commits suicide after informing on the Resistance.

More than any other actress of the period, Lollobrigida sought to consolidate her position in national culture with a series of films in which she played the parts of acknowledged beauties of literature and history. In *La donna più bella del mondo* (The most beautiful woman in the world), she played the beautiful opera singer Lina Cavalieri, to whom she bore a resemblance and to whom she lent her own voice for two arias. Made in 1955, the film was released at the height of Lollobrigida's popularity and consolidated her position as an emblematic figure. She starred in the film version of *La bellezza d'Ippolita* (The beauty of Ippolita), Elio Bartolini's successful novel of a lusty Friulian peasant who finds work in Trieste as a servant and then puts her particular talents to more profitable use as a prostitute. Subsequently, she played Napoleon's sister Paolina Bonaparte Borghese in *Venere imperiale* (imperial Venus). The release of the film was accompanied by a full-colour spread in an illustrated weekly in which the actress posed not only as Borghese but as several other well-known Roman beauties of the past, including Lucrezia Borgia and Beatrice Cenci.[20]

The trajectory of Lollobrigida's career proved influential. Her success in playing peasants and Italian types was imitated by others and notably by Loren, who would become her great rival. Born Sofia Scicolone to an unmarried mother in Pozzuoli, near Naples, in 1934, Loren was seven years younger than Lollobrigida. She also began her movie career playing a variety of minor parts, although in her case they were predominantly exotic and included, for example, the title role in the opera film *Aida* (in which she was dubbed by Renata Tebaldi). Curiously, Lollobrigida also took ethnic parts in some early roles, something that would occur only very infrequently in her later career. The racism of the Fascist period was too recent a memory for a prominent national actress to be cast comfortably in African or gypsy roles.

Loren began working in photoromances and then appeared in a variety of genre films, thanks to her liaison with Carlo Ponti, one of the most influential Italian producers. She

51 Promotional booklet for the film *La donna più bella del mondo*, in which Lollobrigida played opera singer Lina Cavalieri, 1956.

was an introverted personality who only blossomed when the actor and director Vittorio De Sica turned her into a loud, sexy and unfaithful pizza girl in an episode of his cinematic celebration of his adoptive city *L'Oro di Napoli* (Gold of Naples). Far from being a natural, she had to be coached by the director into her extrovert screen persona.[21] Her lower-class screen image was consolidated in *La donna del fiume* (Woman of the river), a melodrama set in the eel-fishing community of Comacchio. Her big break came when she was offered the lead role in *Pane, amore e . . .* (*Scandal in Sorrento*) after Lollobrigida refused to play *la bersagliera* for a third time. The final film in the series shifted the location to Sorrento and turned the peasant girl into an exuberant and sensual fishwife, a part Loren played with verve. Both women developed screen personae that were passionate, unrefined and extrovert. This endeared them to the lower classes who constituted the big new audience for cinema in post-war Italy. People could identify with the way they shouted, talked in accented Italian, put their hands on their hips and asserted their female prerogatives. Since she was marked as Neapolitan, Loren was at first a more sectoral figure than her rival, but Naples was nonetheless a place with its own music, customs and atmosphere, all of which had made a vital contribution to the national image.

52 Philippe Halsman's iconic portrait of Sophia Loren.

The down-to-earth qualities of the stars' main roles created an accessible and familiar set of identifications for Italians. Italy was not yet a mass society, but still a country of peasants, white-collar workers, artisans and workers. It therefore preferred recognisable types as its idols. In contrast to the manufactured products of Hollywood, Italian stars preserved a certain accessible quality that was much appreciated by the public. Silvio Guarnieri argued that:

> Italy expresses itself or is represented by a football team, by a racing cyclist, by a boxer or by a beautiful and shapely woman. This is because we celebrate gifts and qualities that are absolutely natural, spontaneous, the fruit not of research, study or commitment but rather of a gift had from birth and spontaneously grown, or that suddenly reveal themselves, and that bring the individual forcefully to the fore, like a stroke of luck or a lottery win.[22]

This meant that simple, everyday qualities were preferred. 'Even our most popular, most loved actresses, those who the public seeks out and prefers, those who embody it and its preferences,' he continued, are those who are 'least like actresses, the least talented and even the least intelligent'. If one of them tried to overcome her limitations and raise the quality of her craft, the audience no longer identified with her, because her efforts had the effect of distracting it from what it cared about and what interested it most, that is her beauty and ordinariness.

Like Pampanini and Mangano, Lollobrigida and Loren offered an image of prosperity, health, fertility and simplicity. To Italians they combined qualities of beauty that varied slightly from actress to actress – increasingly petit bourgeois in the case of the former and more lower class and southern in the case of the latter – with a sexuality that was overt but not in any way perverse.[23] It was unquestionably their bustlines that initially brought them so much attention. Despite this, there was consternation at an impromptu comment by actor and director Vittorio De Sica at the London Italian film festival of 1953. 'Outrage and revolt among our actresses at De Sica's accusation that they are "just curves"' headlined Rome newspaper *Momento-sera*.[24] The director was quoted as saying 'Italian beauties are "all curves", Lollobrigida, Mangano, Pampanini: their artistic talent really cannot compete with their physical attributes. It is sad to say it, but the Italian film industry tends today above all to make a show of legs and eye-catching, opulent, enormous breasts'. De Sica subsequently apologised but, as an editorial in *Cinema Nuovo* admitted, with few exceptions, Italian actresses were 'more beautiful than talented'.[25]

This criticism was odd because few more than De Sica contributed to the success of Lollobrigida and Loren. As an actor, playing the avuncular and charming Carabinieri marshal in *Pane, amore e fantasia* and its sequels, he proved an ideal screen foil for both actresses. By 1953, he had already made the first of these films. Moreover, as a director, he would be responsible for turning Loren into a fully-fledged star. He first directed her in *L'Oro di Napoli* and then in a series of films beginning with *La ciociara* (*Two Women*) in 1960 that would confirm her as a sensual dark beauty and emotionally explosive woman.[26] It can only be assumed that De Sica, like many of his colleagues, initially viewed dismissively the new wave of female stars. He then came to appreciate their potential in marking out a specifically Italian identity at a time of rampant Americanisation.[27]

Post-war Italian cinema was made mostly by men in which stories and images of women were paramount. Where films did not have a rural background, they had a provincial or local setting. The names of women or feminine qualities appeared very frequently in the titles of films, sometimes coupled with place names.[28] Beauty, too, was often highlighted directly or indirectly in titles such as *La bella indiavolata* (Devilish beauty), *La bellezza d'Ippolita*, *Bellezze in bicicletta* (Beauties on bicycles), *La bella mugnaia* (The beautiful miller), *Bellissima* and *La bella di Roma* (Beauty of Rome). These films, it has been said, unified a film-going audience that had been divided by political events and contrasting experiences of liberation in the north and south.[29] The passage of many beauty pageant participants to the resurgent Italian cinema, and the consequent

53 The features of Sophia Loren are employed in this advertising illustration for Italian fruit.

development of a star system, introduced an important American-style element of distraction into a field of entertainment production that was beginning once more to take on the features of an industry. Rural comedies, such as *Pane, amore e fantasia* and its two sequels, were controversial because they abandoned the social concerns of neo-realism for a rose-tinted view of life impregnated with optimism and good humour. This dovetailed perfectly with the Christian Democrats' pragmatic policy. The Virgin Mary might have been the true Catholic ideal of feminine beauty, but the minister responsible for cinema in the late 1940s, Giulio Andreotti, had happily exhorted Italian cinema to adopt a more terrestrial programme, which he reputedly summarised in the dictum: 'less rags [i.e. the ragged clothes of the protagonists of neo-realist films], more legs'.[30]

In fact, it was breasts rather than legs that symbolised the female appeal of post-war Italian cinema. According to the journalist Marisa Rusconi, writing in the mid-1960s:

> Our home-grown, well-stacked girls, from Gina to Sophia, embody a proletarian need for direct, obvious sexuality available to all. The comely girls of Ciociaria and the shapely village women depicted on the screen spoke to the collective instincts of a mass population that was as yet unconcerned with Freudian and intellectualistic complications. But at the same time they were manoeuvred rather effectively by the puppeteers who held the strings of political life in a country that was still fundamen-tally fascist. The films based on the breasts of cheery peasant wenches are a sign of disengagement and social indifference that stands against the dangerous problematic of neorealism and the first intellectual films.[31]

Large breasts were identified in American cinema with the lower class, 'the busty woman using every ounce of mammary flesh to attract an affluent husband and move up the socioeconomic ladder'.[32] There were elements of this in the Italian case, too, although Marilyn Yalom notes that 'Italians Anna Magnani, Gina Lollobrigida, and Sophia Loren offered an alternative vision of passionate and even vengeful sexuality smouldering beneath their dark hair and heaving bosoms'.[33] The Italian bosom was not just an ornament but the primary signifier of female power in a culture that was still organised on the basis of conventional gender divisions. It was therefore identified not just with femininity but also with place. For Giovanna Grignaffini, certain 'typically Italian' figures emerged from comedies that were set in locations that were highly recog-nisable and deemed typical. Of all the actresses of the period, the most typical was Lollobrigida, the star who fixed a look and a manner of being that were identified with the Italian woman. Within this way of being, sexuality was 'an inoffensive weapon' that was wrapped up in disarming innocence. Her vitality was expressed in a repertoire of superficial gestures and attitudes, a shapely body and physical beauty, which together communicated a promise of compromise and reconciliation. Emotion, instinct and common sense transpired from her body in a way that connected directly with an idea of social interaction that had no dimension beyond that of the family and the village community.[34] This was also the reason why her fame would begin to decline as Italy changed and became a predominantly urban consumer society.

Italian actresses and international cinema

After the huge success of *Riso amaro*, magazines and newspapers the world over devoted many covers and articles to Italian actresses. One of the most memorable was the issue dedicated to 'Hollywood on the Tiber' published by *Time* in August 1954.[35] This described the extraordinary growth of the film industry in Rome as Italian cinema recovered from the crisis of the post-war years and underwent a great expansion in production. In the 1950s and 1960s the Italian film industry was the second most important in the world, producing half as many films as Hollywood and distributing them to 86 countries. In Britain, these decades saw the exhibition of between twenty and forty Italian films per year.[36] In contrast to the films of any other country, Italian cinema promised realistic qualities and a flavour of true life.[37] For the American weekly, this growth was essentially modelled on the example of Hollywood. The American idea of the star had been transplanted in Italy, with both positive and negative results. 'This boom is really a series of busts', one onlooker was quoted as saying,[38] and to prove the point, the accompanying thumbnail sketches of all young actresses included their vital statistics. Sophia Loren (age nineteen and measuring – in inches – 38, 24, 37), it was stated, 'has a thick Neapolitan accent, and in the sultry Roman evenings, loves to turn on the record player, throw off her clothes and dance'.[39] For her part, Pampanini (37, 24, 36) was reported as complaining that producers always wanted her to do scenes in the near-nude as if she were a prize pig. In general, Italian cinema was said to be 'offering a kind of beauty new to the US eye – an earth-heavy Italian beauty as rich as roses in an olive dusk'.[40]

The cover of the magazine was dedicated to Lollobrigida, since she was the most prominent new Italian actress at this time. The article inside was filled with compliments, such as that of Humphrey Bogart who was reported to have commented that 'she makes Marilyn Monroe look like Shirley Temple' or photographer Philippe Halsman who asserted that 'she has the finest figure of any actress I have known'.[41] Although the Americans accepted the sex appeal of Lollobrigida easily, it was a matter of some controversy in Italy. Although off-screen she cultivated a highly respectable image, there was debate about how far her elevation to the status of sex symbol was compatible with an idea of Italian feminine beauty. As the magazine *Le ore* wrote in 1954: 'According to the Americans, Gina's beauty is a special beauty. Everyone admits it is "sexy", i.e. "provocative", but her fiercest supporters have defined her as a "typical Italian brunette", a definition that, understood in the traditional way, should rule out a "sexy" content; rather it is used to refer to types of women whose beauty is serene, pure and a little ingenuous'.[42]

The reasons why Mangano, Lollobrigida and company enjoyed such popularity abroad may seem obvious. But it is worth looking at the issue more closely to understand the specific dynamics of their impact since it occurred simultaneously abroad and at home. The various influential factors relate to the international star system, the image of Italy, and the social and cultural climate of English-speaking countries. First of all, while the younger Italian actresses were different from the Americans, they also, crucially, possessed similarities. Although Anna Magnani was a unique reference point for all the new actresses, they shared some features with Rita Hayworth, Jane Russell and other stars who had emerged in the war years. The fact that they had come to light in Italy mainly through beauty contests, at a time when Hollywood was forcefully present on Italian screens, meant that they were indirectly endowed with some American characteristics. The shift from face to body that in America was marked by the demise of Greta Garbo and the rise of war-time favourite Betty Grable was followed after the war in Italy by the disappearance of the young modest *signorine* of the Fascist-period 'white telephone' films and the emergence of curvy beauties of more popular origins. At times of hardship, the desire for uncomplicated female abundance seemed to be universal.

Thus, while the Italian stars were regarded by foreign audiences as different, because of their darkness, their foreign accents and their shapely figures, they were also recognisable as being in tune with a prevailing trend in star types. Male critics drooled over the shapely forms of the new stars and these remained their most identifiable characteristic. In 1962, *Newsweek* referred to Loren as 'a Mount Vesuvius' and in the same year *Time* described her body as 'a mobile of miscellaneous fruits and melons'.[43]

This physical emphasis signalled a disruption of the rigid hierarchy that marked the American concept of a star system. Despite the shift mentioned above, the general rule – identified in the late 1950s by the sociologist Edgar Morin in his pioneering account of film stardom *Les Stars* – that stars unveil their souls while the lesser figures of starlets must unveil their bodies, still applied.[44] With the sort of figure-hugging dresses and low-cut tops that Lollobrigida and Loren wore, they made their physical shapes, and in particular their busts, a key signifier of their stardom, thus violating an established norm. To foreigners, they had the prominence and individuality of stars while conserving the 'cheesecake' appeal of starlets. In this sense, they inserted themselves into a process that was already occurring and that would be accelerated as a result of their emergence. One of the appeals of Marilyn Monroe, for example, was that she moved her body (the famous 'wiggle') in a provocative way; she had also done nude pin-up work.[45] To older stars, like Joan Crawford, this was a denial of the lady-like elements of the Hollywood star persona and was therefore to be deplored. It also implied a shift away from the elements that were guaranteed to appeal to a female audience (fashion, cosmetics, hair-styling) towards attributes that aroused male interest. For this reason, Lollobrigida was presented in America as a European Marilyn Monroe. In the mid-1950s she was often photographed in Monroe-style garb and poses, pouting and looking seductively at the camera.[46] For Vittorio Spinazzola, she was 'the perfect image of a national reaction to the Hollywood vamps and pin-ups'.[47]

One of the main reasons that Italian actresses appeared abroad as starlets rather than stars was that they had passed from beauty contests to screen prominence quickly and without many intermediate stages. In contrast to the Hollywood studio practice of grooming and preparing many young people and carefully selecting the few who would gradually move up the ladder of stardom, the Italians had been placed directly in films and quickly passed from bit parts to leading roles. They had minimal training as actors, their voices were usually dubbed by professionals, and they had undergone precious little glamorisation. In America, sex appeal was a manufactured quality that diffused sexuality through a complex set of signs and techniques. It relied on grooming, fashion, hair styling, cosmetics, studied flirtatiousness and lighting. The Italian actresses, by contrast, offered something more raw and unpolished. This difference was marked by their more or less uniformly dark hair colour, as opposed to the bottle blonde that since the 1930s had been a Hollywood sign of virtue, honesty and acceptability.

Lollobrigida and Loren frequently made promotional trips abroad for premières or Italian film festivals. On these occasions, they became ambassadors not only of Italy and Italian cinema but of the Italian people and the Italian lifestyle and character. This was perceived as much at home as abroad. Silvio Guarnieri noted the extraordinary attention that the Italian press had paid in 1955 to Lollobrigida's visit to Britain and Loren's to Scandinavia. These, he said, 'have not just confirmed but consecrated officially not so much a beauty or special capability of these actresses as a taste, a preference, an acceptance on the part of the whole of our people'.[48] The success of Italian stars aroused 'the interest not of a part of the public but of the whole public, in a unanimous solidarity'.

The emphasis on the breasts of the stars became an official marketing device of Italian cinema in the United States. Italian Film Export, a promotional tool set up with the financial support of the American film industry to help Italian films transfer into the commercial arena, published bulletins for distributors and exhibitors that promised 'sex, spectacle and showmanship'. Italian films, the first bulletin stated, 'thrilled [audiences] by provocative picture layouts revealing the off-beat allure of Italian beauties'.[49] 'Italy's secret weapon' was 'fresh new faces and box-office figures': 'Italy has emerged as the testing ground for modern star beauties with half a dozen answers to Marilyn Monroe in each new crop of signorinas'. The appearance of the actresses became a brand feature of Italian cinema abroad, to the extent that *Variety* spoke of 'that now well-identified and highly merchandisable "Italo-style" build' being a guarantee of box-office success.[50]

Was the beauty of the stars as natural as it seemed? There were certainly some unre-fined elements, but their photogenic qualities were paramount. Lollobrigida liked to refer to herself as 'a simple country girl' who came from the people, but she exercised a tight control over the distribution of photographs featuring her, censoring those that did not contain the right doses of glamour and simplicity.[51] The British journalist Joe Hyams, who met her in 1956, was amazed at the 'cold detachment' with which the actress selected the images. 'Gina is not a beauty, according to American "standards"', he wrote, 'but she has the inner strength that pushes her to seek success, a typical quality of the Americans'. In the flesh, he found her disappointing: 'too small in stature, the figure too ordinary, the legs too heavy. Only the eyes are beautiful. . . . Examined bit by bit, Gina does not make a great impression. But if you put together all those imperfect bits, you have the photogenic mystery that is Lollobrigida'.[52]

There were significant differences between the two stars. Lollobrigida was much more in line with the conventionally accepted criteria of Italian beauty. At first, Loren seemed too assertive and Neapolitan to be acceptable as a beauty to mainstream opinion. She was like 'an intensive development of the proportions of Lollobrigida: taller, wider, more vulgar, more explosive', observed Renzo Renzi; 'she has a bigger mouth, more open eyes, a more overwhelming bust'.[53] Put another way, she seemed like Jayne Mansfield as compared to Marilyn Monroe. Others made similar observations. For Spinazzola, 'the irregularity of her features underlined a femininity that was fleshy and robust in a lower class manner, without any Raphaelesque aura, to which were matched animated facial expressions and gesticulation that maybe were ungraceful but which were rich with a Neapolitan physicality'.[54] He argued that, although she employed the same blend of innocence and sexuality as her rival, avoiding the pitfalls of the vamp, she developed more fully a certain lower-class directness, combined with an element of sexual provocation.

Loren had not had much success in beauty contests precisely because she was regarded as excessive, that is to say, her looks were seen as irregular and aggressive. Arturo Lanocita noted that 'objectively, especially if seen in profile, it can be said that she is not beautiful'.[55] But her great strength was that she was not modelled or constructed. Not conventionally beautiful, she was 'more than beautiful'. 'She is the bearer of a glorious, triumphant physical personality, that draws her irregularities into a whole that is unquestionably her, and that is familiar to whoever looks at the world's magazines, from *Vogue* to *Harper's Bazaar*,' he argued. Loren's naturalness can be over-stated. She was certainly artfully presented, in a way that commercially exploited her physique. But precisely this emphasis on the physical was a cinematic rather than a social phenomenon. Her celebrated playing of a sexy and unfaithful pizza girl in *L'Oro di Napoli* had established her as a vibrant, authentic force on screen. But, as the writer Anna Garofalo pointed out, she was placed behind her counter 'wearing a very low-cut dress with which no real pizza girl would present herself to her miserable fellow countrymen'.[56]

Although her physical beauty would enable her to achieve considerable social mobility in the type of characters she played on screen, Loren could never establish the sort of connection with the pictorial tradition that her rival managed. When Italian painters had been asked in 1938 to produce a portrait of their ideal woman the result bore a striking resemblance to the Lollobrigida type.[57] Instead, Loren made herself the expression of another cultural strand, that of the eternal woman. The long-established idea of the Bay of Naples as the origin of humanity, a place rich with a past of female pagan deities, gave her a quite different pedigree. One of her precursors could be said to have been

54 In June 1938, *Le Grandi Firme* invited artists to submit a sketch of their ideal woman. Several of those published, including Boccasile's (top right) bear a striking resemblance to Gina Lollobrigida.

De Lamartine's Graziella. Loren, like Magnani, was regarded abroad as a typical Mediterranean woman because of her emotional force, her defiance in the face of adversity, her exuberance and her vitality. Later she would also develop a maternal appeal. 'The whole world likes her because she embodies in a typical way the femininity of her country', Spinazzola noted, 'therefore her popularity is more international than it is Italian'.[58] For Lanocita, 'The luminous topaz of her eyes is the noble coat of arms of a figure that is completely majestically aristocratic; that is, the aristocracy, accentuated by a way of being and moving, of flexible felines'.[59]

Curves and clichés

Because American film companies regularly made films on location in Italy from 1950, Italian actors were often given the opportunity to join a supporting cast of figures whose task was to add to local colour. Although blockbusters like *Quo Vadis* and *Ben Hur* excluded Italians from all but the most minor parts, the potential of Italy's new actresses was soon grasped. Loren, for example, was cast in three films with a Mediterranean setting, *The Pride and the Passion*, *Boy on a Dolphin* and *Legend of the Lost* before she was offered a contract by Paramount to make a series of films in Hollywood. The resulting films were often clichéd and backward in their portrayals of Italy and of Italian women. Designed to appeal mainly to foreign audiences, they concentrated on well-known locations and tourist sights. Always sunny and upbeat, they offered as selective a view of Italy as the travellers' portraits of a century previously. Shot in English and in colour, they were distributed through commercial circuits and reached much wider audiences than all but the most successful Italian films. Although they were rarely of great quality, they had production values, picturesque features and romantic story lines that appealed to mainstream audiences. Thus they were important in establishing Italian actresses as international stars.[60]

Italian intellectuals expressed qualms about the way the country's actresses were being used in American productions. As the Neapolitan critic Giuseppe Marotta was swift to point out, they were frequently reduced to playing stereotypical parts. In her American films, he wrote, Loren had been turned into a grotesque parody of the Mediterranean woman, all 'olive skin and rags'.[61] Films such as *It Started in Naples*, in which she played a wayward nightclub dancer with a heart of gold to Clark Gable's practically-minded American businessman, confirmed the American idea of Italy as a charming and beautiful country that was hopelessly backward. Even in films that avoided such obvious commonplaces, the physical beauty of the actresses was objectified in ways that were pronounced even by American standards. For example, in *Never So Few*, the spectator is introduced to Lollobrigida by a tracking camera that gradually works up her body from her feet to her face. The viewpoint is that of her co-star, Frank Sinatra, who catches his first sight of her from a position lying on the floor. After this eyeful, he is shown sweating at such a potent erotic spectacle. In *Solomon and Sheba*, Lollobrigida's title character performs an orgiastic dance sequence of a particularly daring stamp. It might be suggested that Lollobrigida and Loren were subjected not only to the 'male gaze' that Laura Mulvey has identified as a feature of all Hollywood cinema, but a quasi-colonial gaze in which American cinema eroticised according to its own codes the talent of a dependent country.[62]

The actresses were not always cast as Italians. Lollobrigida was significantly more 'Italian' than Loren in her American films.[63] In fact *Solomon and Sheba* is the only film in which her character is not Italian. By contrast, Loren was Italian in only eight of the fourteen American films she made between 1957 and 1966.[64] For example, in *The Pride and the Passion* she played a Spaniard and in *Boy on a Dolphin* she was Greek. But to audiences abroad, her 'Italianness' was signified by the lines of her body, the shapeliness of which was dramatically highlighted in the latter film, in a scene in which she emerged from the sea, her shirt clinging closely to her ample bosom. Significantly, neither actress ever played an American; the ethnic difference remained fundamental.

The whole phenomenon of the Italian actresses was perceived abroad to be a homogeneous one. They were seen as a category of women bearing similar features in which single individuals were not necessarily easily distinguished from each other. When Loren first met Cary Grant, her co-star in *The Pride and the Passion*, she found herself being asked if her name was Miss Lorbrigida or Miss Brigloren.[65] This 'joke' was repeated on other occasions. Acerbic radio commentator and journalist Walter Winchell invented the term 'Lollopalooza' to suggest the particularly physical appeal of Italian actresses, while in France 'les Lollos' became a slang word for breasts. The cosmetics company Revlon tied the launch of its Fire and Ice range to the general influence of the Italians, who were seen as being responsible for bringing ideas of passion and earthiness to the American mainstream.

The actresses were not condemned forever to be picturesque in rags or other scanty costumes. For the American studios, Lollobrigida and Loren made historical and costume films as well as contemporary ones, as did Mangano and another young actress of delicate, fair appearance, Rossana Podestà. In a significant number of the former, and occasionally also in the latter, they were cast in regal and aristocratic roles. Pampanani, Eleonora Rossi Drago and others also adopted the trappings of movie star royalty in the middle of the decade. This added variety and complexity to their earlier images and paved the way for a process of normalisation. From being purely attractive bodies, they evolved into stylish and highly-groomed women who could also act as role models for female spectators. Both on and off-screen they wore sumptuous costumes, pioneered new hairstyles and were shown in luxurious surroundings.[66] Yet unlike Isa Miranda in the pre-war years, Loren and Lollobrigida managed to resist Hollywood homogenisation and to preserve a large measure of their identities. Far from being pliable creatures compelled to accept subordination to studio dictats, they imposed limits and remained largely themselves. This was because they never gave up Italy for Hollywood. Even at the height of their American fame, they continued working in Italian cinema and it was for the latter that they made their best films. Broadly speaking, they remained close to the people. But while the popularity of Loren steadily increased, Lollobrigida turned into a temperamental diva. In 1958 she sued the producer Rizzoli for millions following a delay in the start of filming on *Venere imperiale* (*Imperial Venus*) (which would eventually made in 1962), leading to a certain resentment in a country in which poverty was still widespread. She was criticised for becoming too aloof and detached from her ordinary fans, who preferred 'the simple and kind National Gina'.[67]

Beauty and Italian culture

The centrality of female beauty in Italian identity after 1945 was underlined by two other cultural forms, both of which served to situate post-war beauty in relation to the Italian past. The first of these was a competition for painters that was staged from 1949 in parallel with the Miss Italia competition. The purpose of this was to 'engage the talents of our best artists to underline the grace of the Italian woman'. This was a real challenge because Italian painting in this period was divided between two currents, the figurative and the abstract, neither of which placed emphasis on conventional female portraiture. The intent, moreover, was explicitly unengaged. 'The competition ... expected, and continues to expect, from the artists', wrote Dino Villani in 1953, 'a serene view of life that can act as a comfort amid the anxieties of the modern era'. For the few years of its existence, the prize enjoyed a degree of prominence. Around 70 artists entered each competition, and their works were featured in *Illustrazione italiana* and exhibited in a gallery in Milan. The winner was chosen by a mixture of a jury and a popular vote.

The paintings that were submitted, some by leading artists of the day, were of the most varied type. They included nudes, portraits, abstract works and the occasional example of socialist realism. Leonardo Borgese, a regular contributor to the *Corriere della sera*, was a member of the jury, along with Carlo Carrà and other painters. He received notes from acquaintances recommending this or that work but he exercised his own opinion.[68] He particularly disliked paintings of rice weeders, of which there were two in the 1952 competition. These, he noted with disgust in his catalogue, were simply Communist propaganda. Two works submitted for the 1951 competition merited brief hand-written comments. An ugly nude by Luigi Bartolini received simply an exclamation mark, while the striking semi-nude portrait by Pietro Annigoni, that recalled the figure of Italia and which won the popular referendum, was dismissed with the observation: 'in the final analysis he is just an artisan'.

If the painting competition was a direct product of the Miss Italia pageant, a more generic reflection of the symbolic role of female beauty was provided by literature. Of the popular writers of the period, Moravia was the one who most consistently engaged with cinema. He often featured cinematic references in his novels and tales (no fewer than eight of his *Racconti romani* (Roman tales) refer to the medium) and several of his

Two entries to the 'bella italiana' painting competition:
55 *Adriana* by Giuseppe Tampieri;
56 *Portrait of a rice Weeder* by Ampelio Tettamanti, denounced by Leonardo Borgese as 'communist propaganda'.

57 *La bella italiana* by Pietro Annigoni, 1951.

novels, including *Gli indifferenti* (Time of indifference), *La romana* and *La provinciale* (The provincial girl) were turned into films. A selection of the *Racconti romani* were themselves turned into a Cinemascope movie in 1955. Moravia was a writer with a special interest in cinema and for many years he was the film critic of the political weekly *L'Espresso*. It is reasonable to say that he both contributed to the definition of the cinematic type of the beautiful Italian woman of lower-class origin and that he incorporated into his writings some traits that had been defined on screen by the new wave of actresses. *La romana*'s heroine, Adriana, for example, was already a cinematic type on the page before she was given a screen identity by Lollobrigida. The same can be said of Bartolini's heroine Ippolita, who was also played by the actress. The Florentine writer Vasco Pratolini also enjoyed a multi-faceted relationship with cinema. Some of his prose works contain references to the medium, most notably his 1948 novel, *Le ragazze di San Frediano* (The girls of San Frediano), in which the male hero is nicknamed 'Bob', on account of his resemblance to handsome American actor Robert Taylor. The screen version of the novel, shot in 1954 by Valerio Zurlini, featured Rossana Podestà and a Roman actress, Giovanna Ralli, as the feckless Bob's long-suffering girlfriends. After having been repeatedly tricked by him, they conspire to give him a memorable comeuppance at the conclusion of the story. Unlike Moravia, Pratolini also worked directly with cinema, collaborating on screenplays and writing subjects.

The most striking case of the influence of screen beauty on literature was provided by the historical novel *Il Gattopardo* (*The Leopard*). Published posthumously in 1959, it was the work of a previously unknown author, Giuseppe Tomasi di Lampedusa, and was unconnected to a literary climate that was still impregnated with realism. An instant bestseller, it was translated into sixteen languages. The theme of the novel was the destiny of the aristocratic Sicilian house of Salina in the period of the Risorgimento. Filled with regret for a fast-disappearing order, it explored the alliance established by Prince Salina's nephew Tancredi, who had distanced himself from tradition by following Garibaldi, with the rising bourgeois class that would become the dominant force in the new nation and take the place of the feudal aristocracy.

Il Gattopardo placed strong emphasis on the theme of feminine beauty and there seems little doubt that the author was directly influenced by the cinema of the period, with which he had a great familiarity. Angelica, the beautiful daughter of the newly-rich mayor of Donnafugata, Don Calogero Sedara, is the symbol of the new order of society. It is her engagement to Tancredi that seals the pact between old and new. The seventeen-year-old Angelica is variously described as a 'very beautiful female', 'a flower of a girl', 'a woman of sure beauty' and a 'lusty adolescent'.[69] 'Her eyes, her skin, her magnificence are explicit and can be understood by everyone', wrote Lampedusa. 'She was tall and well-made, on the basis of generous criteria; her complexion should have had the taste of the fresh cream that it resembled, her childish mouth that of strawberries. Beneath the mass of night-coloured hair wrapped in soft waves, were her green eyes, motionless like those of statues and, like those, a little cruel.'[70] When she first bows to the Salina family, this greeting, unusual in Sicily, 'conferred on her the allure of the exotic, combined with that of peasant beauty'.

Although she has been sent to school in Florence and has acquired the exterior manners of a lady, Angelica is of peasant stock. Her beauty is inherited from her mother, who is said to be very beautiful but who is never presented in public by Sedara because she is ignorant and ill-mannered. This humble root is manifested in occasional lapses from refinement in Angelica's behaviour and in the 'sensual aura' that surrounds her. Lampedusa contrasts her with the Prince's own daughter, Concetta, who Tancredi had been expected to marry. Blonde and light-skinned like the Prince himself, rather than dark and olive-skinned like the majority of people, including Angelica, Concetta is 'timid, reserved, coy'.[71] The aristocratic girls in general are described as short and ugly, like frogs, save for a handful of more presentable ones. 'It was as well that Angelica had emerged from the depths of Donnafugata to show the Palermitans what a beautiful woman was', thinks the Prince to himself at one juncture.[72]

In fashioning his novel, Lampedusa drew on his own family history (the figure of the prince is said to have been based on his grandfather), his memories of the Sicilian nobles he had met as a young man, and European literature and painting. Among his preferred authors were Stendhal, the first systematic admirer of Italian beauty in the Romantic period, and Proust, an author who had employed numerous Italian pictorial references in his descriptions of the character of Odette. No less important than these two background sources were the events of the post-war years, in which once again the representatives of an old system were compelled to search for ways of preserving their power in a new Italy. Some critics viewed *Il Gattopardo* not as a historical novel but as a contemporary one that reflected the author's own preoccupations.[73] Certainly, the cynical depiction of a transition from one order to another would seem to owe something to the experience of the passage from Fascism to Christian Democracy. Cinema was another contemporary influence. Although dark beauty played a role in the imagery of the nation around the time of the Risorgimento (see Chapters One and Two), events did not favour its being taken up in a full way by the new ruling elite. Only in the 1940s did beauty contests and the cinema fully facilitate the recasting of the iconography of the nation on the basis of the physical beauty of lower-class women. The writer was not an admirer of beauty pageants but nonetheless he did spend summer evenings watching the Mondello 'Miss Italia' competition.[74] He was also a very keen film-goer. There can be little doubt that when Lampedusa composed the figure of Angelica he had actresses like Lollobrigida and Loren in mind. They embodied the displacement of aristocracy by a cult of popular celebrity and they symbolised the new democratic era.

Like all Sicilian novelists, Lampedusa felt the need to explore the events of the Risorgimento. But the stress placed on Angelica's beauty distinguishes *Il Gattopardo* from the two nineteenth-century novels that provided Lampedusa with precedents for his analysis of the compromises and disappointments of the process of unification. These were Verga's *Mastro Don Gesualdo* (1889) and De Roberto's *I vicere* (The viceroys) (1894). Both of these novels feature, like *Il Gattopardo*, a marriage between a representative of a declining class seeking to perpetuate its influence and a figure from the new, rising class that is sure of its destiny and keen to acquire the patina of aristocracy. But in neither of them is dark, olive-skinned female beauty used to symbolise the vitality of the new class, a choice that in the context in which the authors were writing would have amounted to an overt political statement.

When *Il Gattopardo* was made into a film, the casting of Claudia Cardinale, a young actress of Sicilian origin, in the role of Angelica brought the cinematic dimension of the novel to the fore. The director, Visconti, personally identified with Lampedusa and his character of the prince. He was also drawn by the 'pure poetic emotions' he felt when faced with a range of the book's features, including 'the beauty of Angelica' to which, as a former jury member at beauty contests, he was not immune.[75] As a Marxist, Visconti did not seek to read the present into the events of the past. Rather, the past, in the form of the founding moment of national history, the Risorgimento (rendered topical once more by the publication between 1948 and 1951 of Gramsci's prison notebooks, which contained ample reflections on the southern question), merited examination on its own terms. For this reason, the director went to great lengths – greater even than Lampedusa,

58 Giuseppe di Lampedusa's character Angelica, played by Claudia Cardinale in Visconti's film of *The Leopard*, was informed by the film stars of the 1950s.

one might say – to ensure complete authenticity of costumes, settings, make-up and even perfumes in his film. Visconti made sure that Cardinale was clothed in period costumes and that she walked and even washed in the manner of women of the time.[76] However, she was perfect in the role not only because she was seen to have the same feline quality, and the mixture of earthiness and refinement, that marked Angelica, but because the literary character was created with precisely an actress like her in mind.[77]

The beautiful and shapely young women who had been recruited from the beauty pageants to provide new faces for Italian cinema conquered a place at all levels of European and American cinema. More significantly, they became a cultural fact, an emblem of Italian identity. 'The whole Italian people identifies with them,' Guarnieri noted, albeit with some regret.[78] Not even the left, which had hoped to be able to shape the development of cinema in a more socially engaged direction, could object to the emergence of women who rose up from below and who symbolised in some way the progress of Italy's rural and urban lower classes. Although older and more conservative women did not like most of the new stars, whose overt physicality and screen roles they disapproved of, they had a huge appeal for the younger women in provincial and rural locations. These women, who were going to the cinema and reading the press regularly for the first time, found in them an accessible and familiar example of emancipation and material progress. Only the Catholics cared little for the likes of Lollobrigida and Loren

– one Catholic journal, for example, referred to 'that most heavy manifestation of stardom that are the "maggiorate" made, unfortunately, in Italy'.[79] However, they decided mainly to keep their counsel. These actresses renewed the identification of Italy with female beauty at a time when the country needed a new cordial image and new symbols to show to the world.

CHAPTER EIGHT

MASS CONSUMPTION AND IDEALS OF BEAUTY

The years of the economic boom signalled the most rapid transformation in the history of Italy. In a few short years, a country that had been mainly rural in its economic profile suddenly became one of the leading industrial nations. The lives of many Italians changed radically, as people migrated from the countryside to cities and from the south to the north. The experience of economic growth was by no means always positive, especially in the short term, but either as aspiration or reality, most of the country was drawn into the new world of the nuclear family, domestic appliances and motorised transport. There was a striking emphasis in this period on blonde women, whose chromatic aura was attributed with a variety of meanings that were all associated with the American model of the consumer society, prosperity and modernity. In the illustrated press the image of the housewife, the key mediator between the family and the market, was predominantly presented as Americanised in this way. The slim, urban woman who was the symbol of economic aspiration in this period was the heir of the *donna crisi* of the 1920s. Like her predecessor, she fuelled a new current of accessible, imitable beauty that was, however, never represented in a way that was daring or decadent. In contrast to the inter-war years, she was not associated with any crisis, but rather with the promise of prosperity for all.

The shift of focus from the south to the north, and the deployment across the whole country of northern cultural models, represented a sharp break with the recent past. The Christian Democrat party, with its special relationship with the United States, believed that it was nonetheless possible to contain change within a broad pattern of continuity in values and culture. In such a conservative context, it was foreign figures and stars who became signifiers of the extent of the transformation. These included Brigitte Bardot, whose style was unprecedented in Italy and whose highly-charged presence both on and off-screen provoked censorious reactions when she gained exposure there. The abundant exuberance of Anita Ekberg, a Swedish actress who arrived in Italy via Hollywood and made her name in Fellini's *La Dolce Vita*, symbolised the arrival of a new era of leisure and pleasure. These women broke the rules and occupied an imaginative terrain that was widened by their presence. They were the complement of the modernised domesticated women who represented the ordinariness and accessibility of the consumer society. Both types of women, however, were different from the kind of androgynous beauty that became a feature of youth culture as it took shape in the 1960s. The new generation was indifferent to established patterns of dress and behaviour. Its iconic female figures were surly and rebellious rather than maternal and consolatory. They were imprinted with the mood of the time, its mobility, its emancipatory charge, its group ethos and its interest in fashion.

However, the years of the economic boom in Italy were not all about the new. Rapid change also produced a desire for memory, continuity and roots, to which cinema catered. While there was some attention to the contradictions and complexes of industrial society, it was mainly the focus on the rearguard that characterised its output. It was thanks to a nostalgic current that Sophia Loren eclipsed her rivals and established herself as the pre-eminent Italian actress of the period. For foreigners, she was a big star, the one Italian name everybody knew. At home she faced some younger challengers. Claudia Cardinale, for example, was strongly reminiscent in her physical characteristics of those stars who emerged earlier. In this way, she provided a continuity, a physical reminder of the qualities of the Italian people at a time when foreign influence was strong. Like Stefania Sandrelli, she also appeared in modern roles and developed a complex screen persona that was imbued with contemporary qualities. Far more than overtly metropolitan personalities, these women were taken as icons of an Italian beauty for new times.

Beauty and neo-capitalism

The lightness and emptiness of blondeness in the 1950s was primarily identified with white America, and especially Marilyn Monroe, who has been called 'the most important architect of blondeness in our culture'.[1] Fair hair had a lightness and airiness that, like foam, suggested luxury. In a celebrated essay on soap powders, Roland Barthes asserted that foam had this meaning because 'it appears to lack any usefulness'; it is 'abundant, easy' and 'can even be the sign of a certain spirituality, inasmuch as the spirit has the reputation of being able to make something out of nothing, a large surface of effects out of a small volume of causes . . .'.[2] In Italian advertising and on television, blonde femininity offered a new point of departure. As Katia Ferri argues, 'instead of poverty and underdevelopment beneath Vesuvius, the busty North American brought with her the perfume of the richest country in the world that had won the war and invented Coca Cola'.[3]

Sometimes the blondes represented in the mass media were home-grown like the comedienne Sandra Mondaini, who promoted a locally-produced liquor called Stock and Permaflex mattresses, or the young actress Virna Lisi, who endorsed talcum powder and toothpaste.[4] The most striking examples, however, were foreign. Ekberg first appeared in a television advertisement for Splügen beer as the moll of tough guy singer Fred Buscaglione. While the singer rasped a series of quips, she acted as a lazy, spoilt kept woman and tossed her blonde mane back with feigned indignance. She brought her special quota of eroticism to other advertisements, including Lux soap. She was a key figure in the Italian imagination of the economic miracle and her abundant figure would come, due to her role as a film star in Fellini's 1960 extravaganza *La Dolce Vita*, to symbolise the headlong rush to prosperity. The director was fascinated by her exuberance and opulence that were marked in his imagination as foreign.[5] She also featured as a real-life fantasy figure on a huge billboard advertising milk in an episode of the 1962 film *Boccaccio 70*, that Fellini made as a comment on critical responses to *La Dolce Vita*.

The typology of the Hollywood star had for at least two decades found a reflection in Italian culture. In variety theatre, the blonde, sequin-clad *soubrette* had had the function of offering spectators an escape from the everyday and the humdrum. Postwar Italian cinema reserved only a small space for such women; however, they found a much larger place on television and became a vital presence in television advertising from the moment it began in 1957. Blonde women featured prominently because of certain values that were associated with blondeness such as glamour, leisure and exoticism as well as luxury.[6]

The first RAI television broadcasts in 1954 were from studios in Milan and the medium was predominantly northern in its self-representation. Announcers nicknamed *signorine buonasera* (Miss Goodevenings) introduced the schedules and provided links between programmes.[7] A key broadcasting figure, Sergio Pugliese, who had been with RAI since the Fascist period, wanted announcers with blonde hair and the seven women who performed this task, all aged around twenty-four when they were first employed,[8] generally had light-brown or blonde hair and fair complexions. Their white skin, radiant expressions and respectable clothing gave them an aura that connected with the traditional role of the white woman in western culture.

Economic and technological development opened several new roles and professions for women. The television announcer, the air hostess, the secretary, the fashion model, the tourist guide, the receptionist and the interpreter were mainly concerned with public relations and presentation. They combined a certain professionalism with the traditional feminine values of cordiality and sympathy. The women who performed these roles were much envied for their economic independence and polished manner. The focus on grooming and appearance that was typical of the boom years provided an impulse to the fashion and cosmetics industries. American-based companies such as Elizabeth Arden and Helena Rubinstein aimed 'to transform the Italian woman into a modern cosmetic user, as cosmetic-shy, first-time users [were] targeted along with the "habituées" following fashion or searching for variation'.[9] Throughout the period there was a steady increase in the volume of advertising for beauty products in magazines like *Grazia* and *Annabella*. Between 1955 and 1959, the number of pages of *Grazia* devoted to cosmetic and related advertising rose from 13 out of 76 pages to 34 out of 132. A greater proportion of editorial content was also given over to matters of personal appearance and care, beauty and grooming.[10] The Italian market was not as developed as the French or British one, but it was growing. Mainly, it was concentrated in the north, where 58 per cent of spending on beauty products occurred, compared to 27 per cent in the centre and 15 per cent in the south.[11]

In their advertising, international companies relied on the appeal of their foreign-sounding brand names and light-skinned models with a perfectly polished appearance. Such advertisements were founded on a radically different image from the 'casa e chiesa' (home and church) stereotype of the traditional Italian girl and offered a more contemporary popular ideal. Faced with such images, the addressee was placed before a potential or finished version of herself, with use of a system of referrals based not simply on rejection of a norm, and attraction of the daringly different, but also on a modern model of femininity that was superficially reconciled with conservative, middle-class values by mainstream magazines.[12] This was a big shift with respect to the inter-war years when writers like Pittigrilli had depicted such women as cocaine addicts and nymphomaniacs.

The impact of American-style consumerism was apparent even in the Miss Italia competition, that is to say the institution that had championed modest, traditional femininity in the previous decade. Several announcers had emerged through beauty contests. In 1961 there was widespread shock when the first blonde Miss Italia was elected. Franca Cattaneo, a twenty-two-year old from Genoa who was endowed with a figure that was compared to that of Monroe, won a prize of a million lire and an Alfa Romeo Spider. '1.70m tall, she has very blonde hair, dark eyes and a white skin', wrote *Oggi*.[13] Despite the break with tradition, her victory did not divide either the jury or the public, since she was 'a blonde and majestic Miss Italia who is liked even by her rivals'. To ease any alarm, the magazine reported the comforting news that the winner was 'a quiet girl of simple habits'. The break, however, was significant, as Natalia Aspesi wrote in *Il Giorno*:

> No-one had ever seen a representative of Italian beauty who was so little like the homely and Latin stereotype that the jury members of the most important Italian beauty contest usually end up selecting in order to satisfy those who demand that Italian beauty be modesty, simplicity, a girlish figure and blushing cheeks. On this occasion, the jury was not fearful and so, after a dispute, opted for one of those girls that would make even a short-sighted Englishman turn his head in the street.[14]

Although it would remain far more frequent for women of Mediterranean appearance to win the title, candidates who were groomed, polished and presented according to the dominant values of consumer society were no longer penalised. Young women no longer took part to escape poverty; rather, they saw it as a leisure activity that carried with it the possibility of achieving recognition and fame.

Despite the vogue for shapely female bodies in the era of nascent prosperity, the decline of the rural ideal of abundant, curvaceous femininity was a long-term trend. As Cecil Beaton wrote as early as 1957: 'We are still very much in the "age of bones". Gone for the moment is the fleshy padding, with the exception of Gina Lollabrigida (*sic*). Mortification is today's signpost. Fat is not only a solecism, but many modern women, svelte by nature, restrict themselves to ruthless dieting in order to arrive at some more cadaverous appearance'.[15] The preference for 'fleshy padding' to which Beaton referred had its origin in scarcity but it was more geared to male fantasies than female preferences. In Italy, the enthusiasm with which women embraced the models of artificial femininity and the products that were associated with their realisation showed a desire for autonomy and self-determination that broke with tradition. Even the shapely stars responded to it. Most of them slimmed down and refined their images at this time.[16] The most prominent example of female rejection of the canon of florid beauty was provided by Silvana Mangano. The actress very deliberately sought to achieve a refined appearance after her first pregnancies and put herself beyond the type of beauty she had helped create on the screen. By 1960, she had evolved into an ethereal presence, more spirit than body, whose film roles bore no resemblance to those of her early career. Paradoxically,

59 By the 1960s, the girls in the fruit advertisements had a distinctly urban look. Note the earrings, make-up and lacquered nails.

she was also the most family-oriented of the stars, who was often featured in magazines with her husband, the producer Dino De Laurentiis, and her four children.

The new actresses who emerged in the mid-to-late 1950s were aligned with the contemporary ideal of beauty. Although they were only a few years younger than the *maggiorate fisiche*, Elsa Martinelli and Rosanna Schiaffino were much less physically imposing. Martinelli was an important figure of the period because she began as a fashion model and, not unlike Audrey Hepburn – to whom she was compared – always retained an identification with the world of fashion.[17] Although she was born in Rome in 1935 to a humble Trastevere family, Martinelli had the physique and grace to embody dreams of social mobility and refinement. The youngest of eight sisters, she worked in coffee bars and then for a hatter before being signed up as a model. At the age of only seventeen, she made her first trip to America on a promotional tour for the Italian fashion industry. Recruited by Kirk Douglas for her first film, *The Indian Hunter*, she built a film career mainly in Hollywood. None of her films was memorable but she starred alongside legendary actors including John Wayne in *Hatari* and Robert Mitchum and Jack Hawkins in *Rampage*. She led a highly cosmopolitan life and was often photographed by leading photographers for international magazines like *Life* and *Vogue*. She travelled between continents, mixing with the stars in Hollywood and on Rome's Via Veneto. She acted as a testimonial for Chanel, Yves Saint Laurent and Pierre Cardin. Her image was that of the 'aristocratic-style anti-*maggiorata*',[18] who was more international than Italian.

A former Miss Liguria, Rosanna Schiaffino was physically very similar to Martinelli; her body was also slim and toned, although slightly more curvaceous. In 1958 Francesco Rosi cast her in his debut film, *La sfida* (The challenge). In the movie, Schiaffino played Assunta, a humble Neapolitan girl who marries Vito, an ambitious man from the same background who challenges the hold of organised crime over the local fruit and vegetable market. At their wedding, a woman shouts after Assunta, 'She is beautiful like a queen!'. Neither Vito (Jose Suarez) nor Assunta look like slum dwellers and their world is shot through with money values and the attributes of consumption.

Martinelli and Schiaffino appeared together in *La notte brava* (*Bad Girls Don't Cry*), Mauro Bolognini's adaptation of Pasolini's *Ragazzi di vita* (*The Ragazzi*), along with two other minor stars, Antonella Lualdi and Anna Maria Ferrero. They play tough Roman street prostitutes who embark on a night of adventures with three inexperienced pimps. Although both Martinelli and Schiaffino hailed from ordinary backgrounds, they were derided as implausible by the real prostitutes who gathered to watch the filming of the roadside scenes.[19] Their physiques were devoid of external signals of their lower-class origins and indeed suggested sophistication and fashionable beauty. Clad in split-thigh skirts, they had the angular arms and legs that were preferred by fashion houses, while figure-hugging tops revealed the outlines of their pert breasts. Their presence in this film showed that fashionable beauty was taking the place of realism in the representation of women in Italian cinema.

Youth and beauty

For youth, the upheavals and changes of the period brought a new measure of freedom. According to the Catholic sociologist Achille Ardigò, the participation of especially young women in migration was the most visible aspect of a general tendency of the modern woman to associate her own emancipation with the attainment of an urban style of living.[20] Even girls living in villages no longer pictured themselves as rural dwellers, but as participants in an expanding industrial civilisation.[21] In the freer atmosphere of the city, young women succeeded in throwing off some traditional social controls and achieving a degree of self-determination. Industrialisation found a correspondence in a culture that attributed value to big cities and removed it from rural and small town environments. This culture, he argued, prioritised individual freedom. By this, he meant that socialisation through consumption and commercial leisure, including the mass media, accelerated levels of aspiration in a way that drew the mass of the people into the mental universe of the middle class.

Youth culture developed in Italy before the idea of individual freedom really took hold. In the late 1950s, Italian cinema produced a series of light low-budget comedies set among the Roman working class to convey the dilemmas and aspirations of youth. The *Poveri ma belli* (Poor but beautiful) series of films won a huge following and brought popularity to its lead actors, Maurizio Arena and Renato Salvatori, who played two beefy tough guys with hearts of gold, and Marisa Allasio, a teenage *maggiorata* with blonde hair and a breezy manner. Even Lorella De Luca and Alessandra Panaro, who played the boys' mousy younger sisters, attracted a following. The actors physically embodied the aspirations of lower-class youth for material improvement; their carnality and good looks were their sole resource, their only lever in seeking mobility. However, they were completely bounded by conventional morality, family and a tight social order. Allasio's character, in particular, never showed any desire to transgress conventional codes. For this reason, the actors who starred in these films did not survive the rapid transformation of the years of the economic boom. They quickly dated and were eclipsed in popularity by more contemporary figures who did not evoke a recent past of poverty and who explored some of the tensions that characterised the youth condition. Among these was sex, which was no longer a prerogative solely of young men who had been accustomed to having their first experiences in state-licensed brothels, prior to their abolition in 1958.

Italian cinema found it difficult to recruit home-grown actresses able to give expression to the aspirations and behaviour of girls and young women. Foreign actresses were usually used to convey these novelties. A key example of the way Italian cinema dealt with this problem was the case of Catherine Spaak, a Belgian actress of fair appearance who made numerous films in Italy in the early 1960s and subsequently embarked on a television career. Spaak's screen persona was that of the free, amoral girl who was open to erotic experience. She was less provocative than Bardot and more subtle in giving form to sly adolescents of a graceful and bourgeois demeanour. She was in this respect a refined version of another Francophone actress, Jacqueline Sassard, who a few years earlier played a teenage Lolita in Alberto Lattuada's film *Guendalina*. The Milanese director developed a special interest in exploring adolescent female desire. There was no doubt that Sassard and Spaak belonged to a world of prosperity and choice; they had no connection at all to the sort of lower-class settings that were still very popular in Italian cinema. This extraneousness from any specific Italian background meant that the uninhibited behaviour of their characters was less shocking and more digestible.[22] The girls they played usually rejected but were not really critical or overtly rebellious. Spaak, who was only fifteen in 1960, tantalised audiences in Lattuada's *I dolci inganni* (Sweet deceptions), and played the teenage temptress in several classic films of the boom period, including *Il sorpasso* (*The Easy Life*), *La voglia matta* (Crazy desire) and *La parmigiana* (The girl from Parma). She highlighted the displacement of formal behaviour and clothing with relaxed mores, miniskirts and blue jeans. She often appeared in bikinis at a time when beach wear was becoming much more widespread as more people went on holidays. Bodies were routinely exposed much more and the democratic promise of the decade meant that every young woman believed she could be beautiful. This was an aesthetic promise rather than a political one; one that individuals put into practice by wearing make-up, dyeing their hair and practising depilation of their legs.

The only Italian actress who to some extent conveyed in her roles and in her physical presence the tensions and aspirations of young women in this phase of transition was Stefania Sandrelli. She was willowy and tall but also quite conventional in her indolence and seductive warmth. At the age of sixteen, she made her debut as a teenage temptress in Pietro Germi's Sicilian satire *Divorzio all'italiana* (*Divorce, Italian-Style*), a role she reprised in the director's second Sicilian film *Sedotta e abbandonata* (*Seduced and Abandoned*). When Francesco Rosi had highlighted corruption and criminality in the Naples of the economic boom, he did so as a left-wing Neapolitan who wished to promote reform. Germi tackled the customs and manners of Sicily with the same detachment as Lattuada and with even more cynical contempt. The films were grotesque parodies, even if they were brilliantly made as choral works. Sandrelli, who was born in Viareggio and was not therefore a southerner, played teenage girls who were pretty enough to be the objects of desire of older men and clever enough to know how to get free of them. She also had a sexual allure that was natural rather than constructed. According to Elio Girlanda, she and her roles, which were mainly in social comedies, played a most significant part in 'breaking down traditional and conventional images of Italy'.[23]

Sandrelli was part of a scene that was defined by pop music, vacations and mobility. Her affair with the singer-songwriter Gino Paoli turned her into a personality. When he attempted suicide after she abandoned him, her reputation as a woman of special allure was sealed. His recovery and subsequent song about her 'Sapore di sale' (Taste of salt), which became one of the biggest hits of the decade, confirmed this. In this sense, she belonged to a youth environment that was increasingly defined by pop singers and the ideas they communicated in their songs. The blonde Caterina Caselli, whose declaration of autonomy in 'Nessuno mi può giudicare' (No one can judge me) struck a widespread chord, was a tomboy who broke all the accepted canons of femininity. The alluring Venetian singer Patty Pravo, whose slim, elongated body, pale skin and long fair hair set her apart from almost all others, was identified with the Piper music venue in Rome. Mina, a singer whose aggressive manner led her to be dubbed 'the tiger of Cremona', also dyed her hair blonde and established her own rules, scandalising public opinion by becoming an unmarried mother in 1963.

Like many other actresses, Sandrelli emerged due to her participation in beauty contests. Although she was at her best when playing the parts of provincial girls, she did not play teenagers for long. She was soon playing women who were drawn into the contradictions of a fast-changing world. In *Io la conoscevo bene* (I knew her well), she offered a splendid portrait of the downfall of a girl whose hopes for an entry into show-business lead only to compromise and failure. In *La bella di Lodi* (The beauty from Lodi), in 1963, Sandrelli played a dynamic businesswoman whose modern appearance does not seem Italian at all. Her hair dyed blonde and styled in a bob, she dresses in tailored suits, employs an authoritarian tone and uses a good-looking mechanic as a sexual plaything. Her rapid transformation from teenage Lolita to modern woman, and the loss in this

60 Stefania Sandrelli, one of the young starlets of the 1960s who embodied the spirit of the era.

process of some of the exterior and behavioural indicators of the Mediterranean woman, illustrates the way Italy experienced the arrival of the modern world of neo-capitalism. Desirable and desired, it could seemingly only be embraced at the cost of a series of cultural and aesthetic breaks with a past that was still determinant in the elaboration of Italian identity.

The rise of Italian youth culture occurred in a context in which ideas of how young women should look and behave were increasingly shaped by the media and its foreign-inspired notions. In particular the prominence enjoyed by London fashions was accompanied by a new attention to models, who were no longer confined to the rarified world of haute couture. The popularity in Italy of Twiggy (*Grissino*) and Jean Shrimpton (*Gamberetto*) signalled the emergence of a new type of youth and fashion-oriented beauty that was associated with Swinging London. 'Perhaps the female type who is most imitated, even in Italy, is called Jean Shrimpton', commented one writer.[24] Fantasy figures like the women of James Bond, Barbarella, and many comic book heroines marked the emergence of a new type of artificiality that reflected the atomised relations of industrial society. The rise of spaghetti westerns, too, marked the rise of money values and violence as entertainment in an atomised society. For the sculptor Emilio Greco and the painter Toti Scajola, the new models proposed by the mass media were frigid and inexpressive.[25] They were like Ursula Andress, a blonde siren who Scajola found cold and masculine in contrast to the warm Italians. In Elio Petri's science fiction film *La decima vittima* (*The Tenth Victim*) the Swiss actress was a modern Diana who hunts her male prey with a gun. Other critics, inadvertently echoing their predecessors of the inter-war years, bemoaned a certain standardisation and the rise of an international type of beauty. In *L'Europeo* in 1965, Nerio Minuzzo deplored an 'emblematic but ordinary and stereotyped beauty that circulates on the Via Veneto as it does in Chelsea or on the Kurfuerstendamm. This is a beauty that is codified and proposed with infinite repetition by the means of communication; it has emerged from the pages of women's magazines, television screens and advertising posters and now lives alongside us, in serial form, at all levels'.[26] The ubiquity on billboards and in the media of slim young women with a northern European air heralded a decisive shift in canons of beauty. Some observers were convinced that foreign fashions could not be adapted well to Italy. Women of Mediterranean build who were not suited to the miniskirt were seen to be as distant from the French *yé-yé* singer Françoise Hardy and the slim girls of Chelsea as they were from the statuesque beauties of the belle époque.[27]

Modernity and identity

The position of Italian beauty in all this was complex. Although it seemed as if Italy was losing its specific identity, in fact this was not the case. The rapid turnover in ideals of beauty moved faster than popular tastes and perceptions, for which the typical Italian woman, and specifically her representation on the silver screen, was still defined by her generous curves.[28] This can be illustrated in a number of ways. First, it is worth considering some actresses who have already been mentioned. Although Martinelli, Schiaffino and Sandrelli each carved out a niche for herself, none but Sandrelli – for the reasons mentioned above – succeeded in winning broad popularity. Italian producers were keen to sign up Martinelli because of her international reputation, but they chose for her launch a vehicle that took no account of her individuality. Her first Italian film, *La risaia* (*The Rice Girl*), was a remake of *Riso amaro*, in which she played a role similar to the one that had made Silvana Mangano a star. It was a rural film typical of the period. However, with her lean, willowy physique, Martinelli could not achieve the same symbiosis of body and landscape that had made the earlier film such a landmark. In fact, the rice fields acted merely as a picturesque backdrop to a conventional melodramatic plot. More appropriate to her profile was *Donatella*, a modern-day Cinderella story, also made in 1955, in which Martinelli is given access to the luxurious wardrobe of a wealthy American woman while she is away from Rome. The dresses she wore were all designed by the Roman dress designer Capucci. Both films were reasonable successes but very few offers followed. For producers, Martinelli stood outside the range of figures and types deemed to be recognisably Italian. Although she was well known and reasonably popular, she simply did not carry sufficient Italian connotations to construct a lasting career in national cinema. Nor did she have the advantage of being the protégée of a producer or director.

Martinelli's career, consequently, was largely international. She was the one prominent Italian actress who was identified with the colourful nightlife of the *dolce vita* and she married a Roman aristocrat (from whom she would soon separate). She played expensive mistresses in several American films and her looks as well as her lifestyle were more cosmopolitan than Italian. Moreover, she contributed to the rise of informality and helped define the style of the 1960s. She personally preferred casual clothing to haute couture and, even when wearing the latter, opted for designers with a modern edge like Courrèges or Saint Laurent. At home and abroad, she stood for the ideal of the modern unencumbered, free-living woman who was in favour of emancipation and personal freedom. For Italians, she seemed to embody both left-bank Paris and London's Carnaby Street. Precisely because she lay outside the recognised framework of Italian womanhood and was never endowed with a specific Italian aura, she was able to pursue an emancipated lifestyle, showing complete disregard for conservative public opinion. Considerably ahead of her time, she acted as a trailblazer for the sexual revolution.[29]

Rosanna Schiaffino had the advantage of being personally involved with a producer, Alfredo Bini. Yet she too failed to achieve a broad-based popularity. As an actress, she was defined by her moderate variation on the established canons of Italian cinematic beauty. She was a younger, quieter, more urban version of Lollobrigida. Like Martinelli, she appeared in many international productions, of the type that was popular at the time, although usually only in supporting roles. Perhaps her most memorable role as a beauty was as the air hostess Anna Maria in the episode 'Illibatezza' (Purity) in the collective film

Rogopag. Directed by Rossellini, she played a reserved, conventional girl who works on long haul flights and who dutifully films Super8 images to send back to her jealous Calabrian fiancé in Rome. However, she attracts the attention of a boorish American businessman who, sated with the buxom blondes of Hollywood, is aroused by her simplicity and naturalness. She is the pure, maternal girl of his dreams. She only manages to discourage his unwanted attentions when, in exasperation, she adopts the guise of a glamour girl, complete with platinum blonde wig, cigarette habit and tight-fitting cocktail dress. Repelled by this polished exterior, he curses the disappearance of the simple, reassuring Italian girl who had fascinated him. Conversely, her fiancé, seeing the film of her in her glamour guise, is excited by the overt sexiness of the persona she has temporarily embraced. Schiaffino's beauty was also employed explicitly in the plots of Mauro Bolognini's tale of corrupted innocence *La corruzione* (Corruption) in 1963 and Lattuada's adaptation of Machiavelli's *La mandragola* (*Mandragola: the Love Root*) in 1965.

Antonella Lualdi, Anna Maria Ferrero and many other young actresses also served to reinforce the reputation of Italian cinema for female beauty, even though they never came fully to the fore in their own right. The problems that all these women faced were twofold. On the one hand, they were not young enough to benefit from the trend towards youth. By 1960, they were all in their twenties. On the other, they were not individual enough to displace the actresses who had emerged in the defining moment of the post-war years and who had come to be seen as embodiments of the new Italy. These women were still relatively young and it was they who monopolised the best roles.

The star system that Italian cinema formed in the 1950s evolved relatively little in the years that followed, although the personalities who composed it modified their images and took on more varied roles. The stars balanced their sexy screen images with lifestyles that were certainly visible and attractive but basically conventional. Despite the advent of television, they were the aristocrats of the media system and they confirmed this by transferring attention from the shapeliness of their bodies to their elegance and the luxury of their lifestyle. People looked to them for examples of ways to dress, wear make-up, decorate a home, conduct family life and travel.

Sophia Loren emerged as the premier Italian actress of the period, thanks both to a significant shift in her image as she came to be seen as more maternal, and a series of historical roles. History films became popular in Italy around 1960, as censorship weakened and controversial episodes in the country's past could be tackled. This was a genre in which another actress, Giovanna Ralli, became prominent. Ralli played De Sica's young lover in Rossellini's *Il Generale Della Rovere* (*General della Rovere*), a black market girl in *Era notte a Roma* (*Blackout in Rome*) and a Calabrian peasant in *Viva l'Italia*. In *Carmen di Trastevere* (Carmen '63), she appeared in an updated version of Merimée's classic story in which the melodramatic structure was preserved intact. In these films, she was tough and courageous, loyal and strong, like Magnani. Unlike some of her colleagues, she acted using her own voice and, as an actress, was possessed of a variety of registers. Although Ralli would continue to work for many years in Italian and international cinema, she

61 Giovanna Ralli, a second-rank actress of Italian cinema's golden age.

never consolidated her position as a leading actress. One of the main reasons for this was that the historical current within cinema, that began as a highly controversial exploration of neglected or difficult episodes from recent history, soon evolved into a more self-congratulatory evocation of the past in a nostalgic key. It incorporated elements of comedy that would be harnessed and developed by Sophia Loren, who would turn out to be the key female figure in this genre.

Loren first proved her worth as a serious actress in *La ciociara* (*Two Women*).[30] Released in 1960, the film secured an Oscar for Best Actress as well as a variety of other awards at Cannes, London, Tokyo, Madrid and Berlin. Based on a best-selling novel by Italy's most popular writer, Alberto Moravia, the film described the period leading up to the liberation of Rome from the point of view of a woman evacuated with her daughter to the surrounding countryside. Although the women escape the vengeance of the retreating Nazis, they are trapped and raped by a band of Moroccan soldiers enrolled in the French army. It is therefore a crude aspect of the liberation that is underlined at the expense of the more conventional triumphant dimensions. Originally, Magnani had been considered for the role of the mother and Loren for the daughter. However, the older actress rejected the proposal out of hand. The parts were therefore re-written to lower the mother's age from fifty to thirty (Loren in fact was twenty-six) and that of the daughter from eighteen to thirteen.

La ciociara had the look and feel of a neo-realist film (and like several classics of that era was directed by De Sica and scripted by Zavattini). It was crucial to Loren's career in that it enabled her to step into the role of dishevelled woman of the people. Widely seen as 'a brutal but honest film', as *Time* magazine called it, it fitted with the new wave of films that Italian cinema made between 1959 and 1962, tackling the themes of Fascism and war. In fact, *La ciociara* was one of the least controversial movies of those years. The tragedy at its centre was strictly personal rather than political or social and it did not raise any issues, unlike other historical films of the early 1960s which tackled sensitive themes relating to Italy's role in World War One.[31]

That De Sica was moving in a direction quite different to neo-realism was evident from the films he subsequently made with Loren, several of which also starred Marcello Mastroianni. Unlike some other directors, De Sica took refuge in a celebration of an Italian spirit that belonged to the past and which the two actors embodied. Like the Neapolitan critic Giuseppe Marotta, he had not appreciated the Americanisation of Loren's image that occurred in the international productions in which she was involved in the mid-1950s. Her director in *L'Oro di Napoli*, he saw her as a figure able vividly to bring to life a common sentiment that he identified with Naples. He cast her in the episode 'La Riffa' (The Raffle) in *Boccaccio 70*, about a fairground girl who gives herself every Saturday night to the winner of a raffle; the three part film *Ieri, oggi, domani* (*She Got What She Asked For*), in which the actress played a happy-go-lucky Neapolitan slum dweller, who escapes imprisonment for trafficking contraband cigarettes by being constantly pregnant, a Roman prostitute and a Milanese society woman; and *Matrimonio all'italiana* (*Marriage Italian-style*), an adaptation of Eduardo De Filippo's play *Filumena Marturano*. Despite variations of social class – although the preferred environment remained that of a spirited southern lower-class world – all these characters were distinguished by their independence from official morality and, at the same time, their conformity to a normative system that matched the easy-going impulses of a recognised popular sentiment. In short, even in their transgressions, they aroused popular sympathy and approval.

Although they were made between 1962 and 1964, a period in which the processes of urbanisation, modernisation and motorisation were all well-advanced, these films were for the most part set in an Italy that was mainly southern and in any event rural or pre-industrial. There were no signs of the recent, rapid transformations that had altered the face of the country; consumerism and modernity in general were notable by their absence. To this extent, it may be argued that, far from representing an element of renewal, they constituted a regressive current in a cinema that in other respects was beginning to recover its critical edge after a phase in which passive entertainment had been the norm. The image of the country offered in these films was not problematic, but cheery, sunny and timeless.

These films helped Loren to deepen her connection with the history and customs of the south at a time when it was seen as the repository of memory and identity in a

62 Sophia Loren, the best-known Italian actress in the world.

fast-changing Italy. Thoroughly Italian in feel and visual language, they helped consolidate the country as an imaginative territory for foreign audiences in which Loren herself was an integral part. As a result, she not only eclipsed Lollobrigida as the leading embodiment of Italian beauty, she also supplanted Anna Magnani as the most popular dramatic incarnation of the spirit of the Italian people. Spinazzola's analysis of the distribution of box office takings reveals that De Sica's films of the early 1960s were highly successful in the more industrial regions and in particular in the provincial centres of the north and centre of the country.[32] In the south, the region that featured most frequently in this type of cinema, reactions were mixed. Vittorio Ricciuti, critic of the Neapolitan daily *Il Mattino*, was particularly vociferous in his attack on what he saw as its false authenticity. In his view the films lacked human vitality and in any case a celluloid creation like Loren was not a worthy successor to Anna Magnani or the star of the stage version of *Filumena Marturano*, Titina De Filippo.[33]

Abroad, De Sica's films of the 1960s did especially well. *Ieri, oggi, domani* unexpectedly took the Oscar for best foreign film in 1964 while Loren won a Best Actress nomination for her role in *Matrimonio all'italiana*, as well as a Golden Globe from the Hollywood foreign press corps and other awards. One of the reasons for the success of these films was their close connection with Hollywood convention.[34] In both, Italy was presented in exactly the same way, as a country that was defined in terms of a set of unchanging stereotypes recognisable to all. The Italians appeared as a roguish but essentially lovable people whose principal defect was that they were irredeemably ill-suited to the ways of modern, industrial society. To the Americans, this seemed like an authentic portrait. As *Time* wrote, 'the country fair that formed the backdrop of "la Riffa" is alive with superb detail, from the smallest of the watermelon seeds to the largest of the paunchy farmers with hot breath and sausage fingers. In this milieu, Sophia is not a star showing off but a figure that belongs'.[35] Loren was so well known at this time that Bob Dylan included her in a line of his 1963 song 'I Shall Be Free'. Dylan receives in the song a friendly call from President Kennedy, who asks him, 'What do we need to make the country grow?'. 'My friend John, Brigitte Bardot, Anita Ekberg, Sophia Loren' is his reply.

Claudia Cardinale

The continuing appeal of Mediterranean beauty was shown by Claudia Cardinale, who was seen by some as Loren's natural successor when the latter graduated to maternal roles. Cardinale should also be seen in relation to Monica Vitti, who emerged in the 1960s as the favourite actress of the director Michelangelo Antonioni. Both actresses benefited from the great international success of the Italian art house cinema and owed their international standing to this. Antonioni was one of very few directors to explore modernity from the inside. Often criticised by left-wing observers for creating a bourgeois cinema, he detached himself completely from the aesthetic that arose out of the neo-realist movement and the ethic of commitment on which it was predicated. As his preferred actress, Vitti developed a screen persona that was largely forged and contained within his universe. Her acting style was minimalist and interiorised. In other ways, too, she largely eradicated 'Italian' elements from her persona. Her appearance alone – blonde, pale-skinned, and waif-like – situated her in the industrialised world of mass consumption and its contradictions. A somewhat depersonalised screen presence, only her full lips and expressive eyes suggested something of the Mediterranean woman. This dematerialisation of her presence was more filmic than personal (unlike Mangano) and it ensured that, although she also made some memorable comedies, she was never considered in relation to the Italian actresses who came to prominence in the post-war years.[36] Her films with Antonioni made her an icon of a certain type of cinema *d'auteur* but she was too complex and cerebral to be embraced as a national symbol.

Cardinale, by contrast, was thoroughly Mediterranean in appearance even if she did not only play southerners. She had no training as an actress, although she did attend the Centro Sperimentale after beginning her film career. It was her physical beauty that marked her out. The producer Franco Cristaldi, who first spotted her and who became her partner, used this as a basis to plot a highly successful career strategy. The daughter of Sicilian parents who had been born and raised in Tunisia, Cardinale had once won the title of 'the most beautiful Italian girl in Tunis'. Her screen presence was initially reliant solely on her Mediterranean beauty, before she graduated to more complex and contemporary roles. Cardinale contributed to the consolidation of the idea that feminine beauty was an unlimited resource of Italy that Italian cinema was especially skilled at discovering and presenting. While she was often placed on screen in backward or lower-class southern environments, her physique was modern. As a personality, she was largely reassuring and protective. More composed than Loren and Lollobrigida, she was at home playing bourgeois women, as she did in Maselli's adaptation of Moravia's novel *Gli indifferenti* and Visconti's *Vaghe stelle dell'Orsa* (*Of a Thousand Delights*). In fact, art directors regarded her as pliable but quite distinctive. She had a rough voice, a certain otherworldly quality, and an air of melancholy.

Visconti cast Cardinale as a typical southern beauty in *Rocco e i suoi fratelli* (*Rocco and His Brothers*), his epic drama about the destruction of a family of southern peasants who migrate to Milan during the economic boom, and in his screen version of *Il Gattopardo*. In both these films, she had little more than cameo roles. Yet her profile grew. Although she was rarely the biggest source of a film's box office appeal, between 1958 and 1963 she took part in over twenty high-profile Italian and foreign films. She was a significant presence in the social comedy *Il bell'Antonio*, the decadent *I delfini* (*The Dauphins*) and many other movies, including Sergio Leone's *C'era una volta il West* (*Once Upon a Time in the West*) and a variety of international adventure films. Valerio Zurlini's *La ragazza con la valigia* (*Girl with a suitcase*) and Luigi Comencini's dramatisation of Carlo Cassola's Resistance novel *La ragazza di Bube* (*Bebo's Girl*) provided her with more opportunity to shine.

Cardinale did not consider herself really to be an actress. 'I have never thought of myself as an actress. I am only a woman with a certain sensibility and it is with that that

63 Claudia Cardinale, who combined a traditional physique with a contemporary attitude.

I have always worked', she declared. However, the fact that she was an instinctive performer, who used her physical presence and emotional repertoire to give rise to her screen identity, made her appealing to many directors. They saw her as pliable and available for their moulding, a body on which could be inscribed a variety of meanings. She worked with an extraordinary variety of directors and was the only actress to work in the 1960s with both Visconti and Fellini, who were considered to be polar opposites in terms of their style, values and approach to the business of film-making. Visconti was the director who taught her most. 'Among all the things he taught me', she wrote:

> there is the awareness of my body, my legs, my shoulders, my arms, my chin and my eyes. He taught me to guide my body and not allow myself to be guided blindly by it. He restored to me, if I can put it like that, a look and a smile. Today, I am more than ever united with him. It is him I continue to refer to whenever I speak, think, cry or laugh in front of a camera.[37]

In *Il Gattopardo*, he encouraged her to walk with long strides, taking possession of the ground with the soft yet strong confidence that animals have.

Cardinale's body was a key feature of her individual yet Italian appeal. Reviewing one of her early films, Pasolini commented that her eyes 'looked only into corners'.[38] She had a mobility that was of the moment. However, the graceful curves of her body were central to her identity. 'I have got attractive breasts, I know; they have always been like that', she later declared. 'They are a part of my body that has never been a problem and for that I thank Mother Nature – it is all her merit. It is also Mother Nature who made me a gift of a body that, fortunately, is not a tree trunk. I have always had this slim waist, round hips and a bust that allows me to wear any sort of neckline'.[39]

On screen, she played a wide variety of women, from southern girls of peasant origin to temptresses and dark ladies in the films of Bolognini, and also career women, bourgeois women and the beautiful object. Her lack of a technique made her flexible. However, there was a constant in the tension between her closed, aggressive personality, which was highly defensive and combative, and the inviting reassurance of her soft curves and feminine appearance. Her character, 'closed and rebellious', was her distinctive feature; it put her in tune with the 1960s and lent her autonomy and complexity. By contrast to, say, Vitti, Cardinale was both traditional and contemporary.

Her adaptability to a variety of screen roles was memorably illustrated by Moravia in an interview that was based on the premise that she was 'an object'.[40] In conversation with the actress, he defined her long hair as matching, in its movements, 'the curves of her body'. Her bust was 'very evident and full', her skin 'constantly brown as if always sun-tanned', her eyes 'very dark brown but very bright and very luminous'. For the writer, her mouth had a hard, cross expression that was 'a bit rustic, a bit rural'. It was a mouth that 'one imagines in the act of biting a piece of fruit or spitting out a pip, or chewing a blade of grass'. When she laughed, her eyes 'become two black, glittering openings, with a mischievous, passionate, intense and southern quality'. This objectification did not mean that the writer was wholly in control. Recalling this interview in her autobiography, Cardinale said that she did not object at all to being considered as a body since this was the tool of her labour as an actress. 'I amused myself a little by making him feel ill at ease, because I understood that my physical appearance embarrassed him more than a little. Physically in fact, I was very close to his world, to his female characters, as he thought of them and described them. I was in some way part of his writing since I was, and I appeared, so dark, moody, argumentative and also a bit indifferent to him'.[41]

Spinazzola argued that Cardinale did not develop a precise profile as a star.[42] In fact she was different from Lollobrigida and Loren while also clearly stemming from a similar root. She had a certain mystery about her that contemporary observers felt owed more to Mangano. In addition, she was photogenic in a striking modern way. This made her especially appealing to the art-house directors of the early 1960s. Her presence may have been understated by comparison with others, but she constructed an exceptionally long career that has lasted down to the present. While the actresses who had first emerged when cast as buxom rural beauties slimmed down and struggled to conform to a bourgeois ideal of refinement and elegance, balancing home-grown and cosmopolitan qualities, Cardinale easily bridged the gap. She had grown up speaking French and her idol was Brigitte Bardot, a free spirit for whom there had been no equivalent in Italian cinema in the 1950s. She walked like a model and offered an unusual mixture of temperament and introversion.

Cardinale cultivated a certain mystery by ensuring that her body was never exposed on screen. Her silhouette was suggested, dresses were low-cut, her back was seen naked and her full lips and unkempt hair gave her a wild, untamed look that suggested sex. But she never stripped for the camera. Like other female stars, however, she found that her fans fantasised about her naked body. They wrote to her to request photographs, sometimes making no secret of their desire that these should depict her unclothed, like the teenage Swedish boy who wrote informing her that 'I want to see your breasts, legs and thighs' or the Frenchman who informed her that 'I am a fervent admirer of your body'.[43] It was only foreigners who referred explicitly to her body. The letters she received from Italian fans reveal that it was the early films in which she played pure, idealised women that made most impact with them. It was a partly imagined version of Cardinale as a sweet, reassuring brown-haired, dark-skinned beauty that exercised most attraction. Repeatedly, her small, supporting roles in *I soliti ignoti* (*Big Deal on Madonna Street/ Persons Unknown*) and *Rocco e i suoi fratelli* were mentioned. However, she was also an object of aspiration. Girls wrote saying they wanted to be beautiful like her, while men asked for pictures or for financial help. The authors were very varied and included students and mothers, as well as a Catholic priest. According to the critic Giovanni Grazzini, who edited the letters, 'the Italian audience, that is still influenced by the cult of the Virgin Mary and the national obsession with motherhood, is more sensitive to the values of a femininity that is lovingly protective'.[44] Like others before her, Cardinale appeared in a variety of international productions and also made several films in Hollywood. Although she was offered an exclusive contract by Universal, she only ever agreed to make films one at a time. She found herself faced with demands that she lose weight, lighten her hair, and undergo cosmetic surgery. When she rejected these, she was prescribed massages, a diet and corrective make-up. 'Their aim, that besides was very explicit, was to transform me totally into an American actress, with curls, tight dresses and breasts flattened. . . . But after having been patient with them for a while, I said No, I refused'. Like her predecessors, she regarded such attempts as contrary to her 'natural' Italian persona.[45]

CHAPTER NINE

EMANCIPATION, EROTICISM AND NOSTALGIA

Between the 1970s and the 1990s, no actress in Italy was more popular than Ornella Muti. Born in Rome to a Neapolitan father and a Russian mother, Muti offered a cross between some characteristic features of Italian beauty and a certain exotic appeal. With her blue, slightly slanted eyes, high cheek bones, light skin, long light brown hair, and adolescent physique, she had very little in common with the dark and shapely ideal of beauty that was associated with Loren and Lollobrigida. On the contrary, she owed more to the youthful stars of the early 1960s like Catherine Spaak, who had brought to Italy the sort of free-spirited seductiveness that had not, up until that point, been conveyed in Italian cinema. Muti was the sort of beauty who was often employed in photoromance magazines – that is to say, she looked both unusual and recognisable, familiar and yet individual. While she made a number of *auteur* films, particularly early and later in her career, she emerged as the ideal screen partner of many of Italy's most popular comedy actors. Observers commented on her 'natural Italian-style sensuality',[1] her 'innocent sensuality',[2] and her status as 'the beauty preferred by most Italians'.[3] She regularly featured in lists of Italy's most beautiful women. According to the journalist Maria Stella Conte, she was the 'quivering incarnation of a sex appeal with an ordinary flavour, devoid of allusions and very much in the Italian style' and a 'priestess of cinematic sensuality'.[4]

Muti's popularity occurred during a time of great changes to sexual mores, the position of women in society and the configuration of the mass media. Between the late 1960s and the late 1970s, society was traversed by collective protest and demands for change. These did not generally bring reform on the scale desired but they heralded a far-reaching transformation of customs and values. With the adoption of a divorce law in 1970, that was overwhelmingly confirmed in a referendum in 1974, the way was opened to further changes to family law, the legalisation of abortion and less official changes in the pattern of gender relations. As the economic stagnation of the 1970s gave way to a second economic miracle in the mid-1980s, permissive attitudes and practices were conditioned by a wave of consumerism in which individuality, the body and seduction were central. With her unconventional personal lifestyle and frequent playing of independent, but usually unthreatening, women, Muti was the star who was most identified with these changes.

Italy's sexual revolution was a partial and distorted affair that brought a certain tolerance and freedom to some. However, it left older generations behind and created uncertainty around gender roles. After the divorce referendum, there was an extraordinary explosion of soft pornographic magazines and films that mostly worked on the hypocrisies of the period and the opportunities provided by a weaker climate of censorship. Film-makers did not only exploit the new situation but also reflected on it. However, cinema as a medium lost its dominant role in leisure at this time. This meant that the progressive treatment of sexual themes was accompanied by a recourse to pornography as a means of warding off crisis. In fact, virtually all forms of cinematic eroticism contained strong elements of masculine nostalgia for a largely mythical pre-consumerist sexuality. The women who were cast in their films often reflected the nature of this nostalgia in their generous curves and comforting acquiescence to male desires.

Sex and society in an era of rapid modernisation

In the period following the end of the war, the domination of the Christian Democrats and the Church allowed a censorship machine to function effectively. Sexual imagery in the public sphere was very limited in the period between 1948 and 1960. Although a subdued eroticism in the form of the bodies of the *maggiorate fisiche* was permitted and encouraged by Andreotti as a counter to the political themes of neo-realism,[5] this was an exception in a climate in which repression prevailed. In so far as the body and sexuality were represented, it was in a way that was informed by certain established perceptions deriving mainly from Catholic culture. The crumbling of the compromises on which this system rested occurred as a result of urbanisation, the spread of a culture of consumerism that was infused with products marketed on the basis of desirability and displaced sexuality, the abolition of the system of publicly-licensed brothels, and the growth of liberal public opinion, and international pressures.

Women also made a particular contribution. Even conventional women's magazines such as *Grazia* and *Gioia* cautiously engaged with issues such as the pill and changes in internal relations within the family that were raised by modern society. New publications including *Amica*, created by the *Corriere della sera* in 1962 and *Arianna* (which would later evolve into the Italian edition of *Cosmopolitan*) were more open. These magazines not only held debates; they secularised personal problems, replacing the page of the father confessor with an agony aunt who addressed them in a pragmatic way. At the time of the divorce referendum, most women's magazines aligned with the campaign to preserve the law against the Catholic militants who wished to abolish it.

The journalist Milena Milani hailed these changes. 'Italy has entered the big international circuit, it has lost its provincialism. It does not matter that it is a sexy Italy and that some might be shocked to hear this definition', she argued. 'A sexy Italy means a young Italy, in the vanguard and conscious of its vitality and of its problems; an Italy with its eyes uncovered, without taboos and without falsehood'.[6] However, permissiveness also brought some distortions. The 'para-pornographic' press that developed in the 1960s, in which titles like *Men* were selling up to 600,000 copies per week, did not portray sex and eroticism as 'essential, natural, eternal components of Man . . . but as components of manias, deformations, obsessions that act as a stimuli to vanity, to adultery, to superficiality in human relations and as a filler for emptiness and boredom'.[7]

If, in the 1960s, the promoters of liberation were a small band of writers and journalists who enjoyed challenging dominant prejudices and hypocrisies, this changed early in the following decade. When Italian *Playboy* began publishing in 1972, it was able to involve cultural figures, just as the American edition had done. The first issue in November of that year contained goodwill messages from Sophia Loren, Vittorio De Sica, the footballer Gianni Rivera, the singer Mina, the composer Luciano Berio and the leaders of two political parties: Bettino Craxi of the Socialist Party and Giorgio Almirante of the neo-Fascist Italian Social Movement. Contributors during the first year included major writers such as Italo Calvino, Pier Paolo Pasolini, Alberto Moravia, Alberto Arbasino and Luigi Malerba. The magazine's 'philosophy', in line with that of its parent edition, was based on 'an open, vital, aggressive, American-style liberal attitude, in other words progressive in its perspective on the great themes of our time'.[8]

In its first issues, *Playboy* included much American material and all its centrefold models were foreign. From 1974, it ran a series of interviews with Italian actresses and performers under the title '*Playboy* has tried it on with . . .'. The articles were accompanied by veiled photographs of the subjects in which the suggestion of nudity was more present than the reality. Among the first interviewees were Elsa Martinelli and Rosanna Schiaffino. A popular television quiz assistant, Sabina Ciuffini, was also among the pioneers. Whereas at one time anyone who appeared on television had been expected to conform scrupulously to official standards of moral behaviour, on and off-screen, Ciuffini's partial nudity caused little scandal. As the quizmaster Mike Bongiorno put it, 'No one pays any attention to those attitudes that at one time gave rise to scandals on television. It is understood now that people only care about the spectacle'.[9] Soon after, the actress Eleonora Giorgi, the pop singers Loredana Berte and Patty Pravo, and the dancing Kessler sisters appeared, almost always photographed by Angelo Frontoni. Led by these examples, from mid-1975, the first Italian playmates appeared in the magazine. However, competition remained intense from *Playmen*, a magazine started in 1967 that, despite sustained legal action from *Playboy*, which halted its distribution in the English-speaking world, maintained a readership by means of a locally-based approach. It regularly featured stars from the lower rungs of the showbusiness ladder.

During the 1970s, Italian feminism staked claims to liberation, to female freedom of expression and to a different perception of the body. Its core campaign around the issue of abortion was designed to assert women's right to control their own sexuality and reproduction. Feminism emerged initially within the far left that was itself spawned by the student movement. It therefore had an aggressive, radical edge that was felt not only within society and the institutions but also within the left itself. The influence of French ideas of difference was marked among the educated women who formed the leading cadres of the movement. Their campaigns had a wider impact due to the presence of many women activists in industrial and urban protests. The Communist party was at first reluctant to adopt the feminist term 'liberation' alongside, or in place of, the historic idea of emancipation. However, it eventually accepted it, while never embracing all aspects of the feminist campaign on abortion. The leadership was not willing to imperil its strategy of compromise with the Christian Democrats by pushing for anything more than a cautious legalisation with numerous institutional controls. In this way, feminists found that their core issue was taken over by mainstream politicians and turned into a moderate law that commanded broad support. A similar cultural appropriation and distortion of their ideas on female sexuality also took place. Nina Rothenberg writes that 'as a consequence of feminist claims for liberation of the body, sex [became] a product of consumerist and hedonist culture, trapping the imagery of women in the category of the always available sexual object'.[10] This engendered a deep suspicion of the media amongst feminists. Journalism remained, in the 1970s, a heavily male profession; moreover, male domination of the media more generally meant that 'feminism was translated into a male version of women's liberation that was very often interpreted in terms of sexualisation of film, television and the press. The female body became a symbol of sexual liberation and a sellable expression of modernisation and secularisation'.[11] This became a matter of special concern as the media extended their presence in society with the liberalisation first of radio waves and then, through two historic rulings of the Constitutional Court in 1974 and 1976, of broadcast frequencies. As women's representation in the media continued to be stereotyped and increasingly objectified, critics identified what American feminists had called a 'gender ideology', that is, a 'system of stereotyped messages instilled by the mass media that legitimised the injustices of the patriarchal system'.[12]

Ornella Muti (born Francesca Revelli) began her career at precisely the moment when old values were crumbling. As a result, she reflected the opportunities that women now had, as well as the discrimination they faced. In her first film, Damiano Damiani's *La moglie più bella* (The most beautiful wife) in 1969, she took the part of Franca Viola, a Sicilian girl from Alcamo. The eighteen-year-old daughter of poor peasants and, it was said, the most beautiful in her village, the real-life Viola had been kidnapped and raped by a would-be suitor in 1965. At that time the penal code exempted from prosecution a man who, in similar circumstances, married his victim. Viola stood out against community pressure and refused the *matrimonio raparatore* (marriage of repair). Aged just fourteen, Muti played Viola opposite Michele Placido. In many of her subsequent roles, including, many years later, *La ragazza di Trieste* (Girl from Trieste) in 1983 and *Io e mia sorella* (Me and my sister), with Carlo Verdone, in 1987, she played women who rejected conventional models of behaviour.

Muti's own private life was independent and unconventional. At the age of nineteen, she became pregnant by a man whose name she never revealed. She had two further children with a businessman, Federico Fachinetti, who she only married in 1988. While engaged in this relationship, she had affairs with the popular singer and actor Adriano Celentano (her co-star in *Il bisbetico domato* (The taming of the male shrew) in 1980 and *Innamorato pazzo* (Madly in love) in 1981) and Tuscan comic Francesco Nuti (with whom she starred in *Tutta colpa del paradiso* (All the fault of paradise) and *Stregati* (Bewitched) in 1985 and 1987). She left her husband after he was revealed to have used her name in financial dealings that led to his bankruptcy.

Because of the decline of Italian cinema, few opportunities came Muti's way to star in Hollywood productions. In fact, an appearance in *Flash Gordon* in 1980 and a role in *Oscar*, opposite Sylvester Stallone, in 1991, were her only American parts. More significant were the roles she played in French and Spanish cinema. From the start of her career she maintained a European profile, although rarely appearing in the films of front-rank directors. Perhaps only her roles in *Un amour de Swann*, in which she played the courtesan Odette, and in Francesco Rosi's adaptation of Gabriel García Márquez's *Chronicle of a Death Foretold*, were major international productions. As a result, Muti's best-known films were Italian and it was this that contributed most to her national profile. Although she was never regarded as an actress of particular talent, over the years she starred in box office hits alongside the country's leading comic actors. For several years in the 1980s,

64 Ornella Muti's natural sensuality was widely praised in the 1970s and 1980s.

Carlo Verdone, Nuti and others competed to cast her as their partner in comedies destined for release over the Christmas season, sure that her presence would add the lightness of touch and a quota of feminine beauty that would make their films attractive to a broad audience.

Muti was a contemporary star with a domestic focus whose task, in her heyday, was to provide reassurance that recent changes in customs and behaviour could be absorbed in a manner that was broadly compatible with an Italian idea of homeliness, naturalness and authenticity. She was modern, but not in a way that was disruptive or disturbing. Only a few of her films were in costume or set in the past and attempts to place her in the tradition of the neo-realism of the 1940s were extremely rare.[13] In contrast to other actresses of her generation, she was never turned into a spectacle to be admired solely for her physical attributes. At a time when the naked body became, paradoxically, a symbol both of progressive politics and of the reduction of woman to sex object, her nude scenes were few and usually fleeting. Although her manner was soft and her presence quiet and pleasing, she often played headstrong girls. The key characteristic of her characters was youth and, even into her 40s, Muti was playing the part of youthful women. She kept her slim, toned physique in shape with several hours of gymnastics every day and preserved her good looks. Magazines frequently held her up as an example of success in the battle against advancing years. This fitted perfectly with the ideology of privatised hedonism that developed in the prosperous 1980s, as the political involvements of the previous decade declined following the killing of Aldo Moro in 1978. For readers of the illustrated weeklies *Gente* and *Oggi*, Muti was the embodiment of serene and ageless beauty, a woman who, as she prepared to become a grandmother at the age of 40, still possessed the radiance of youth. She was a mother, a wayward sister, a sensual woman and a model of natural beauty all rolled into one. In keeping with the fashion emphasis of the 1980s, she became a model of elegance and was often photographed in the company of Giorgio Armani.

In the 1990s, she increasingly made films with young European directors, a courageous choice that, however, ensured she became less visible to the mainstream audience. To offset this, she took the part once more of a woman who in the past had been unafraid of defying convention, starring in a RAI-TV film about champion cyclist Fausto Coppi's affair in 1953 with Giulia Occhini, a married woman who was known as the 'dama bianca' (white lady).

Fellini and the cinematic imaginary

The growing public presence of women did not undermine the powerful role played by male journalists, film directors and film and television producers in determining the nature and uses of female beauty. Leaving aside De Sica's long collaboration with Sophia Loren, which was crucial to establishing her as an iconic figure, Fellini was the director who did most to place his own idealised vision of women in the national consciousness. Only De Santis, whose *Riso amaro* had been fundamental to the reconstruction of Italian identity around female imagery in the post-war years, and Alberto Lattuada, who cast Silvana Mangano (*Anna*), Martine Carol (*La Spiaggia* – The beach) Jacqueline Sassard (*Guendalina*), Catherine Spaak (*Dolci inganni*), Rosanna Schiaffino (*La mandragola*) and Sophia Loren (*Bianco, rosso e . . .* – White, red and . . .) in a series of films centered on women, could be considered as rivals. Unlike these directors, however, Fellini's women were explicitly described as projections of the director's desires and fears, and therefore, to some extent, of all men of his generation and background.

With the release of *La Dolce Vita* in 1960, Federico Fellini became the best-known Italian film director in the world. The highly personal vision that he elaborated in his subsequent films, which increasingly set aside the neo-realist practice of the social enquiry and documentation in favour of fantasy and memory, was taken by foreigners to be more or less synonymous with Italian culture itself. The world he explored in his best-known films, from the crises of a film director (*8½*), his childhood in Rimini under Fascism (*Amarcord*), his adoptive city of Rome (*Roma*), masculinity (*Casanova*) and femininity (*La città delle donne* – City of Women), touched themes that seemed related to core issues in Italian history and identity. At the centre of Fellini's oeuvre, and perhaps his most recognisable authorial trademark, alongside the parade and a soundtrack composed by Nino Rota, was his representation of women.

Fellini's attitude was not very progressive. In 1965, he declared that: 'we have still not freed ourselves of the old Catholic and moralistic cliché about women, that oscillates between two opposed images – the Madonna, the mother and the angel on the one hand and prostitution, the devil and son on the other'.[14] This outlook he developed first and perhaps most fully while he was making *8½*, his partially autobiographical film about the existential crisis of a film director. The film reflected Fellini's discovery of Jung, an author whose works also inspired the depiction of women in the film. According to the celebrated psychologist, men projected on to women the unknown part of themselves, to the extent that woman became 'the part with which man needs to re-unite in order to find a complementary dimension, a spherical wholeness . . .'.[15]

The protagonist of *8½* is surrounded by a variety of women, a monstrous prostitute who first awakened him to sex (La Saraghina), then the lover, the wife, the muse. After Anita Ekberg in *La Dolce Vita*, La Saraghina was the first of a series of excessive, opulent female figures who would appear in the director's films. He claimed that such an obsession with immense, carnal women was the result of a repressive Catholic education, the consequence of which was a permanent adolescent pursuit of 'a huge quantity of woman, like the poor man who, when thinking of money, fantasises not about thousands of Lire but about millions or billions'.[16]

For Fellini, the mother figure was the crucial female archetype in Italian culture. 'In our country', he argued, 'there is a real idolatry of mothers; mummies, mums, great mothers of all types dominate our private and public firmaments in a fascinating iconography: virgin mother, martyr mother, Mother Rome, the she-wolf, motherland, Mother Church'.[17] The prostitute was the essential counterpart to the Italian mother. While the mother feeds and dresses the child, the prostitute initiates (or intitiated those of the director's generation) into sexual activity. She was at once the projection of male fantasies and unknowable, something immense that was responsible for both stealing desires and realising them. However, he believed that the spread of commercial eroticism and pornography was the consequence of 'an absence of mother'. 'I believe therefore that we have not had enough "good mother" and for this reason we feel the lack of it and we feel too often like small helpless children'.[18] His own universe was a reflection of this and, although many actresses aspired to work with him, they were rarely allowed to escape one of these clichés or some variant on them.

In *8½*, Fellini explored a variety of female figures. His favourite was undoubtedly the character of Carla, played by Sandra Milo, an actress who he encouraged to put on weight until she met his idea of the role (she embodied, he once said, 'the dirty-minded school-mate'),[19] but there was also a special place for an actress who had already established herself as a *bella italiana*: Claudia Cardinale. Her character represents 'Grace' or inspiration, it has been said, qualities that derived from the actress's 'pleasing and earthy aspect'.[20] The film, or at least the idea of the harem that is contained within it, grew out of an earlier film, *I vitelloni*. Fellini took his starting point for the later film from a scene in which one of the young men from *I vitelloni*, Moraldo, is in a barn belonging to his grandmother and he fantasises: 'I would like to end my life in this barn, surrounded by all women'.[21] In Fellini's films, memory, fantasy and social comment were always interwoven. Even in the most highly personal of films there was some connection to a wider world, or at least a wider national psychology.

In *Amarcord*, the film that was an evocation of his childhood in fascist Rimini, a variety of women are presented as populating the visual universe of a growing boy. These include grotesque figures, such as the prostitute Volpina and a massively busty tobacconist, but also the local object of desire, Gradisca (Magali Noël). As the director later recalled:

> Outside the Café Commercio Gradisca used to walk. Dressed in black satin that flashed in a steely, glittery way, she was one of the first to wear false eyelashes. Inside the café, everyone had his nose to the glass. Even in winter, Gradisca looked as if she had just stepped out of a band-box, with curls, the first permanent wave. . . . When Gradisca walked by all sorts of enormous appetites were called into being: hunger, thirst, a longing for milk. Her broad hips looked like railway engine wheels when they moved, they suggested such powerful movement.[22]

Gradisca is unusual in Fellini's canon because she is clearly a fashionable woman of her time, similar to Boccasile's Signorina *Grandi Firme*.[23] In other films, like *La Dolce Vita*, the fashionable woman – in that instance the bored aristocratic nymphomaniac Maddalena (Anouk Aimée) – is not presented as desirable. However, in Gradisca it is not her 'carnival glitter', her polished exterior, that prevails, but rather her strong, shapely figure. The part was that of 'a mythical opulent beauty' who, in the director's original intentions, was to be cast only following a nationwide search.[24] She was a woman who emerged with an individual profile whereas many others were reduced to a generic phys- icality. As an example of the latter, Fellini recalled waiting outside a church on Sundays for the moment when the countrywomen would emerge and mount their bicycles, another memory that was evoked in *Amarcord*: 'the sharp saddles slipped rapidly under the shiny black satin skirts, outlining, selling, expanding, with dazzling gleams and sparkles, the biggest and finest bums in the whole of Romagna. Lots of them burst out altogether, left, right and centre, and we couldn't swing round fast enough'.[25]

Nostalgia was a strong theme in the director's work. He often explored or celebrated worlds that were on the point of extinction or which already belonged to a past that remained vivid in his memory. *Luci del varietà* (*Variety Lights*) examined the universe of touring variety troupes, recalling the *avanspettacolo* on which Fellini had written as a jour- nalist on *Cinemagazzino* in the 1930s. *La Strada* dealt with a touring circus, *Il Bidone* (*Swindle*) with the confidence tricksters who briefly flourished in the post-war years, *La Dolce Vita* with the displacement of an old, familiar Rome with showbusiness, fame and decadence, *Amarcord* with his Fascist childhood. In interviews he loved to evoke the experiences of his youth and his early jobs as journalist, screenwriter and cartoonist. He revealed that his cinematic idols were not Greta Garbo, Joan Crawford nor other major stars of the 1930s, but rather Mae West and some of the minor stars of Italian cinema. It was large women, forgotten by the 1970s, who appealed to him, including Greta Gonda and Elli Parvo. Gonda, he said, 'was a sumptuous lady, not in the first flush of youth, a classic aging beauty who was impressive and severe and who had that maternal and threat- ening aspect that was typical of the female imagery that was evoked as a contrast to the castr- ation imposed by an education shaped by Catholic values, Fascism, the bourgeois family and provincial life'.[26] Gonda, he said, was a sort of Mae West, who did not have exactly the same qualities of a brothel madam or saloon bar owner, but who was nonetheless 'a bit of a circus animal-tamer'. In his view, boots and a whip would have suited her.

In his work up until the mid-1970s, Fellini's nostalgia connected with the collective culture. It gave him a way of looking at himself and the surrounding society. His working title for *Amarcord*, for example, was *Viva l'Italia*. The same would also be true later, when memory and fantasy became more important than social comment. But his films of the last fifteen years of his life tended to take on a certain conservatism. This was felt widely to be the case with *La città delle donne* (*City of Women*), a 1979 film that was in part at least an exploration of feminism, even though the director insisted that it was more a reflection on femininity. It was, he said, 'a journey through the female universe, that is constantly seen through the eyes of an Italian male who is Catholic, vaguely sexist and at one and the same time attracted, fascinated and frightened by what he encounters, like a male version of Little Red Riding Hood in the forest'.[27]

The climate, however, had changed since the 1960s and women did not occupy the same position in society. A male artist could no longer expect simply to be given free reign to comment on them in general as reflections of his own subconscious. Marcello

Mastroianni, who in *La Dolce Vita* and *8½* had played the director's alter ego, and, as Snaporaz, returned to the role in this film, noted the difference: 'In *8½* there was the harem but in the end there was this sort of general "let's all love each other". This time the journey through the female universe is much more marked by crisis, there is no possible harmony, and so a sense of nostalgia is born, along with regret for how uncomplicated things used to be at one time'.[28] The film took seven months to shoot and during that period there were several attacks on the director by feminists. Indeed, among the two hundred women who took part in the scene of the feminist congress that takes place at the Grand Hotel Miramare, there were numerous feminists who sought to challenge the director or involve him in a continuous debate. However, they found themselves sharply criticised in the feminist press for collaborating with him.[29]

The female ideal in the film is played by Donatella Damiani, a dark-haired young actress of extremely ample charms. As the women collectively seek to rationalise the situation of their sex, she 'encapsulates all the dark, obscure, combustive, fervent, burning passion of the feminine,' as Fellini put it. She is the projection of Snaporaz's desires and dreams and he encounters her everywhere. For the director:

> Donatella, who he encounters all the time in the film because she is the feminine in all its forms, a sort of fake Arianna who is also a real Arianna who tries to lead him to safety but in the end ties him up in her string and fires a machine gun at the hot-air balloon in which he is supposed to escape. She is a femininist, a terrorist, one of Katzone's guests, a showgirl, a hot-air balloon, a mamma, a helper, a killer . . . .[30]

She was the ideal Fellinian woman: soft and abundant, sensual and innocent, profoundly erotic but reassuring and maternal. But by the end of this film, the director clearly felt that no such comforting image existed in reality and that his fantasies had been destroyed. In fact, Fellini's influence would persist. Until he died in 1993, he continued to be considered the spokesman of a certain type of male point of view on women and he was called on to comment on every single female object of desire who entered the public imagination.[31]

Laura Antonelli and eroticism Italian-style

Fellini's influence also made itself felt, although probably not in a way he would have acknowledged or recognised, in the soft-pornographic films that flourished in the 1960s and 1970s. The trend towards sexual explicitness in cinema occurred as a result of changes in society and the desire of directors to push back the barriers of the permissible. However, there was also a strong drive towards the commercial exploitation of nudity. Producers were quick to follow in the steps of art-house directors including Fellini, Pasolini and Bertolucci by offering male audiences the spectacle of female nudity.[32] The trend was accelerated by the decline of cinema itself. As the collective movements of the 1970s declined and commercial television developed on a massive scale, cinema lost its place at the core of Italian leisure and became, as it had been before the 1950s, an entertainment that was predominantly urban.

The erotic comedies that prospered at this time were set in institutions that were familiar to all, such as the school, the hospital, the hotel or the military barracks. They owed a debt to Fellini that was not wholly indirect. One of the most popular protagonists, Alvaro Vitali ('Pierino'), had appeared in several of the director's films, including *Satyricon, Roma, Clowns* and *Amarcord*. 'Everything I know was taught me by Fellini: the timing, the walk, the staring, the bodily movements', he declared.[33] Fellini's ideal woman, Damiani, whose shapely figure and dark hair gave her a special appeal to domestic audiences, also made a handful of these films. The low-budget comedies were extremely popular with provincial audiences for their pairing of old comedians with attractive starlets, who would often be seen naked through a key hole. For their source material and male performers, they drew on variety theatre and the popular films of the past. Fleeting female nudity, voyeurism and male frustration were typical themes of this cinema. Older men, military conscripts, schoolboys and students watched them and bought cheap weeklies that were filled with still photographs of the stars. Many of these were foreign: Barbara Bouchet, Edwige Fenech and Corinne Cléry were all French, while Sylva Koscina was Slovenian and Janet Agren Swedish. Trim and middle class, they mostly recalled the blonde tourists that filled seaside resorts in the summer.

One or two Italians, notably the star of the cheeky schoolgirl series, Gloria Guida, were also fair-haired and Nordic in appearance. But others had a more familiar, curvaceous earthiness that was not at all exotic. These included Laura Antonelli, Lilli Carati, Michela Miti and Carmen Russo, who had a small role in *La città delle donne* and who was the last star of a genre that continued until the mid-1980s. The only one of these women who succeeded in combining a strong connection with erotic cinema while also developing a career in mainstream comedies and in *auteur* films was Laura Antonelli. Her success came not because she was more talented than her colleagues, but because her physical qualities were familiar and because she was the first Italian to work the genre. An Istrian who had moved at a young age to Rome, Antonelli had dark hair, a soft, shapely figure and a slightly melancholic face which differentiated her from the current of actresses who had emerged in the post-war years.

The film that defined her, *Malizia* (*Malice*), was made by a young director named Salvatore Samperi in 1973. Set in a middle-class Sicilian household in the 1950s, it starred Antonelli as a domestic servant to the family of a recently widowed proprietor of a draper's store and his three sons. The film was different from the type of eroticism that had permeated Italian cinema since the 1960s, and to which the actress had contributed. It had some of the flavour of an *auteur* work and was photographed with artistry by the cinematographer Vittorio Storaro, who had worked with Bertolucci and who would go on to collaborate with Francis Ford Coppola and Warren Beatty. The film, moreover, was a sort of cinematic *bildungsroman*. Antonelli's character is a sweet-natured and dutiful

65 Laura Antonelli and her
suspenders in *Malizia*.

family help whose melancholic sensuality arouses the interest of the fifty-year-old
widower and becomes the focus of the burgeoning desires of his adolescent son, Nino. In
the course of the film, she undergoes the erotic torments of Nino, before she finally
marries his father.

The film was a huge hit in Italy and abroad and Antonelli won a David of Donatello
award for her performance. What struck many commentators was the use of a setting
that evoked a period that was still vividly present in the minds of older spectators. This
permitted the exploration of erotic atmospheres that belonged to an earlier era. Four key
elements of these were the unspoilt natural sensuality of a country girl who had found
work in the city; the tempting presence of a young female servant (a phenomenon that
was on the point of disappearance in the 1970s); the fact that the girl concedes only a
little while protesting and modestly asserting her innocence; and the depiction, even in
the image chosen for the illustrated poster used to advertise the film, of stockings and
suspenders under the skirts of the protagonist. With 'her soft body and 1950s-style
beauty', Antonelli fitted perfectly in this bygone world.[34]

The actress's body was in fact hinted at and alluded to more than it was shown. In
comparison to the expansion of explicit nudity in magazines and films, *Malizia* was
understated. Nevertheless, Oreste Del Buono hailed Antonelli as 'this highly unusual
figure in Italian cinema, this irresistible incarnation of eroticism'.[35] The Italian edition of

Playboy declared that, 'for years Italian cinema was looking for a type like Laura', that is to say, an actress with an erotic appeal that was neither imported and boyish, nor lost in the mass exposure of flesh of certain art films, nor compromised by the vulgarity of low-budget comedies. The rapid liberalisation of mores and of legal restrictions over what could be shown produced as a reaction 'not only a generic return to the fashions of the 1950s', but a desire to recreate 'the pre-tights era, when a glance that succeeded in finding its way up a skirt was not lost in a rather unpromising shady area but could rest itself firmly on a pair of suspenders and fantasise about the mystery that would be unveiled by proceeding further'.[36]

Antonelli was in many respects an erotic spectacle, an object of pleasure for male spectators as for her male partners on screen. In her subsequent films, she played a series of roles that made ample recourse to her classical physical appeal and original combination of innocence, melancholy and seduction. She appeared in middle-of-the-road comedies directed by Dino Risi (*Sessomatto* – Sex mad) and Luigi Comencini (*Mio Dio come sono caduta in basso* – my God! how low I have sunk) as well as several French films, before taking the place of the pregnant Romy Schneider in Visconti's adaptation of D'Annunzio's *L'innocente* (The innocent) and starring in Giuseppe Patroni Griffi's 1920s drama *Divina creatura* (Divine creature) whose very title seemed tailor-made for her. As an erotic star, she belonged unequivocally to the 1970s. She was almost a textbook case of the way the female subject in cinema was a product of the male gaze, an actress who, it has been argued, was 'the image of submissiveness, never objecting to her role as an object of pleasure: she let herself be touched, fondled, looked at and used in any way'.[37] However, even though she may have been 'perfect for the parts of maids, waitresses, housekeepers', in fact her characters were rarely wholly passive. Even in *Malizia*, where Antonelli's servant is subjected to the whims of her employer's son, in the end it is she who finally takes the game in hand and seduces her tormentor. This gave her a certain following among women, who appreciated in her an adventurous erotic spirit that seemed contemporary.

Yet the majority of her films, and certainly the most successful ones, were set in the past. They were infused with the sepia tones of nostalgia. It was this relationship with the past that enabled Antonelli to become, for several years, one of the most popular Italian actresses, twenty years after the emergence of the stars of the1950s. Several male directors believed nostalgia could be a source for atmospheres and cultures that could be counterposed to the dominant ethos of consumerism. However, it was also a terrain on which politics could be displaced and the sexual revolution subjected to commercial exploitation. Nostalgia offered a way of avoiding the problems of the present, of providing a channel for aesthetic pleasure through the recognition of characters, physiques and locations that belonged to a timeless Italy. In this way changes in mores were not embraced but bypassed and sex was turned into 'a product of consumerist and hedonist culture, trapping the imagery of women in the category of the available sexual object'.[38]

The contradiction between culture and commerce was played out through the bodies of actresses, which could be displayed more than ever before precisely because of the breaks in an old framework of customs and values. Antonelli was caught in these contradictions as a figure who carried a certain emancipatory thrust while embodying a yearning for a past that offered an escape from changes that were difficult, challenging or unpalatable. These consisted equally of commodified, artificial or liberated femininity. Pasolini was the first to denounce the new consumer civilisation and to seek to delineate a new cleavage between those who were internal to it and those who could in some way be considered oppositional. The homogenisation of the Italians in line with the values of consumerism was something that, in his view, occurred through mass hedonism. 'Peasant and pre-industrial Italy has collapsed, it has dissolved, it has gone, and in its place there is an emptiness that will probably be filled by complete bourgeoisification', he argued.[39] More than Fascism, this changed the character of the Italians and rendered them subject to consumerist ideology. Yet Pasolini was by no means immune from contradictions. An *apocalattico integrato* (a critic who was also part of the cultural establishment),[40] he was even *Playboy*'s resident film critic for the first few months of 1974.

Because Antonelli was cast in leading roles by several art house directors, her screen persona could be interpreted in different ways. But there is no doubt that many of the other erotic stars were entirely functional to the hegemony of permissive capitalist values that fell into place after 1974. This was exemplified by Carmen Russo, who became one

66 Glamour model Carmen Russo adopts a pin-up pose reminiscent of Boccasile's Signorina *Grandi Firme*.

of the leading pin-ups in Italy in the late 1970s and 1980s. There was a nostalgic dimension to her persona. A photographic model and sometime actress who featured regularly in soft pornographic magazines, she once reprised some of the poses of Boccasile's Signorina *Grandi Firme* for *Playmen*. However, she developed her career as a fantasy object with determination and methodical calculation. In contrast to the gauche nudity of some models, she exploited her firm and pneumatic physique in a highly contemporary way. Following roles in several minor erotic comedies, she moved into television. After regular slots on the programmes of Silvio Berlusconi's Fininvest channels, including *Risatissima* and *Grand Hôtel*, in which she appeared in the briefest of costumes, she was taken up in 1990 by RAI-1's ultra-respectable Sunday afternoon container show *Domenica In*. It was announced that, instead of highlighting her curves, 'she will present herself to the respectable micro-bourgeois audiences of a Sunday afternoon in honest little tailored suits typical of any married lady'.[41] In the illustrated magazines the new 'family-issue Supercarmen' was portrayed with her companion and dance partner Enzo Paolo Turci at home in domestic settings.[42] On the RAI show, she danced, joked to a script and acted the part of the dumb brunette. For the veteran journalist Maria Venturi, the model of femininity she presented was nothing short of reactionary. She was 'a woman who has overturned all the points that were assumed to have been won after the barricades of the feminist movement'. She was a sort of 'counter-guerilla' who, instead of working for social progress, worked against it.[43]

Tinto Brass and the allure of nostalgia

The sexual preoccupation of Italian cinema in the period of its historic decline was nowhere more evident than in the work of the director Tinto Brass. After a respectable but not very remunerative career as an experimental director, the Venetian Brass discovered the appeal of sex at the box office and became the champion of the art house sex film. Two films, *Salon Kitty*, a blatantly exploitative drama mixing Nazism and sex, but without the intellectual sophistication of Liliana Cavani's *The Night Porter*; and the notorious *Caligula*, a shambolic spectacle of perversion and excess produced by *Penthouse* magazine's Bob Guccione, conferred on the director a scandalous aura. From 1983, he made a series of overtly erotic films, many of which were based on literary texts and most of which were enormously successful. These included *La chiave* (The Key), *Miranda, Capriccio, Paprika, Cosi fan tutte* and *Senso 45*. Dismissed as pornography by most critics, they were popular with the public and served to project a series of actresses into the public mind as figures evocative of the ideas and aesthetic preferences of Brass. Due to her collaboration with him, Stefania Sandrelli relaunched her career, while Serena Grandi, Francesca Dellera, Debora Caprioglio, Claudia Koll and Anna Galiena became icons of a certain type of Italian-style female beauty that was drenched in nostalgia but which was also highly sexualised in keeping with the explicit nature of the cinema of the period. 'The movie industry was creating a new type of woman. After the sunny but chaste eroticism of the well-endowed *maggiorata* of the 1950s, counterparts of the Italian economic boom, the new goddesses of eroticism were perverse and malicious exhibitionists. References to sex were obsessive,' wrote the critic Stefano Masi.[44] But this was to suggest that somehow it was the actresses who were responsible for the sexualisation of cinema. In fact it was male directors and the film industry's fear of decline that led to this insistent focus.

Unlike many directors, who preferred to let their works speak for themselves, Brass was concerned to provide an ideological justification for his films. He adopted the attitude of a champion of sexual freedom, although some critics saw him more as a 'very calculating encourager of a certain strain of national voyeurism'.[45] In fact, Brass was ideally suited to the 'return to the private' that was a hallmark of the period. A former anarchist and rebel, he abandoned his political concerns for a focus on personal issues. He declared that working on the theme of sex within marriage in *La chiave* led him to a reflection:

immersing myself in that story and reflecting deeply on it, I came to the conclusion that some of my revolutionary political instincts derived from the need to revolutionise my private life. Now I am inclined to think that the only revolution that will not end up in a stupid bloodbath or in a dictatorship of narrow-minded bureaucrats will be the revolution that is made by those who have first succeeded in revolutionising themselves. Only those who have learned how to live in harmony and on the basis of mutual respect without prudish constraints will be able to attempt to build the utopia of a world freed from the exploitation of man by man.[46]

A striking feature of Brass's films, which undoubtedly became one of the cultural phenomena of the hedonistic 1980s, was that all of them were set in the past and mostly in the period between the 1930s and the 1950s. These settings favoured florid beauty rather than the adolescent bodies that were associated with the cinema of Lattuada. Dismissed as 'cinema glamour' by Brass, Lattuada's films reflected his personal preference for 'the slight, quite androgynous girl' rather than 'great Rubensian masses of flesh'.[47] Brass claimed personally to prefer mature women, like the 40-year-old Stefania Sandrelli, who he cast opposite Frank Finlay in *La chiave*. But in fact, several of his stars were beautiful young actresses with soft curvaceous bodies who hailed from a variety of regions and cities including the Veneto, Friuli, Emilia-Romagna and Rome. They were all associated in the films with Brass's idiosyncratic conviction that peasant women in the decades before the economic miracle were sexually free and unconditioned by morality and inhibition.

Miranda, released in 1985, was based loosely on Carlo Goldoni's *La Locandiera*. The flirtatious games of the Venetian playwright's character Mirandolina with her four suitors were transferred by Brass into a rural 1950s setting in Emilia-Romagna. Mirandolina became a voluptuous inn-keeper whose multiple copulations with four lovers constituted the core of the film. According to the director, the film was a hymn to the 'joyous sexuality that is unaware of the sex of sin, remorse and repentance'.[48] The explanation offered for the choice of period was that he preferred the post-war decade to the present, 'so as to ensure that the universal theme of the film would not be contaminated and muddled by the unavoidable conditionings of present pressures, such as feminism, terrorism and neo-hedonism . . .' The universal theme was that of the 'new woman': 'An enterprising, courageous woman who wants to enjoy everything, take the best, choose instead of being chosen, give herself rather than waiting to be conquered, use her charms as a weapon of seduction and power, mixing silk stockings and peasant innocence, basques and emancipation'. 'I like the 1950s', Brass continued; 'I think that at that time everything was lived in a calmer way. We were less "contaminated" by culture and more willing to live in a joyous way the most varied experiences.'[49]

The actress chosen to bring to life Brass's character was Serena Grandi, a twenty-six-year-old Bolognese woman whose strikingly opulent body and enormous breasts corresponded to his idea of fertile sexuality. 'I like to see women in all their attributes: bum, tits and vagina; smells, moods and flavours', he asserted. 'What do you want from me? Am I a pornographer? Pornography is a reproduction of sex, whereas I express it. I am the first artist of the thaw, the one who broke the sexual ice age of Italian cinema.'[50] Grandi lived up to her image. 'Personally, I am like that, from the Romagna region, carnal and passionate', she said.[51] She went on to make a series of literary-inspired erotic films, including *La signora di notte* (Lady of the night) by Piero Schivazappa as well as *Desiderando Giulia* (Desiring Giulia), based on Svevo's *Senilità* (Senility) as well as several sexy comedies, that consolidated her reputation as one of Italy's favourite pin-ups. According to the respected journalist Natalia Aspesi, she became 'the symbol of a dirty, excessive femininity that has its legs permanently spread'.[52]

The persona that Grandi embodied was that of the *maggiorata*, that is to say, she was seen to evoke the golden years of Pampanini, Lollobrigida and Loren. She was aware that she had 'the physique of a 1950s-style shapely beauty' and that this recalled the film stars of the past.[53] As an adolescent, she said, 'I kept by my bed pictures of La Lollo, Loren and Mangano, and I was very pleased to be a bit like them, something that is rare today in a world of skinny and androgynous women'.[54] Grandi claimed that her character in *Miranda* was nothing like those of Fellini: 'My Miranda is a strong, characterful woman. Fellini's actresses, like Milo and Noël are big dolls without any personality. . . . I would be very fearful of making a film with Fellini; he has a vision of women that I do not like'.[55] The veteran Bolognese critic Renzo Renzi, however, noted her character's resemblance to the outsize tobacconist in *Amarcord* and decreed that both were stereotypical versions of the women of Bologna of the type that had long been in circulation among men from outside the city.[56]

At a time when the fashion model was emerging as the dominant bearer of female beauty, and the gym was becoming the new temple, the explosion within Italian cinema of fleshy female forms was a marked contrast. 'What an abundance of breasts, hips and

67 Serena Grandi was the most memorable of Tinto Brass's fantasy female figures.

buttocks in Italian cinema! What enormous tits and long, large legs marked by cellulite, as if gymnasia and break-dancing, aerobics and Jane Fonda were nothing more than exhibits from the nineteenth century!', asserted Francesco Massa in *L'Espresso*.[57] Cellulite, suspender belts and reinforced brassières recalled the 1950s, Andreotti and sinfulness, he continued. This re-emergence was linked to national identity, because it was permeated by a 'homely feel and national pride'. At a time of foreign hegemony, 'you go back to the basic elements that in the historical memory of both Italian customs and cinema have always remained fresh, that is to bottoms and breasts'.[58] Not by chance, the Italian qualities of these films were underlined by the presence of spaghetti, bread, cheese, pizza, and macaroni, foodstuffs that had nothing to do with the contemporary ideal of the lean, toned physique. From this point of view, Grandi was a 'spaghetti Venus' who was similar to the stars of the past but who had the attitudes and outlook of a woman of her own generation.

After the *succès de scandale* of *Miranda*, Brass made *Snack Bar Budapest*, a commercial thriller that flopped at the box office. In the aftermath of this, he returned to more familiar territory in 1987 with *Capriccio*, adapted from Mario Soldati's 1953 novel *Lettere da Capri* (letters from Capri). This time the theme concerned the relations between four characters, as an American married couple on vacation meet up again with their former lovers in order to relive the memories of earlier erotic experiences. His star, Francesca Dellera, who played Rosalba, a prostitute who has had a liaison with the husband, was in Brass's view, 'a very young, sensual little animal devoid of any cultured superstructure . . . a pagan thing'.[59] If Grandi seemed like a soft-pornographic re-edition of Loren, then Dellera brought to mind another star of that era. 'She reminds me a great deal of Gina Lollobrigida at her most magnificent' the director declared.

Brass returned to his favourite decade four years later, with *Paprika*, a homage to the world of state-licensed brothels, that was released in 1991. The film was notorious for the nostalgia with which it looked on an institution whose abolition in 1958 was the result of a long, hard campaign by the Socialist senator Lina Merlin. The film's publicity was explicit: 'Tinto Brass reopens the state-run brothels' exclaimed the poster above a picture of the star, Debora Caprioglio. The film brought the director on to the wavelength of Fellini, who wistfully recreated the world of the brothels in *Roma*. Brass's co-author on the film's script was Bernardino Zapponi, who co-wrote *Roma*, *Casanova* and *La città delle donne*. However, Brass differentiated himself from a director with whom some associated him. 'Yes, we both like women a lot, but unlike him I have never sought mother-figures at the brothel', he asserted.[60] Brass recalled the delights of the brothels of his youth and in interviews praised the prostitutes as practitioners of 'a skilled and socially useful trade': 'Those women without any contract, whose lives were regulated by the periods of two weeks they spent in each brothel, were women who were naturally inclined to pleasure and to an idea of sexual pleasure that I have never ceased to practice'.[61]

In the film the 22-year-old Caprioglio plays Nina, a young country girl who is persuaded by her boyfriend to work in a brothel so that they can save enough money for him to start his own business. 'Paprika' is the name given to her by the madam of the establishment. However, she enjoys the work and begins the series of two-week sojourns in the brothels of different cities that was the life of the prostitutes who worked in state-licensed brothels. After experiencing every type of sex, she meets an elderly count who marries her shortly before dying and leaving her his fortune. On the last day of the brothels before their abolition, she temporarily abandons her now respectable and comfortable existence to return to her first brothel to offer her services free of charge.

Caprioglio, whose 'youthful little voice and cute adolescent face probably caught the director's attention on account of the way they contrasted with her shapely figure', according to the journalist Michele Anselmi, was no novice.[62] She had appeared with the *monstre sacré* Klaus Kinski in *Pagannini* and, despite a 40-year age gap, had become his lover. The youngest of the sex symbols launched by Brass, she was also, with Grandi, the one whose appeal rested most exclusively on an unusually curvaceous physique. With her endowments and angelic face, she, too, recalled a star of the 1950s: the actress Marisa Allasio, who had appeared in the comedies *Poveri ma belli* (Poor but beautiful), *Povere ma belle* (Poor but beautiful girls), *Marisa la civetta* (Marisa the flirt) and *Le diciottenni* (The eighteen-year olds) Caprioglio appeared destined to work only in erotic cinema until Francesca Archibugi cast her as Ghisola in her version of Federico Tozzi's *Con gli occhi chiusi* (With closed eyes). Her work in this nineteenth-century set film won critical and popular acclaim. In the wake of this, she began a career as a presenter and actress on television that offered proof of her considerable personal charm.

The two women that Brass would cast in his two subsequent Italian period films were less exclusively carnal in their appeals. In *Così fan tutte*, Claudia Koll played the part of Diana, a sexually voracious wife whose infidelities are encouraged by her at first furious and then complicit husband, Paolo. He only becomes jealous beyond tolerance when she becomes sexually involved with a poet who takes a passionate interest in female bottoms. Rejected by Paolo, Diana engages in wild sexual excesses with her sister and some friends. A dark-haired, white-skinned woman of Hungarian-Italian background, Koll was curvaceous and cerebral. Alone among Brass's actresses, she appeared to regret that she had found it necessary to indulge in the explicit eroticism of his cinema in order to win recognition and secure parts in more mainstream theatre and television productions.[63] Nevertheless, it is doubtful if, without the launch that his film provided, she would have become a recognised Italian beauty whose gentle features and courteous smile would win her lead roles in several series of the RAI-TV production *Linda e il brigadiere* (Linda and the brigadier).

Like Sandrelli, Anna Galiena was an actress who had made several important films before being cast by Brass in 2002. Born in 1954, she had made her debut in 1981 and had starred opposite Jean Rochefort in Patrice Leconte's *Le mari de la coiffeuse* and with Sandrelli and Penelope Cruz in Bigas Luna's *Jamon Jamon*. In *Senso 45* Galiena plays Livia Mazzoni, the mature, alluring wife of a senior government official who has been conducting a secret affair with a god-like young officer of the Wehrmacht. She endeavours to reach him in Venice but, once in the lagoon city, she finds herself drawn into a vortex in which the desperate climate of the closing phase of the war weighs on individual destinies. The film was an explicit return to the period and environments of both *Salon Kitty* and *La chiave*. It served to renew interest in the sensual charms of Galiena, that few would have suspected as being so powerful in an actress of her age. Her acting brought class to the film and served to revive her European film career.

Brass's heroines were strong and in his films they were usually the leaders in the erotic situations in which they were placed. But the whole surrounding fantasy and the guiding hand in the representation was Brass's own. That the films were less than progressive was concealed by their period setting. For all the brothels, suspender belts and underarm hair, Brass's films were as polished as the soft pornographic magazines in which stills from his films usually appeared before their release. The artistic illusion derived in part from this excellent confection.[64] The only person to contest the focus on the 1950s was Giuliana Gamba, the one woman who joined the camp of erotic cinema directors. Brass, Samperi and others were fixated with the 1950s, she argued. 'It is like hiding behind a windscreen. Why do they not show us what a man and a woman of today really think and do?'[65]

Nevertheless, some observers felt that the erotic cinema of the 1980s was an authentic product of Italian culture. The sociologist Francesco Alberoni, whose own book *Erotismo* (*Eroticism*) was a bestseller of the period,[66] argued that a genre had been discovered by the Italians, 'a theme that is more consistent with their culture, with the reality of their society, with their problems and sentiments than puritan American-style comedies'.[67] The image of Italy as sexy and sinful that erotic cinema cultivated was not casual, he argued, rather it derived from a pagan undercurrent in national culture. It was 'the manifestation of a fundamental cultural tendency that belongs specifically to us'. What he failed to add was that it was a consequence of a male ideology that contributed to the maintenance of the established gender order in society.

Cicciolina and Moana

Cinematic eroticism flourished in a context in which film-going was in steep decline as a leisure activity. Pornography proved to be the sole product capable of attracting sufficient customers to ward off closure for many film theatres. By offering a high erotic content, film-makers like Brass could draw a part of the audience of hard-core pornography back into mainstream circuits. However, far from damaging the pornography industry, this strategy accorded it a measure of legitimacy. Highly sexualised imagery became commonplace on posters, at news kiosks and even in newspapers and on television. From the late 1970s until the early 1990s, pornography flourished on a remarkable scale. It grew into a major industry supplying films for theatre release, videocassettes, magazines and live shows. In 1988, half of all cinemas in Lombardy and 25 out of 90 cinemas in Rome showed only hard-core films.[68]

At times of rapid change, modern Italy had always been susceptible to cultural inputs from outside. In the 1970s, hard-core pornography was a phenomenon that was mainly associated with the United States (*Deep Throat* and *The Devil In Miss Jones* were both released in 1973). It arrived in Italy first in a clandestine form (repeating the pattern of *Playboy* and men's magazines) and then developed as a local industry in a context in which censorship was losing force and laws against obscenity were no longer being applied with consistency or rigour. It benefited from a climate in which liberals and the left were absorbing the ideas of lifestyle change that had emerged from the student and alternative movements and in which feminists were disinclined to take over the mantle of censors. For their part, Catholics and conservatives preferred to ignore it rather than try to suppress it. Pornography was not subject to the censorship that resulted, for example, in the total ban on Bertolucci's *Ultimo tango a Parigi* (*Last Tango in Paris*) because it was regarded as a sectoral sub-product of no cultural value or influence. While this may have been true for a brief period, developments would show that pornography could escape the ghetto to which many assumed it would remain confined.

Within this industry, one impresario, Riccardo Schicchi of Diva Futura, occupied a strategic place and two of his protégées became household names: Illona Staller, a blonde woman of Hungarian origin better known as Cicciolina, and the Catholic-educated Moana Pozzi, whose soft, curvaceous figure and wavy blonde hair gave her the appearance of a Marilyn Monroe lookalike. Neither Cicciolina nor Moana (who was widely known by her first name only) bore any resemblance to the Italian ideal of beauty in appearance, attitude or behaviour. As a foreigner, Staller cultivated an image that was iconoclastic in every respect with regard to Italian customs. Both became household names and Moana eventually came to be considered something of a traditional consolatory figure, who in men's fantasies combined elements of various feminine roles. She was at once a mother, lover, wife and sister, although never a daughter.

Staller achieved huge worldwide attention when she was elected to the Italian Parliament on a Radical ticket in 1987. Campaign pictures of the marble-skinned and bright red-mouthed Cicciolina, her long straight blonde hair flowing in the wind, her arms raised high and her low-cut dress pulled down to expose her small breasts, were printed in newspapers across the world.[69] Contrary to all expectations, she secured 19,886 preference votes and won a seat representing Rome. Never before, in any part of the world, had a porn star been elected to Parliament. To foreigners, her election seemed to say something about the status of women in Italy, although they were unsure if this was a message of emancipation or a sign that Italy's sexual revolution had led to a commodification of all the primal and predatory male instincts that female tourists were obliged to contend with when they visited the peninsula. The day Staller arrived at the Montecitorio Palace to take her seat, she was demurely adorned in the colours of the Italian flag: her long sea-green dress featured ruffled touches of green, red and white.

Cicciolina's adoption of the tricolour, although ostensibly modest, was merely the latest in a long line of stunts designed to provoke controversy. From the moment she arrived in Italy in 1973, she had attracted attention with her uninhibited promotion of sexual freedom and nudity. Guided by her agent, Schicchi, she first hosted a radio show entitled *Voulez-vous coucher avec moi?* on the station Radio Luna, on which she talked of sex and took live phone calls from listeners. With her unusual accent and mock-infantile voice, she enticed her audience into a world that was at once transgressive and playful. During this show, the nick-name Cicciolina was born. At first, she used the term to refer to her clitoris, however it was soon extended to her whole person and then to everyone else too, so that listeners were addressed as *cicciolini*. A photographer by background, Schicchi next published explicit nude photographs of Staller and organised live appearances for her in discotheques. Her notoriety suddenly increased in 1978 when she exposed her breasts live on national television. Her film career began with supporting roles in soft-core pornographic films such as *La supplente* (The supply teacher), and *La liceale* (High school girl), the latter starring Gloria Guida. After appearances in a number of erotic art films, including Miklos Jancso's *Vizi privati, pubbliche virtù* (Private vices, public virtues) and *Cuore di cane* (Dog heart), an Alberto Lattuada film based on a Bulgakov novel, failed to lead to

68 The Hungarian porn star Ilona Staller (Cicciolina) provocatively employs the Italian tricolour.

more promising roles, she specialised in sex films. Her first showcase was *Cicciolina amore mio* (Cicciolina my love) in 1979, which was co-written by Schicchi. There then followed a long series of hard-core productions in which she almost always played the by now well-known character of Cicciolina.

Staller was a shrewd businesswoman who co-founded Diva Futura with Schicchi and played a part in discovering and launching new hard-core talent. She carefully managed her personality as a figure of erotic fantasy and even directed one film. Her live shows, in which she masturbated, performed a penetrative act with a live python and urinated on her audiences, were frequently raided by the police and closed down on grounds of obscenity. However, she acted the part of an innocent, a latter-day hippy with nothing but peace and pleasure on her mind. Although she was born in 1951, and therefore was already aged 29 in 1980, she adopted some of the mannerisms of an adolescent or even a child. She was often photographed in white, sucking her thumb and holding a fluffy toy.

As Cicciolina, Staller took delight in baiting establishment figures and buttoned-up politicians, who she amused the public by referring to as *cicciolini*. She campaigned against nuclear power and censorship. However, she did not side with the left or with the women's movement. Indeed, she explicitly counterposed to the feminists' slogan *Io sono mia* (I am mine) a slogan of her own that was aimed exclusively at her fans: *Io sarò vostra* (I will be yours).[70] Every star of stage and screen offers his or her audience a similar unfulfillable promise, but in this case her adoption of the role of sex object was programmatic and polemical. She was not a symbol of her sex, but of sex as a voyeuristic commodity. Every inch of her anatomy was literally available to all as a spectacle. When she was once asked in an interview if she had ever been in love with one person, she replied, 'No. No . . . no. I am still looking for that person. But I am always looking for them among my audience'.[71] However, there were contradictions within her persona. Staller was articulate, albeit in a sloganistic way, and sought to mobilise her audience as a collectivity. Her first flirtation with politics came in 1979 when she stood as a candidate for the Lista del Sole. In 1985, she adhered to the Radical Party, a force of the liberal left that had won a following by campaigning on civil rights issues such as divorce, abortion and the legalisation of drugs. After joining campaigns against nuclear energy and for civil rights, she was selected, largely for publicity reasons, to stand for Parliament.[72] Her election, with a quantity of preferences that placed her second only to the party founder and leader Marco Pannella, caused a sensation. It was interpreted as an anti-politics vote on the part of disaffected men who had no interest in the Radicals' agenda. As a member of Parliament, she tried to continue with her shows and films but found that her fame worked against her. Public protests, bans on the part of local authorities, police raids, cancellations by nervous impresarios and falling interest brought her hard-core career to a close in Italy, if not abroad.[73]

Although Staller would quickly lose interest in Parliament and served for only one legislature as a deputy, she did not abandon the political scene. In 1992, she founded the *Partito dell'amore* (Love party) together with other performers from the Diva Futura stable. At a time of great political change and uncertainty, she manipulated a certain disaffection from politics and indeed contributed to the banalisation of what had been, for much of the history of the republic, a sphere dominated by middle-aged and elderly male professionals. The Love Party never succeeded in electing any of its candidates, but it received a vast amount of publicity and won a public platform for the woman who, following the fall in Cicciolina's box-office appeal, had emerged as Italy's leading porn star. Moana Pozzi shared with her colleague a passion for her calling and frequently defended her right to practise it. She appeared with Cicciolina in several films including, most famously, *Cicciolina e Moana ai mondiali* (Cicciolina and Moana at the World Cup) in 1990. In this hard-core feature, the two performers help the Italian team win the cup final by inducing their opponents to have sex with them in the changing room at half-time and thereby tiring them out. The male performers were disguised as leading footballers of the day, including Maradona and Falcao.

In contrast to Cicciolina, Moana Pozzi was neither provocatively controversial nor an effective campaigner. Her involvement with the Love Party was short-lived and unconvincing.[74] Born in Genoa, she was brought up strictly by her Catholic parents in several countries, since her father's work as an engineer often involved long periods abroad. By some accounts, her uninhibited ways had already brought her into conflict with her family before she moved to Rome in 1980. While she worked in commercials and took small parts in comedy movies, she became the lover of many famous actors and entertainers as well as politicians, including the leader of the Socialist Party, Bettino Craxi, who would become prime minister in 1983. Due to his influence, she was given a job presenting a children's television programme on state television. The same year, 1981, she took an uncredited part in her first hard-core movie, *Valentina, ragazza in calore* (Valentina, girl on heat). It was not long before someone noticed the television presenter on the screen. In the ensuing scandal, she denied she had appeared in the film but was anyway suspended from working on television.

The press coverage brought her notoriety and led to further small roles, including one in Fellini's satire on the world of commercial television, *Ginger e Fred*. In 1986, she joined Schicchi's Diva Futura agency and embarked on a career in hard-core in which her fame was a key lure. As with Cicciolina, viewers of films such as *Fantastica Moana* (Fantastic Moana), *Tutte le provocazoni di Moana* (All Moana's provocations) and *Moana l'insaziabile* (Moana, the insatiable) were sold a double guarantee of authenticity: not only were the sex acts real but the personality on screen was one they had already learned much about from newspapers and magazines. In fact, with Pozzi, the guarantee became threefold since she adopted no fantasy persona and appeared always as herself. It was this lack of the customary artifice and distancing typical of the sex industry that rendered her intriguing, especially to educated men. While the military conscripts, students and white collar workers who were the habitual consumers of pornography found in her the beautiful, pliable, always available submissive woman of their dreams,[75] intellectuals and journalists were fascinated by a woman who defied every cliché and was sexy, open-minded, worldly and sophisticated.

Over a short but intense career, Pozzi established herself as a national personality, who was a regular television performer and talk-show guest, the author of books, and a friend and lover of the famous and the powerful. Unlike the sleazy or banal personalities who are typically associated with the world of hard-core, she was charming and polite, well-read and forever smiling. Although she enthusiastically performed virtually every variety of sex with numerous partners in her many films, she appeared to the public to be an elegant middle-class young woman who would not have been out of place at any respectable function. A tall blonde, she had a natural, easy-going air and conversed readily. She also professed religious beliefs, although she was careful to specify, 'I feel Christian, not Catholic'. 'Christ never said anything about sex', she added; 'they invented everything to get control over believers and make them feel guilty'.[76]

The emergence of the world of hard-core from the shadows into the mainstream was occasioned by the entry of Cicciolina and Moana into spheres that would normally have been closed to them. Hard-core pornography had previously been an anonymous world close to prostitution whose practitioners, once they had crossed its threshold, could never return to mainstream cinema or television. Staller's election was sensational, but it brought about the end of her hard-core career. Pozzi, by contrast, succeeded in combining the life of a porn star with that of a celebrity and television personality. Antonio Ricci, one of the more inventive spirits at Berlusconi's Fininvest empire, used her as the mascot for the comedy show *Matrjoska*. She would come on wrapped in a transparent plastic veil, or

69 Moana Pozzi, the middle-class porn star who became a national personality and, after her early death, a secular saint.

even totally naked. Later she was invited by the RAI-3 programme *Jeans 2* to give cookery tips to housewives. Immediately, the *Federcasalinghe* (Housewives' Union) denounced the move as 'offensive to our category' and threatened legal recourse against RAI.[77] Each new role was greeted with some disapproval and protest. Catholic opinion was especially hostile to a woman who, without the slightest compulsion or shame, had embraced the most immoral of activities and exercised it without repentance. However, she became a familiar figure, a sort of porn-star-next-door, who was regarded with a certain wary affection. She seemed normal, reassuring and good. Although, behind her, there was an industry that thrived on exploitation and degradation, none of this transpired from Moana's cordial and relaxed face.[78] The comedienne Sabina Guzzanti, who bore a striking resemblance to her, underlined her paradoxical normality with a highly successful satirical imitation on a popular television show.

Pozzi's place in the public sphere was a strange and in some respects unique phenomenon. On the one hand, she was a product of the rapid breakdown in censorship and the affirmation in significant quarters of an attitude of absolute openness on sexual matters. The emergence of new views about the self and the body were related to this. The particular conjuncture in the entertainment industry was also relevant. The rapid decline of film-going and the sudden explosion of commercial television broke all previously established broadcasting conventions, brought new talents to the fore and created a climate in which shocks and sensations were ready currency. At the same time, there were strongly conservative aspects to the way this particular middle-class porn star became tentatively domesticated. Much may have changed rapidly in Italy but mentalities do not evolve quickly. Pozzi keyed in with masculine ideas identifying all women primarily with sex. She conformed to the pacific idea of the non-conflictuality of the sexes and did so by being malleable and pleasing. Ostensibly, she did not seek to trespass on a masculine terrain but rather occupied the conventional female sphere of intimacy and pleasure. These attributes brought her back within the field of recognition of Catholic culture and made her an odd, anomalous Italian beauty of her times.

When Moana died suddenly from liver cancer in 1994, there were rumours that she had contracted AIDS. This proved not to be the case, but the many public expressions of sadness seemed to veil a feeling that she had paid the price for her lifestyle. The newspapers talked of the silence that surrounded her final illness and the private reconciliation with the Church that preceded her death. She became in death a sort of secular saint who had passed through the most corrupting of environments and had emerged unscathed.[79] The fact that she had died at the same age as Christ seemed to carry a meaning. The Archbishop of Naples referred in his weekly homily to 'that poor child' and others compared her to Mary Magdalene. Her brief life carried a warning about the consequences of flouting social norms. Finally, the champion of transgression and guilt-free sex, who came from a solid Catholic background, was reabsorbed into a national Catholic paradigm. 'Paradoxically, the sudden demise of Moana transformed an "impure" dream into a "chaste" need for her' commented the social observer Roberto D'Agostino; 'As a result, her icon has been purified in a Catholic manner with the features of a precise liturgy. One minute we have the Porno-saint after the lights have gone off. The next we are hailing Saint Moana of the Sacred Taboo'.[80]

Reflecting on this period some fifteen years later, the writer Giuseppe Genna recalled the central place Moana Pozzi had occupied in the male imagination. 'You are the epiphany that exploded into the vision, the minds and the flesh of an entire nation and you challenge with your narrow, knowing and vaguely blue eyes the mass of human material that gathers at your feet to kiss them.'[81] 'You enchant a country that is in the process of transformation . . .', he wrote.[82]

In this year 1989 the flow of articles and celebrations has shocked the loyal followers of the cult, the shapeless mass of flesh that wants you to endow it with a shape, a limit, some satisfaction. Your skin is the cloth of the stars, you are the first and the last, the most revered and most loathed, you are barren and have never been pregnant; you are surrounded by generations of rejected and misunderstood sons who demand to be your husbands, who seek your milk, who seek your blood.[83]

Women were less enamoured of the way the stars of Diva Futura came to occupy a place in mainstream culture, from chat-shows to debates, round tables and literary juries.[84] While women's magazines felt unable to ignore the phenomenon, they interviewed Staller with little sympathy.[85] It was recognised that the sex industry was enormous and that its ever more specialised products were also bought by couples.[86] But there was also suspicion of the way porn stars were identified with liberty and praised as bearers of a positive lifestyle. While they talked of freedom and the abolition of taboos, such women ultimately only won a place in the public sphere because they catered to male fantasies and visions of women. Only in a country in which the political sphere, broadcasting, cinema and the press were still firmly dominated by men could they have received so much complicit attention.

The sociologist Luigi Manconi did not believe that the election of Staller 'has been an expression of sexual liberation and emancipation'. 'Rather I see a victory of sexual consumerism', he added; 'an outcome of a modernisation. It is a phenomenon without labels, neither good nor bad'.[87] It bore witness to the peculiarities of the transformations that Italian society underwent between the 1970s and 1980s. These included the rise of feminism and the sexual revolution, the ascent and decline of the left, and the re-ordering of the media system and the re-casting of its relationship to the economy and society. The ruptures in the pattern of social relations brought many new figures to the fore but they also created a nostalgic urge. This was not just felt by the older generations, since nostalgia is as much a vague yearning as a desire to recapture a known place or past. Within the pattern of desires that fuelled this urge were many that found some outlet in creating, or more commonly consuming, consolatory images of femininity that were at once exciting and reassuring to men who were struggling to digest the changes in patterns of work, family life and gender roles. The numerous actresses who won recognition as *belle italiane* in this period all had more professional and personal options than their predecessors. They enjoyed a new freedom of expression and opinion, even if they were no less constrained by assumptions that their beauty was a banner of the community. While this would change little in the years that followed, it will be shown in the next chapter that conventional ideas of Italian beauty were at this time subjected to unprecedented challenges. First, mention must be made of one final figure who represented some of the contradictions of the period.

Alessandra Mussolini

Mussolini's grand-daughter Alessandra embraced a surprising number of issues involving women's rights in the political career that she embarked on in 1992, when she was elected to Parliament in a Naples constituency as a candidate of the neo-Fascist Italian Social Movement. Although her party was always the least progressive in Italy on matters concerning the family, the emancipation of women and gay rights, Mussolini did not hesitate to join left-wing parliamentary colleagues in protesting against a judge who had ruled that a woman wearing jeans could not have been raped since her assailant would have been unable to remove them without cooperation. She supported a bill to grant legal recognition to de facto couples and another to allow parents to choose whether to pass on to their children the surname of the father or the mother. She was a woman born in the early 1960s who shared some of the sensibilities and attitudes of left-leaning women of her generation. However, for Italians she was an awkward figure who literally embodied a complex heritage and who reminded everyone, often against their will, of the recent past of their country. She was an example of how such contradictory elements as history, nostalgia and sex appeal could be combined in an unpredictable way.

Alessandra Mussolini first came to public attention as a teenager when she won some small parts in films. The daughter of the Duce's third son, Romano, and Maria Scicolone, Sophia Loren's younger sister, she had a unique double claim on public curiosity. Although not conventionally beautiful, she had a distinctive and not displeasing face, with a strong jawline that vaguely recalled that of her grandfather, combined with the full lips and physical appeal of the Scicolone family. It was inevitable, given her background and appearance, that her every move would be scrutinised and evaluated in relation to her family heritage. Initially, she embarked on a showbusiness career, aided by her famous aunt. From the start, she attracted attention on account of her surname. Although Loren never manifested any support for neo-Fascism, and indeed, as a firm supporter of the introduction of the divorce law in 1970, was usually loosely identified with the left, she generously helped her niece. Alessandra had a small role in Lattuada's *Bianco, rosso e . . .* (in which Loren played a sexy nun) and *Una giornata particolare* (*A Special Day*), an acclaimed film by Ettore Scola made in 1975 that was set during Hitler's visit to Rome in 1938. It is centred on a down-trodden housewife, played by Loren, who enjoys a day-long platonic courtship with another individual marginalised by the regime, a homosexual played by Marcello Mastroianni. Among the other films in which the two women appeared were *Qualcosa di biondo* (something blonde), directed by Maurizio Ponzi in 1984, in which Loren's son Edoardo also featured, and *Sabato, domenica e lunedì* (*Saturday, Sunday, Monday*), a 1990 television film by Lina Wertmuller based on Eduardo De Filippo's play about a matriarchal family in Pozzuoli.

Mussolini's efforts to make a career independently of Loren were not very successful. Without exception, her films were minor comedies or made-for-television productions. The only one in which she took the leading role was a film biography of the Neapolitan organised crime leader Pupetta Maresca. She also appeared with veteran comic Alberto Sordi in his 1983 film *Il Tassinaro* (The Taxi Driver), in which the actor-director encounters a variety of famous people (including Fellini, Silvana Pampanini and others) who happen to get into the back of his taxi. Of some historical interest was *The Assisi Underground*, an international production starring James Mason and Irene Papas about the role of the Catholic Church and the people of Assisi in helping Jews escape from the Nazis in 1943. Although Mussolini only played a small role, as a nun, her family connections brought the film some publicity.

In a climate in which eroticism of one variety or another was dominant in cinema, an attractive young actress of ambition inevitably received more offers to reveal her body than to develop her talent. The prospect of marketing topless pictures of the Duce's grand-daughter was especially enticing to producers and magazine editors. She appeared on the cover and in a photographic spread of the Italian edition of *Playboy* in August 1983 and then in the German edition four months later. The Italian magazine made the most of her family background, using the title 'Sensational: the grand-daughter of the Duce – Alessandra Mussolini – the determination of Grandpa Benito and the sex appeal of Aunt Sophia Loren'. These pictures, routine shots of an aspiring starlet, attracted worldwide attention purely for their curiosity value.

Alessandra Mussolini was aware that her surname had a profound effect in a country that, since 1945, had struggled to come fully to terms with the execution of her grand-father and the public exhibition of his dead body in Milan's Piazzale Loreto.[88] Even those who had no sympathy for Fascism saw her as a connection with a past that still had a certain undeniable, if undesirable, resonance. She deliberately played on this, choosing, for example, to marry in Benito Mussolini's birthplace of Predappio on 28 October 1989, the anniversary of the March on Rome. At the same time, her allure was complex and far from one-dimensional. Her youth and beauty attracted attention while her famous aunt

70 Alessandra Mussolini's controversial pictorial spread for the Italian edition of *Playboy.*

linked her to Italy's cinematic heritage and the star system. Although she was born in Rome, she considered herself to be a Neapolitan and embraced the passionate, expressive feminine style that was associated with her aunt. In television appearances and interviews, she was polemical and articulate and did not hesitate to espouse her political views even while she was engaged in showbusiness. Seeing her, many found themselves feeling a bizarre mixture of attraction and repulsion. She was at once a contemporary figure, a modern woman who belonged within the everyday political and cultural frame, and on the other a throwback who belonged to an Italy that was heavily redolent of an awkward and violent past. She embodied a whole heritage that was eminently contradictory and whose antinomies were exacerbated by her alluring appearance and her gender.

Brown-haired and only barely distinguishable from others at the start of her career, she later dyed her hair blonde and adopted a persona that was explicitly southern and lower class. Although she was a university graduate, she was earthy and direct in her expressions and gestures, as though she was striving to become the physical expression of her constituency. Her blondeness was a sign of modernity, but it was a modernity that was of a qualified, provincial kind. In the 1950s, dyed blonde hair had signified foreignness, modernity and sex appeal. By the 1980s, however, it was more associated with the way these qualities had been absorbed and mixed with conventional values and social patterns. For example, no one imagined that, by dying her hair, Mussolini was cutting herself off from the traditional femininity that was part of her maternal family background. On the contrary, despite her Roman accent, she somehow resonated with the archaic femininity that was identified with Naples, and in particular with the area around Pozzuoli. De Filippo's play *Sabato, domenica e lunedì* explored precisely the resonance of the ancient great mother cult in an area known for its seismic instability and strong women. In Mussolini's case, this was combined with her being a modern career woman. She had three children by her husband, but he remained in the background while she occupied the public scene.

As a politician, Mussolini was not primarily known for her beauty and nor was her beauty the object of public discourse. To many northern Italians, she looked as vulgar and unrefined as she sounded. However, her appearance needs to be considered in relation to context. Aged just 30 when she was first elected, for several years she was the youngest and best-looking figure on the political scene and, by comparison to the men around her, she exuded sex appeal. While most representatives of the Italian Social Movement were hardened old men, she was young, female, assertive and blonde. A tenacious defender of her grandfather's reputation and legacy, she was at once one of the most progressive and most reactionary members of her party.[89] For her party, she was a valuable ornament, a feminine face that connected it with Italian female beauty at a time when it stood outside the constitutional arc of the party system.

For Italians, no one else presented so many problems and contradictions as Mussolini. She tantalised the public by, at one and the same time, looking like a young woman of her time and sounding like a latter-day propagandist for her late grandfather. By being a physical reminder of both Mussolini and Loren, she possessed a special, oddly compelling aura. As a public figure, she personalised Fascist nostalgia and mixed it with elements of both archaic and modern femininity. Her aura derived from the fact that she alone could embody these incompatible aspects of history and society, with effects that were at turns familiar and unsettling.

CHAPTER TEN

BEAUTY AND ETHNICITY IN THE ERA OF GLOBALISATION

In 1996 the annual Miss Italia beauty pageant was won by Denny Mendez, an eighteen-year-old naturalised Italian citizen born to parents of African descent who had been raised in the Dominican Republic. In a nationwide telephone poll, in which no fewer than nine million Italians took part, Mendez secured her victory over nearly 60 other finalists to become the first ever black winner of the contest. This event was not unmarked by controversy. The winner's triumph was marred by an unseemly polemic that had raged over the simple fact of her candidature. Observers were divided in their judgements over the purpose of a contest that had become an institution. For some, including the organiser Enzo Mirigliani, the pageant was simply a national ritual like the Giro d'Italia or the New Year lottery. Every year its purpose was to capture the attention of a vast television audience with a range of selections, tests and eliminations to whittle down the field of young women, most of whom aspired to some career in showbusiness. The winner went on to a year of promotions and personal appearances organised by commercial sponsors before either returning to an anonymous life in the provinces or going on to occupy a niche on some television show. For others, however, the contest was a competition with a specific function in the maintenance and renewal of a certain national idea of female beauty.

The question of ethnicity had not been raised in debates about Italian beauty since the Fascist period. But in the 1990s it came to the fore for a variety of reasons that had to do with inward immigration, greater awareness of the legacy of colonialism, and internal political divisions. Italy was a country that historically had exported its surplus labour but in the period from the 1980s it had increasingly drawn workers from North and Central Africa, China, the Philippines, Albania and other countries of Eastern Europe. These headed mostly for northern regions, where they were likely to find opportunities for work. In this sense, they followed in the steps of southern Italians who had migrated to the cities of the north during and after the economic boom. Yet, even for them, integration had not been an easy process. After thirty or forty years, some northerners still resented the southerners who lived in their midst and who they regarded as culturally different. Consequently, black and Arab immigrants did not find a ready welcome. They were often forced to live on the margins of society, unrecognised and subject to a variety of forms of discrimination, hostility and violence. Their skin colour was the primary indicator of their status of being exterior to the nation, even if in reality the steady flow of immigration meant that some second-generation immigrants were already present in schools, public employment and even some national sports teams.[1]

The way Italians reacted to Denny Mendez threw into the light a colonial legacy that had never been the subject of widespread critical reflection or repentance. Even goodwill towards her was sometimes expressed in patronising terms. But the debate over her candidature and victory also served to bring to the fore wider issues concerning the ethnic identity of the Italians, as well as the role of feminine beauty in providing a connecting tissue to the nation. In the opinion of many, the maintenance of a specifically Italian canon of beauty was a core issue in national identity, the sign of an irreducible specificity that persisted over time and which distinguished the Italian people even in an age when foreign and commercial ideals of beauty held considerable sway in the country. Mendez highlighted the existence of a multi-cultural Italy that was more diverse than this conception allowed.

In truth, the prominence of traditional southern imagery in the iconography of the nation was already under attack from the right-wing Northern League. As a challenge to the dominance of Mediterranean beauty in the Miss Italia pageant, the League launched a rival competition, Miss Padania, that was intended to promote a model of beauty specific to the northern regions. It was scarcely accidental that, at precisely the time when it was being placed under strain from various sources, there was a strong rearguard restatement of traditional beauty. This was centred on the Sicilian actress Maria Grazia Cucinotta. The extraordinary attention that was paid to her utterly conventional beauty of olive skin, long dark hair, large brown eyes and opulent bosom was at once a reassertion of identity in difficult times and the sign of a desire to escape the complications of the present.

Miss Italy 1996

While countries such as Britain and France witnessed a substantial influx of people from actual or former colonies in the 1960s, the ethnic profile of Italy changed significantly only three decades later. Although immigrants made up only 2.5 per cent of the national population, by the end of the decade, 10 per cent of the population of Milan was made up of immigrants.[2] In schools in the northern regions, approximately 5 per cent of pupils were of immigrant families. Once largely a 'mono-cultural and mono-colour society', Italy was quickly forced to contend with diversity of religion, culture and ethnicity.[3] Like Germany, Italy did not grant citizenship to its immigrants, and their existence was not

officially recognised. On the one hand, there
was a laissez-faire attitude towards the arrival
of workers who filled an economic need especially in low-status manual employment. On
the other, government and society were less
than welcoming in providing facilities and
assistance in terms of housing, health and
education.[4]

Miss Italia 1996 was probably the first occasion on which a black person had competed
in a prominent field to be selected as the sole
representative of Italy. Because of the importance of the tradition of feminine beauty and
the symbolism of the annual competition,
this moment was a significant one in which
fears and anxieties about identity came
dramatically to the surface.[5] At the outset it
did not seem that there would be any special
reason for controversy. The shape of the
contest was in fact flexible. Almost every year
since the 1980s there had been a small modifi-
cation to the rules, for example to abolish

71 Denny Mendez, the first Miss Italia of colour.

the measuring of vital statistics or to allow mothers to take part. Moreover, variety in
the selection of winners appeared to have become the norm. In the previous three years,
two fair-haired women (Arianna David and Alessandra Meloni) had won, as had one
darker Mediterranean beauty (Anna Valle). However, the issue of ethnic origin had never
been raised, even though the country was increasingly the destination of economic
migrants.

There was a further ambiguity in the way the pageant was perceived. The rules stated
that the competition was open to all women of sound moral standing aged between
sixteen and twenty-five who held Italian citizenship. Yet every year the organisers sought
to win publicity for the contest by encouraging the press to evoke the past glories of the
contest, and especially the golden year of 1947, which saw the participation of several
women who would go on to become film stars. In the 1990s, Gina Lollobrigida, Sophia
Loren and Claudia Cardinale all acted as presidents of the jury. Moreover, intellectuals
and artists were urged to reflect on the nature of female beauty and to debate its importance in Italian culture. 'We are always looking for the new Lollobrigida and the new
Sophia Loren' declared Enzo Mirigliani, who had organised the contest for 38 years.[6] Yet
at the same time the basic aim remained that of the 1940s: to select a girl-next-door who
jurors saw as having the qualities of an ideal wife or daughter-in-law. 'The Miss as I see
her should, yes, be a girl-next-door but her aim should not be to appear on TV but rather

to have a family,' asserted Mirigliani.[7] In short, he was looking for an ordinary girl with the potential, but not the ambition, to be a star.

In reality, virtually all the contestants aspired to a career on the small screen or on the catwalk. For all Mirigliani's assertions that the competition was merely a game, the prizes included several fashion engagements and endorsements. For many contestants, the ideal of beauty that they looked to was unrelated to the Italian past. Rather, it was an international one that was embodied by supermodels such as Claudia Schiffer and Cindy Crawford or, for the more provincial, the *soubrettes* of Italian television. It was easier for the well-nourished and physically fit Italian girls of the 1990s to aspire to this ideal than it had been for previous generations. Italian television offered a homely translation of the cosmopolitan ideal in figures such as the surgically-enhanced half-Finnish presenter Anna Falchi or the curvaceous Sardinian Marilyn Monroe lookalike Valeria Marini. Even a more commonplace young presenter, Lorella Cuccarini, a dyed-blonde from the working-class Prenestino district of Rome who avoided the manufactured sex appeal of her colleagues, did not look remotely Mediterranean. In 1995 the make-up artist Diego Della Palma, who worked with the Miss Italia participants for a month, protested that 'the girls who come here have all been "Schiffer-ified"... or "Marini-fied" because they are convinced that the only model is that of the micro-stars of the television'.[8] Despite this, intellectuals and commentators looked to the contest to find proof of what they saw as authentic Italian beauty. The veteran film director Dino Risi, who was commissioned to make a television film about Miss Italia, affirmed that, in looking for a new face, 'I only looked at the brown, Mediterranean beauties'.[9] The potential contradiction between the cultural pretensions of the competition and the pragmatic view of the contestants was manageable as long as there was a certain variety in the choice of winners.

The 1996 contest was different because the variety that potentially had to be taken into account was suddenly widened beyond the ethnically homogeneous. Italy's imperialist ambitions had taken shape in the 1880s and come to an end in 1943, although a continuing involvement in North Africa in the years that followed tempered the brusqueness with which the empire was brought to a close. However, the residual cultural influences of that phase were not so easily eradicated. Throughout its twenty-year rule, Fascism had proudly asserted that it was reviving Italian civilisation and fulfilling the promise of the Risorgimento. The invasion of Ethiopia in 1935 was seen as finally remedying the humiliation of the 1896 Battle of Adowa and putting Italy on an equal footing with France and Britain. By imposing a government on Ethiopia and encouraging settlers, Fascism believed it was fulfilling the civilising mission that had marked the cause of Italian nationalism. While press coverage of resistance by tribesmen and atrocities by Italian soldiers (including the use of poison gas on civilians) was minimised, there was a mass diffusion within Italy of accounts of peaceful progress in the battle against backwardness, disease and chaos. With the Liberation in 1945, racial discourses were officially swept aside and former Italian colonies were placed under international jurisdiction. But since the republic marked a new political phase, and this period witnessed emigration rather than immigration, there was no assessment of past responsibilities. In the 1980s, pioneering work by the historian Angelo Del Boca brought to light the brutality and inhumanity of Italian colonialism, but little of this penetrated into official representations of the experience or into popular consciousness.[10] The absence of any debate meant that it was still widely assumed that Italy was superior to, and more civilised than, many other countries. The colonial experience allowed Italians to eradicate once and for all any confusion over the issue of how white they themselves were. The consequences of this, and of the way it was achieved, were revealed by Paola Tabet in an extraordinary study of the racist attitudes of small children. In answering in written form questions about what they would do if their parents were black and so on, the children revealed that they naïvely associated blackness with dirt and evil.[11]

Against this background, it is not surprising that Denny Mendez gave rise to such controversy. On account of her news value, the press commented on her more than on any other candidate. In the run-up to the final, controversy reared its head when two prominent members of the jury, the German photographer Rob Krieger and the television showgirl Alba Parietti, questioned on live television whether a woman of colour could adequately represent an ideal of Italian beauty. The point of view of the 60-year-old photographer was that of a foreigner enamoured of a traditional idea of Italy and its inhabitants. 'I would like the chosen girl to be emblematic and to be a mirror of this eternal Italy. I do not want her to be copied from some other country or other culture. She must be an Italian girl; I insist on this point', he declared.[12] For her part, Parietti asserted bluntly that the victor needed to be 'a physical type who embodies certain traditional requisites'.[13] The thinly-veiled implication was that blackness was not among these characteristics. Although Krieger was forced off the jury and Parietti was obliged to withdraw her comments, the impression remained that some general issue of national self-perception had been raised by their clumsy interventions. The event caused what the veteran journalist Nello Ajello called 'a little national psycho-drama'.[14] Due to the controversy, nearly 14 million people watched the final evening of the contest on television, a record 80 per cent share of the total audience.[15]

The doubts voiced by two prominent jury members about the representativeness of Denny Mendez were echoed in far less civil tones by others. There were reports of her being insulted or pointed at in the street (she overheard people say 'Look, there's a negro girl!' as she paraded with the other girls at Salsamaggiore).[16] The mothers of some contestants disputed her right to represent Italy. Her coronation was greeted with whistles and hundreds of protest calls were registered by the RAI switchboard. Mendez was well aware of the potential controversy of her candidature and indeed had deliberately chosen to challenge the Italians (in her biographical statement she had written: 'I would like to take part to see what effect a girl of colour has among all the others').[17] She defended her position by pointing out that 'the regulations state that Miss Italia must be Italian, not that she must be white. I have been Italian for four years. Inside, I am one of you even if on the outside I am different . . . I am a black Italian'.[18]

There were several black winners of beauty pageants in Western Europe in the 1990s and early 2000s. A black Miss Finland was elected in 1996, two black Miss Germanys in the 1990s, a black Miss France in 1999 and 2003, and a Muslim Miss England in 2005. In each case the event gave rise to comment, but only in Italy did it attract widespread attention on account of the specific tradition of feminine beauty that is associated with the peninsula. Even the London *Times* published an editorial on the topic, in which it warned Italians against parochialism by citing the precedent of the multi-ethnic Roman empire. Even if some would have preferred that the scandal of Mendez's election had never happened, it served to bring to the surface issues that were difficult and problematic. Among these was the question of whether it was possible to be black and Italian in anything other than a legal sense. 'I know that I don't represent Italian beauty', Mendez declared in *La Repubblica* of 9 September 1996; 'but they have elected me; what was I supposed to do, refuse?' By not refusing, she compelled Italians to take cognisance of the presence in their midst of immigrant communities. In fact, Denny Mendez's victory in 1996 did not constitute a major disruption of a consolidated tradition, merely an interference in a discourse that would soon resume as if nothing had happened. But, due to it, the Italians found out that in the Dominican Republic, despite the fact that the vast majority of the population is black, the national beauty contest had always been won by a white woman, and that a white woman had been elected Miss Uganda. Some other anomalies were also highlighted. Giuliano Zincone pointed out that many people of foreign origin occupied places in Italian public life and that the Italians themselves were the product of the most complex cross-fertilisation of ethnicities. Even the Sardinian who was the runner-up, Illaria Murtas, was no Mediterranean beauty since, she was 'tall and blonde like a viking . . . like the Sardinian [showgirl] Valeria Marini'.[19]

Yet there were other, less reassuring aspects to the whole matter, including Italy's relationship with its colonial heritage. For Enzo Biagi, Mendez's victory offered an insight into the ways Italians viewed black women. 'Perhaps now we can understand the secret reason for our having become a colonial power. It was the unconfessed love that the Italians had for the Eritrean girls that they had only seen on postcards'.[20] In the era of globalisation, old and new representations of black people appeared in ways that were not always easy to distinguish. The black person as exotic outsider enjoyed a special status in the Italian entertainment media. Black models appeared more frequently in Italian *Vogue* than in other editions of the magazine and were regularly used in advertising and television.[21] But towards black and East European immigrants there was a crescendo of racial discrimination, violence and abuse. 'Since 1989, there has been a veritable catalogue of violent racist attacks and murders in Italy', R. King and J. Andall write, 'perpetrated especially against Africans, Asians and gypsies, and in some cases clearly orchestrated by the extreme right'.[22] They blame the media for the anti-immigrant frenzy, but also indicate the role of the Northern League in creating a siege mentality.

How, then, should the overwhelming plebiscite in Denny Mendez's favour be interpreted? For Enrico Mentana, a senior television journalist who was also a member of the jury, the vote was a case of 'imposed political-correctness'. In an interview published in *La Repubblica*, he declared that it was a way 'of cleansing our consciences because a suspicion of racism hung over all of us for the simple reason that we had dared to say that Denny, who was certainly gorgeous, was not representative of Miss Italia'.[23] Other commentators confirmed the view that it was a cost-free way of affirming that Italy was modern and open, a fully paid-up member of the global village.[24] For the philosopher Gianni Vattimo, 'It is like inviting a black person to dinner in order to show how open you are but then treating him the same as before in the workplace'.[25]

In another interpretation, the election of Mendez could be seen as an ornamental annexation of a para-colonial type. Although her Dominican origins meant that she had no connection with territories belonging to Italy's former empire, the emphasis on her blackness over all other qualities – including even beauty – inevitably revived memories and unconscious assumptions. The choice of an 'exotic girl as the representative of Italian allure', as the *Corriere della sera* expressed it, had little to do with Italian identity.[26] Newspapers referred to Mendez quite unthinkingly as a 'black Venus' or 'the black gazelle', echoing the terminology of the colonial period. *Panorama* referred to her 'exotic face', her 'Tuscan accent and coal-coloured skin', while the *Corriere della sera* repeatedly spoke of 'the black pearl'. Others spoke of 'the Dominican panther', 'the gorgeous lady with chocolate-coloured skin' or referred to 'her appearance that has the flavour of the jungle and the tropics'. From this point of view, her victory was an aesthetic tribute not so much to Italy's tolerance and inclusiveness as to its historical pre-eminence as a country able to select and evaluate global beauty. The fact that Mendez was Catholic (although not practising), allowed Italians to situate her according to a sort of Italo-centric world outlook.[27] Nevertheless, her victory raised the question of whiteness and ethnicity in national identity. It showed that anxieties were still triggered by associations between Italy and ethnic darkness.

Miss Padania

In all the debates that occurred over Denny Mendez, the Northern League was a spectre that hovered in the background and that was used either to justify or to oppose her candidature. For some, her victory was a gesture of defiance in the face of the purist and vaguely racist discourses of the League. 'A Miss Italia with black skin could be seen as an emblematic reply to the delerious secessionist impulse of [League leader] Bossi that is all the more significant because it is not inspired by a political design' argued Vattimo.[28] The objections showed that many had either not realised that Italy had become a multi-ethnic country, or still refused to recognise it. By contrast, the photographer Krieger affirmed, 'With this decision, we run the risk of having made a gift of a lot of votes to Bossi. He'll seize the opportunity to say to the country: "Do you want the Italy of the future to be like this?"'.[29]

The Northern League did not solely oppose the influx of foreign immigrants. It also, and indeed primarily, campaigned against the negative influence of Rome and the south

72 Mediterranean beauty in a modern glamour version, with model in place of peasant girl, from *Illustrazione italiana*, 1993.

on the northern economy. The primacy of Mediterranean beauty in the compound of images that made up national identity was, in the view of its spokesmen, one of the indicators of this dominance. The League attacked the Miss Italia pageant for privileging southern beauty, but what perhaps no one expected was that it would launch its own beauty contest. Yet this is what happened in 1997, with the launch of the first edition of Miss Padania. The contest was certainly a stunt, but it also revealed something of the efforts of the League to give shape to a restricted ethnic identity based on the Italian north. Heats were held throughout Lombardy, Piedmont and the Veneto, with over a thousand girls taking part. However, the League's contest had some disturbing elements that appeared to derive from a Fascist heritage, including the use of the body as a basis for a political project to contrast the dominance of Mediterranean beauty.[30] This was rendered explicit in an article in the League's magazine *Il Sole delle Alpi*, which sought to employ the tools of what in the past was called physical anthropology to establish the ethnic qualities of the three girls who were crowned winners. The author was pleased to announce that the three girls corresponded to the three principal 'spirits' of the Padanian ethnic group: the Adriatic Padanian, the Alpine Padanian and the Ligurian Padanian.[31]

The success of this initiative convinced the League's charismatic leader, Umberto Bossi, that it could be useful. The following year it became a major event in the movement's calendar. As the League was keen to avoid charges of discrimination, a set of rules was adopted that was surprisingly open. Candidates were only required to have lived within the Padania region for five years (later extended to ten). However, in compensation, a declaration of support for the League was called for. A series of other dispositions delineated the cultural project that stood behind the competition. It was decided that the chosen girl should have light skin and no trace of the olive tone that might conceal a southern background. She also had to be at least 1.70m tall, a rule that discriminated indirectly against southerners, who were more likely to be shorter. In fact some contestants did have one southern parent but this was deemed unimportant so long as their appearance was acceptable and they were sympathisers or members of the League. Several of the Piedmontese girls who took part in one of the 1998 heats were happy to declare their political faith. 'I have never taken part in other contests; I am only interested in Padania' pledged Carol Ghio; 'I want to stand up to Miss Italia to give her a metaphorical slap', added Silvia Boncristiano. Tamara Motterle announced that her dream was to 'become a real Padanian woman'.[32] However, some of them could not help but confess their tastes for Roman entertainers like Christian De Sica and Renato Zero. Such compromises were unlikely from Tania Viaggi, who was elected Miss Camicia Verde (a title reserved for the most militant) in the local competition in Marina di Carrara. The proud bearer of Umberto Bossi's signature on her bosom, 'She truly carries Padania in her heart'.[33]

The most detailed requirements were set out by the film director Tinto Brass, who was the president of the jury in 1998. 'If the emblem of Italy is a woman with a castle on her head and a generous bosom, the emblem of Padania must be a beautiful piece of fanny with a well-rounded bottom', he proclaimed.[34] For the director, the bosom was nothing other than a poor copy of the buttocks, that were more sensual on account of their being completely disassociated from reproduction. 'The beauty from Padania', he continued, 'cannot have the careerist ambitions of someone who is eager to get on. Nor can she have swelled, sticking-out lips like Parietti'. According to Bossi, such collagen-filled lips were to be considered symbolic of *Roma ladrona* ('thieving Rome'). Brass outlined his view that the winner should be an authentic natural beauty and not a sub-product of the fashion world. The task was to locate and reward 'hips of the type you do not see anymore because the dominant female ideal is the model'. The winners, he said, would be those who 'more than any others are far-removed from the Barbie ideal that is imposed by the mass media'.[35]

In fact foreign and showbusiness influences were by no means absent, although these seemed mainly to reflect a delight in politically incorrect behaviour. One of the preliminary competitions, mutated in fact from an American college spring break practice, was for Miss wet T-shirt – a custom designed to maximise the pleasure of the male spectator by revealing under a dampened garment the contours of the breasts of the participants. Flavio Arensi could scarcely contain himself after his experience administering the buckets of water. 'What bodies these Padanian girls have! Who would ever have imagined being able to touch almost with one's hands the genial perfection of our women – and, what's more, with their permission', he wrote.[36]

The pride taken in the display of beauty was notable. In the League's newspaper *La Padania*, one correspondent wrote on the eve of the 1998 final:

> If it was necessary to demonstrate the quota of pulchritude and the healthy, youthful exuberance of the Padanian weaker sex, then there has been no better opportunity before today. It seems to me, after having viewed (for professional reasons relating to the present article) the photographs of hundreds of girls in competition suits, that the category of surgeons who dispense various silicone roundnesses (see Parietti) can calmly shut up shop and take an interest in horse-racing instead.[37]

The final competition was held at Cernobbio with 38 participants, all of whom paraded in bathing costumes, evening dress, and the green shirts of the League. At the end of the final parade, the latter were to be removed in a sensual manner 'perhaps accompanied by gentle movements of the hips' to the accompaniment of Joe Cocker's 'Keep Your Hat On',[38] best known from the soundtrack of the erotic Hollywood movie *Nine and a Half Weeks*. Umberto Bossi and his wife, together with the mayor of Milan, were in attendance. At the conclusion of the evening, the title of Miss Padania was conferred on Sara Venturi, an eighteen-year old from Boario Terme and a 'convinced League supporter'. However, evidently her convictions were not very strong since she renounced the title not long afterwards, on the grounds that it might have hindered rather than helped her career. 'The League for me is a hindrance,' she declared; 'I am apolitical and I need to detach myself from the image of Miss Padania that could limit me regionally'.[39] Curiously, the runner-up, Miss Sole delle Alpi (Anastasia Komasova), was not in fact Italian but a seventeen-year-old school student born in Russia who had lived in the Lombard town of Crema for eight years.

These contradictions, which recalled the problems that the Communists had encountered in the 1950s with the *Vie Nuove* competition, somewhat undermined the purpose of the contest. It proved impossible to use it to challenge the dominant values in the media world when most girls were influenced by these and indeed embraced them. In the years that followed, similar contradictions persisted. The title of Miss Padania 2001 was won by a twenty-year-old professional model with a southern surname, Francesca De Rose, who cheerfully announced that her favourite food was pizza, a dish of Neapolitan origin. The 2003 winner, Alice Grassi declared that her aspiration was to 'work in the entertainment industry', while the 2004 winner wanted to become a model. Amid general relief from League supporters, the 2005 winner, Laura Albertin from the Veneto, declared her delight at being chosen to 'represent the typical northern girl, who is respectful of family values and of the traditions of her region'.[40]

Small-screen sex appeal

There were various signs in the 1990s that the conventional idea of Italian beauty was coming under strain. Contemporary standards of beauty were not determined so much within nations but were international and commodified, with the fashion and cosmetics industries, the press and other media taking a leading role in proposing desirable typologies of weight, height, hair colour, and body shape. Increasingly, a type of artificial beauty resting on cosmetic surgery and other physical modifications set the tone. One Italian investigation into 'the feminine ideal of the mediatised body' found that 'it has the smooth skin of Cindy, the well-shaped legs of Claudia, the magnetic eyes of Naomi, the flat stomach of Linda and the charisma of Kate', that is to say, it was a composite of the supermodels of the moment.[41] Modern ideals of beauty were translated into Italian culture through a variety of media, but especially through the prism of television. Ever since the 1950s, the medium had presented the country with people and images that combined traditional values with cosmopolitan appearances. The world of the small screen was filled with women who were recognised and much-loved figures, but who had little of the appearance or spontaneity of the conventional Italian beauty. The leading showgirl-presenter, Raffaella Carrà, who made her debut in the early 1970s, sang, danced and presented various quiz and variety shows. By the early 1990s, Carrà, whose androgynous body and fixed smile were capped by the dyed-blonde helmet hairstyle that was her trademark, was one of the most popular people on television. Her down-to-earth manner and low voltage sex appeal constituted a model for those who aspired to follow in her footsteps. There were many of these, since the explosion of private television and the consolidation of the sector under the control of Silvio Berlusconi had expanded the role of television in consumption and leisure and placed it at the centre of social life. The faster rhythms, entertainment emphasis and focus on artificial sex appeal that Fininvest brought to Italian television were soon also adopted by RAI in its efforts not to be left behind in the ratings war.

In a context in which the key television format was the variety show, the hybrid figure of the *soubrette* (part presenter, part dancer and showgirl) was central. Challenging the by now mature Carrà were a series of younger personalities who appealed to the domestic audience. Among these was Lorella Cuccarini, who was another – much younger – bottle-blonde dancer of humble origins who was first thrust in 1985, at the age of twenty, into the limelight of the Saturday evening variety *Fantastico*. With her long legs, honey-coloured hair, angelic face and delicate manner, she soon became the idol of the conservative half of the country. A practising Catholic who made no secret of her support for the Christian Democrats, even at a moment when the party was disintegrating after more than forty uninterrupted years of power, Cuccarini was seen as the embodiment of the glossed-up girl-next-door, the woman every man would be happy to have as a fiancée or wife and who every woman would be happy to have as a friend, daughter or daughter-in-law.

After abandoning RAI for Fininvest in 1989, Cuccarini hosted Saturday evening and Sunday afternoon shows and took over from Carrà in promoting a popular brand of built-in kitchens. Her religious wedding was amply covered in the press, as was her family life after the birth of her children. A woman who made no secret of being 'old-fashioned' in her values,[42] she was seen as a 'cartoon fairy rather than a woman made of flesh'.[43] As an approachable small screen star who, according to Isabella Bossi Fedigrotti, 'smells of the weekly wash but also of spaghetti sauce', she was the idol of family audiences who preferred their stars to be polite and conventional in their outward behaviour. As a dancer 'she too shows her legs and nearly her knickers too', continued Fedigrotti, 'but both legs and knickers are rather homely, like those of a beautiful cousin or of a younger sister who has enrolled at dance school'. She was sexy 'but without being arousing, without keeping anyone awake at night, rather like a fairy who encourages and blesses sleep'.[44]

While Cuccarini preserved the inoffensive, domesticated erotic appeal of Carrà, another fair-haired, white-skinned *soubrette*, the Sardinian Valeria Marini, provided male audiences with an infantile illusion of available and uncomplicated womanliness. Like Marilyn Monroe, to whom she bore a superficial resemblance, Marini emphasised her curves and played the dumb blonde.[45] In RAI variety shows like *Saluti e baci* (Greetings and kisses) and *Bucce di banana* (Banana skins) she smiled, simpered, danced and spoke a few lines of dialogue with the resident comedians. The fact that she towered over them lent her a magnificent, statuesque quality. At a time of political uncertainty, Marini, who made no secret of her sympathies for Berlusconi after he entered politics in 1994, offered a comforting illusion of joy and abundance. The *soubrette* was neither mysterious nor truly fascinating. Nor, it was widely rumoured, was she the glorious natural beauty that she seemed to many of her male admirers.[46] She simply satisfied in the most banal way the none-too-complex demands of the collective male imagination. With her youthful, exuberant body and cheerful manner, she transmitted a promise of fun and pleasure. She also appealed to families and children, since she had an ironic and theatrical sense of her role as a televisual object of desire, something that was underlined by her frequent wearing of red, the colour par excellence of drama, passion and provocation. She played the femme fatale with humour, while reassuring her audience that she was really a good girl by posing for family magazines like *Oggi* and *Gente* while she lent a hand in the kitchen or chatted to her mother. She drew a veil over her private life and spoke earnestly of the difficulty of finding the right man. She feared that she had betrayed her audience when she posed for a calendar of the petrol company IP which featured glamour photographs of her by Helmut Newton.

Marini looked like a cosmopolitan beauty composite but she did not endorse the contemporary vogue for aerobics, physical fitness and the toned body at all. She was carefree and relaxed; she put on weight and did not appear troubled by it. Far from undermining her popularity, it seemed that this actually increased it.[47] In this sense, she formed part of the tradition of shapely Italian women. Her breasts, but most especially her generous bottom, were the object of public appreciation and press discussion.[48] The whiteness of her skin, a characteristic she shared with Cuccarini, recalled the purity and limitlessness of mother's milk.

Television stars bore witness to the limited impact of feminism. Emancipated women were much rarer on the screen than women who mixed elements of emancipation with older, more familiar feminine models.[49] One inquiry found that the way women were presented on screen was heavily stereotyped and conceived in relation to clear-cut roles such as the housewife, the mother, the career woman and the *soubrette*.[50] While women read the news and presented programmes by the 1980s, there was nonetheless a marked emphasis on their physical appearance. 'The female body in most cases is portrayed and shown as an object subordinated to the gaze of the audience, like a spectacle to be admired', observed Cristina Demaria: 'The gaze of the media, in particular the gaze of television, favours a process of objectification that transforms a woman into a body without roles or specific tasks, an object of desire purely and simply, which is simply "incorporated" as a decorative element'.[51] Women commonly took supporting roles, provided light relief or brought a sentimental dimension to programmes. Only rarely did they present programmes or take on roles that differed from this general pattern. However, there were a small number of anomalous cases.

The showgirl par excellence during this period was none other than Alba Parietti, the jury member who later caused so much controversy at Miss Italia 1996. A divorced mother with a turbulent private life, Parietti made a few minor television and cinema appearances before achieving a wider impact on *Galagoal*, a football programme on Tele Montecarlo in the early 1990s. She was recruited by the left-wing channel RAI-3 for a variety show and from there she graduated to a number of other shows and prominent one-off engagements. She presented the 1993 edition of the annual San Remo song competition with Cuccarini and added a pin-up dimension, together with Marini, to RAI's coverage of the 1994 football World Cup. The two women opened each show with a less than sophisticated dance routine for which they wore revealing swimming costumes the same shade of blue as the shirts of the Italian team. Parietti was paired with her colleagues and rivals on these occasions because she was in several respects an alternative to them.

There was something about Parietti's steely determination to succeed, even in the absence of any particular talent or gift, that recalled the stars of the past. Brown-haired, green-eyed and unconventional, she was famously deemed to have a quality of 'wildness' that other television personalities lacked.[52] The popular writer Alberto Bevilacqua observed that 'she would have done better in the day of Loren, Mangano, Lollobrigida and company, when an actress, in order to succeed, needed the earthy stubborn-ness of a Bartali the many times winner of the Tour of Italy cycle race and the erotic flight of the light-blue eagle Coppi, Bartali's historic rival, that is to say in an Italy that was still savouring the return to normal life after the ruins of war'.[53] She had 'the determination of a variety theatre debutante', he noted. Bevilacqua and others commented on the 'imperfection' of the *soubrette* and suggested that this rendered her an accessible figure

73 Valeria Marini (left) and Alba
Parietti (right) add a showgirl touch to
television coverage of the 1994 World
Cup.

in whom everyone could see something of themselves. For the RAI-3 manager, Arnaldo
Bagnasco, 'her beauty is a possible beauty, an imperfect beauty, a genuine beauty. . . . She
represents an Italy that laughs at its defects, its lapses of taste and its vulgarity and that
seeks transgression and diversion'.[54]

In fact, the resemblance between Parietti and the stars of the past was rather tenuous
and very limited indeed on the physical plane. In terms of her appearance, she was not
easily situated in the tradition of Italian beauty. As a seventeen-year old, she had won a
beauty contest that gave her the right to participate in the finals of Miss Universe in
Australia. However, she had rejected the demand of the organiser that she should
darken her hair and have her teeth adjusted in order to look more conventionally
Italian. By the 1990s, though, her appearance was anything but natural. Although she
was tall, slim and endowed with good, long legs – that were always the key focus of her
scenic presence – she offered an image of re-made beauty.[55] At a time when most Italian
personalities strenuously denied having plastic surgery, she was a case where denial was
impossible. It was evident that she had had breast implants and rhinoplasty. Moreover,
she was one of the first celebrities to have collagen injected into her lips, leading to a
plump pouting effect which was highly artificial. In this, she had a do-it-yourself look
that was indeed accessible but not remotely reassuring or maternal. The role of the

latter-day dark-haired *maggiorata* or temptress was in fact played on television by Pamela Prati, a second-division showgirl who was never fully taken to heart by the public.

Parietti was well aware of the way her beauty was perceived and she made full use of controversy to attract publicity. Her outspoken intervention in the Miss Italia competition in favour of Italian beauty suggested that she saw herself as being somehow a modern version of what it might be. The point of departure for this consideration had nothing to do with her actual appearance. In this sense, Parietti exercised a subjective judgement that disregarded the collective view of male-dominated public opinion. She was happy to use the issue as a platform while in effect subverting several of the cardinal features of conventional beauty. She thus exercised a rare subjectivity in completely redefining the terms within which beauty was usually considered. Any woman, in her view, who was of Italian parentage could choose to model her beauty as she preferred and remain within the paradigm of Italian beauty. This was not, of course, a rejection of the discourse of beauty itself, and her view was ultimately a personal one, but it was striking and iconoclastic.

Parietti was different from her colleagues in that she was highly opinionated, aggressive and left-wing. Moreover, her rollercoaster private life was out of sync with the more orderly pattern that Italians generally preferred from their small-screen celebrities. On one occasion, she engaged in an outspoken defence of the law on abortion on RAI-3's current affairs show *Il rosso e il nero*, while stating that she considered herself to be 'a true Catholic'.[56] This merited her stern criticism in the Catholic press.[57] Further criticism followed when Bologna's Cardinal Biffi observed with disdain, at the time she was presenting the Sunday show *Domenica In*, that 'she declares that she is a Christian but then disrobes with rather too much ease'.[58] Needless to say, the showgirl failed to repent: 'I am a Christian. I follow the example of Mary Magdalene' she bluntly responded; 'what terrorises them is that a woman who is independent and free-living has proclaimed that she is a Christian'.[59] Only after the polemic over Denny Mendez, was her attitude contrite. 'I take note that the contest, reflecting changes underway in the country, embraces the perspective of a multi-ethnic, multi-racial society,' she affirmed.[60]

Parietti was singled out as a target as the parties of the right attacked the public broadcaster RAI in the run-up to the 1994 elections. 'Parietti acts the communist with public money', complained the Northern League senator Achille Ottaviani, as he labelled her, in an epithet that stuck, 'the long leg of the PDS [Democratic Party of the Left]'.[61] Yet the *soubrette* was not an acritical supporter of the successor force to the Communist Party, which formally ceased to exist in 1991. Moreover, as a woman who broke barriers and happily mixed political commitment, religious belief, overtly sexy dress, artificial beauty and sexual freedom, she had little truck with a certain left-wing Puritanism. She declared that she could not bear 'the morbidity and hypocrisy of the left, this boring and conformist left that forced its beautiful women to hide their bodies beneath manly jackets before it accorded them respect'.[62]

74 Red hair, green eyes, a smooth skin, lightly-tanned, and full lips. The virtual beauty created by referendum on the Miss Italia website, with the collaboration of the RAI-1 TV channel, reflects contemporary aesthetic preferences.

The unusual attention that was lavished by the print media on Marini and Parietti showed the absolute centrality that television had assumed in public life. Even the most trivial personality or controversy received endless press coverage. Yet popular interest was wide rather than deep. Although they played the part of erotic lightning conductors on television, the audience was insufficiently interested to want also to pay to see them on the large screen. Marini's cinema debut in *Bambola* (Doll), a film directed by the Spaniard Bigas Luna (who had directed her in some memorable advertising shorts for IP), set in an eel fishing community that had strong echoes of *Riso amaro*, was a flop.[63] After three years of on-off negotiations, Parietti decided against making her debut as a protagonist in a Tinto Brass movie that had the working title 'Madame Pipi'. Instead she made *Il Macellaio* (The butcher), a strongly erotic film by Aurelio Grimaldi in which she played a bourgeois woman who throws off all her inhibitions. The film's modest box office taking showed that Parietti's charisma did not extend beyond the limited confines of the small screen and the press that concerned itself with TV events and personalities.

The rise of Maria Grazia Cucinotta

Even though television became, in the 1980s, the dominant mass medium, the very ubiquity of its programmes, personalities and peculiarly distorted picture of society gave rise to disaffection. Among traditionalists, there was some hostility to the exaggerated, artificial beauty of its leading ladies that did not seem either natural or Italian. This mood was not limited to any one political faction. It was more a feature of a deep Italy that identified with a conventional current of authenticity and attachment to roots. It is unwise to connect unlinked events in too mechanical a fashion, but there can be little doubt that the sudden rise to popularity of Maria Grazia Cucinotta was a disguised conservative backlash against all the forces and episodes that had undermined the privileged place occupied in national culture by Mediterranean beauty. It offered a welcome escape from the present that had the added advantage of reinforcing the country's export image. A few years previously, this model of beauty seemed destined for decline, save for nostalgic revivals. However, in the 1990s it re-emerged as a symbol of Italy at a time when the iconography of the nation was changing and when the country was fashioning a distinctive set of images with which to identify itself in the international marketplace.

More than any other woman, Cucinotta, a Sicilian from Messina, the daughter of a postman and a florist, became the embodiment of the country in the distinctive global mediatic context of the 1990s. She achieved international recognition following her emblematic performance as Beatrice, the object of desire of Massimo Troisi's timid postman in Michael Radford's multi-Oscar-nominated film *Il Postino* (*The Postman*). The film was set on the small Mediterranean island of Lipari in 1952. Philippe Noiret played the exiled Chilean poet Pablo Neruda, who takes up residence there for a few months. He employs the poor and nearly illiterate Mario (Troisi), the son of a local fisherman, as his personal postman, but takes no interest in the man who, for his part, develops a great curiosity in the poet. Gradually Neruda softens and teaches Mario about poetry and the importance of emotion. He also conveys to him his belief in communism. Mario uses his knowledge to woo the beautiful waitress Beatrice, who finally marries him, with the poet serving as their witness. After his return to his homeland, Neruda fails to maintain contact with Mario, much to the consternation and disappointment of the latter, who lives in adoration of a man whose ideas and beliefs he has embraced as his own. He comes to the conclusion that the poet sees him as a man of little worth who has failed to absorb his lesson about emotion. Mario sets about recording the sounds of the island to send Neruda to remind him of his and Beatrice's existence. This emotional gesture awakens his creative spirit and leads him to compose a poetic tribute to the poet. When word of his work spreads, he is invited to Naples to read it to a left-wing gathering. He plans to record this act as the final part of his recording. However, as he mounts the stage, shots ring out and the police charge the gathered leftists. As a result, Mario dies and the tape recording is never sent to Neruda. Only several years later, when the poet makes a return visit to the island and comes asking after Mario does he discover what happened. He meets Mario's son Pablito and Beatrice hands him the tape of sounds of the island, the final part of which records the violence of the police attack, gunshots and screams.

Il Postino offered a timeless story of friendship, love and poetry in an idyllic setting that was beautifully captured by the cinematography of Franco di Giacomo. The success of the film, which received five Oscar nominations in 1995 and won the Oscar for best original soundtrack, owed something to its original use of the theme of nostalgia. This is embedded in the film, in the sense that, after Neruda's departure, Mario feels his absence intensely and reflects on a friendship that has changed his life for ever. Even Neruda, who appears to have forgotten his time on the island, eventually returns and relives it through Mario's tape recording. Nostalgia also binds the audience into the film's themes. This was most readily felt by the Italian audience. At a time of political turmoil and instability, the film offered a familiar image of a poor and simple but not too remote Italy. For the first time, the Communists, whose dissolution as a party provoked genuine feelings of loss and sadness, are included in the picture of the past. However, their inclusion is not solely a wistful one, as Mario's death underlines. The sudden death the day after the end of filming of the much-loved comedian Troisi, who had postponed heart surgery to make the film, added a note of poignancy. For the international audience, it is the landscape, the humour, the simplicity, the photogenic poverty and the emotional issues that connect with a long-established idea of Italy.

Both audiences found a shared source of identification in the figure of Beatrice. The 25-year-old Cucinotta's character has little to say, but she occupies a key place in the film as the beautiful woman who is the object of Mario's dreams and desires and the subject of his discussions with Neruda. Her abundant dark hair, olive skin, large nut-brown eyes and opulent breasts were evocative of the tastes and smells of the island. Her graceful deportment made her seem like a queen. A native Sicilian, Cucinotta seemed at home in the Mediterranean setting and a perfectly natural love interest for the shy Mario. The film turned the actress into an icon. Before *Il Postino*, she had appeared on television on Renzo Arbore's RAI variety show *Indietro tutta* (All backwards), she had made numerous advertisements and she had taken small roles in a series of minor comedy films. After the film, she became instantly recognisable and one of the most in-demand models for magazine covers and photographic shoots, roles for which she had previously been turned down. For the recently-founded Italian and international monthly men's magazines, like *FHM*, *Max* and *Maxim*, she was the perfect subject, a woman whose eroticism required little underlining by artifice or pose, since it transpired directly from her supremely curvaceous figure, her sultry Latin looks and her large eyes. Photographed customarily *deshabillée* in black underwear – the uniform of choice for sexy Italian stars since the time of neo-realism and Sophia Loren's famous striptease for Marcello Mastroianni in *Ieri, Oggi, Domani* – she became a global pin-up. Various publications drooled over her generous charms, while in 1997 the British edition of *FHM* declared her to be the winner of its lingerie awards.

In Italy and abroad, Cucinotta was hailed as 'the new Loren', that is the woman who was the most valid and attractive successor to the actress who for four decades had been the leading bearer of the image of the country. Cucinotta relaunched the type of woman associated with Loren and projected it once more to the forefront of national consciousness. She was the symbol of the time when full-bodied female beauty seemed to be a rare natural Italian resource to be supplied in limitless quantities to the world. For the playwright Ugo Chiti, she was 'the symbol of the full and exuberant Italian beauty of the

LAVAZZA
E I FOTOGRAFI MAGNUM

Caffetteria Palazzo delle Esposizioni - Roma, 5 aprile 10 luglio 2000

Ferdinando Scianna - Calendario Lavazza 1996

75 Maria Grazia Cucinotta, photographed by Ferdinando Scianna for the 1996 calendar for the coffee brand Lavazza, was the most representative Italian beauty of the late 1990s.

1950s'.[64] Even *Vogue Italia* commented on her 'unending legs, generous bosom, shining black eyes and long silky hair that reaches almost down to her waist'.[65] She offered 'a typically Mediterranean allure to which are added freshness, spontaneity and determination. Maria Grazia Cucinotta is the latest representative of that stock of beauty that has its archetype in Sophia Loren and that is recognised by the whole world as "Italian"'. Expert observers refined this judgement to draw attention to the similarity not only to Loren, but also to Silvana Mangano and Claudia Cardinale, actresses whose quiet class balanced the splendour of their beauty. The only person to pretend not to have heard of her at the apex of her success was Loren herself. Reportedly, when asked what she thought of 'the new Sophia Loren', the actress replied 'Who is Maria Grazia Cucinotta?' Nevertheless, she won plaudits from traditionalists. As the self-appointed guardian of convention, Krieger, put it: 'I find La Cucinotta marvellous as an example of an Italian woman'.[66]

One of the keys to Cucinotta's appeal to Italians was that her beauty was deemed to be 'reassuring' and 'calming'. For Arbore, the man who discovered her, she was 'the girl we would all like to have as a girlfriend'.[67] She was widely hailed as the most beautiful woman in Italy. In 1996, an opinion poll revealed that she was the ideal wife of 22 per cent of Italian men aged between eighteen and thirty-four, ahead of Ornella Muti, who was placed second, with 14.5 per cent.[68] Her success was partly due to the fact that she originated from the region that was deemed in the same poll to be most representative of sincerity, beauty, fidelity and passion.

Cucinotta became almost a national mascot. Her homely-sounding surname, like Lollobrigida's, possessed a down-to-earth flavour. It was said to be evocative of country kitchens, fresh vegetables and flavoursome home cooking. She was adopted as a favourite cover girl by family weeklies like *Oggi* and *Gente*, as well as by daily newspapers that could not resist adorning their columns with her image.[69] In 1996 an extraordinary total of 1,045 photographs of her appeared in the eight leading newspapers and the twenty top magazines, a total that made her far and away the most visible woman in Italy.[70] At a time when Italian fashion was affirming its pre-eminence in the world, Cucinotta joined Loren as a key promoter of Giorgio Armani. The designer found that their Mediterranean beauty was as similar as their characters; they were both emblematic of a type of 'true woman' that was no longer widespread.[71] Like Italian stars of the past, Cucinotta usually dressed elegantly, with simplicity and without either jewellery or any special hairstyling.

In interviews, she explained how her physique had prevented her from realising her early ambition to be a fashion model. Although she was very tall and thin, her large breasts obstructed her success. During this period, she later revealed, she was repeatedly the target of obscene approaches, proposals to make pornographic films and threats that if she did not have sex with X or Y her prospects were zero. In fact, one of her characteristics was that she did not strip either on screen or for magazines. 'I have never stripped; I have always thought it was not useful. It is better to seduce, to move and to suggest', she declared in 1995.[72]

Her career after *Il Postino* went in two directions, domestic and international. In Italy, she made two films, *I laureati* (The graduates), by an emerging comic Leonardo Pieraccioni, in which once more she played a dream woman, and *Italiani*, a forgettable light comedy by Maurizio Ponzi. Her first film role of any consequence was in Ugo Chiti's *La seconda moglie* (The second wife), a 1998 film set in rural Tuscany in the 1950s in which she played Anna, a single mother from Sicily who becomes the wife of Fosco, a lorry driver. She is more reserved than either her husband or the easy-going local women, yet when Fosco is jailed for selling Etruscan relics, she falls for his son Livio. In contrast to the directors of explicit erotic films, Chiti did not seek to exploit her physique in sex scenes. For this, the director won her approval. 'He was looking for femininity and sensuality not nudity or vulgar sex . . .', she affirmed; 'I do not believe in nudity; in that case where is the space for the imagination?'[73] In fact the film was not a success. Less challenging than *Il Postino*, it used over-familiar locations and fell into clichés. Moreover, it used visual teases – such as a well-oiled cleavage and passionate stares – that evoked not the opulent beauty of the *maggiorate* of the 1950s, but the unattractive climate of bigotry in which they prospered.

The Americans were initially enthusiastic about Cucinotta's potential for a Hollywood career. The actress sensed that producers were interested because they were tired of 'certain stars who, let us say, are a bit plastic'. 'And I am not referring to silicone curves so much as to the heart', she continued: 'Women who only think about their careers and very little about feelings. They told me that it was the fact that I am instinctive, Latin and not at all manufactured that won them over. My Mediterranean shape and black eyes correspond to a character who is sentimental and unambiguous. . . . My real weapon of seduction is not the fact of being shapely but my being an old-fashioned woman'.[74] However, the only role she secured in a major foreign film was as a cigar girl in the dramatic opening sequence of the James Bond film *The World is Not Enough*. Despite a serious effort to launch a Hollywood career, she only appeared in a handful of independent films including *Picking Up the Pieces*, in which she starred opposite Woody Allen and Sharon Stone and was directed by Alfonso Arau, and *Just One Night*, an implausible caper in which her co-star was a second-rank actor, Timothy Hutton.

Between 1995 and 2000, Cucinotta was Italy's great international hope. However, the expectations that were placed in her were at best only partially fulfilled. The actress's marriage and desire for a family meant that she was unable to invest the time or bear the long absences from home that would have been necessary to build an international career. Her limited talent and poor English reduced opportunities (her screen test for Allen's *Celebrity* was, by her own testimony, a disaster).[75] At the same time, her refusal to contemplate any nudity closed the doors of much European cinema to her. This stance won her the approval of the Church but meant that she was obliged to work mainly in television productions and on small films, often set in Sicily.

A poll conducted by an illustrated weekly in 1999, after the French had decided that the model Laetitia Casta would lend her face to the emblem of the Republic Marianne, once more confirmed Cucinotta's popularity in Italy. Invited to select a woman who would be worthy of representing the face of the Italian Republic, 18 per cent indicated Cucinotta, while 11 per cent opted for Ornella Muti and 8 per cent for Monica Bellucci.[76] Cucinotta was deemed to be a star with an international profile who embodied the best and most typical features of Italian womanhood.

Yet the idea of typicality was inevitably somewhat out-of-date in a diverse, multicultural world. Moreover, Cucinotta could never really have become a new Sophia Loren because the conditions in which the latter became a star no longer existed. Changes in society, cinema and the nature of collective dreams meant that that era was unrepeatable.[77] In contrast to Loren, who constructed a career and placed herself at the centre of Italian identity with roles in a variety of high-quality dramatic and comedy films, many of which touched common chords in the history and character of her fellow citizens, Cucinotta was merely a beautiful presence. The memory of the golden age of Italian stars lived on, though, and she profited from it. After 1995, she was primarily known for appearing in photographs and magazine articles. She became an example of a virtual star, whose image and celebrity have little to do with a movie career that had few highlights. An evocative figure, there seemed only to be a future for her as a talismanic permanent example of conventional Italian beauty.[78]

CHAPTER ELEVEN

THE RETURN OF THE 'BELLA ITALIANA'

In contemporary culture, the body has become an adjustable project, a focus of identity and a vehicle of status. 'In the decade that we have just gone through', wrote the author and journalist Lidia Ravera in 1990,

> the body has been transformed from an instrument of pleasure into a bizarre and demanding God that demands extreme sacrifices without offering even a hint of paradise. The consequence is a uniform, homogenised quasi-beauty, a bit standardised, a bit empty, that has not practical purpose and which no one looks at since they are busy looking at themselves, checking the curve of their stomach, their hair nourished with pollen, their surgically-corrected nose and their fantastic buttocks. In brief, the body God offers us an empty, blind and lonely paradise. The stupidity of the health mania, the absurdity of the gym Narcissus lies in having allowed a means to become an end. That is, not to become healthy and beautiful in order to be seduced, conquered and courted but to be healthy and beautiful for the sake of being healthy and beautiful.[1]

This trend was crystallised in television, as the medium that most reflected trends in consumption and leisure. 'TV propagates armies of bodies and supplies images of bodies on a daily basis', argue two Italian observers of the medium;[2] 'Fashion and sport, for their own needs, produce "well-made bodies", sequences of robust physiques, processions of beauties, an uninterrupted flow that has a quasi-industrial rhythm.'

The impact of media-related and commercial beauty ideals is no less marked in Italy than in other countries, even though they clash directly with the conventional idea of the beautiful Italian woman.[3] They even had some impact on the women who, after Cucinotta, came to the fore because they bore a physical resemblance to the iconic beauties of the past. Monica Bellucci, Sabrina Ferilli and Manuela Arcuri were women of their time, even if at some level they shared traditional expectations and values. Each of them acquired a particular resonance by simultaneously conforming to some prevailing mediatic values and situating herself in relation to the national canon of beauty. There were elements of play-acting and staging involved in this process because all these women were determined professionals who were highly ambitious. This reality did not always sit easily with the fact that the *bella italiana* is, at an imaginary level, everybody's neighbour, the girl-next-door, your friend's sister, the girl at the bus stop or in the market. The celebrity figures who will be considered in this chapter provide proof of a complex process of blending. The actresses who were deemed by the collectivity to embody the qualities of national beauty both reinforced and undermined stereotypes by simultaneously trading off them, performing the roles that were expected of contemporary personalities, and seeking to maintain original, individual profiles.

Monica Bellucci: the international diva

Monica Bellucci (whose very surname is resonant of beauty) has been said to incarnate 'a more complex, allusive and intimate type of beauty, closer to transgression and sin' than her colleagues.[4] It has also been said that she 'incarnates the modern liberated woman who has much to offer beyond traditional attractions'. While these observations are supported by the facts about Bellucci's career and personal choices, they need to be balanced with a recognition that the actress has consciously constructed a multi-faceted image that is both highly contemporary and related to conventional perceptions of the Italian beauty. As one of what the journalist Corrado Augias calls 'the only two Italian actresses worthy of embodying the style of our country',[5] Bellucci has inevitably been attributed national qualities. The reputation she has acquired as 'arguably the world's most beautiful actress',[6] a label similar to that attached to Lina Cavalieri, has not only given her a global resonance but has also perpetuated interest in Italian feminine beauty.

Although it was cinema that made her famous, Bellucci first came to public attention as a model, a job she began while still a student. By the early 1990s, she was a highly-paid professional earning $10,000 per day, living in Monte Carlo and working in Paris, Milan and New York. Her image adorned the covers of magazines including *Elle* and *Vogue France* and the advertisements of Christian Dior, Revlon and Florentine designer Chiara Boni. She appeared with Alain Delon in a video advertising Annabella fur coats and worked with leading photographers, including Richard Avedon, Fabrizio Ferri and Oliviero Toscani. Initially under contract to the Milan model agency of Riccardo Gay, she was later taken on by the top New York agency, Elite. Her presence in this world of cover girls and top models was unusual since no other Italians broke through and Mediterranean features and full breasts were not normally regarded as compatible with the type of beauty privileged by the fashion world and the international media of the time. Bellucci succeeded because of her photogenic qualities, her poise and refinement, and also because the success of Italian fashion designers brought about a shift in the

76 Monica Bellucci used her beauty to build a career first in modelling and then in cinema. She has featured on numerous magazine covers and in many photo shoots.

ideals of beauty and created an aura of fashionableness around Italian products and qualities. 'If my image appeals it is because my face expresses something', she said in 1990, aware that her Italian origins were no longer a handicap.[7]

Part of her success was due to the place occupied in the collective memory by the female stars of the past. For an industry that regularly drew on the repertoire of visual culture, this was important. According to the photographer Marco Glaviano, who worked with her at the start of her modelling career, she 'recalls the cinematic mythologies of Silvana Mangano and Claudia Cardinale. In the fashion world there has never been a personality like that. With Monica's appearance, typical Italian looks have finally exploded among the top models'.[8] For Oliviero Toscani, she was the opposite of a Cindy Crawford whose 'celebrated sensual beauty, her mouth, her widely advertised curves are almost a stereotype compared to Monica Bellucci', who was 'a real personality, at last, a bit old-style, with a well-rounded bottom and something of Anna Magnani at the height of her powers'.[9]

Bellucci made her film debut in *Vita coi figli* (Life with children), by the veteran director Dino Risi, who also compared her fulsome beauty to that of Silvana Mangano in *Riso amaro*. In her first major role, in Francesco Laudadio's *La Riffa* (The raffle) in 1991, the commercialisation of her beauty was the film's theme. Bellucci played a young high-society widow left penniless by her husband. In order to obtain money for herself and her daughter, she organises a lottery between ten wealthy men with herself as the prize. Inspired by an episode of *Boccaccio '70*, in which Loren played the part of a fairground girl who auctions herself to the highest bidder every Saturday, the film presented Bellucci as the quintessential beautiful woman who is desired only for her body. Yet in the end, she runs away with her daughter to avoid surrendering herself to the lottery winner.

As a result of this film, Bellucci came to the attention of Francis Ford Coppola, who cast her in a small part in *Bram Stoker's Dracula*. Finding that there were few roles for her in Italian cinema, where she was considered too perfectly beautiful to become a proper actress, she moved to Paris, where she did many auditions before winning a role in the thriller *L'Appartement* in 1996, for which she received a César nomination. This led to a variety of other roles, mainly of little note, with the exception of the postmodern thriller *Dobermann*. In 1999 she made four films (two French, one Spanish and one Italian) and was called to appear with Gene Hackman and Morgan Freeman in the thriller *Under Suspicion*. Then in 2000 she was cast in the lead role in the Miramax-financed and internationally-distributed *Malena*, a film by the Oscar-winning director of *Cinema Paradiso*, Giuseppe Tornatore. In her biggest Italian film to date, she was once again introduced as a widow, the daughter of a Latin professor, who lives alone in a Sicilian village. This time she is an erotic fantasy figure for young boys, who spy on her washing and dressing, as well as the recipient of glances and attention from older men and jealous stares from women. In the film, dreams are spun around her and her desirability, elaborated in numerous nude scenes, is repeatedly underlined. The film was similar in some respects to the Laura Antonelli vehicle *Malizia*, but the fact that it was set in the Fascist and wartime period lent it a political dimension absent in the former film.

The film further raised Bellucci's international profile and brought her to the attention of leading figures in Hollywood. She was cast in *The Matrix 2* and *The Matrix Reloaded*, as well as in Mel Gibson's controversial *The Passion of the Christ* (as Mary Magdalene). She remained, however, a fundamentally European actress, able to act in French, English and Spanish, as well as Italian. She has made her home in Paris, where she lives with her husband, the actor Vincent Cassel. The couple have made several films together, often with a violent or controversial edge. Indeed, brutal scenes have become a speciality. As Malena, she was beaten and shaved on account of her alleged collaborationism and Bellucci's character was subjected to a long, dramatic rape scene in Gaspare Noe's *Irréversible*, which caused some to walk out of its showing at the 2002 Cannes film festival. All these associations lend her a special appeal for experimental young film-makers. Her work in France has stressed a controversial dimension that has not found adequate expression in the more conservative Italian cinema. In several ultra-violent thrillers, for example, her dark looks have taken on a comic-book simplicity. However, she has also featured in lighter films, including *Astérix et Obélix: Mission Cléopatre* and *The Brothers Grimm*, in which she was the Mirror Queen. In 2003, she acted as official hostess of the Cannes festival.

Physically, Bellucci has the perfection and iconic stillness of a Renaissance beauty, although her Mediterranean looks lend an earthy dimension to her coolness and self-containment. She is tall, has long dark hair, often ruffled in a state of casual disorder, an oval face, dark brown eyes, full lips, light olive skin, and a sinuous body. Her womanly figure is the core of her appeal. 'I will never be skinny. . . . I love to eat. Who cares? I am natural', she proclaimed.[10] Like the Italian stars of the 1950s and 1960s, she has never played girls but only women. For British observers, her 'curvy Loren-like figure is a refreshing change from the usual stick-thin Hollywood stereotype'.[11] She acts like a trigger on the memory of men of a certain age. To see her on screen, writer Geoff Dyer remarked, 'is to be transported back in time and space to *La Dolce Vita*'.[12] Her beauty is not of the uncomplicated, sun-drenched type, rather it is more regal and untouchable. But it is still recognisably Italian and possesses numerous antecedents. 'We Europeans wear on our faces the weight of history' she has observed: 'ours is an original beauty, even when we are of a sunny disposition we have in our eyes the signs of melancholy, of a depth that renders us different from all the others. There is something antique about us and it is that characteristic that most fascinates'.[13]

It has long been customary for foreign film directors to cast Italians as temptresses and femmes fatales. Isa Miranda, Alida Valli and Gina Lollobrigida all played gold-diggers and occasionally murderesses in American movies. But Bellucci is unique in revelling in these roles, and in accepting them without fear of being typecast. In her film roles, dialogue is often limited and she invariably uses her physical beauty as a tool of seduction. Men are attracted to her and the spectator is frequently drawn into a voyeuristic complicity with them. She is always either middle or upper class or an outsider (for example as the deaf-mute gypsy in *Dobermann*). On occasion there is an air of impending doom about her. It is often remarked that Bellucci is a poor actress. Her playing is wooden and one-dimensional it is said, and she is frequently inexpressive. But this has little bearing on her stardom or her star quality. She has established herself as a type, and is instantly recognisable and consistent in her choice of roles, and she has carved out a unique niche for herself in international cinema.

From early in her career, Bellucci forged a relationship with the designer duo Dolce & Gabbana, whose explorations of the heritage of the Italian stars of the past and the years of the *dolce vita* provided them with a distinctive fashion imagery. Their clothes enjoyed the reputation of looking as good on shapely figures as on supermodels. The experience of the fashion world and of working with leading photographers shaped the whole of her subsequent career. She has maintained a consistent presence in the press, in particular in contemporary men's magazines, for which she is ideal cover material. Frequently shot naked or in black lingerie, she is happy to adopt bizarre or surrealist poses for photographers she trusts. Her first topless photograph was taken by Richard Avedon and appeared in the 1997 Pirelli calendar. This spare upright black and white portrait, revealing a rounded bust, was the only one in the calendar not to be condemned in the British press for encouraging anorexia. In the following years, she posed for a variety of strikingly suggestive and daring shots, often with a perverse tone. For *GQ*, Fabrizio Ferri photographed her naked, save for a light covering of caviar, and with her face dripping with olive oil.[14]

Although the limited edition Pirelli calendar enjoys a prestigious status in Italy, the models have rarely been Italian. In 1991, *Max* magazine began the custom of engaging a leading domestic female celebrity to pose for its annual calendar. The extraordinary sales success of the initiative led a series of other illustrated weeklies and monthlies to follow suit. In 1998 and 2000, Bellucci posed for two calendars, respectively for *Max* and the Italian edition of *GQ*. Photographed by Ferri and Gian Paolo Barbieri, in poses and settings that were imbued with a strong Italian flavour, Bellucci achieved a symbolic symbiosis between the harmonious curves of her mostly naked body and the natural landscape. The two calendars were bestsellers, reaching sales of between 400,000 and 500,000 copies each.

The actress has appeared in few films in which her perfectly-proportioned body has not been at least briefly unveiled. 'I have posed naked without any difficulty', she confessed in 1999; 'working as a model gets you used to a natural relationship with your body. . . . An actress should not have limits, her face and her body are the tools of her trade'.[15] 'Most women in Italy rarely get to be free birds. I have shown my body on screen because I do not object to nudity on screen', she later commented.[16] Such attitudes and the controversial roles she has played place her at odds with mainstream opinion and make her a disconcerting figure for many conservative Italians.[17]

In one of her first press articles, Bellucci expressed disinterest in Loren, Lollobrigida, Magnani and Mangano. She staked out a precocious claim to originality by stating: 'I'm not a Bicycle Thief. I don't like Bitter Rice. I didn't know this Dolce Vita'.[18] Later, she adopted a more diplomatic position, claiming that 'as a child I dreamt about actresses like Sophia Loren. When I was young I sat in front of the TV watching all these incredible films. I grew up with this kind of sensuality. Maybe that is why they are comparing me to Claudia Cardinale and Sophia Loren'.[19] In reality, it was a more recent actress who was her model: 'When I was 14 I fell in love with Ornella Muti. She stood for everything that was erotic. . . . I was also fascinated by the gracefulness of Isabelle Adjani in *One Deadly Summer*.'[20] In fact, it is Adjani that physically she most closely resembles. Although her parts in period films and her classical beauty suggest a link to the tradition of Italian screen icons, she is in many respects a more modern figure.

One reason for Bellucci's ambivalence about being located in relation to previous stars lies in her struggle to assert her originality. 'I have never sought, not even when I was less famous than I am now, to conform to the beauty ideal proposed by my milieu . . .', she declared.[21] She evidently felt that she did not reject one ideal only to become the prisoner of another. However, like other Italian beauties of the past and present, she wears little make-up and minimal jewellery. She is also a vocal defender of natural beauty: 'Today, I say with complete sincerity, I am very disturbed by the number of surgically-enhanced women you see around. They are all dramatically the same, they look as though they have come from the same mould . . .'. In her opinion, 'extreme surgery is the negation of femininity; it represents the passive adaptation of women to the erotic imagination of the male; it is a tangible sign of the standardisation of tastes and the renunciation of mental independence'.[22]

For all her cosmopolitanism, the actress's origins are provincial. She was born in 1968 in Città di Castello, near Perugia in the Umbria region. Her father owned a road haulage company while her mother was a housewife. She was given a relaxed upbringing, without undue parental constrictions, and received a classical education. Invited to contribute in a special issue of a travel magazine dedicated to her native region, she praised its unique fusion of modernity and tradition: 'my roots are in Umbria, the place of the spirit and of memory . . . I go "home" whenever I can, to feel at one with myself, to experience the atmospheres of my childhood, and to feel a sense of pride'.[23] Bellucci underlined both her similarity to her character in *Malena* and her distance from a dated model of femininity:

> I can understand Malena because I come from a village and I know what it is like to walk down the street and have everyone look at you. In the Sicilian society of this time women only existed through men. And Malena has an antique femininity. Even if I'm not like her, I know very well her character. She harks back to Italian actresses like Sophia Loren. Those actresses were really sexual but also protected; they had a femininity close to the earth.[24]

Only very rarely has Bellucci played a mother, a role normally thought to be essential for an Italian actress seeking to consolidate her position. However, on one of the occasions she did, in Gabriele Muccino's choral generational drama *Ricordati di me* (Remember me) in 2003, she was a pivotal presence. In the supporting role of Alessia, the old flame and new lover of Carlo, a professional man who is having doubts about his life, she brought subtlety and depth to a part that in the screenplay was merely sketched. Although she does not owe the recognition she has won to Italian cinema and is not restricted by the options it offers her, this performance gave an insight into how it could have employed her to advantage.

Sabrina Ferilli: the domestic goddess

If Bellucci is remote and perfect, the Roman actress Sabrina Ferilli, by contrast, is accessible, familiar, earthy and genuine. Although unknown abroad, Ferilli is an extremely popular personality in Italy. She is a film, theatre and television actress, a presenter, a photographic model and an all-round celebrity. She, too, is of provincial origin although the village where she grew up, Fiano Romano, is not far from Rome. Her father was a local Communist politician and her mother a housewife. She spent much of her leisure during her youth at the local Casa del Popolo (left-wing recreational centre) and at open-air left-wing festivals. She has remained faithful to her left-wing roots and, unlike many showbusiness personalities, is not coy about expressing her sympathies.

Ferilli's early aspirations were encouraged by Giuseppe De Santis, the director of *Riso amaro*, who was a family friend and a resident of the same village. After a few small parts in the 1980s, she began her film career proper in the early 1990s, winning her first significant role in veteran director Marco Ferreri's *Diario di un vizio* (Diary of a maniac), in which she played an easy-going waitress. She continued the working-class theme in *La bella vita* (the good life), Paolo Virzì's drama set in Livorno, in which she played a dissatisfied working wife. With this part she won attention for her full figure and conventional beauty. In neither Ferreri nor Virzì's film was her character faithful, yet she nonetheless attracted sympathy and won plaudits for the apparent naturalness with which she played ordinary women. In the bitter-sweet holiday comedy *Ferie d'agosto* (Summer holidays), also directed by Virzì, she once more played an unfaithful wife. In two further films, the Taviani brothers' *Tu ridi* (You laugh*)* and *Americano rosso* (Red american), both set in the inter-war years, she took very similar roles. Rather than leading to her condemnation as a vamp, as had sometimes been the case in the 1940s and 1950s with actresses who took such parts, they did nothing to undermine her appeal to women. Meanwhile, a comedy film she made in 1998 with the Tuscan comic Francesco Nuti, *Signor Quindicipalle* (Mr Fifteenballs), flopped.

Ferilli's television career prospered as her film career stalled. Cinema was responsible for her emergence and for the definition of aspects of her public persona, but her work in theatre and above all on television turned her into an all-purpose celebrity. In two television drama series, she underscored her lower-class allure. In the very popular series *Commesse* (Shopgirls), she adapted easily to a minor role, playing a shop assistant, while in *Almost America* she played a poor woman who travels to Canada to look for her long-absent emigrant husband, only to find that he has established a new family. This character suffering added a new dimension to her repertoire. In the early 2000s she became the leading star of television drama, with a series of films and mini-series including, in 2005, a trilogy of female portraits and a biographical film of the singer Dalida. She has also presented variety shows on television, including one called *La bella e la bestia* (beauty and the beast), in which she, naturally, was Beauty. She also appeared in theatre productions, including a revival of *Un paio d'ali* (a pair of wings), a comedy about an ordinary girl who wants to break into cinema, that was first staged with Giovanna Ralli in the lead role in 1957, and the Roman musical *Rugantino*.

Ferilli is precisely the sort of actress who, in the 1960s or 1970s, would have been a domestic film star. Her decision to diversify and build a career in television is indicative of the central place that this medium occupies in everyday culture. Remarking on the reversal of roles that has occurred between film and television more recently, Ferilli asserted that television drama provides a way of addressing a wider audience and engaging it in a process of considered reflection. 'Cinema in Italy and elsewhere today is the language of pure entertainment, for a young audience that goes in a hurry', she once said in an interview; 'television uses a deeper language and is for people who have the time and want to be moved or to experience lasting feelings'.[25] This is not a widely-held view of Italian television, which is mainly distinguished by its incessant advertising breaks and the consequent distracted channel-hopping of viewers.[26] Television films, however, are an exception in a broadcast diet that consists mainly of talk-shows and variety entertainment.

A natural beauty with a tendency to put on weight, Ferilli makes no secret of her love of pasta or of her dislike of diets. She has a dark, Mediterranean beauty and a shapely figure that she happily flaunts in presenting herself as an erotic object. Like Loren who, in her day, was turned into a loud, exuberant Neapolitan for the screen by De Sica, Ferilli has evolved into a modern-day woman of the people through a combination of proletarian and lower-middle-class roles and the cultivation of a cheerful, outgoing manner. In contrast to the moody and unsmiling Bellucci, Ferilli often wears a broad grin and clearly transmits a sense of joy. Her public personality is warm and open and is based on a friendly, accessible manner. Her attitude towards sex is uninhibited and democratic. She claimed that she had never had 'affairs with famous people. They don't interest me. A butcher's boy who delivers the meat or a soldier encountered by chance while on tour have more chance with me'.[27] Good-humoured and even-tempered, her everywoman image has brought her a popularity that has commercial value at the middle and lower levels of the market. Whereas Bellucci has endorsed luxury and beauty products including Cartier, Dolce & Gabbana's fragrance Sicily and Breil watches, Ferilli has advertised a wide variety of not very prestigious consumer products, including Ferrone clothing, Paul & Shark sailing wear and De Cecco pasta.

In interviews, the actress stresses the fact that she does her own shopping and cooking, that she rides a bicycle and that she is happy among people. She wears little make-up and

77 Roman actress Sabrina Ferilli
has built an image based on
warmth and familiarity. 'Me, a
lover? Not likely, I'd make an
excellent wife' reads the title.

rarely styles her hair. Like Anna Magnani in the past, Ferilli thrives on interaction with
the public, who love her for her apparent spontaneity. Physically, she is dark and florid,
a brunette with deep golden skin, dark eyes and a very large bust which, she is well aware,
is her main feature.[28] 'Her secret?' asked one journalist rhetorically. 'It is the least secret
thing about her: her bosom, abundant and soft, exuberant but not vulgar, maternal yet
somehow mischievous'.[29] 'She is beautiful and, as one used to say, "natural", not only in
her appearance, with a bounty that is documented by our history of art, but also in her
language and habits', remarked the veteran journalist Enzo Biagi; 'her bosom is among
the largest of this Republic, founded on labour, but also . . . on tits'.[30]

'Sensuality is not something that can be concocted in a laboratory; either you have it
or you don't', Ferilli has declared.[31] Because of her natural manner, and radiant and
relaxed outlook, she was the opposite of the stereotype of the manufactured sex symbol.
'People like me because I don't do anything to seduce men. I court them in a reassuring,
friendly, almost adolescent way.'[32] Her status as an object of desire was confirmed when
one magazine conducted a poll to find out which man and woman were most likely to
induce Italians to betray their partner. In the female category, Ferilli came out first, with
23 per cent of votes. The runner-up won only 7 per cent.[33] However, Ferilli was swift to

neutralise any suggestion that she might be a home-wrecker, by affirming that she was more likely to be an ideal wife than a lover.

Although some elements of Ferilli's public persona are real, such as her support for the Roma football team and her much-publicised left-wing sympathies, her career has been marked by a calculated strategy to widen her fan base. Decisions that, at first glance, appear casual or surprising are strictly related to this objective. One of these was her acceptance of an invitation to co-present the annual San Remo song festival on prime-time television directly after shooting a film with the off-beat director Ferreri. Her decision to pose naked for the 2000 calendar of the magazine *Max* was another. Ferilli was known to have refused such offers before 1999.[34] *Max* paid her a reported Lit. 800,000 ($60,000) after its opinion polls showed that she was the woman whose image Italians of all ages and classes most wanted to accompany them through the year.[35] Her reason for agreeing to do this, she claimed, was twofold. She wanted to expand her appeal to youth and also to reach a wider male audience. Her roles as modest, ordinary women won her the sympathy of women, while calendar work was 'a means to make contact with another section of the public that want to see me like that'. 'It is very important for someone who works in my field', she reasoned.[36] The calendar, a masterpiece of erotic construction that demanded the contribution of no fewer than four photographers, demonstrated the power of the male gaze by turning the actress into an object to be surveyed and possessed. It was the bestseller of the year. It not only displayed her generous curves more fully than ever before, it also situated her firmly in the tradition of the warm and available Italian beauty.

Ferilli tantalised her fans in 2001 with a rash promise that she would perform a public striptease in the event that her beloved Roma football team should win the Italian league title. The promise itself provided confirmation of the role of football in the perpetuation of a male-dominated culture. 'Football is an ideal game for a family-centred nation', Paul Ginsborg observes, 'because it links almost effortlessly childhood and adulthood, both within the same person . . . and within the family'.[37] It confirms an established gender order because 'while women are not totally absent from it . . . they nearly always appear, at least in Italy, in subordinate roles: at the ground as the girlfriend or sister *of* someone, or else simply dressing up in the team's colours in order to be noticed; at home, during the televised games, in support roles'.[38] To these roles, Ferilli added those of cheerleader and warrior's repose.

When Roma did indeed secure the title, she announced that she would fulfil her promise. The event at the Circus Maximus, at which an estimated one million supporters were present, was the subject of an extraordinary week-long media build-up. The climax transfixed the audience. To the accompaniment of dancers, noise and music, Ferilli slowly removed layers of clothing in the colours of the Italian flag. First she took off a white bath robe, next a red evening dress, and then a flimsy green garment. Finally, she revealed her curvaceous figure that, however, was still partially covered by a modesty-protecting flesh-coloured bikini. Roland Barthes is most unlikely to have had anything like this in mind when he wrote his famous essay on striptease, but he did remark that in France striptease became nationalised and desexualised through its indirect association with sport.[39] Ferilli cannot exactly be said to have regained 'a perfectly chaste state of the flesh' through her disrobing, but her strip was certainly a 'mystifying device' in which eroticism was 'absorbed in a reassuring ritual that negates the flesh as surely as the vaccine or the taboo circumscribe and control the illness or the crime'.[40]

While she is widely considered 'the natural heir to the Italian beauty incarnated for so long by Loren',[41] Ferilli acknowledges the influence of a wider group of actresses, including Anna Magnani, Giovanna Ralli and Eleonora Rossi Drago. Yet, in some respects, she resembles more closely another, less important actress of the 1950s, Silvana Pampanini. Corrado Augias suggested that Ferilli belonged to a current of carnal, joyous female beauty that went from Pampanini to Serena Grandi and which was associated in the popular mind with Fellini. The archetype of this model, he added, was that of the great Mediterranean mother.[42] Pampanini was the first of the shapely starlets of the post-war years, a cordial, cheerful actress who often played amoral women with a heart. While Loren won international fame and desperately wanted a stable family life, Pampanini was only ever a domestic success and she remained unmarried. In contrast to Loren and Bellucci, Ferilli has never manifested a desire to build an international career. Once asked if she was tempted by Hollywood, she replied: 'Let's not be foolish. I am a queen where I belong . . . I am a simple human being who needs simple things like contact with people

78 Sabrina Ferilli performing her striptease after A.C. Roma won the Italian football league in 2001.

in the street, the flattering comments of the market stallholder . . . '.[43] So strong is her association with her native Rome and so important is this context to the projection of the warm, sympathetic personality that is her trademark, that it is difficult to imagine her outside this frame of reference. To this extent, she is a star who is perfectly suited to the 'distinctive pattern of personal relationships and social networks' based on regular daily contacts that Ginsborg identifies as Italian.[44] While playing modern women, she appears to hanker for a traditional role. Although she did not marry until 2003 (and was separated in 2005) and has not experienced motherhood, she has often played the parts of mothers and is at ease doing so. For many Italian men, Ferilli is quite literally the woman of their dreams. For the psychologist Maria Rita Parsi, she is 'a new Mediterranean Venus in whom men can find the lost paradise. First of all, she has a maternal body and the welcoming bosom of a woman who is a friend, a soft reassuring presence'.[45]

Manuela Arcuri: the Child-Woman

With both Bellucci and Ferilli approaching the age of forty in the mid-2000s, the entertainment industry began seeking new women to groom to take their place as young bearers of Italian beauty. Of the various young women who were working at lower levels of the film and television industries, Manuela Arcuri stood out for her long experience playing small parts in film comedies and for her burgeoning erotic appeal. After a handful of strategic appearances, she was consecrated by the press and television as a personality possessed of a conventional sex appeal combined with youthful wholesomeness. By 2005, she had emerged as one of the few actors with sufficient appeal to the domestic audience to guarantee on her own the success of a television mini-series.

Arcuri was born in 1977 in Anagni, a small town of 20,000 people some forty miles from Rome. She subsequently lived in Latina, a town founded in 1932 following Fascism's bonification of the Pontine marshes. She made her film debut in 1995 in Leonardo Pieraccioni's light comedy *I laureati*, that starred the director himself and Cuccinotta. Subsequently, she had a small part as a teenage goth with one armpit shaved and one not in Carlo Verdone's successful multi-episode comedy *Viaggi di nozze* (Honeymooners). She then appeared in a long series of comedies in supporting roles. In Vincenzo Salemme's hit film *A ruota libera* (Freewheeling), she appeared in a cast headed by Ferilli. In all these films, she usually played the petulant but fundamentally sweet teenager. Fresh-faced and endowed with candid looks, she offered a minor distraction for young male spectators.

While developing her film career, Arcuri worked as a glamour model, posing for topless photographs and advertising material for sunglasses and underwear. Directors also began to present her as an object of male desire. The culmination of this process was *Bagnomaria*, an infantile seaside comedy starring and directed by the comic Giorgio Panariello. As the salesgirl, *la bombolonaia*, she was spied on by the lead male character in much the same way that Edwige Fenech or Carmen Russo had been keyhole candy in

79 Manuela Arcuri
endorsing Gorgonzola in
a press campaign.

the early 1980s. However, instead of condemning her to a career in B films, as would have been the case in the past, the success of this film led to her first major television role. This in turn would open up several new opportunities. The role was the title one in *Alla ricerca di Sheherezade* (Looking for Sheherezade), an Italian–Spanish co-production of Manuel Vasquez Montalban's crime drama featuring the detective Pepe Carvalho (Juanje Puigcorbé) and starring the showgirl Valeria Marini. Arcuri had a small but significant part as a sexy young temptress involved in a bribery scam. Extensive nude scenes, including a lingering one that featured her swimming and then sunbathing on a yacht while the title credits rolled, highlighted her long dark hair, prominent bust and long legs. The role led to two parts in Spanish films (the costume drama *Juana la loca* in 2001 and the thriller *Cosa de brujos* in 2003), more television work and a calendar in 2001 for the newsmagazine *Panorama*.

The calendar was important in situating Arcuri in relation to the national canon of beauty. Photographed by the experienced Conrad Godly, the shoot placed a splendid and even more abundant than usual Arcuri in a variety of evocative Sicilian landscapes. The photographs were highly erotic in a way that played to the Italian imagination. The golden glow of the warm sun, the burned sandstone of the buildings and the magnificent deep blue of the sky and the sea all served to highlight the iconic status of the model. In one pose, she was featured sitting naked on some outside steps, her long dark hair cascading in an unkempt manner over her shoulders, while she held a basket of fruit in her lap. In another, she was seated topless on an ass beneath a natural pergola. In yet another, her body was loosely draped in a red lace shawl while dark gloves and an expression of pain introduced a passing suggestion of widowhood. By means of this staging, Arcuri was turned into a magnificent animal, a creature of passion and instinct, a figure unencumbered by modern worries or constraints whose only aim was to run wild and whose sole needs were primary.

The calendar marked the culmination of Arcuri's career as a glamour model and the beginning of a fortunate series of television roles that would see her transgressive charge diffused in contexts that were heavily conditioned by backward-looking Italian stereotypes. She starred in two editions of the RAI series *Carabinieri*, in which she played Paola Vitali, the officer whose professional and private life offered most plot material. In 2002, she co-presented the San Remo song festival. Subsequently, she took the title role in RAI-1's *Regina dei fiori* (Queen of flowers), in which she was once more a young woman of lower-class extraction with a heart of gold. In a story-line that owed something to *Cinderella* and a little to *Pretty Woman*, she played the part of Regina, a young flower-seller with a stall in Rome's Campo dei fiori. In her spare time, she helps an old and sickly noblewoman take care of a small group of orphans in her large apartment. Among other voluntary helpers is a retired Carabinieri marshal. During a trip to Venice with the Countess, Regina meets and falls in love with a young businessman, Federico, who takes her for a rich girl. When the countess dies and leaves her fortune to Regina, so that she can carry on caring for the orphans, Federico is revealed to be her frustrated descendant. The subsequent legal battle between Federico and Regina provides the terrain on which their love once more blossoms.

Co-scripted by Patrizia Carrano, a veteran feminist journalist and author of a biography of Anna Magnani,[46] the film was clearly intended to consecrate Arcuri as a national icon, the natural successor not only to Ferilli but also to a long series of earlier actresses. Critics saw traces in her role of Loren's pizza girl in *L'Oro di Napoli* and of Magnani's role as a crusading housewife in *L'Onorevole Angelina* (The honourable Angelina). Arcuri's physical presence was crucial to the drama. With her long hair, grey-green eyes, generous bust and adolescent enthusiasm, she provided an anchor to a story of disarming simplicity. Within a choral context populated by stock characters, she took her place as the beautiful *popolana*, just like the actresses whose beauty was highlighted by the titles of the films of the 1950s. The absence of any significant reference to real-life Italy also recalled some of the movies of that decade. The weakly sketched environments and the lack of any proper characterisation suggested that, far from being one of the thought-provoking dramas to which Ferilli referred, this was a demonstration 'that Italian television was profoundly *lazy*'. Its controllers did not encourage analysis of what was happening in society; instead Ginsborg argues that 'radical transitions were coaxed into traditional and reassuring cultural schemes'.[47]

Arcuri cultivated an off-screen image that confirmed her status as a popular national beauty. She was close to her mother and loyal to her family. As with some other television sex symbols, she was popular with children. She cheerfully opened fashion shops in Rome's Via Condotti and fragrance stores in less visible locations. She also fronted a national campaign for Gorgonzola cheese. Although Giorgio Armani made appreciative comments about her, she preferred to model the clothes of a lesser-known designer, Lorenzo Riva, who was a personal friend. Her private life became an object of intense interest as her fame increased. With the candour of a teenager, she happily confessed to a healthy appetite for sex. After having been romantically linked to two businessmen of Middle Eastern origin, she was associated with a series of footballers, including Francesco Totti of Roma and A. C. Milan's Francesco Coco. In this way she both evoked previous affairs and marriages between showgirls and sportsmen that were commonplace in Italy in the post-war decades and provided further confirmation of the established gender order.

Arcuri may be the most recent *bella italiana*, but there is little that is contemporary about her save for the emphasis in her career on youth. She has the look of a teenager, even in her late twenties, and is one of few Italian beauties to have made this a trademark. This owes much to her genuineness and transparency. While there are aspects of Ferilli and of Ornella Muti in her professional persona, she also evokes the atmospheres of the *Poveri ma belli* series of the late 1950s. In those films, that were heavily conditioned by the conformism of the society of the period, Marisa Allasio played the angel with the body of a temptress. Working-class men fell over themselves to win her favours, but despite their efforts, at the end of every day Marisa always went home to her mother. With the due adjustments of mores and period, Arcuri is a star who, while by no means disassociated from sex, is predominantly conservative in her meaning.

The women who are connected by commentators, directors and writers to the tradition of feminine beauty can be compared to their predecessors but they operate in a fundamentally different context. Their stardom is not simple but complex and multi-faceted. Stars today are modern multi-media celebrities whose fame is constructed through the deployment of a conscious media strategy. Within the range of available media, film still occupies a special place and has a unique capacity to render actors iconic and endow them with an aura. But television has a more ready capacity to place them at the centre of the general culture. If contemporary female stars are continuously compared to their predecessors, women who impressed themselves indelibly on the national and international consciousness, it is because memory and tradition provide a paradigm that is infused with ideas about national identity. It is also because Italian society has been permeated less at all levels by feminism than other western societies.[48] This means that women who are not themselves mothers are pressed into playing maternal roles, that the language employed to describe women in the public domain has evolved relatively little and that, for good or ill, female beauty continues to occupy a central place in the national culture.

CONCLUSION

One of the most striking features of Italian feminine beauty is continuity or, more accurately, the semblance of continuity. A crucial part of the appeal of this cultural configuration lies in the fact that the beautiful Italian woman is considered to be timeless, a figure who bears some of the hallmarks of the 'eternal feminine'. From the time of the Grand Tour, northern Europeans looked to the peninsula and its women, hoping to find there a sense of the wholeness that they were convinced had disappeared from their own countries. Italy was a country in which ruins and archaeological sites testified to the existence of ancient civilisations and Italians as a people bore the imprint of this extraordinary heritage. They were the contemporary survivors of much older forms of humanity and their beauty and bearing apparently testified to this. Visitors found in Sicilian women traces of the Greek heritage of the island, while the inhabitants of the Roman countryside were seen as being directly descended from the ancient Latin people. Italians in these and other areas were regarded as being at one with nature and somehow rooted to their physical context. The sky, the sea and the land were their natural environment; their dark complexions signalled that they were a people whose proper dimension was out of doors. Italian women were predominantly seen to have a beauty that was dark and fascinating, although some were fair-haired. Typically, they had black flashing eyes, thick hair, full lips, curvaceous figures and a natural grace.

This sort of image was one that provided foreign males with the pleasure of difference. Compared to the refined and artificial Frenchwoman, the remote and composed English rose and, later, the sporty and emancipated American, the vital and untamed Italian woman offered a promise of warmth and passion, a sense of full acceptance of her biological destiny, a strong link to place and a comforting refusal to encroach upon the prerogatives of men. Similar sentiments shaped the manner in which male Italians looked at the women of Italy in the period from the late nineteenth century. As the country experienced the impact of modernity, intellectuals and artists grasped at traditional ideals of the feminine to resist some features of the modern and establish certain conventional female attributes as core aspects of identity. Part of this project involved resisting the demands of women for equality of treatment and citizenship. By rejecting foreign models of modernity in favour of a national model that was slower, less disruptive and always combined with strong elements of tradition, conservatives attempted to situate female emancipation outside the nation.

Still today, Italian femininity, in so far as it is articulated as a national typology, is often counterposed to contemporary visions of beauty that emanate from abroad. While millions of Italian women have embraced lifestyles and roles that are in every way equivalent to those of women in other European countries, the conventional image of the Italian woman as a beautiful, dark-haired, olive-skinned force of nature persists, albeit in a much-evolved form. An ideal of naturalness is a key value. The ideal Italian beauty does not diet to the point of emaciation, pursue physical fitness as a goal in itself or engage in plastic surgery. She is authentic and comfortable with herself. At a time of increasing globalisation and narrowing of the beauty canons which are presented in the mass media, the Italian beauty's enjoyment of her food and of the pleasures of life provides a humane counterpoint to dominant models. It offers a vision of sex appeal not as a manufactured construct but as a quality that is related to physical being, a particular pattern of gender relations and a relaxed lifestyle.

A number of factors bear on the conceptualisation and appreciation of Italian female beauty. These include the remote background influence of pagan mother cults in the south; the secularisation of artistic and intellectual discussions of beauty, so that they centred on appearance, rather than on the soul; the production of the country's artists, writers, photographers and film-makers; the foreign view of Italy as a feminine land of art and imagination; and national pride and patriotism. A diffuse sense of the beauty of the physical strongly conditions the way ideals of femininity have been formed and subjected to collective discussion and evaluation. Guglielmo Ferrero emphasised this aspect in his reflections on national specificities in masculine culture. For the southern European male, beauty was a quality to be appreciated through sight, smell and touch. It was not filtered through abstract ideas or sensations and nor was it the result of a process of idealisation.[1] This particular approach persists even in the present. Physical qualities are prized in the dominant culture and are culturally acknowledged. In this sense, the impact of the otherwise strong influence of Catholic culture in Italy encountered a limit. Catholicism reinforced the centrality of motherhood and the notion of a protective female function, while systematically downgrading female sexuality. However, the Catholic negation of the flesh, while it was very influential in the nineteenth century and for several decades of the twentieth, never suppressed or eliminated this substratum of popular culture. Nevertheless, Catholic efforts at repression shaped ideas of beauty and resulted in its being linked to approved female roles.

There is a political history of feminine beauty, which has been highlighted in this book. It is by no means a straightforward one, since beauty has been harnessed and employed by a wide range of forces, some of which have used it decoratively or opportunistically, while others have regarded a particular model of beauty as a visualisation of a wide-ranging programme of gender reform. In the political context of nineteenth-century Italy, the secular image of the beautiful young woman of the people became identified with the left. It was taken up as a symbol by nationalists and explicitly embraced by Garibaldi as a metaphor of the qualities and potential of the Italian people. The beauty was the embodiment of the true, deep Italy, a popular Italy that was to be drawn into the life of the nation by a revolution leading to the foundation of a democratic republic. The fact that unification did not occur in this way meant that she became the symbol of a nation still to be made and a representational trope that could never be completely annexed by power. Even though the political right also later embraced dark Italian beauty as a symbol of Latin supremacy, this earlier association with democracy was never cancelled.

The allegorical use of the female image was rooted in an age in which women were not drawn fully into the political life of the nation. The promise of collective affirmation and emancipation it offered therefore could have come to an end in 1946, when women acquired the vote and entered public life. However, the concept of the *bella italiana* persisted, on account of the many facets of Italian culture that informed the idea and that had come to bear on it. As the case of the French Marianne shows, it is possible for allegorical female figures to preserve a role even in a context of female citizenship. Marianne, for example, evolved into a universal symbol of a happy and dynamic France.[2] In the period after Fascism, when Italy finally did become a democratic republic, feminine images were useful in re-fashioning collective symbols and values. Film actresses became one of the main bearers of national unity and identity in a way that did not occur to the same extent in any other European country. They also became ciphers of modernisation and consumption, reconciling change on the cultural plane with tradition. This was something that triggered political and cultural disputes, because both the Communist left and the Catholics were unhappy about the growing role of the film industry in determining the way in which female beauty was projected as a badge of national identity. However, while the Catholics remained diffident, the left came to accept the women of post-war cinema. To have rejected them would have been as unthinkable as opposing motherhood or Garibaldi.

Up until the 1940s, it was commonplace for the beauty of women to be evaluated in relation to the heritage of Renaissance art. The nobility and beauty of Queen Margherita, for example, was always referred to in these terms, but so too were the looks of the first Miss Italia, Rosanna Martini. From that time, pictorial references became markedly less frequent and instead, cinema became the principal vehicle for the formation and perpetuation of a national ideal of feminine beauty. This was mediated by the press, which had always been a vital vehicle of debate and comparison. The rise of cinema was appropriate to the mass age when the vast majority of the peninsula's inhabitants finally acquired a sense of collective belonging. Their involvement was not with the nation in any conventional patriotic sense and so a symbol like the *bella italiana*, that had always been more an image of the people than of the state, could easily find a contemporary application.

Historically, the capital has been the most influential place in Italy, in terms of the production of both ideals and examples of Italian womanhood. While Naples and Sicily also have special claims to make in that regard, the capital, and its surrounding country-side, have either given rise to, or been particularly associated with, emblematic females. It is the working class and popular districts, such as Trastevere, rather than the aristo-cratic and bourgeois districts of the Eternal City, which have had special resonance. It was in Trastevere in 1875, that the most significant representative of Italian female beauty was born. Today, Lina Cavalieri is not widely remembered either in her homeland or abroad. Yet, of all the women who have been linked to the idea of Italian beauty, she was without doubt the most influential. A woman of medium height and slender build, she was seen in her time as a great beauty in the classic mould.[3] One of the first multi-media celebrities of the modern age, who was in succession identified with the demi-monde, European aristocracy, the opera world, cinema and the beauty industry, she was a woman of humble social extraction who had a noble bearing and unusual grace. She was the first figure in unified Italy to bring together the regal and spiritual ideal of beauty that was sustained by the pictorial heritage and the popular dark idea of beauty as the physical expression of the Italian people. Cavalieri was also the first Italian woman of the modern era to give rise at home and abroad to elaborate discussions of beauty that mirrored the emergence on the international scene of the nation.

Because there are few examples of Cavalieri's beauty that remain in current circula-tion, or which triumph over the limitations of the photographic culture of her day, it is rare, to say the least, to find her name employed among the comparisons and cultural references that are habitually used to situate contemporary women in relation to a national pantheon of beauty. Yet, in Monica Bellucci, it is possible to identify the same 'Italian aura of sad perfection . . . dominated by large eyes, compassionate and sombre, set beneath eyebrows raised not in question but in inner sorrow' that Cecil Beaton saw in Cavalieri.[4] The two women also have in common an 'equally sombre but sensuous mouth'. While the joyous exuberance of the unpolished woman of the people is perhaps the best-known Italian female attitude, melancholy is no less bound up with the female imagery of the nation. From Francesco Hayez's sad, bare-breasted 'Italy in 1848', there has been a sad, regretful strain to Italian beauty that is a reflection, not of the fundamental qualities of the Italian people, but of the inadequacies and failures of the country's leaders.

Cinema produced many iconic women whose attitude was more positive and exuberant. Italian cinema of the 1950s and 1960s produced an extraordinary quantity of actresses, almost all of them women of humble backgrounds who, in the numerous post-neo-realist films of the period, projected an image of the country that was vital, aspira-tional and cordial. In the 1950s, Gina Lollobrigida was acknowledged as the most valid example of feminine beauty. However, by far the most influential screen actress over time has been Sophia Loren, who continues to this day to shape national and international perceptions of the Italian woman.[5] Loren was not, at the start of her career, considered to be a typical Italian beauty. A series of films produced by Carlo Ponti and directed by De Sica turned her into the contemporary representative of the woman of Naples, one of the most enduring and richly significant locations in the peninsula. Her international career, her growing success in the early 1960s as a dramatic and comic actress, and her early casting in maternal roles all aided her emergence as a national icon. That she is still, some 56 years and 90 films after her debut, a paradigm for younger actresses, and an unavoidable point of comparison in all discussions of Italian beauty, is a testimony to the unique resonance she has had. Indeed, it may be said that Italy's deep-seated identification with the feminine has been underscored by the international profile of this actress. Towards the end of the first decade of the twenty-first century, she is still regarded as one of the world's most beautiful women. Because the Bay of Naples is the unrivalled location of an archaic, archetypal femininity, Loren knows that an identification with her home region is vital to her identity. She carries within her celebrity persona a post-card of Naples. In every interview she refers to her humble origins as an illegitimate child in Pozzuoli. She is also one of the chief champions of beauty as a natural rather than a man-made quality. In a beauty guide she authored in 1984, she claimed that beauty depended not on youth, physical perfection or techniques, but charm, warmth, wisdom, intelligence and imagination.[6]

Reference has been repeatedly made to male discourses in the course of this book because it has been principally through the writings and speeches, as well as the paintings, films and photography of men, that the culture of Italian beauty has been formed and perpetuated. In recent decades especially, women journalists have taken part in these discourses and in some respect have made them their own. Because beauty is widely appreciated, the hidden gendered mechanisms of selection are rarely exposed. Yet particular women have often been drawn into the system of representations because they stimulated men's dreams and fantasies. The emphasis on a type of femininity that is conventional and apparently un-modern is a demonstration of how deeply entrenched male dominance is. Although Italy ceased in the second half of the twentieth century to be a land of backwardness and underdevelopment, the idea of the emblematic female changed surprisingly little. This is so, even though there have been numerous challenges to, breaks with, and departures from tradition.

In the past, the emphasis on beauty was accompanied by a concern to exclude ideas of female emancipation from the national space. Today, the cultural emphasis on female beauty occurs in a context in which women do not have the same influence in the public sphere, the media or the cultural realm that they do in most other advanced industrial countries. While it is undoubtedly true that the women's movement was a crucial agent in modernising Italian society in line with the standards of a modern industrial society,[7] its influence was incomplete. In 2001, the female presence in the Italian Parliament amounted to 8.9 per cent, compared to a world average of 13.7 per cent. While only 10.9 per cent of the French Parliament was composed of women, the percentage for Spain was 28.3 per cent, for Germany and Holland 30 per cent and for Sweden and Denmark 42.7 per cent and 37.4 per cent respectively.[8] The distorted representation of women in the media is merely one aspect, albeit the most evident, of a profound sexual asymmetry in Italian society. There have been numerous public interventions and commissions appointed to address this issue, many of which have done valuable work, but the persistence of male-dominated structures of power and cultural conceptions of separate male and female spheres have seriously limited their impact. In the media itself, the female presence has increased notably in the last 25 years. Since the 1980s, female anchors of news programmes have become commonplace and women journalists have increasingly tackled political and other hard news. In 1978, there were just 721 women journalists in Italy, around 10 per cent of the total. By 2002, there were 5,386 or around 35 per cent of the total.[9] This demonstrates that the female presence goes well beyond conventional decorative or performative functions. Yet this progress is still well short of equality, especially if the minimal presence of women in managerial and leadership positions is taken into account. Moreover, the increasing presence of women is concentrated in visibility rather than power.[10] In a patriarchal system, moreover, visibility automatically privileges youth and beauty, operating a further selection amongst the ranks of women. The reasons for this situation are complex and include the primacy of the political in the media and the particular structure of the journalistic profession in Italy.

80 Miss Italia 2005, Edelfa Chiara Masciotta, faces photographers after her victory.

Visibility is a complex phenomenon which confirms existing structures of power through a process of visual annexation. In the web of representation and consumption, relations of power are implicated that are always gendered. However, in the form of modern celebrity, visibility is an attribute that is widely sought and much envied. The film or television star is the bearer of collective dreams also because many believe that, with luck, they could one day occupy the position that she does. Visual images of beauty invariably blend ordinariness with the exceptional. The 2006 Miss Italia calendar, published by the event's organisers, features photographs of the then holder of the title, Edelfa Chiara Masciotta, going about her everyday life. She is shown studying, sleeping, visiting a museum, applying her make-up, taking a drink in a café and so on. Three images, however, relate to her victory in the 2005 competition. One depicts the canonical moment she was crowned by the American actor Bruce Willis. She stands, as convention demands, in a bikini, barely holding back the tears, while the outgoing holder of the title stands in an evening gown to her right and the organisers, Enzo and Patrizia Mirigliani, are positioned to her left. A further image illustrates what the fairytale moment of the coronation obscures. It pictures the newly-crowned winner from behind as, still in her bikini and crown, she faces an entirely male pack of photographers. Such an image appeals to the vanity that is widespread among so many contestants, while simultaneously revealing how the fragile body of the year's chosen emblem of Italian beauty is turned into an object to be posed, snapped, packaged and sold along commercial lines.

81 Edelfa Chiara Masciotta, Miss Italia 2005, surrounded by the inhabitants of an unidentified village, to which the viewer is supposed to assume she belongs.

The third photograph shows Masciotta, who was born and lives in Turin, in the main piazza of an unidentified village. She is standing in the foreground, a smile on her face and dressed inconspicuously, save for the sash that proclaims her title. Behind her is gathered a large crowd of curious and uniformly white older men and women, mothers and children, young girls, single men and Carabinieri officers. The image presents Miss Italia as an ordinary girl from the provinces who has been briefly raised up from the anonymity of a normal life but who will soon return to that life, almost as if her participation in the contest had been a dream. It encapsulates the core ideological presupposition not only of the pageant but of Italian beauty in general, namely that it is accessible and familiar. The beauty is not an aloof diva but 'one of us', someone we could meet in the street or talk to in a bar. She is a young woman of domestic inclinations who is embedded in a network of interpersonal relations centred on the family. Even the most famous of actresses cultivate this perception. In this way, beauty is linked to place, community and identity. It appears to be an entirely natural phenomenon. However, in the complex and rapidly changing Italy of the early twentieth century, no less and perhaps even more than in the past, this is a fiction. It implies that the community is compact, ethnically homogeneous and comfortable in its conformity to tradition. In this fashion, beauty bolsters an image of the country which is long-established. However, it is ultimately a consolatory image that provides pleasure and reassurance by excluding dissonant elements from the picture. The radiant young woman who in theory should stand for the future in fact is more representative of the past.

NOTES

Introduction

1. See *Telegraph magazine*, supplement to the *Daily Telegraph*, 18 January 2003.
2. As such, she features on the cover of G. Malossi (ed.), *Volare: the Icon of Italy in Global Pop Culture* (New York: Monacelli Press, 1999).
3. *Il Messaggero*, 3 September 1996, p. 35.
4. G. Melli, 'Che complesso avere il seno più sognato d'Italia', *Oggi*, 22 January 1997.
5. M. L. Giovagnini and G. Melli, 'Eminenza stia tranquillo, saremo sexy come dice lei', *Oggi*, 16 April 1997.
6. M. Bellucci, 'È il giardino del mondo', *Riflessi*, March 1998, p. 17.
7. The series is published by Il Mulino. The opening volume was E. Galli della Loggia, *L'identità italiana* (Bologna: Il Mulino, 1998). By the end of 2005, there were forty-four books in the series. Mario Isnenghi adapted the idea of the *lieu de mémoire* in *Luoghi di memoria*, 3 volumes (Rome-Bari: Laterza, 1996–7). Another book on Italian identity containing no references to beauty is S. Bertelli (ed.), *La chioma della vittoria: scritti sull'identità degli italiani dall'Unità alla seconda repubblica* (Florence: Ponte alle Grazie, 1997).
8. The only exception is the important chapter dedicated to 'La bella italiana' in M. De Giorgio, *Le italiane dall'Unità a oggi* (Rome: Laterza, 1992). I raised the issue of beauty in 'Il Bel paese: art, beauty and the cult of appearances' in G. Bedani and B. Haddock (eds), *The Politics of Italian National Identity* (Cardiff: University of Wales Press, 2002) and 'Feminine Beauty, National Identity and Political Conflict in Postwar Italy, 1945–54', *Contemporary European History*, 8:3, 1999, pp. 359–78.
9. On male beauty, see G. Malossi (ed.), *Latin Lover: the Passionate South* (Milan: Charta, 1996).
10. See the extended treatments of the issue in J. Landes, *Visualizing the Nation: Gender, Representation and Revolution in Eighteenth-Century France* (Ithaca, NY: Cornell University Press, 2001) and A. M. Banti, *L'onore della nazione: identità sessuali e violenze nel nazionalismo europeo dal XVIII secolo alla Grande Guerra* (Turin: Einaudi, 2005).
11. R. Romano, *Paese Italia: venti secoli di identità* (Rome: Donzelli, 1994), p. 13.
12. G. Ferrero, *L'Europa giovane* (Milan: Treves, 1897), p. 141.
13. Ibid., p. 141.
14. Ibid., p. 129.
15. M. Yalom, *A History of the Breast* (London: Pandora, 1998), p. 3.
16. For an extended treatment of this theme, see M. d'Amelia, *La mamma* (Bologna: Il Mulino, 2005).
17. D. Gros, *Il seno svelato* (Milan: SugarCo., 1988), p. 17.
18. *Marianne au combat: l'imagerie et la symbolique républicaines de 1789 à 1880* (Paris: Flammarion, 1979; trans. *Marianne into battle: Republican Imagery and Symbolism in France 1789–1880*, Cambridge: Cambridge University Press, 1981); *Marianne au pouvoir: l'imagerie et la symbolique républicaines de 1880 à 1914* (Paris: Flammarion, 1989); *Les métamorphoses de Marianne: l'imagerie et la symbolique républicaine de 1914 à nos jours* (Paris: Flammarion, 2001).

19. See, for the two most widely-cited views, S. de Beauvoir, *The Second Sex* (London: Vintage, 1997; first published 1949), p. 175 and L. Mulvey, 'Visual Pleasure and Narrative Cinema', *Screen* 16, no. 3 (1975), p. 11. Also important is John Berger's small but influential book, *Ways of Seeing* (Harmondsworth: Penguin, 1989), which highlights on p. 47 the contrast between masculine 'doing' and feminine 'being'.
20. On this double-edged aspect of female representations in the nation, see, with reference to France, Landes, *Visualizing the Nation*, p. 19.

Chapter One

1. R. Graves, *The White Goddess* (New York: Random House, 1948).
2. P. Tinagli, *Women in Italian Renaissance Art*, pp. 85–6. See also M. Rogers, 'The decorum of women's beauty: Trissino, Firenzuola, Luigini and the representation of women in sixteenth century painting', *Renaissance Studies*, 2:1, 1998, pp. 47–88.
3. F. Petrarca, 'Ad Italiam' in *Epistolae Metricae*, translation from G. Contini, *Letteratura italiana delle origini* (Florence: Sansoni, 1994).
4. J. Hale, *England and the Italian Renaissance* (London: Fontana, 1996; first published 1954), p. 16. See also A. Brilli, *Un paese di romantici briganti* (Bologna: Il Mulino, 2003).
5. J. Black, *Italy and the Grand Tour* (New Haven and London: Yale University Press, 2003), p. 37.
6. Ibid., pp. 125–6.
7. Ibid., pp. 119, 126–7.
8. C. P. Brand, *Italy and the English Romantics* (Cambridge: Cambridge University Press, 1957), p. 20.
9. See J. C. Herold, *Mistress to An Age: A Life of Madame De Staël* (London: Hamish Hamilton, 1958), pp. 299–310.
10. Black, *Italy and the Grand Tour*, pp. 223–4.
11. Mme De Staël, *Corinne, or Italy* (Oxford: Oxford University Press, 1988; first published 1807), pp. 27 and 93. For Nelson Moe, *Corinne* 'constitutes the first full-blown expression of this dual interest in the southern landscape and southern people . . . in the early Romantic period'. Moe, *The View from Vesuvius: Italian Culture and the Southern question* (Berkeley: University of California Press, 2002), p. 67
12. De Staël, *Corinne*, p. 23.
13. Ibid., p. 23.
14. M. Gutwirth, *Madame de Staël, Novelist* (Urbana: University of Illinois Press, 1978), p. 212.
15. See B. Anderson, *Imagined Communities: reflections on the origin and spread of nationalism* (London: Verso, 1983).
16. See, for example, I. Blom, K. Hagemann and C. Hall (eds), *Gendered Nations: Nationalisms and the Long Nineteenth Century* (Oxford: Berg, 2000), J. B. Landes, *Visualizing the Nation: Gender, Representation, and Revolution in Eighteenth-Century France* (Ithaca: Cornell University Press, 2001) and A. M. Banti, *L'onore della nazione: identità sessuali e violenze nel nazionalismo europeo dal XVIII secolo alla Grande Guerra* (Turin: Einaudi, 2005).
17. S. Wenke, 'Gendered Representations of the Nation's Past and Future', in Blom, Hagemann and Hall, *Gendered Nations*, p. 67.
18. Landes, *Visualizing the Nation*, pp. 5–6.
19. R. Sennett, *Flesh and Stone: The Body and the City in Western Civilisation* (London: Faber and Faber, 1994), p. 287.
20. Ibid., pp. 288–9.
21. M. Warner, *Monuments and Maidens: the Allegory of the Female Form* (London: Weidenfeld and Nicolson, 1985), p. 289.
22. J. J. Preston, 'Conclusion' to Preston (ed.), *Mother Worship: Themes and Variations* (Chapel Hill: University of North Carolina Press, 1982), p. 335.
23. The permutations of representation and their meanings are explored in detail in Banti, *L'onore della nazione*, chapter one. Allegorical females were depicted in several ways. If they had one or more bare breasts and bore arms, their source was Minerva. If they had one or more bare breasts and bore no arms then they communicated peace and fertility. They could be exhorting and on their feet, or seated and composed. The most common image was of the nation as a mother nourishing her children with the political values of freedom and equality. Various attributes were sometimes added, including a cornucopia, a turreted crown, a flag and a mace. Radicals embraced more readily images like that of Delacroix's revolutionary Liberty, in his 1830 painting 'Liberty leading the people', in which the women were solid and realistic. By contrast, conservatives preferred more purely classical imagery in which the figures were more abstract and idealised.
24. Herold, *Mistress to An Age*, p. 306.

25. De Staël, *Corinne*, p. 27.
26. Ibid., p. 27.
27. Ibid., p. 91.
28. This observation is taken from H. T. Finck, *Romantic Love and Personal Beauty* (London: Macmillan, 1887, 2 vols), vol. 2, p. 402.
29. Gutwirth, *Madame de Staël*, pp. 272–8.
30. The unhappy love affair between the poetess and Oswald is based on de Staël's experiences with Dom Pedro de Souza e Holstein, a Portuguese nobleman with whom she fell in love while in Italy.
31. On this theme, R. Casillo's *The Empire of Stereotypes: Germaine de Staël and the Idea of Italy* (London: Palgrave, 2006) was about to be published as the present book was going to press.
32. J. Buzard, *The Beaten Track: European Tourism, Literature, and the Ways to Culture, 1800–1918* (Oxford: Oxford University Press, 1993), p. 134.
33. Quoted in ibid., p. 134.
34. De Staël, *Corinne*, p. 102.
35. A. Chapman and J. Stabler, 'Introduction' in Chapman and Stabler (eds), *Unfolding the South: Nineteenth-Century British Women Writers and Artists and Italy* (Manchester: Manchester University Press, 2003), pp. 1–2.
36. See R. Cronin, '*Casa Guidi Windows*: Elizabeth Barrett Browning, Italy and the poetry of citizenship' in Chapman and Stabler, *Unfolding the South*.
37. Herold, *Mistress to An Age*, p. 301.
38. Moe, *The View From Vesuvius*, p. 67.
39. R. N. Coe, translator's preface to *Rome, Naples and Florence* (London: Calder, 1959; first published 1817), p. xx. See P. Marcenaro and P. Boragina, *Italie, il sogno di Stendhal* (Cinisello Balsamo: Silvana, 2000).
40. A. E. Greaves points out that Stendhal had read De Staël and took some of his cues from her. See *Stendhal's Italy: Themes of Political and Religious Satire* (Exeter: University of Exeter Press 1995), p. 7.
41. Stendhal, *Rome, Naples and Florence*, p. 41.
42. Ibid., pp. 42–3.
43. Ibid., pp. 370–1.
44. I. Calvino, Introduzione in Stendhal, *Dell'amore* (Milan: Rizzoli, 1996; first published 1822), pp. 17–18.
45. Ibid., p. 41.
46. Ibid., pp. 41–2.
47. Stendhal, *Dell'amore*, p. 55.
48. Ibid., p. 72.
49. Stendhal, *Rome, Naples and Florence*, pp. 108–9.
50. Coe, Introduction to ibid., p. xxi.
51. Stendhal, *The Charterhouse of Parma* (London: Zodiac, 1980; first published 1839), p. 5.
52. According to Indro Montanelli and Beniamino Placido, who cite approvingly a comment by Calvino, she was 'the only real Italian woman in the nineteenth-century novel', *Eppur si muove: cambiano gli italiani?* (Milan: Rizzoli, 1995), p. 87.
53. Stendhal, *The Charterhouse of Parma*, p. 94.
54. Ibid., p. 208.
55. Ibid., p. 227.
56. Ibid., p. 95.
57. Ibid., p. 227.
58. Ibid., p. 227.
59. Ibid., p. 229.
60. Ibid., p. 228.
61. For a presentation and discussion of these positions, see Gutwirth, *Madame de Staël*, pp. 287–92.
62. A. de Lamartine, *Souvenirs et portraits* (Paris: Hachette, 1871), p. 226. Quoted in ibid., p. 291.
63. Moe, *The View From Vesuvius*, p. 56.
64. A. de Lamartine, *Graziella* (Paris: Albin Michel, 1979; first published 1852), pp. 62–3.
65. See de Lamartine, *Mémoires inédits 1790–1915* (Paris: Hachette, 1881), pp. 180–219.
66. N. Penny, Introduction to Hale, *England and the Italian Renaissance*, p. ix.
67. Brilli, *Un paese di romantici briganti*, p. 24.
68. J. Dickie, 'Murder by Stereotype: Contessa Lara's "Un omicida" and the two faces of the imaginary South', *The Italianist*, 15 (1995), pp. 103–15, 103–4.
69. H. Bhabha, 'The Other Question: stereotype, discrimination and discourse of colonialism' in Bhabha, *The Location of Culture* (London: Routledge, 1994), p. 70.
70. See Banti, *L'onore della nazione*, chapter four.

71. V. R. Jones, *Le Dark Ladies Manzoniane* (Roma: Salerno, 1998), p. 90. See also S. B. Chandler, 'Manzoni's Originality in the Character of Lucia Mondella' in A. Testaferri (ed.), *Donna: Women in Italian Culture* (Toronto: Dovehouse editions, 1989).

72. For example, L. Parisi, *Manzoni e Bossuet* (Alessandria: Edizioni dell'Orso, 2003).

73. On the importance of virginity and purity in the nationalist discourse, see A. M. Banti, *La nazione del Risorgimento: parentela, santità e onore alle origini dell'Italia unita* (Turin: Einaudi, 2000), p. 131.

74. See A. Leati, *Alessandro Manzoni e le arti figurative* (Lecco: Bartolozzi, 1958), pp. 71–3.

75. Jones, *Le Dark Ladies Manzoniane*, p. 102.

76. Ibid., p. 103.

77. F. De Sanctis, *La letteratura italiana del secolo XIX*, vol.1 (Bari: Laterza, 1962; first published 1870–1), p. 69.

78. See G. Parisi, *Nella terra di Lucia* (Rome: Signorelli, 1964), pp. 23–4.

79. The close relationship between travellers' accounts of Italian vices and the perceptions of patriots has been illuminatingly highlighted by S. Patriarca in 'Indolence and Regeneration: Tropes and Tensions of Risorgimento Patriotism', *American Historical Review*, 110:2 (2005), p. 2 (downloaded version).

80. A. M. Banti and R. Bizzocchi, 'Introduzione' to Banti and Bizzocchi, *Immagini della nazione nell'Italia del Risorgimento* (Rome: Carocci, 2002), pp. 17–19. For a more detailed reflection see Banti, *La nazione del Risorgimento*, pp. 65–119, 162–9.

81. F. Mazzocca, 'L'iconografia della patria trà l'età delle riforme e l'Unità' in Banti and Bizzocchi, *Immagini della nazione*, pp. 100–1.

82. See I. Porciani, 'Stato e nazione: l'immagine debole dell'Italia' in S. Soldani and G. Turi (eds), *Fare gli italiani: scuola e cultura nell'Italia contemporanea*, vol.1 (Bologna: Il Mulino, 1993).

83. See Mazzocca, 'L'iconografia'.

84. Quoted in ibid., p. 100.

85. Quoted in ibid., p. 101.

86. Ibid., pp. 105–7.

87. On the issue of beauty, see Banti, *La nazione del Risorgimento*, p. 191; on the breast, M. Yalom, *A History of the Breast* (London: Pandora, 1998), p. 105. See also Blom, *Gendered Nations*.

88. Mazzocca, 'L'iconografia', p. 106.

89. Banti, *L'onore della nazione*, p. 271.

90. D. Beales and E. F. Biagini, *Il Risorgimento e l'unificazione dell'Italia* (Bologna: Il Mulino, 2005; revised edition first published 2002), pp. 187–90.

91. Ibid., pp. 189–90.

92. Ibid., chapter two.

93. See the section 'La costruzione pedagogica della nazione' in C. Collina and others (eds), *Bandiera dipinta: il tricolore nella pittura italiana 1797–1947* (Milan: Silvana, 2003), pp. 153–70.

94. G. Meredith, *Sandra Belloni* (London: Constable, 1996; first published 1864), p. 92.

95. G. Meredith, *Vittoria* (London: Constable, 1902; first published 1867), pp. 515–16.

96. E. and J. Goncourt, *L'Italie d'hier: notes de voyage 1855–1856* (Paris: Editions Complexe, 1991; first published 1894), pp. xxiii.

97. Ibid., p. 25.

98. Ibid., p. 196.

99. Théophile Gautier, *Italia* (Paris: Hachette, 1860), p. 180.

100. Ibid., p. 181.

101. Ibid., p. 181.

102. H. Taine, *Voyage en Italie*, Tome 2: *Florence et Venise* (Paris: Hachette, 1921; first published 1865), p. 42.

103. Ibid., p. 188.

104. Ibid., p. 187.

105. Ibid., p. 188.

106. Ibid., p. 19.

107. See, for example, the illustrations in A. Comandini, *L'Italia nei cento anni* (Milan: Vallardi, 1929), pp. 5 and 155.

108. L. Braudy, *The Frenzy of Renown: Fame and Its History* (New York: Oxford University Press, 1986), p. 453.

109. Ibid., p. 453.

110. M. Warner, *Monuments and Maidens* (London: Weidenfeld and Nicolson, 1985), p. 292.

111. M. De Giorgio, *Le italiane dall'Unità a oggi* (Rome-Bari: Laterza, 1993), p. 147.

112. G. Garibaldi, *Manlio: romanzo storico politico contemporaneo* (Savasola: International Institute of Garibaldian Studies, 1982).

113. G. Garibaldi, *Clelia ovvero il governo dei preti* (Milan: Societa editoriale Milanese, 1867), p. 340.

114. Ibid., pp. 69 and 142.

115. Ibid., pp. 5–7.
116. G. Garibaldi, *Cantoni il volontario* (Milan: Societa editoriale Milanese, 1870), p. 140.
117. Ibid., p. 25.
118. Ibid., p. 54.
119. Banti, *L'onore della nazione*, pp. 328–31. Banti in fact omits this passage from his discussion of the novel.
120. Ibid., p. 109.
121. Quoted in E. Gentile, *La grande Italia: ascesa e declino del mito della nazione nel ventesimo secolo* (Milan: Mondadori, 1997), pp. 43–4.
122. S. Sighele, *Il nazionalismo e i partiti politici* (Milan: Treves, 1911), p. 31.
123. S. Patriarca, 'Indolence and Regeneration' pp. 10–11.

Chapter Two

1. Quoted in A. Truffa and others, *La bella Rosin: regina senza corona* (Moncalvo: private publication, 1969), p. 27.
2. Quoted in C. Casalegno, *La regina Margherita* (Turin: Einaudi, 1956), p. 66.
3. Ibid., p. 67.
4. The episode is recounted in detail in R. Bracalini, *La regina Margherita* (Milan: Rizzoli, 1985; first published 1983), pp. 93–8. See also, C. Duggan, *Francesco Crispi: from nation to nationalism* (Oxford: Oxford University Press, 2002), p. 442.
5. Quoted in ibid., p. 91.
6. C. Brice, 'I viaggi della Regina Margherita', in D. Corsi (ed.), *Altrove: viaggi di donne dall'antichità al Novecento* (Rome: Viella, 1999).
7. A character in Matilde Serao's novel, *La conquista di Roma* (Naples: Perrella, 1910) affirms: 'this beautiful queen who greets, with such loveliness, friends and enemies, monarchists and republicans, is also a woman who feels, thinks, knows and listens; but this king, so heavily burdened, obliged dutifully to be continuously obedient, is not a man' (p. 133).
8. U. Alfassio Grimaldi, *Il 're buono'* (Milan: Feltrinelli, 1973), p. 60.
9. V. De Napoli, *L'eterna bellezza della Regina Margherita di Savoja* (Naples: Gargiulo, 1894), p. 52.
10. Ibid., p. 54.
11. Ibid., pp. 236 and 52–3.
12. Quoted in Bracalini, *La regina Margherita*, p. 86.
13. H. T. Finck. *Romantic Love and Personal Beauty* (London: Macmillan, 1887, 2 volumes), vol. 2, p. 376.
14. On the place of blondeness in Italian culture and society, see A. Niceforo, *La fisionomia nell'arte e nella scienza* (Florence: Sansoni, 1952), especially pp. 323–36.
15. D. Mack Smith, *Italy and Its Monarchy* (New Haven and London: Yale University Press, 1989), p. 72.
16. Bracalini, *La regina Margherita*, p. 292.
17. G. Gigliozzi, *Le regine d'Italia* (Rome: Newton Compton, 1997), p. 45.
18. The importance attached to this by Francesco Crispi, among others, is referred to in Duggan, *Francesco Crispi*, pp. 440–2.
19. Ibid., p. 27.
20. Quoted in Casalegno, *La regina Margherita*, pp. 67–8.
21. Grimaldi, *Il 're buono'*, pp. 50, 108.
22. Ibid., p. 170.
23. Cited in R. Drake, *Byzantium for Rome: The Politics of Nostalgia in Umbertian Italy, 1878–1900* (Chapel Hill: University of North Carolina Press, 1980), p. 19.
24. De Napoli, *L'eterna bellezza*, p. 21.
25. Ibid., p. 54.
26. See S. Gundle, 'Mapping the Origins of Glamour: Giovanni Boldini, Paris and the Belle Epoque', *Journal of European Studies*, XXIX (1999), pp. 269–95.
27. Quoted in Casalegno, *La regina Margherita*, p. 70.
28. Gigliozzi, *Le regine d'Italia*, pp. 55–6.
29. G. D'Annunzio, *Breviario mondano* (Milan: Mondadori, 1994), pp. 11–12. For an example of the fashionableness of blonde hair, see the novel by Salvatore Farina, *Capelli biondi* (Rome and Turin: Casa Editrice nazionale, 1876).
30. M. Praz, *La carne, la morte e il diavolo nella letteratura romantica* (Florence: Sansoni, 1986), chapter one.
31. G. Pieri, 'D'Annunzio and Alma-Tadema: Between Pre-Raphaelitism and Aestheticism', *The Modern Language Review*, 96:2 (2001), pp. 361–69, p. 365.

32. Pieri, 'D'Annunzio and Alma-Tadema', p. 366.
33. G. D'Annunzio, *Il Piacere* (Torriana: Orsa maggiore, 1995; first published 1889), p. 6.
34. Ibid., p. 105.
35. Ibid., p. 285.
36. Ibid., p. 299.
37. Ibid., p. 154.
38. Ibid., p. 263.
39. Ibid., p. 53.
40. G. D'Annunzio, *Il trionfo della morte* (Rome: Newton Compton, 1995; first published 1894), p. 18.
41. Ibid., p. 129.
42. Ibid., p. 131.
43. Ibid., p. 19.
44. Ibid., p. 205.
45. Ibid., p. 205.
46. Ibid., p. 209.
47. Ibid., p. 210.
48. Ibid., p. 210.
49. P. Mantegazza, *Fisiologia della donna* (Milan: Treves, 1893), p. 219.
50. D'Annunzio, *Il Piacere*, p. 102.
51. The influence of Crispi on D'Annunzio, albeit with reference to the latter's later oratory, is mentioned in Duggan, *Francesco Crispi*, p. 449. More generally on the desire to instil patriotism and reform the Italian character in the 1880s, see pp. 426–32.
52. D'Annunzio, *Il trionfo della morte*, p. 124.
53. Ibid., p. 172.
54. Ibid., p. 172.
55. Ibid., p. 211.
56. C. Salinari, *Miti e coscienza del decadentismo italiano* (Milan: Feltrinelli, 1959), pp. 30–2.
57. K. Theweleit, *Male Fantasies* vol. 2 (Cambridge: Polity Press, 1987; first published 1977), pp. 73–5.
58. G. D'Annunzio, *Le vergini delle rocce* (Rome: Newton Compton, 1995; first published 1895), pp. 306–9.
59. Salinari, *Miti e coscienza*, p. 38.
60. Ibid., pp. 38–9.
61. Bracalini, *La regina Margherita*, p. 23.
62. Mack Smith, *Italy and Its Monarchy*, p. 72.
63. Grimaldi, *Il 're buono'*, p. 357.
64. Duggan, *Francesco Crispi*, p. 715. Crispi was concerned about the effects of intermarriage within the Savoy family. Montenegro offered a good solution because a royal alliance would not give it any leverage over Italy.
65. Quoted in Gigliozzi, *Le regine*, p. 72.
66. Grimaldi, *Il 're buono'*, p. 370.
67. Neera, *Profili, impressioni, ricordi* (Milan: Cogliati, 1920), pp. 237–9.
68. W. Weaver, *Duse; a biography* (London: Thames and Hudson, 1984), pp. 128–30.
69. For an analysis of this relationship, see L. Re, 'D'Annunzio, Duse, Wilde, Bernhardt: Author and Actress between Decadentism and Modernity in L. Somigli and M. Moroni (eds), *Italian Modernism: Italian Culture between Decadentism and the Avant-Garde* (Toronto: University of Toronto Press, 2004), pp. 86–118.
70. J. Stokes, 'The Legend of Duse' in I. Fletcher (ed.), *Decadence and the 1890s* (London: Edward Arnold, 1979), p. 155.
71. Ibid., p. 156.
72. Neera, *Profili, impressioni, ricordi*, p. 239.
73. This discussion of Tommaseo is based on M. D'Amelia, *La mamma* (Bologna: Il Mulino, 2005), pp. 137–41.
74. See J. Dickie, *Darkest Italy: the nation and stereotypes of the Mezzogiorno 1860–1900* (Basingstoke: Macmillan, 1999).
75. The following are examples: 2 August 1885 'La pescatrice', 6 December 1885 'Chi mi ama mi segue' (the shepherdess), 29 November 1885 'La ciociara' (woman of Ciociaria), 10 January 1886 'La zingara' (the gypsy), 30 May 1886 'La fioraia'. On 5 September 1886 two engravings from the Brera Exhibition of 1886 by Angelo Dall'Oca-Bianca featuring young women were reproduced.
76. N. Moe, *The View From Vesuvius: Italian Culture and the Southern Question* (Berkeley: University of California Press, 2002), p. 206.
77. Ibid., p. 219.
78. Ibid., p. 220.

79. Ibid., p. 188.
80. Finck, *Romantic Love and Personal Beauty* (2 volumes), vol. 2, p. 381.
81. Ibid., p. 387.
82. Ibid., p. 402.
83. S. Olson, *John Singer Sargent: His Portrait* (London: Barrie and Jenkins, 1986), p. 69. Olson reports that Rosina Ferrara later married an American painter, George Randolph Barse and lived with him in Westchester, New York.
84. Quoted in S. Lanaro, *Nazione e lavoro: saggio sulla cultura borghese in Italia 1870–1925* (Venice: Marsilio, 1979), p. 59.
85. Ibid., p. 62.
86. See C. Lombroso, *L'uomo criminale* (1875), *L'uomo delinquente* (1876), and, with G. Ferrero, *La donna delinquente* (1893).
87. A. Niceforo, *L'Italia barbara contemporanea* (Palermo: Sandron, 1898).
88. See, for example, Niceforo on the Germans in *I Germani: storia di un idea e di un a "razza"* (Rome: Società editrice periodici, 1917) and Ferrero on English women in his *L'Europa Giovane* (Milan: Treves, 1897), pp. 140–7.
89. P. Mantegazza, *L'anno 3000: sogno* (Milan: Treves, 1897).
90. On Mantegazza, see C. Reynaudi, *Paolo Mantegazza: note biografiche* (Milan: Treves, 1893).
91. Mantegazza, *Fisiologia della donna*.
92. P. Mantegazza, *Le donne del mio tempo* (Rome: Voghera, 1905).
93. Mantegazza, *Fisiologia della donna*, p. 66.
94. Ibid., pp. 317–18.
95. Ibid., p. 305. For comparison, see Finck, *Romantic Love and Personal Beauty*, pp. 391–438.
96. Ibid., pp. 183–4.
97. Ibid., p. 185.
98. Ibid., p. 185. For Ferrero's view, see *L'Europa giovane*, pp. 143–7.
99. Ibid., p. 142.
100. Ibid., pp. 182–3.
101. Ibid., p. 189.
102. Ibid., p. 310.
103. C. Rochet, *Traité d'anatomie, d'anthropologie et d'etnographie appliquées aux beaux arts* (Paris, 1886), pp. 233–4. Quoted in ibid., p. 189.
104. Ibid., p. 329.
105. Mantegazza, *Fisiologia della donna*, p. 329.
106. Ibid., p. 188.
107. P. Artusi, *La scienza in cucina e l'arte di mangiare bene* (Florence: Giunti Marzocco, 1960; first published 1891), p. 6.

Chapter Three

1. The film in fact bears only the most superficial relationship to the reality of Cavalieri's life. See F. Di Tizio, *Lina Cavalieri – la donna più bella del mondo: la vita 1875–1944* (Chieti: Ianieri, 2004), pp. 475–7.
2. Erté, *Things I Remember* (London: Peter Owen, 1975), p. 46.
3. E. D. Rappaport, *Shopping for Pleasure: Women in the Making of London's West End* (Princeton: Princeton University Press, 2000), p. 185.
4. L. Cavalieri, *Le mie verità* (Rome: S. A. Poligrafica Italiana, 1936), pp. 171–5.
5. C. Beaton, *The Book of Beauty* (London: Duckworth, 1930), p. 6.
6. N. Yuval-Davis, *Gender & Nation* (London: Sage, 1997), p. 47.
7. P. Portoghesi, *La donna Liberty* (Rome: Laterza, 1983), p. 254.
8. V. Steele, *Paris Fashion: A Cultural History* (New York: Oxford University Press, 1988), p. 75.
9. Ibid., p. 298.
10. O. Uzanne, *Parisiennes de ce temps en leurs divers milieux, états et conditions* (Paris: Mercure de France, 1910), pp. 18–20.
11. P. Adam, *La vie des élites: la morale de l'amour* (Paris: Méricault, 1907), p. 333.
12. Neera, 'Le donne milanesi' in Luigi Capuana and others, *Milano 1881* (Milan: Allegretti di Campi, 1976), p. 39.
13. M. Serao, *Saper vivere* (Naples: Perrella, 1905), p. 310. Her booklet on grooming, *Fascino muliebre*, was published by the cosmetics company Bertelli (Milan, undated but approximately 1906).

14. M. Antelling, *Al vento: per le signorine* (Milan: Agnelli, 1900), p. 10.
15. Ibid., p. 10.
16. Ibid., p. 98.
17. See, for example, M. Proust, *Remembrance of Things Past I* (Harmondsworth: Penguin, 1989), p. 254. The whole of 'Swann in Love' is permeated with comparisons of this type.
18. Paul Adam, *La vie des élites: la morale de L'amour* (Paris: Méricaut, 1907) p. 334.
19. Cited in S. Candela, *I Florio* (Palermo: Sellerio, 1986), p. 326.
20. Donna Franca shared this preference and did not like her own dark features. See A. Pomar, *Franca Florio* (Palermo: Novecento, 2002), pp. 11 and 46.
21. M. Serao, *I Mosconi* (Naples: Delfino, 1974), p. 117.
22. Cavalieri, *Le mie verità*, p. 21.
23. Di Tizio, *Lina Cavalieri*, pp. 26–7. Her son Alessandro would remain in the background throughout her public life and he would never learn from her the name of his father. He was seriously wounded in the First World War but recovered to live to the age of 101. He died in Florence in 1993.
24. According to V. Paliotti she made her debut in the Caffe Torre Belisario which was located near Porta Pinciana. See *Il Salone Margherita e la belle époque* (Rome: Benincasa, 1975), p. 187.
25. See P. Jullian, *D'Annunzio* (Paris: Fayard, 1971), p. 250.
26. Cavalieri, *Le mie verità*, p. 26.
27. Ibid., p. 32.
28. Ibid., p. 59. Recent research by Paul Fryer and Olga Usova has shown that there is no legal record of this marriage ever having taken place. They conclude that a private marriage ceremony may have occurred but that it was either never formalised or was rendered null and void by the court authorities. See *Lina Cavalieri: The Life of Opera's Greatest Beauty, 1874–1944* (New York: McFarland, 2004), pp. 27–9. The singer's Italian biographer, Franco Di Tizio, agrees. See *Lina Cavalieri*, pp. 69–74.
29. Fryer and Usova, *Lina Cavalieri*, pp. 32–3. Just two months passed, in fact, between Cavalieri's last variety performance in November 1899 and her Lisbon debut in January 1900.
30. Quotations from *Il Mattino* are taken from Paliotti, *Il Salone Margherita*, pp. 189–92.
31. See Fryer and Usova, *Lina Cavalieri*, p. 80.
32. *Illustrated London News*, 27 June 1908.
33. Jarro (G. Piccini), *Viaggio umoristica nei Teatri* (Florence: Bemporad, 1909), p. 252.
34. Ibid., p. 8.
35. Fryer and Usova, *Lina Cavalieri*, pp. 148–9.
36. Paliotti, *Il Salone Margherita*, p. 193.
37. The face of Marta 'was truly worthy of an artist's brush. . . . Taller than average, shaped like a statue, with thick brown, naturally wavy hair and very dark eyelashes and brows, blue eyes, a milk and roses complexion she seemed, and truly was, enchanting'. Maria-Luisa was delicate and aloof, 'it was said that there was a drop of aristocratic blood in that girl, so noble and pure of spirit was she that her superb head would truly have been worthy of a crown'. C. Invernizio, *La regina del mercato*. (Turin: Tipografia della Gazzetta di Torino, 1903), pp. 6 and 78.
38. M. T. Contini and others, *Café-chantant* (Florence: Bonechi, 1977), p. 51.
39. Anon., 'Fra voi belle brune e bionde: una proposta', *Il café-chantant*, 8 January 1907, p. 1.
40. U. Tegani, *Cantanti di una volta* (Milan: Valecchi, 1951), p. 315.
41. C. Beaton, *The Glass of Fashion* (London: Weidenfeld and Nicolson, 1954), p. 65.
42. Ibid., pp. 65–6.
43. Ibid., p. 66.
44. Fryer and Usova, *Lina Cavalieri*, p. 13.
45. Algernon St Brennon of the *New York Daily Telegraph*, quoted in ibid., p. 81.
46. Di Tizio, *Lina Cavalieri*, p. 189.
47. Gajo, 'La bellezza sulla scena: Lina Cavalieri', *Il Marzocco*, 13 October 1901.
48. Jarro, *Viaggio umoristico*, pp. 2–3.
49. Ibid., p. 7.
50. Reproduced in Di Tizio, *Lina Cavalieri*, p. 104.
51. Quoted in A. Mazza, *L'Harem di D'Annunzio* (Milan: Mondadori, 1995), p. 34. See also Di Tizio, *Lina Cavalieri*, pp. 446–50.
52. Cavalieri, *Le mie verità*, p. 65.
53. Quoted in Di Tizio, *Lina Cavalieri*, p. 12.
54. *Verde e azzurro*, I:24 (undated).
55. *Verde e azzurro*, I:21 (undated).

56. *Verde e azzurro*, II:10–11, 28–9 February 1904., pp. 4–5. A further vote was announced to choose the overall winner but no evidence of the result has been found.
57. *La Donna*, 20 February 1908, p. 13.
58. *La Donna*, 5 August 1908, p. 13.
59. *La Donna*, 5 November 1908, pp. 11 and 22.
60. *La Tribuna Illustrata*, 28 September–1 October 1911, p. 633.
61. E. Biagi, *Quante donne* (Turin: ERI-Rizzoli, 1996), p. 55.
62. Piccini, *Viaggio umoristico*, pp. 253–4.
63. U. Notari, *Signore sole: interviste e ritratti delle celebri artiste* (Milan: Edizioni del Giornale Verde e Azzurro, c.1903), p. 18.
64. Ibid., p. 23.
65. E. Ghione, *L'ombra di Za la Mort* (Milan: Bietti, 1973; first published 1933), p. 270.
66. Paliotti, *Il Salone Margherita*, p. 185.
67. 'L'elezione della regina di Roma', *Il Travaso delle idee della domenica*, 17 September 1911, p. 3.
68. 'Corriere della moda', *La Tribuna Illustrata*, 5 February 1911, p. 6.
69. Quoted in Fryer and Usova, *Lina Cavalieri*, pp. 15–16.
70. Ibid., p. 27.
71. Cited in Paliotti, *Il Salone Margherita*, p. 192.
72. Ibid., p. 193.
73. Jarro, *Viaggio umoristico*, p. 6.
74. V. Colonna di Sermoneta, *Memorie* (Milan: Treves, 1937), p. 97.
75. Altea, 'L'arte e la bellezza di Lina Cavalieri', *La Donna*, 20 January 1903.
76. Beaton, *The Glass of Fashion*, p. 67.
77. Ibid., p. 70.
78. Notari, *Signore sole*, pp. 20–1.
79. V. Martinelli, 'L'avventura cinematografica di Lina Cavalieri', *Il territorio*, II:3 (1986), pp. 285–99, 291–2.
80. Donna Paola, 'Venere vincitrice', *La Donna*, 5 February 1908, pp. 18–19.
81. L. Cavalieri, *My Secrets of Beauty* (New York: The Circulation Syndicate, 1914).
82. See Di Tizio, *Lina Cavalieri*, p. 432.
83. Her fame was fuelled by the release in 1930 of a film version of *Romance*, a play by Edward Sheldon that featured a young priest's unconsummated love for a scandalous opera diva, who he named Rita Cavallini. The Catholic Sheldon had as a younger man been obsessed with Cavalieri and his play drew its inspiration from this idolisation. First performed in 1909, the drama enjoyed a long Broadway run and a successful American tour.
84. Di Tizio, *Lina Cavalieri*, pp. 435–7.

Chapter Four

1. The 'discursive obsession with female identity' during the inter-war years was not limited to Italy. See M. L. Roberts, *Civilisation Without Sexes: Reconstructing Gender in Postwar France, 1917–1927* (Chicago: University of Chicago Press, 1994).
2. The changes and conflicts of the era in Italy, most especially with reference to the impact of commercial culture, are most fully explored in V. De Grazia, *How Fascism Ruled Women: Italy 1922–1945* (Berkeley: University of California Press, 1992).
3. Roberts, *Civilisation Without Sexes*, p. 10.
4. See R. Curci (ed.), *Dudovich: oltre il manifesto* (Milan: Charta, 2002).
5. Quoted in ibid., p. 111.
6. F. T. Marinetti, 'Contre le luxe féminin: manifeste futuriste', Milan 11 March 1920, pages unnumbered.
7. F. T. Marinetti, 'Contro il lusso femminile', *Roma futurista*, II, n.77, 4 April 1920, p. 1. On this and related issues, see E. Mondello, *La nuova italiana: la donna nella stampa e nella cultura del ventennio* (Rome: Editori Riuniti, 1987), chapter one (this quotation on p. 45).
8. De Grazia, *How Fascism Ruled Women*, p. 211.
9. I. Brin, 'La moda nel cinema' (1943) in M. Verdone (ed.), *La moda e il costume nel film* (Rome: Bianco e Nero, 1950), p. 57.
10. *Eva*, 5 March 1935, cover.
11. R. Calzini, *La bella italiana: da Botticelli a Tiepolo*, special issue of *Domus*, December 1934, pp. 5–6.

12. For a comparison with Britain, see J. Stacey, *Star Gazing: Hollywood cinema and female spectatorship* (London: Routledge, 1994), Chapter 5.

13. *Cinema Illustrazione*, 26 August 1931, p. 6. De Grazia gives a similar example of a girl observing in the magazine *Kines* that 'if Leonardo came back and had to choose a model, he would certainly take Bébé Daniels over Mona Lisa', *How Fascism Ruled Women*, p. 212.

14. N. Scalia, 'Dove non si parla di dattilografe', *Il Primato artistico italiano*, 1919, pp. 15–18.

15. D. Banfi Malaguzzi, *Femminilità contemporanea* (Milan: Alpes, 1928).

16. Ibid., p. 23.

17. Ibid., pp. 133–4.

18. Ibid., p. 22.

19. A. Spadini, 'Pareri sulle belle donne', *Galleria*, 20 January 1924, p. 113.

20. E. Cecchi, 'Pareri sule belle donne', *Galleria*, 20 February 1924, pp. 192–3.

21. For example, Pittigrilli wrote in his novel *Cocaina*: 'the modern Venus no longer has the soft chubby graces that our grandfathers sought (with their hands); the Venus of today must evoke thoughts of the androgynous girls who belong to English gymnastic troupes'. (Milan: Bompiani, 2000; first published 1921), pp. 92–3.

22. See B. Cartland, *We Danced All Night* (London: Hutchinson, 1971), p. 183.

23. 'Moda', *Enciclopedia italiana* (Rome: Treccani, 1951; first published 1938), p. 508.

24. Cited in M. Cesari, *La censura nel periodo fascista* (Naples: Liguori, 1978), p. 47.

25. Taken from *Panorama*, 23 July 1984, pp. 124–32.

26. Quoted in Cesari, *La censura nel periodo fascista*, p. 50.

27. E. Sturani, 'La dove s'incarna il simbolo: Boccasile, dalla Signorina Grandi Firme alla R.S.I. e oltre', *La Cartolina*, n.36, 1989, p. 6.

28. Boccasile, *La Signorina Grandi Firme*, ed. Antonio Faeti (Milan: Longanesi, 1981).

29. Ibid., p. 435.

30. G. Boccasile, 'Io e le donne', *Le Grandi Firme*, 1 July 1937, pp. 6–7.

31. Cover of issue of 10 February 1938.

32. Lyrics reproduced in *Le Grandi Firme*, 14 April 1938, p. 2.

33. 'Lettrici! Cerchiamo una diva', *Grandi Firme*, 12 May 1938, p. 2.

34. *Grandi Firme*, 26 May 1938, p. 2.

35. 'Quella che amerei', *Grandi Firme*, 16 June 1938, p. 8. The sculptor featured in the issue of 29 September 1938, pp. 6–7.

36. Mondello, *La nuova italiana*, p. 112.

37. See O. Del Buono (ed.), *Eia, Eia, Eia, Alalà!: la stampa italiana sotto il fascismo 1919/43* (Milan: Feltrinelli, 1971), pp. 369–70.

38. Emmegidi, 'Estetica femminile senza cosmetici', *Almannacco della Donna italiana* 1937, reproduced in Del Buono, *Eia, Eia, Eia, Alalà!*, pp. 329–30.

39. G. Capo, 'Madri feconde', *Illustrazione italiana* 1934, reproduced in Del Buono, *Eia, Eia, Eia, Alalá!*, pp. 224–5.

40. See De Grazia, *How Fascism Ruled Women*, pp. 74–5

41. Mondello, *La nuova italiana*, p. 141.

42. P. Willson, *Peasant Women and Politics in Fascist Italy: The Massaie Rurali* (London: Routledge, 2002), pp. 157–8.

43. Ibid., p. 205.

44. Ibid., p. 204.

45. p.a.m.p., 'Donne d'Italia', *Gente Nostra*, VII:46, 17 November 1935, p. 9.

46. Nepal, 'Bellezza e grazia nell'arte italiana', *Gente Nostra*, VII:3, 20 January 1935, p. 3.

47. R. Calzini, *La bella italiana: da Botticelli a Tiepolo*, supplement to no. 84 of *Domus*, December 1934, p. 5.

48. Ibid., p. 6.

49. See L. Frati, *La donna italiana: nei più recenti studi* (Turin: Bocca, 1928), chapter II 'Il tipo estetico della bellezza femminile'.

50. Ibid., p. 6.

51. S. Ponzanesi, *Paradoxes of Postcolonial Culture: Feminism and Diaspora in South-Asian and Afro-Italian Women's Narratives* (Ph.D. thesis, University of Utrecht, 1999), pp. 171–2.

52. R. Ben-Ghiat, *Fascist Modernities: Italy 1922–1945* (Berkeley: University of California Press, 2001), p. 129.

53. Ponzanesi, *Paradoxes*, p. 178.

54. Ben-Ghiat, *Fascist Modernities*, p. 129.

55. J. Gennari, 'Passing for Italian', *Transition*, 6:4, 1996, pp. 36–48.

56. M. Raspanti, 'Il mito ariano nella cultura italiana fra Otto e Novecento', in A. Burgio (ed.), *Nel nome della razza: il razzismo nella storia d'Italia 1870–1945* (Bologna: Il Mulino, 1999), pp. 75–85.

57. C. Cecchelli, 'Origini ed omogeneità della razza' in Paolo Orano (ed.), *Inchiesta sulla razza* (Rome: Pinciana, 1939), pp. 69–70.
58. F. T. Marinetti, *Notari scrittore nuovo* (Villasanta: Notari, 1936), p. 81.
59. U. Notari, *La donna 'tipo tre'* (Milan: Notari, 1929), pp. 147–52.
60. U. Notari, *Dichiarazioni alle più belle donne del mondo* (Milan: Notari, 1933), p. 20 and p. 16.
61. Ibid., p. 87.
62. Ibid., p. 140.
63. Quoted in B. Spackman, *Fascist Virilities* (Minneapolis: University of Minnesota Press, 1996), p. 10.
64. See U. Piscopo, 'Umberto Notari: A 80 anni dalla fondazione dell' "Associazione Italiana di Avanguardia"', *Cultura e scuola*, XXX:119 (1991), pp. 39–45, 40–1.
65. Notari, *Dichiarazioni alle più belle donne*, p. 161.
66. U. Notari, *A che gioco giochiamo? Autarchia contro xenolatria* (Milan: Notari, 1938), pp. 84–88.
67. U. Notari, *Panegirico della Razza italiana* (Villasanta: Notari, 1939).
68. Ibid., p. 106.
69. Ibid., pp. 106–7.
70. Ibid., pp. 184–85.
71. A. Fraccaroli, *Donne d'america* (Milan: Omenoni, 1930), p. 31. Quoted in M. Beynet, *L'image de l'Amérique dans la culture italienne de l'entre-deux-guerres* (Aix-en-Provence: Publications de l'Université de Provence, 1990), p. 434.
72. M. Gallian, 'Nel mondo delle meraviglie', *Gente Nostra*, VIII:36, 13 September 1936, p. 10.
73. Quoted in A. Ferraù, 'Lettere d'amore', *Film*, 5 April 1941, p. 8.
74. Anon., 'Paola Barbara e il suo nome', *Grazia*, 13 March 1941, 11–17.
75. Emmeci, 'Parliamo un po' delle nostre attrici nuove', *L'Eco del cinema*, January 1941, pp. 3–4.
76. P. Willson, *The Clockwork Factory: Women and Work in Fascist Italy* (Oxford: Oxford University Press, 1993), p. 244.

Chapter Five

1. G. P. Brunetta, *Storia del cinema italiano dalle origini al 1945* (Rome: Editori Riuniti, 1979), pp. 515–24.
2. L. Quaglietti, *Storia economic-politica del cinema italiano* (Rome: Editori Riuniti, 1980), Table A, p. 245.
3. See D. W. Ellwood, *Rebuilding Europe: Western Europe, America and Postwar Reconstruction* (London: Longman, 1992), p. 227.
4. M. Rosen, *Popcorn Venus: Women, Movies and the American Dream* (London: Peter Owen, 1973), p. 158.
5. G. Ringgold, *The Films of Rita Hayworth* (Secaucus: Citadel, 1974), p. 13.
6. P. P. Pasolini, *Amado mio* (Milan: Garzanti, 1982), pp. 191–2.
7. G. Guida, 'Gilda', *Cinemoda*, 6 April 1947, p. 7.
8. B. Paris, *Garbo* (London: Pan, 1995), p. 364.
9. T. B. Hess, 'Pinup and Icon' in T. B. Hess and L. Nochlin (eds), *Woman as Sex Object: Studies in Erotic Art 1730–1970* (London: Allen Lane, 1972), p. 227.
10. Ibid., p. 227.
11. C. Wright Mills, *The Power Elite* (New York: Oxford University Press, 1956), p. 81.
12. M. Gabor, *The Pin-Up: A Modest History* (New York: Evergreen, 1972), p. 151.
13. R. Calzini (ed.), *La bella italiana: da Botticelli e Tiepolo*, supplement to *Domus*, No. 84, December 1934, p. 5. The reprint was published as a book in 1945 by Editoriale Domus with the modified subtitle 'da Botticelli a Spadini'.
14. Ibid., p. 5.
15. *La Domenica degli italiani*, 18 November 1945, p. 3. The *Domenica del Corriere* adopted this alternative title in 1945 to 1946, while the press remained under Allied control.
16. For example, see the issue of 9 December 1945, p. 6.
17. *La Domenica degli italiani*, 30 December 1945, p. 6.
18. *La Domenica degli italiani*, 16 December 1945, p. 6.
19. *La Domenica degli italiani*, 23 December 1945, p. 5.
20. Anon., 'Belle ragazze anche da noi', *Corriere Lombardo*, 18 December 1945.
21. J. Heller, *Catch 22: a novel* (New York: Simon and Schuster, 1961), p. 152.
22. J. H. Burns, *The Gallery* (London: Secker and Warburg, 1948), p. 206.
23. See A. Garofalo, *L'italiana in Italia* (Bari: Laterza, 1956).
24. Ibid., p. 7.

25. On the way women won the vote, see A. Rossi Doria, *Diventare cittadine: il voto delle donne in Italia* (Florence: Giunti, 1996).
26. Cited in L. Cigognetti and L. Servetti, '"On Her Side": female images in Italian cinema and the popular press, 1945–55', *Historical Journal of Film, Radio and Television*, XVI:4 (1996), pp. 555–63, 558.
27. Ibid., p. 97.
28. Ibid., pp. 29–30.
29. See A. Arvidsson, *Marketing Modernity: Italian Advertising from Fascism to Postmodernity* (London: Routledge, 2003), pp. 22–5.
30. O. Vergani, Introduction to D. Villani, *Come sono nate undici Miss Italia* (Milan: Editoriale Domus, 1957), p. 8.
31. For a discussion of the challenge of American advertising in Europe, see V. De Grazia, 'The Arts of Purchase: How American Publicity Subverted the European Poster, 1920–1940' in B. Kruger and P. Mariani (eds), *Remaking History* (Seattle: Bay Press, 1989). A critique of this interpretation is offered in S. Gundle, 'Visions of Prosperity: Consumerism and Popular Culture in Italy from the 1920s to the 1950s' in C. Levy and M. Roseman (eds), *Three Postwar Eras in Comparison: Western Europe 1918–1945–1989* (London: Palgrave, 2002).
32. Villani, *Come sono nate*, p. 43.
33. Ibid.
34. Ibid., p. 10.
35. Quoted in ibid., p. 65.
36. G. D., 'La più bella', *Tempo*, 21 September 1946, p. 25.
37. F. Antonioni, '. . . e le stelline non stanno a guardare', *La Cinematografia italiana*, November–December 1948, p. 5.
38. *Cinestar*, 27 December 1947, p. 2.
39. Antonioni, '. . . e le stelline', p. 5.
40. Quoted in G. C. Castello, *Il divismo: mitologia del cinema* (Turin: ERI, 1957), p. 424.
41. G. D., 'La più bella', *Tempo*, 21 September 1946, pp. 26–7.
42. *Tempo*, 4 October 1947, p. 18.
43. Bosé, quoted in F. Faldini and G. Fofi (eds), *L'avventurosa storia del cinema italiano: raccontato dai suoi protagonisti 1935–1959* (Milan: Feltrinelli, 1979), pp. 147–9.
44. See Villani, *Come sono nate*, pp. 94–5.
45. Quoted in ibid., pp. 94–5.
46. Anon., 'Fulvia Franco ha vinto il titolo', *Giornale di Trieste*, 28 September 1948, p. 2.
47. R. Bacchelli and others, *Donne italiane* (Turin: ERI, 1949), p. 15.
48. Ibid., p. 53.
49. Ibid., p. 25.
50. Ibid., pp. 64–5.
51. Ibid., p. 96.
52. Ibid., p. 46.
53. Ibid., p. 48.
54. Ibid., p. 89.
55. Ibid., p. 71.
56. Ibid., p. 72.
57. Ibid., the first quotation is by Stuparich (p. 69), the second by Titta Rosa (p. 89).
58. G. C. Castello, 'Il cinema senza attori', *Il Ponte*, XIII:8–9 (1957), p. 1391.

Chapter Six

1. Quoted in M. De Giorgio, *Le italiane dall'Unità a oggi* (Rome-Bari: Laterza, 1993), p. 148.
2. Ibid., p. 148.
3. E. B., 'Danze', *Famiglia cristiana*, 14 May 1950, p. 387.
4. See G. B. Guerri, *Povera santa, povero assassino* (Milan: Mondadori, 1987).
5. P. Ginsborg, *A History of Contemporary Italy: Society and Politics, 1943–88* (Harmondsworth: Penguin, 1990), pp. 168–73.
6. Ibid., p. 4.
7. Quoted in R. Manzini, 'Le smanie per la Miss', *Famiglia cristiana*, 15 October 1950, p. 805.
8. Ibid., p. 805.
9. Ibid.
10. P. Serafino Guarise, 'Il fenomeno delle Miss', *Famiglia cristiana*, 18 July 1954, p. 3.

11. Padre Atanasio, 'Bellezza e bontà', *Famiglia cristiana*, 21 November 1954, p. 3.

12. P. Colini Lombardi, 'I concorsi di bellezza', in Don G. Rossi (ed.), *Cento problemi di coscienza* (Assisi: Edizioni pro Civitate christiana, second edition, 1959), p. 438.

13. Lya, 'Sfilata di . . . Miss', *Famiglia cristiana*, 5 July 1953, p. 15.

14. Ibid., p. 4.

15. P. Attanasio, 'La ragazza di campagna', *Famiglia cristiana*, 22 July 1956, p. 3.

16. P. Attanasio, 'Bellezza e bontà', *Famiglia cristiana*, 21 November 1954, p. 3.

17. P. Attanasio, 'Farsi belle', *Famiglia cristiana*, 28 November 1954, p. 3.

18. Anon., 'La fiera della vanità femminile', *Famiglia cristiana*, 6 October 1960, p. 5.

19. M. Boneschi, *Santa pazienza: la storia delle donne italiane dal dopoguerra a oggi* (Milan: Mondadori, 1998), p. 197.

20. For a full discussion of these and all other aspects of Communist cultural policy, see S. Gundle, *Between Hollywood and Moscow: the Italian Communists and the Challenge of Mass Culture, 1943–1991* (Durham, N.C.: Duke University Press, 2000).

21. See, for example, the reference to such a contest being held in Pesaro as late as 1977 in C. Bernieri, *L'albero in piazza: storia, cronaca e leggenda delle feste dell'Unità* (Milan: Mazzotta, 1977), pp. 124–5.

22. Luigi Arbizzani, a party official in Bologna at the time, informed me that the party viewed Miss Italia as a frivolous, even snobbish event whose bourgeois matrix made it unacceptable to Communists. The term *stellina* (starlet) was deliberately adopted as an alternative to the foreign term 'Miss'. Interview with the author, 24 June 1989.

23. Communist party (PCI) Archive, papers of the meeting of the directorate of 13 June 1950; Associazione amici dell''Unità', Grande concorso per l'elezione della 'stellina dell'Unità'.

24. Anon., 'Chi sarà la più bella?', *La Lotta*, 8 September 1950, p. 3.

25. Anon., 'E' necessario curare l'aspetto finanziario delle feste della stampa comunista', *Quaderno dell'attivista*, IV:7, July 1949, p. 2.

26. Togliatti's numerous speeches on the 'Woman Question' are collected in *L'emancipazione femminile* (Rome: Editori Riuniti, 1965).

27. Interview with Marisa Musu, 4 May 1993.

28. See S. Gundle, 'Cultura di massa e modernizzazione: *Vie Nuove* e *Famiglia cristiana* dalla guerra fredda alla società dei consumi' in P. P. D'Attorre (ed.), *Nemici per la pelle: sogno americano e mito sovietico nell'Italia del dopoguerra* (Milan: Franco Angeli, 1991).

29. Information concerning the print run was published in *Vie Nuove* on 24 September 1950, 15 April 1951, 3 February 1952 and 12 September 1954.

30. S. Tutino, '*Vie Nuove*: il nostro grande settimanale illustrato', *La Verità*, 12 January 1952, p. 8.

31. See Gundle, *I comunisti italiani*, pp. 120–4 and 139–49; and Stephen Gundle, 'Il PCI e la campagna contro Hollywood (1948–58)' in D. W. Ellwood and G. P. Brunetta (eds), *Hollywood in Europa: industria, politica, pubblico del cinema 1945–60* (Florence: La Casa Usher/Ponte alle Grazie, 1991).

32. D. Villani, *Come sono nate Undici Miss Italia* (Milan: Editoriale Domus, 1957), p. 131.

33. C. Zavattini, 'Altea Baiardi ovvero l'amore in bicicletta', *Vie Nuove*, 7 March 1954, p. 17.

34. Arbizzani informed me that *Vie Nuove* developed the idea of the competition following the success of Miss Italia in producing names like Silvana Pampanini, who rapidly made a name for herself in cinema. Even the term 'Miss' could no longer be rejected. The Communists felt the need to 'do something for pretty girls' who otherwise might have been subject to corrupt, bourgeois influences.

35. Picture caption, *Vie Nuove*, 24 September 1950, p. 24. She was featured on the cover of *Noi Donne* reading the magazine on 29 October 1950. Villani reported that there had been attempts to persuade the jury not to select her, as such a choice would have seemed political. Villani, *Come sono nate*, p. 148.

36. *Vie Nuove*, 15 October 1950, p. 17.

37. Ibid., p. 17. Musu's letter was probably motivated by an announcement two weeks previously that a young woman chosen as Miss *Vie Nuove* in Novacchio had received a producer's letter; 'one of those letters that every girl dreams of receiving, now that the place of the handsome prince has been taken by the producer or film director', the magazine commented. *Vie Nuove*, 1 October 1950, p. 24.

38. Fidia Gambetti interview, 1 November 1991.

39. Interview with the author, 11 July 1991. It needs to be borne in mind that many older Communists were extremely suspicious of the journalists who worked on party papers and magazines, many of whom were young and middle class and/or former Fascists. Gambetti, Pellicani's successor at *Vie Nuove*, had even been editor of a Fascist newspaper in Asti. His reflections on the Fascist period are contained in *Gli anni che scottano* (Rome: Mursia, 1967). On the world of Communist journalism in the 1940s and 1950s, see M. Venturi, *Sdraiati sulla linea* (Milan: Mondadori, 1991) and Gambetti, *Comunista perchè come* (Rome: Vecchiarelli, 1992).

40. Longo's role was not an active one, indeed Pellicani claimed that, by citing journalistic and promotional justifications for his innovations 'I exercised a sort of violence over him, but he allowed himself to be subjected to this violence'. As he transformed *Vie Nuove* into a popular magazine, Pellicani needed political protection and Longo, he said, 'covered my back'. However, there is some evidence to suggest that Longo rather enjoyed his role. He often acted as president of the jury at Miss *Vie Nuove* competitions in the party stronghold of Emilia-Romagna.
41. Pellicani interview.
42. Victims of this sort of insulting treatment included Musu and Teresa Noce, Longo's wife and herself a member of the PCI directorate (until Longo divorced her – without her knowledge – in San Marino in 1952). By contrast, Togliatti's companion Nilde Jotti, the young deputy Laura Diaz (who was referred to as 'Parliament's Joan Crawford') and Luciana Castellina were seen as unusual examples of elegant and attractive Communist women.
43. Concetto Marchesi in PCI, *VIII Congresso del Partito comunista italiano. Atti e risoluzioni* (Rome: Editori Riuniti, 1957), pp. 142–3.
44. Quoted in *Vie Nuove*, 2 July 1950, p. 17.
45. Ibid., p. 17.
46. L. Repaci, *Peccati e virtù delle donne* (Milan: Ceschina, 1954), pp. 107, 36, 58–9.
47. G. Guareschi, 'Festival', contained in *Gente cosi* (Milan: Rizzoli, 1981; fourth edition), pp. 237–46.
48. *Vie Nuove*, 7 March 1954.
49. C. B., 'A Miss Bologna non piace "Grand Hôtel"', *La Lotta*, 7 September 1951, p. 5.
50. Musu interview.
51. According to Pellicani, this advertising (which also appeared regularly in *Famiglia cristiana*) was placed through the advertising concessionary SIPRA, with which the magazine had a contract.
52. *Vie Nuove*, 16 September 1951, p. 20.
53. Ibid..
54. Casiraghi interview.
55. See R. Coward, *Female Desire* (London: Paladin, 1984), pp. 57–60.
56. See M. A. Macciocchi, *Duemila anni di felicità* (Milan: Il Saggiatore, 2000). Her experiences as editor of *Vie Nuove* are recounted on pp. 253–348.

Chapter Seven

1. Quoted in F. Faldini and G. Fofi (eds), *L'avventurosa storia del cinema italiano raccontato dai suoi protagonisti, 1935–59* (Milan: Feltrinelli, 1979), p. 154.
2. Ibid., p. 154.
3. Ibid., p. 155.
4. I. Calvino, 'Tra i pioppi della risaia la "cinecittà" delle mondine'(1948) in Calvino, *Saggi 1945–1985*, edited by M. Barenghi (Milan: Mondadori, 1995; 2 volumes).
5. C. Lizzani, *Riso amaro* (Rome: Officina, 1978), p. 97.
6. G. Grignaffini, 'Il femminile nel cinema italiano: racconti di rinascita' in G. P. Brunetta (ed.), *Identità italiana e identità europea nel cinema italiano dal 1945 al miracolo economico* (Turin: Edizioni della Fondazione Giovanni Agnelli, 1996), p. 358.
7. Ibid., p. 364.
8. Ibid., p. 372.
9. Compare ibid., pp. 371–2.
10. The debates took place in *Vie Nuove* and *Emilia*. For an overview, see S. Gundle, 'Il PCI e la campagna contro Hollywood (1948–58)' in D. W. Ellwood and G. P. Brunetta (eds), *Hollywood in Europa: Industria, politica, publico del cinema, 1945–60* (Florence: la casa usher/ Ponte alle Grazie, 1991), pp. 121–2.
11. B. Crowther, *New York Times*, 19 September 1950. Cutting contained in Academy of Motion Picture Arts and Sciences, Los Angeles, MPAA Production Code Files: Bitter Rice 1949.
12. AAMPAS, MPAA, Memo Breen to Gordon White, 10 May 1950, contained in ibid. Breen imposed cuts but failed to halt the film's distribution.
13. Faldini and Fofi, *L'avventurosa storia*, p. 155.
14. See R. C. V. Buckley, 'The Female Film Star in Postwar Italy (1948–1960)', (University of London PhD thesis, 2002), chapter 2.
15. See the photograph on the cover of *Lavoro*, 10 May 1952.
16. E. Scarfoglio, *Il Processo di Frine* (Naples: Deperro, 1973; first published 1884), p. 44.
17. Ibid., p. 53.
18. *Sorrisi e canzoni*, 27 December 1953, p. 1.

19. A. Moravia, *La romana* (Milan: Bompiani, 1949), p. 1.
20. *Epoca*, 1 May 1960.
21. See S. Gundle, 'Sophia Loren, Italian Icon', *Historical Journal of Film, Radio and Television*, 15: 3, 1995, pp. 367–85.
22. S. Guarnieri, 'Campioni e dive', *Cinema nuovo*, 10 July 1956, reproduced in G. Aristarco (ed.), *Il mito dell'attore* (Bari: Dedalo, 1983), p. 49.
23. V. Spinazzola, *Cinema e pubblico: lo spettacolo filmico in Italia 1945–65* (Milan: Bompiani, 1974), pp. 124–5.
24. *Momento-sera*, 11 February 1953, p. 1.
25. Anon.,'Lo scandalo delle curve', *Cinema Nuovo*, 1 March 1953, reproduced in Aristarco, *Il mito dell'attore*, pp. 261–2.
26. See M. Landy, *Italian Film* (Cambridge: Cambridge University Press, 2000), pp. 288–95.
27. For a fuller discussion of De Sica's role in shaping Loren's screen identity, see Gundle, 'Sophia Loren'. See also N. Piombino, 'Representations of the South in Postwar Italian Cinema' (University of London PhD thesis, in preparation), chapter three.
28. Grignaffini, 'Il femminile nel cinema italiano', p. 384.
29. Spinazzola, *Cinema e pubblico*, p. 123.
30. For a general statement of Andreotti's views on cinema in this period, see Faldini and Fofi, *L'avventurosa storia*, p. 217.
31. M. Rusconi, 'Il seno', in *Almanacco letterario Bompiani 1967: la bellezza 1880–1967* (Milan: Bompiani, 1966), pp. 85–6.
32. M. Yalom, *A History of the Breast* (London: Pandora, 1998), p. 192.
33. Ibid., pp. 192–3.
34. Grignaffini, 'Il femminile nel cinema italiano', p. 384. The observations on Lollobrigida contained in this paragraph are based on this passage. See also R. C. V. Buckley, 'National Body: Gina Lollobrigida and the Cult of the Star in the 1950s', *Historical Journal of Film, Radio and Television*, 20:4 (2000), pp. 527–47, 543.
35. Anon.,'Hollywood on the Tiber', *Time*, 16 August 1954.
36. E. Marcarini, 'Distribution of Italian Films in the British and American Markets 1945–1995' (University of Reading PhD thesis, 2001), p. 6, figure 1.
37. For the attractions of Italian cinema mentioned here, see G. P. Brunetta, 'Presenza del cinema italiano nel mondo' in G. P. Brunetta and others, *Il cinema italiano nel mondo* (Pescara: XXIX Premi internazionali Flaiano, 2002).
38. Anon, 'Hollywood on the Tiber', p. 32.
39. Ibid., p. 34.
40. Ibid., p. 33.
41. Ibid., p. 32.
42. Anon., 'Lollo degli americani', *Le ore*, 6 February 1954, pp. 12–13.
43. Anon., 'Much Woman', *Time*, 6 April 1962, p. 44.
44. E. Morin, *Les Stars* (Paris: Seuil, 1972; first published 1957), p. 53.
45. See R. Dyer, 'Monroe and Sexuality' in J. Todd (ed.), *Women and Film* (New York, 1988).
46. Buckley, 'National Body', p. 538.
47. Spinazzola, *Cinema e pubblico*, p. 127.
48. Guarnieri, 'Campioni e dive', p. 48.
49. *IFE* (Bulletin of Italian Film Export), n.1 (undated, pages unnumbered). Consulted in the Margaret Herrick library, American Academy of Motion Picture Arts and Sciences, Los Angeles.
50. *Variety*, 11 April 1957.
51. J. Hyams, 'Gina, la ragazza di campagna', *Settimo giorno*, 25 July 1956, p. 32.
52. Ibid., p. 32.
53. R. Renzi, writing in 1955, cited by G. Grignaffini, 'Silvana Mangano/Sophia Loren in Grignaffini (ed.), *Star: tre passi nel divismo* (Modena: Comune di Modena, 1981), p. 86.
54. Spinazzola, *Cinema e pubblico*, p. 128.
55. A. Lanocita, *Sofia Loren* (Milan: Longanesi, 1966), p. 151.
56. A. Garofalo, 'Maggiorate offese', *Cinema Nuovo*, 10 February 1955, reproduced in Aristarco, *Il mito dell'attore*, pp. 263–5.
57. 'Quella che amerei', *Grandi Firme*, 16 June 1938, p. 8.
58. Spinazzola, *Cinema e pubblico*, p. 153.
59. Lanocita, *Sofia Loren*, p. 151.
60. For a full discussion of this phenomenon, see Buckley, 'The Female Film Star in Postwar Italy', chapter three.
61. See 'Sofia Loren rinnova con ogni suo film il miracolo giudiziario di Frine' in G. Marotta, *Marotta ciak* (Milan, 1958).
62. See L. Mulvey, 'Visual Pleasure and Narrative Cinema' in Mulvey, *Visual and Other Pleasures* (London, 1989).

63. See Buckley, 'The Female Film Star', chapter three, which contains a detailed discussion of this issue.
64. See ibid.
65. W. G. Harris, *Cary Grant: A Touch of Elegance* (London: Sphere, 1998; first published 1987), p. 186.
66. See for example, the cover article on Lollobrigida's wardrobe in *Life*, 10 January 1955.
67. A. Corsi, 'I consigli della contessa Clara', *Settimana Incom illustrata*, 29 March 1958, p. 56.
68. This and the rest of the information in this paragraph is taken from materials in the Leonardo Borgese Collection, Getty Research Institute, Los Angeles.
69. G. Tomasi di Lampedusa, *Il Gattopardo* (Milan: Feltrinelli, 1963; first published 1959), pp. 53–81.
70. Ibid., p. 53.
71. Ibid., p. 48.
72. Ibid., p. 149.
73. Critics hostile to the novel, which they saw as fundamentally conservative, including Elio Vittorini and Franco Fortini, detected a variety of contemporary influences that they used to condemn it as a hybrid of high and low fiction that pandered to popular taste. Among these were a variety of popular films, including the specific example of the French film *Moulin Rouge*. See F. Fortini, 'Contro *Il Gattopardo*' in Fortini, *Saggi italiani* (Milan: Garzanti, 1987), pp. 261–71 (essay first published 1959). The author's widow wrote a letter to the press to deny that her husband had seen this film, but his English biographer, David Gilmour, reveals that not only did he visit a cine-club no less than two or three times a week, but that he had engaged in a conversation about this very film. See G. L. Lucente, 'Scrivere o fare . . . o altro: Social Commitment and Ideologies of Representation in the Debates over Lampedusa's *Il Gattopardo* and Morante's *La Storia*', *Italica*, 61:3, 1984, p. 225. D. Gilmour, *The Last Leopard: a Life of Giuseppe di Lampedusa* (London: Quartet, 1988), p. 132.
74. See also ibid. Gilmour bases this information on the author's diary for 1955.
75. F. Faldini and G. Fofi (eds), *L'avventurosa storia del cinema italiano: raccontato dai suoi protagonisti 1960–69* (Milan: Feltrinelli, 1981), p. 258.
76. C. Cardinale and A. M. Mori, *Io Claudia, tu Claudia: il romanzo di una vita* (Milan: Frassinelli, 1995), pp. 102–3.
77. Ibid., p. xiv.
78. Guarnieri, 'Campioni e dive', p. 50.
79. E. Baragli, S. J., 'Su dive, divi e divismo', *La civiltà cattolica*, 1959, pp. 401–7, 405.

Chapter Eight

1. G. McCracken, *Big Hair: A Journey into the Transformation of Self* (London: Indigo, 1997) p. 97.
2. R. Barthes, *Mythologies* (London: Paladin, 1973; first published 1957), p. 37.
3. K. Ferri, *Spot Babilonia* (Milan: Lupetti, 1988), p. 74.
4. Even after she began making films, Lisi never shook off her association with Chlorodont toothpaste. In a celebrated series of advertisements for this product, she played a dumb blonde. In each one, her final quip, after a brief dialogue with a male actor, was 'Did I say something wrong?', to which her partner provided the stock punchline, 'With that mouth you can say what you like'. Ferri, *Spot Babilonia*, pp. 81–2.
5. R. Cirio, *Il mestiere di regista: intervista a Federico Fellini* (Milan: Garzanti, 1994), p. 19.
6. Ferri, *Spot Babilonia*, p. 74.
7. S. Gundle, 'Signorina buonasera: images of women in early television' in Penelope Morris (ed.), *Women in Italy 1945–60* (New York: Palgrave, 2006).
8. For some amusing reflections on them, see A. Campanile, *La televisione spiegata al popolo* (Milan: Bompiani, 1989), p. 80.
9. J. Di Domenico, 'Advertising in Italian Women's Magazines 1815–1980: Gender and Evolving Ideologies of the Middle Class Woman' (University of Strathclyde PhD thesis, 2004), p. 303.
10. Ibid., p. 303.
11. Ibid., p. 36.
12. Ibid., p. 304.
13. Anon., 'Una Miss Italia bionda che piace anche ai suoi rivali', *Oggi*, 14 September 1961, pp. 40–1.
14. Quoted in F. Metz and E. Mondi (eds), *La più bella sei tu* (Rome: Ulisse, 1994), p. 96.
15. C. Beaton, *The Face of the World: An International Scrapbook of People and Places* (London: Weidenfeld and Nicolson, 1957), p. 167.
16. See R. C. V. Buckley, 'The Female Film Star in Postwar Italy 1948–1960' (University of London PhD thesis, 2002), chapter 5.
17. See E. Martinelli, *Sono come sono: dalla dolce vita e ritorno* (Milan: Rusconi, 1995) and R. Buckley, 'Elsa Martinelli: Italy's Audrey Hepburn', *Historical Journal of Film, Radio and Television*, 26:3, 2006, 327–40.

18. F. Pierini, 'Il mito', *L'Europeo*, 12 December 1965, p. 45.
19. Martinelli, *Sono come sono*, p. 208.
20. A. Ardigò, *Emancipazione femminile e urbanesimo* (Brescia: Morcelliana, 1964), p. 22.
21. F. Alberoni, *Consumi e società* (Bologna: Il Mudellino, 1964), p. 29.
22. V. Spinazzola, *Cinema e pubblico: lo spettacolo filmico in Italia 1945–65* (Milan: Bompiani, 74), pp. 195–6.
23. E. Girlanda, *Stefania Sandrelli* (Rome: Gremese, 2002), p. 7.
24. I. Vercelloni, 'Il corpo imposto', *Almanacco letterario Bompiani 1967: La bellezza 1880–1967* (Milan: Bompiani, 1966), p. 67.
25. N. Minuzzo, 'La bellezza', *L'Europeo*, 12 December 1965, p. 69.
26. Ibid., p. 54.
27. Ibid., p. 65.
28. See P. De Tassis, 'Corpi recuperati per il proprio sguardo: cinema e immaginario negli anni "50"', *Memoria*, 6 (3), 1982, pp. 24–31, 31.
29. Buckley, 'Elsa Martinelli', pp. 335–7.
30. See S. Gundle, 'Sophia Loren, Italian Icon', *Historical Journal of Film, Radio and Television*, 15: 3, 1995, pp. 367–85.
31. See S. Gundle, 'Hollywood, Italy and the First World War: Italian Responses to Film Versions of Ernest Hemingway's *A Farewell to Arms*', in G. Bonsaver and R. Gordon (eds), *State, Culture and Censorship in Twentieth-Century Italy* (Oxford: Legenda, 2005).
32. Spinazzola, *Cinema e pubblico*, p. 289.
33. V. Ricciuti, *Il Mattino*, 20 December 1964.
34. Spinazzola, *Cinema e pubblico*, p. 289.
35. Anon., 'Much Woman', *Time*, 6 April 1962, p. 48.
36. See M. Landy, *Italian Film* (Cambridge: Cambridge University Press 2000), pp. 297–8.
37. Ibid., p. 101.
38. Ibid., p. 45.
39. Ibid., p. 223.
40. A. Moravia, *Claudia Cardinale* (Milan: Lerici, 1962).
41. C. Cardinale with A. M. Mori, *Io, Claudia, tu Claudia* (Milan: Frassinelli, 1995), p. 199.
42. Spinazzola, *Cinema e pubblico*, p. 305.
43. G. Grazzini (ed.), *Cara Claudia: lettere dei fans alla Cardinale* (Milan: Longanesi, 1966), p. 17 and p. 67.
44. Ibid., p. 20.
45. Cardinale, *Io Claudia, tu Claudia*, p. 159.

Chapter Nine

1. P. D'Agostini, 'Ornella, l'eterno desiderio', *La Repubblica*, 22 August 1993.
2. E. Pugnaletto, 'Ma vi sembro una nonna?', *Oggi*, 19 March 1997, p. 99.
3. Anon., 'Se non ci fosse Ornella', *Panorama*, 5 July 1992, p. 193.
4. M. S. Conte, 'A lezione di seduzione', *La Repubblica*, 1–2 December 1991, p. 21.
5. C. Cosulich pointed out that Andreotti condemned the social content of *Umberto D*, but replied to a local newspaper that attacked the lax censorship of the early 1950s by asserting that 'the danger of a film cannot be judged on the basis of the presence or otherwise of the odd exposed leg'. See *La scalata al sesso* (Genoa: Immordino, 1969), p. 68.
6. M. Milani, *Italia sexy* (Genoa: Immordino, 1967), p. 118.
7. G. Tedeschi, 'Il giornalismo parapornografico dal boom alla crisi', *Ulisse*, 67, 1970, pp. 150–6, 156.
8. '*Playboy* Tribuna', *Playboy*, I:1, November 1972, p. 35.
9. '*Playboy* intervista: Mike Bongiorno', *Playboy*, III: 6, June 1974, p. 26.
10. N. Rothenberg, 'Women and Mass Communication in Italy' (University of London PhD thesis, 2005), p. 214.
11. Ibid., p. 216.
12. Ibid., p. 217.
13. For a rare example, see C. Llera Moravia 'Diva inclusa', a photographic article with commentary that portrayed Muti as if she were a star of the black and white cinema of the neo-realist era, *Moda*, December 1989, pp. 50–7.
14. Fellini interviewed in a survey entitled, 'La donna in Italia', *L'Europeo*, 12 December 1965, p. 30.
15. F. Fellini, *Sono un gran bugiardo*, edited by Damian Pettigrew (Rome: Elleu, 2003), pp. 64–5.
16. F. Fellini, *Fare un film* (Turin: Einaudi, 1974), p. 83.
17. Ibid., p. 84. On the place of the mother figure in Italian culture, see M. d'Amelia, *La mamma* (Bologna: Il Mulino, 2005).

18. Fellini, *Fare un film*, p. 84.
19. R. Cirio, *Il mestiere di regista: intervista con Fellini* (Milan: Garzanti, 1994), p. 19.
20. T. Kezich, *Federico: Fellini, la vita e i film* (Milan: Feltrinelli, 2002), p. 237.
21. Cirio, *Il mestiere di regista*, p. 145.
22. A. Keel and C. Strich (eds), *Fellini on Fellini* (London: Eyre Methuen, 1976), p. 25.
23. The similarity was acknowledged by Fellini. See Cirio, *Il mestiere di regista*, p. 70.
24. Kezich, *Federico*, p. 303.
25. Keel and Strich, *Fellini on Fellini*, p. 17.
26. Ibid., p. 18.
27. Fellini, *Sono un gran bugiardo*, p. 64.
28. F. Faldini and G. Fofi (eds), *Cinema italiano oggi 1970–1984: raccontato dai suoi protagonisti* (Milan: Mondadori, 1984), p. 262.
29. See Kezich, *Federico*, p. 329.
30. Faldini and Fofi, *Il cinema italiano oggi*, pp. 261–2.
31. Among the women he praised was Valeria Marini (see chapter 10). Marini's reflections on the praise she received are contained in Barbara Palombelli, 'Valeria Marini: Quella notte d'estate inseguita da Fellini', *La Repubblica*, 16 July 1995, p. 11.
32. See G. P. Brunetta, *Cent'anni di cinema italiano* (Bari: Laterza, 1991), pp. 620–4.
33. Faldini and Fofi, *Il cinema italiano oggi*,, p. 341.
34. Anon. 'Grazie Antonelli', *Playboy*, II: 7 July 1973, p. 64.
35. Quoted in ibid., p. 64.
36. Ibid., p. 64.
37. S. Masi, *Italian Movie Goddesses* (Rome: Gremese, 1998), p. 164. 'I have interpreted eroticism in every way: comically, ironically, dramatically', she once said. 'It is something that has never been a problem. On the contrary, I play with it, it amuses me; you cannot take yourself so seriously on this topic'. Quoted in F. Di Giammatteo, *Dive e divi del cinema italiano: agenda 1989* (Florence: la Nuova Italia, 1988), page unnumbered.
38. Rothenberg, 'Women and Mass Communication', p. 214.
39. P. P. Pasolini, *Scritti corsari* (Milan: Garzanti, 1975), p. 48.
40. S. Gundle, 'Un "apocalittico integrato"', *Dopo Pasolini*, supplement to *L'Unità*, 28 October 1995, p. 7.
41. L. Laurenzi, 'Carmen Russo: da maggiorata a mezzobusto', *Il Venerdì di Repubblica*, 21 September 1990, p. 27.
42. G. Visigalli, 'Supercarmen formato famiglia', *Telesette*, 6 November 1985.
43. M. Venturi, 'Un "oggetto" misterioso: Carmen Russo', *Annabella*, 18 January 1986, p. 8.
44. Masi, *Italian Movie Goddesses*, p. 164.
45. C. Lazzaro, 'Italiani, l'erezione vi salvera', *L'Europeo*, no. 6, 1994, reproduced in *L'Europeo*, July 2002, pp. 212–15, 212.
46. Ibid., p. 215.
47. A. Farassino, 'Luci rosse a noi due!: viva l'eros sullo schermo purchè resti misterioso', *La Repubblica*, 11 December 1985, p. 23. For a further denunciation by Lattuada of Brass, see A. M. Mori, 'Basta con l'erotismo e ora di protestare', *La Repubblica*, 3 June 1987, p. 25.
48. Quoted in M. Anselmi, 'Una "maggiorata" per Goldoni', *L'Unita*, 5 May 1985, p. 15.
49. Ibid.
50. F. Massa, 'Signorina Grandi Forme', *L'Espresso*, 10 November 1985, pp. 123–30, 123.
51. Quoted in N. Aspesi, 'Ave Serena siamo tutti pazzi di te', *La Repubblica*, 3 September 1986, p. 29.
52. Ibid.
53. Quoted in S. Barile, 'Dico basta al sesso', *TV Radiocorriere*, 2–8 March 1986, p. 35.
54. A. M. Mori, 'Serena, che ci viene dal mondo dell'Eros', *La Repubblica*, 18 October 1985, p. 28.
55. Ibid.
56. R. Renzi, *L'ombra di Fellini* (Bari: Dedalo, 1994), pp. 189–91.
57. Massa, 'Signorina Grandi Forme', pp. 123–30, 123.
58. Ibid., p. 123.
59. V. Spiga, 'Il sesso per capriccio: Tinto Brass ci svela il suo ultimo film scandalo', *Il Resto del Carlino*, 28 January 1987, Sezione Spettacoli p. IX.
60. M. Anselmi, '"Le case chiuse? Bellissime ma oggi sarebbero uno squallore"', *L'Unità*, 8 February 1991, p. 21.
61. Ibid.
62. M. Anselmi, 'Un Brass alla "paprika" in cerca di successo', *L'Unità*, 16 February 1991, p. 23.
63. See M. P. Fusco, 'Koll, sotto il vestito la voglia di cultura', *La Repubblica*, 16 January 1995, p. 25.
64. See O. Calabrese, 'Ecco il cinema a luce rosa', *L'Unità*, 10 March 1985, p. 13.
65. M. Giovannini, 'Chi dice porno dice donna: intervista con Giuliana Gamba', *Panorama*, 1 February 1987, p. 149.

66. F. Alberoni, *Erotismo* (Milan: Garzanti, 1989).

67. F. Alberoni, 'E torna il cinema italiano . . .', *La Repubblica*, 14 February 1985, pp. 1 and 4.

68. R. Chiodi, 'Porno Italia', *L'Espresso*, 25 September 1988, pp. 24–6.

69. For Italian coverage of this event, see P. Boccacci, 'Cicciolina comizio a seno nudo', *La Repubblica*, 29 May 1987, pp. 1 and 4.

70. L. Irdi, 'In camera mia', *Europeo*, 7 November 1987, p. 40. Staller recalled the slogan in this interview and claimed that it was anti-conformist.

71. C. Castellani, 'Nel paradiso di Cicciolina', *Anna*, 13 September 1986, p. 41.

72. In the previous two election campaigns, the Radicals had put up and secured the election of two public figures, the political theorist Toni Negri and the television presenter Enzo Tortora, who had been imprisoned on questionable grounds. These candidatures were intended to provoke public opinion and dramatise the problems of preventive imprisonment and the rights of the defendant.

73. Gr.b., 'Cicciolina, un business in crisi, adesso è una diva a luci spente', *La Repubblica*, 18 August 1987, p. 4.

74. For an interview with Moana Pozzi as an election candidate, see G. Valentini, 'Moana: "Farò meglio di Cicciolina"', *La Repubblica*, 23 January 1992, p. 13.

75. See A. Longo, 'Solo, 45 anni, impiegato; ecco il pornomane d'Italia', *La Repubblica*, 21–22 June 1992, p. 10. The article contains a summary of an official report into the consumption of pornography.

76. Ibid..

77. Anon., 'Moana in Tv? Le casalinghe diffidano la Rai', *La Repubblica*, 3 October 1987, p. 18.

78. It was said that the stars of Diva Futura, all middle class and educated, transformed the public image of the porn star, while the rest of the industry prospered on the back of declining careers and lost hopes. For the decline of Lili Carati from soft-core actress into drug addiction, hard-core and eventually jail, see R. Salemi, 'Il corpo del reato', *L'Europeo*, 22 May 1988, pp. 60–1.

79. See, for example, E. Arosio, 'Santa Moana Vergine', *L'Espresso*, 30 September 1994, pp. 68–72; S. Pende, 'La doppia vita di Moana', *Panorama*, 30 September 1994, pp. 58–63; N. Aspesi, 'Moana porno e santa', *La Repubblica*, 20 September 1994, p. 29.

80. R. D'Agostino, 'Sogno italiano', *L'Espresso*, 30 September 1994, p. 69. A film based on Pozzi's life, *Guardami*, by Davide Ferrario, was released in 1999. On her life, see M. Giusti, *Moana* (Milan: Mondadori, 2004) and F. Parravicini, *Moana: tutta la verità* (Reggio Emilia: Aliberti, 2006).

81. G. Genna, *Dies Irae* (Milan: Rizzoli, 2006), p. 205.

82. Ibid., p. 207.

83. Ibid., p. 206.

84. D. Gianeri, 'Maîtresses-à-penser nude alla meta', *La Stampa*, 9 June 1993, p. 21.

85. See, for example, Castellani, 'Nel paradiso di Cicciolina', pp. 38–45.

86. N. Aspesi, 'L'eros in tasca', *La Repubblica*, 16 June 1989, pp. 32–3. See also Aspesi, 'Vedo porno', *La Repubblica*, 13 June 1989, pp. 32–3 and 'Se il porno è femmina', *La Repubblica*, 21 June 1989, pp. 28–9.

87. Quoted in R. Leone, 'Cicciolina sposta i confini del pudore', *La Repubblica*, 1–2 March 1992, p. 4.

88. For an investigation into the various meanings and consequences of this event, see S. Luzzatto, *Il corpo del duce: un cadavere tra immaginazione, storia e memoria* (Turin: Einaudi, 1998).

89. She strenuously opposed the proposal of the Italian Social Movement leader Gianfranco Fini to dissolve the MSI and create a new post-Fascist party, Alleanza Nazionale. She nevertheless remained in the party and later stood as a candidate of the centre-right for the post of mayor of Naples. She eventually abandoned Alleanza Nazionale and founded a new party of the far right on whose ticket she was elected to the European Parliament in 2004.

Chapter Ten

1. See M. Ardizzoni, 'Redrawing the Boundaries of Italianness: Televised Identities in the Age of Globalisation', *Social Identities*, 11:5, 1995, pp. 509–30.

2. J. Foot, 'Immigration and the city: Milan and mass immigration, 1958–98', *Modern Italy*, 4:2 (1999), pp. 159–72, 169.

3. F. Daly, 'Tunisian migrants and their experience of racism in Modena', *Modern Italy*, 4:2 (1999), pp. 173–89, 175.

4. R. King and J. Andall, 'The geography and economic sociology of recent immigration to Italy', *Modern Italy*, 4:2 (1999), pp. 135–58, 152.

5. For a broader discussion of the themes of this section, see S. Gundle, 'Miss Italia in Black and White: Feminine Beauty and Ethnic Identity in Modern Italy', in S. Ponzanesi and D. Merolla (eds), *Migrant Cartographies: New Cultural and Literary Spaces in Post-Colonial Europe* (Lanham MD: Lexington Books/Rowman & Littlefield, 2005), pp. 253–66.

6. Quoted in S. Viviani, 'C'è una Miss ideale ma non è tutta di un pezzo', *Oggi*, 4 September 1996, p. 64.
7. Quoted in A. Orlando and D. Burchiellaro, 'E io cerco un'italiana vera', *Panorama*, 12 September 1996, pp. 144–5.
8. Quoted in Anon., 'Ma l'Italia vota le bionde', *La Repubblica*, 4 September 1995, p. 15.
9. Quoted in ibid., p. 145.
10. Among many works, see A. Del Boca, *L'Africa nella coscienza degli italiani: miti, memorie, errori, sconfitte* (Rome and Bari: Laterza, 1992).
11. Paola Tabet, *La pelle giusta* (Turin: Eianaudi, 1997).
12. Quoted in C. Rogledi, '"Mi hanno usato per influenzare il voto"', *Visto*, 20 September 1996, p. 18.
13. Quoted in M. N. De Luca, 'Parietti pentita "Ma non dite che sono razzista"', *La Repubblica*, 8 September 1996, p. 19.
14. N. Ajello, 'La Miss dei buonisti', *La Repubblica*, 9 September 1996, pp. 1, 17.
15. A. Scotti, 'Italiani divisi sulla "Perla nera"', *Corriere della sera*, 9 September 1996, p. 18.
16. M. N. De Luca, 'Miss Cinema e Danny (sic) italiana di San Domingo', *La Repubblica*, 5 September 1996, p. 22.
17. Quoted in M. N. De Luca, '"Non importa per i fischi io mi sento italiana"', *La Repubblica*, 8 September 1996, p. 19.
18. Quoted in M. N. De Luca, '"Ti dicono bellissima e poi ti discriminano"', *La Repubblica*, 6 September 1996, p. 19.
19. G. Zincone, 'Da Gramsci alla Mendez', *Corriere della sera*, 11 September 1996, p. 1.
20. See 'Reginetta nera', p. 34.
21. On programmes presented by members of ethnic minorities, see Ardizzoni, 'Redrawing the Boundaries', pp. 517–26.
22. King and Andall, 'The geography and economic sociology of recent immigration', p. 165.
23. Cited in M. N. De Luca, 'La miss nea divide in due l'Italia', *La Repubblica*, 9 September 1996, p. 17.
24. See the opinions expressed in 'Reginetta nera si reginetta nera no', *Oggi*, 18 September 1996, p. 34.
25. A. Varano, 'Vattimo: "Ma non cancella il razzismo"', *L'Unita*, 9 September 1996, p. 9.
26. Scotti, 'Italiani divisi', p. 18.
27. In fact Mendez's victory was by no means a landslide. She won a relative majority of 1.13 million votes out of a total of 3.94 million. A Sardinian achieved just 28,000 fewer votes to win second place and four other candidates won a combined total of 1.7 million. She received nine out of thirty available jury votes.
28. Varano, 'Vattimo', p. 9.
29. Rogledi, '"Mi hanno usato"', p. 19.
30. See F. Ceccarelli, 'Folklore, ammiccamenti e appelli alla "purezza politica" al maxi-concorso di bellezza organizzato dal Carroccio', *La Stampa*, 3 April 1998, p. 6.
31. A. Rognoni, 'Ma le miss hanno i tratti da vera padana?', *Il Sole delle Alpi*, undated 1997, p. 80.
32. Quoted in Anon., 'Tutti i colori delle miss', *La Padania*, 24 March 1998, p. 23.
33. Anon., 'Quell'autografo sul petto', *La Padania*, 9 March 1998, page unnumbered.
34. Quoted in C. Pilloli, 'E una diciotenne la prima Miss Padania', *Il Messaggero*, 4 April 1998.
35. Ibid.
36. F. Arensi, 'La mia missione di bagnino. Un sacrificio da ripetere', *La Padania*, 24 March 1998, p. 23.
37. M. Parisi, 'Miss Padania, stretta finale', *La Padania*, 21 March 1998, p. 22.
38. P. Pellai, 'Carol, l'amica degli animali', *La Padania*, 24 March 1998, p. 23.
39. 'Miss Padania: addio Lega', *Il Giornale*, 18 July 1998.
40. *http://www.gossipnews.it/mondanita/miss_padania_2005/*
41. The names refer to the supermodels in vogue at the time: Cindy Crawford, Claudia Schiffer, Naomi Campbell, Linda Evangelista and Kate Moss. See L. Bolla and F. Cardini, *Carne in scatola: la rappresentazione del corpo nella televisione italiana* (Rome: Rai-Eri, 1999), p. 13.
42. Quoted in D. Campana, 'Lorella d'Italia', *Il Giorno*, 13 January 1987, p. 3. See also, Claudio Castellani, 'Lorella la candida', *Anna*, 1 August 1987, pp. 46–50.
43. L. Laurenzi, 'Lorella Lorella più zuccherosa che mai', *Televenerdi*, *La Repubblica*, 31 March 1995, p. 28.
44. I. Bossi Fedigrotti, 'Per me pari sono', *Epoca*, 3 March 1993, p. 13.
45. On her appropriation of the mantle of Monroe, see Mimmo Pacifici, 'In TV piaccio a tutti meno che a papà', *Oggi*, 24 January 1994, pp. 68–9. More generally, see S. Gundle, 'Fenomenologia di Valeria Marini e Pamela Anderson', *Altochemestre*, 5, 1997, pp. 35–7.
46. Anon. '"La Marini è tutta rifatta"', *La Repubblica*, 13 July 1996, p. 18; for her response, see E. Bertolotto, '"Ma quale bisturi sono bella e naturale"', *La Repubblica*, 15 July 1996, p. 17.
47. See M. N. De Luca, 'Signorine Grandi forme', *La Repubblica*, 6 February 1995, p. 19; M. Serra, 'Il tuo talento è la quantità Valeria, sei l'essenza della tv', *La Repubblica*, 21 February 1997, p. 45; M. Simonetti, 'L'audience va su con sette chili di più', *L'Espresso*, 24 February 1995, p. 127.
48. The most telling article in this sense was N. Aspesi, 'La rivincita del Sedere', *La Repubblica*, 3 March 1998, pp. 1, 23. See also, Aspesi, 'Valeria, il gioco dell'Oca', *La Repubblica*, 20 February 1997, pp. 1, 42.

49. M. Chiesi and L. Cornero, 'Introduzione' in L. Cornero (ed.), *Una, nessuna . . . a quando centomila?: La rappresentazione della donna in televisione* (Rome: Rai-Eri, 2001), p. 25.
50. L. Cornero, 'Presentazione' in Cornero, *Una, nessuna . . . a quando centomila?*, p. 11.
51. C. Demaria, 'Di genere in genere: le autorappresentazioni del femminile' in Cornero, *Una, nessuna . . . a quando centomila?*, p. 220.
52. The expression was coined by Angelo Guglielmi, director of RAI-3.
53. A. Bevilacqua, 'L'atroce dilemma', *Epoca*, 3 March 1993, p. 12.
54. Quoted in L. Maragnani, 'Sinistra dell'eros', *Panorama*, 30 June 1991, p. 127.
55. G. Melli, A.Ponta, S.Viviani, 'Care dive, siete rifatte?', *Oggi*, 28 January 1995, pp. 36–40.
56. Quoted in D. Matelli, 'Alba, che macello', *L'Espresso*, 16 October 1997, p. 148.
57. M. S. Conte, 'La Chiesa contro Santoro e Parietti', *La Repubblica*, 21–2 February 1993, p. 19.
58. M. A. Mori, '"Senza veli, senza Dio"', *La Repubblica*, 8 September 1993, p. 20.
59. Quoted in Mori, '"Senza veli, senzo Dio"', p. 20.
60. Quoted in A. Scotti, 'La "Perla nera" eletta Miss Italia', *Corriere della sera*, 8 September 1996, p. 17. However, in further declarations, the showgirl offered a further insight into her views: 'There is nothing racist in saying a person cannot be Miss Italia. . . . It is as if an Italian wanted to run for Miss Congo'.
61. C. De Gregorio, '"Parietti, coscia lunga pds"', *La Repubblica*, 5 January 1994, p. 10.
62. B. Palombelli, 'Risorge l'Alba', *La Repubblica*, 5 April 1997, page unnumbered.
63. A typical review was M. Anselmi, 'Bambola sgonfiata', *L'Unità*, 7 September 1996, p. 3, in which the film was described as 'bad, mad and erotically sub-zero'. Marini fared no better when she starred alongside veteran comic actor Alberto Sordi in *Incontri proibiti* in 1998. See S. Fumarola, '"Ma non è colpa mia se il cinema è in crisi"', *La Repubblica*, 24 October 1998, p. 24.
64. Quoted in M. P. Fusco, 'Cucinotta, diva riservata', *La Repubblica*, 12 September 1998, p. 41.
65. Z. Cremonini, 'Una sensuale elegante seduzione italiana', *Vogue Italia*, August 1995.
66. Rogledi, '"Mi hanno usato"', p. 19.
67. Quoted in R. Simone, 'Maria Grazia Cucinotta', *Max*, October 2000, page unnumbered.
68. S. Viviani, 'La moglie ideale esiste: è siciliana, sincera e fedele', *Oggi*, 28 August 1996, pp. 33–43.
69. For a polemical comment on this, see G. Mughini, 'Il bellismo, malattia senile del capitalismo', *Panorama*, 25 January 1995, p. 39.
70. 'Maria Grazia ha vinto la "Guerra delle foto"', *Oggi*, 3 February 1999, p. 57.
71. Quoted in Antonella Amedola and Mauro Suttora, 'Tra Maria Grazia e Sofia' *Oggi*, 7 February 1996, p. 60.
72. Quoted in B. Palombelli, 'Dal Sud con amore una storia made in Italy', *La Repubblica*, 30 July 1995, p. 9.
73. Fusco, 'Cucinotta, diva riservata', p. 41.
74. Quoted in M. C. Crucillà, 'Che tormento avere il seno che manda tutti in estasi!', *Oggi*, 9 April 1997, p. 66.
75. L. Palestini, 'Cucinotta: "Riaprite le case chiuse"', *La Repubblica*, 22 January 1999, p. 46.
76. C. Morvillo, 'Complimenti, Maria Grazia: sei la Marianna ideale degli italiani', *Oggi*, 27 October 1999, pp. 38–43.
77. N. Aspesi, 'Maria Grazia insegue Sophia ma e vera diva?', *La Repubblica*, 29 April 1996, p. 25.
78. Simone, 'Cucinotta'.

Chapter Eleven

1. L. Ravera, 'Belli senz'anima', *L'Espresso*, 7 January 1990, pp. 72–3. Her position recalls that of the theorist Christopher Lasch, *The Culture of Narcissism: American Life in an Age of Diminishing Expectations* (New York: Norton, 1978). For a satirical comment on the contemporary cult of the body, see P. Villaggio, 'Vorrei essere bello, snello e felice . . . come in uno spot', *L'Unità*, 28 February 1993, p. 8.
2. L. Bolla and F. Cardini, *Carne in scatola: la rappresentazione del corpo nella televisione italiana* (Rome: Rai-Eri, 1999), p. 12.
3. For an illuminating account of the impact of television on the appearance and behaviour of viewers, see L. Fantini, *Fare casting: peripezie di un selezionatore di italiani per la tv* (Milan: Feltrinelli, 1996).
4. C. Augias 'Vorrei opporre la Bellucci alla Ferilli', exchange with the reader Mimmo Morabito of Rome in the letters column of *La Repubblica*, 11 February 2001, p. 16.
5. Ibid.
6. Garth Pearce, 'Here's looking at you', *Sunday Times*, Culture supplement, 30 October 2005, p. 5.
7. Pino Buongiorno, 'Bella grinta!', *Panorama*, 25 February 1990, p. 115.
8. Ibid., p. 114.
9. O. Toscani, 'La bella perugina', *Panorama*, 25 February 1990, p. 117.
10. Ibid.

11. J. Nathan, 'Mad About Monica', *Night and Day*, supplement to *Daily Mail*, 24 August 2003, p. 41.
12. G. Dyer, 'And God created Monica . . .', *In Style*, May 2001, p. 122.
13. 'La sfida di Monica', *Inserto promozionale: il cinema italiano in diretta con l'Associazione Philip Morris Progetto Cinema*, n.26 (1999), p. 1.
14. *GQ* UK, February 2002.
15. M. P. Fusco, 'Monica Bellucci: "Con Tornatore sfido me stessa"', *La Repubblica*, 19 September 1999, p. 35.
16. Pearce, 'Here's looking', p. 5.
17. See, for example, the observations in F. Sacchetti, 'Ero una top, sono una splatter', *Panorama*, 4 December 1997, p. 257.
18. 'Bellissima Belluccci by Monica', *Zoom*, November–December 1991, p. 41.
19. Dyer, 'And God created Monica . . .', p. 122.
20. 'Bellissima Bellucci', p. 41.
21. M. Bellucci, 'Belle di natura', *Ulisse 2000*, July 2000, p. 82.
22. Ibid.
23. M. Bellucci, 'È il giardino del mondo', *Riflessi*, March 1998, p. 17.
24. N. Norman, '"I suffer for my beauty"', *Evening Standard*, 21 March 2001, p. 29.
25. R. Romano, 'Totti aspettami che torno', *Panorama*, 16 November 2000.
26. See Paul Ginsborg, *Italy and Its Discontents* (London: Allen Lane, 2001), pp. 86–7, 90–1, 108–12.
27. Anon., 'Sabrina Ferilli, la più desiderata', *La Repubblica*, 5 January 1997.
28. 'Il seno è ancora un protagonista importante', she sighed in E. Bonerandi, 'Sabrina senza veli compagna del 2000', *La Repubblica*, 30 October 1999, p. 24.
29. G. Melli, 'Che complesso avere il seno più sognato d'Italia', *Oggi*, 22 January 1997, pp. 18–23.
30. E. Biagi, 'Anche il décolleté di Sabrina è tradizione nazionale', *Sette*, 23 February 1997.
31. C. Pace, 'Sono la più desiderata perchè non faccio nulla per sedurre', *Oggi*, 31 December 1999, p. 40.
32. Ibid. p. 42.
33. M. C. Crucillà, 'Attenti: nella coppia di amanti ideali sono io a tradire davvero', *Oggi*, 23 August 2000, p. 53.
34. In fact, some staged paparazzi shots of her topless appeared in *Novella 2000*, 13 September 1992, pp. 82–3.
35. E. Bonerandi, 'Sabrina senza veli compagna del 2000', *La Repubblica*, 30 October 1999, p. 24.
36. Pace, 'Sono la più desiderata' pp. 40–4.
37. Ginsborg, *Italy and Its Discontents*, p. 113.
38. Ibid..
39. R. Barthes, 'Striptease', in *Mythologies* (London: Paladin 1979; first published Paris 1957), pp. 86–7.
40. Ibid., pp. 84–5.
41. Anon., *Sabrina come Sophia la piu bella del reame*, in Http://www.kwcinema.it/templates/kwc_popup_stampa/0,2670,2357,00html, 1 November 2000.
42. 'Vorrei opporre la Bellucci alla Ferilli', exchange with the reader Mimmo Morabito of Rome in the letters column of *La Repubblica*, 11 February 2001, p. 16.
43. Romano, 'Totti aspettami che torno'.
44. Ginsborg, *Italy and Its Discontents*, p. 68.
45. Quoted in L. Delli Colli, 'Tutti stretti a Sabrina', *Panorama*, 6 November 1997, p. 188.
46. P. Carrano, *La Magnani* (Milan: Rizzoli, 1982).
47. Ginsborg, *Italy and Its Discontents*, p. 112.
48. Ibid., p. 122, N. Rothenberg, 'Women and Mass Communication in Italy' (University of London PhD thesis, 2005), Chapter 5.

Conclusion

1. G. Ferrero, *L'Europa giovane* (Milan: Treves, 1897), p. 141.
2. M. Agulhon, *Les métamorphoses de Marianne: l'imagerie et la symbolique républicaine de 1914 à nos jours* (Paris: Flammarion, 2001), p. 204.
3. C. Beaton, *The Glass of Fashion* (London: Weidenfeld and Nicolson, 1954), p. 65.
4. Ibid., p. 66.
5. The rivalry between the two actresses was still noticeable in 2006. Following the announcement that Loren would, at the age of 71, pose for the Pirelli calendar, Lollobrigida was asked if she would consider doing the same. The actress, who took up photography, sculpture and dress design after her film career faded, responded: 'No [laughs]. We are quite different. I have different interests. My interest is art. I'm lucky that I have talents'. M. Anderson, 'We Dream of Gina', *Time Out New York*, 17 August 2006.

6. S. Loren, *Women & Beauty* (London: Aurum, 1984), p. 9.
7. C. Pasquinelli, 'Beyond the Longest Revolution: the Impact of the Italian Women's Movement on Cultural and Social Change', *Praxis International*, 4:2, 1984, pp. 136, 132.
8. L. Cornero (ed.), *Una nessuna . . . a quando centomila? La rappresentazione della donna in televisione* (Rome: Rai-Eri, 2001), p. 15.
9. M. Buonanno, *Visibilità senza potere: le sorti progressive ma non magnifiche delle donne giornaliste italiane* (Naples: Liguori, 2005), p. 18.
10. See ibid..

INDEX

Page numbers in italics refer to an illustration.

A ruota libera (film) 257
abortion and feminist campaign in Italy
193–4
Abruzzi: women of 122–3
actresses
as courtesans 60, 62, 64, 76
D'Annunzio and Eleonora Duse 46–8
in Fascist era 103–6
foreign actresses in Italian cinema
170–1, 172, 176–7
Italian actresses in international
cinema 157–63, 180, 190, 195,
243, 248–50
and Miss Italia contest 119–21, 123–4
and Miss *Vie Nuove* contest 133, 136,
138, 140
rise of actress as role model 59, 60,
75–9
see also star culture
Adam, Paul 60, 61
Adjani, Isabelle 251
advertisements
American view of Italians 163
Church opposition to beauty contests
127–8, 128–9
in Communist press 139
and contemporary actresses 250, 253
in mass consumption era 171–3
modern woman in Fascist era 80–1,
82
see also calendar photo-shoots; mass
consumption and ideals of
beauty
aesthetics and feminine beauty xix, 1
aestheticisation of southern Italy 52–4
Grand Tour view of Italian women 4
age and feminine beauty xxiv
Agren, Janet 201
Agulhon, Maurice xxii–xxiii
Ajello, Nello 227
Alberoni, Francesco 211

Albertin, Laura 232
Alfieri, Vittorio 19, 20
Alla ricerca di Sheherezade (TV series)
258
Allasio, Marisa 176, 209–10, 260
Alleanza Nazionale 286*n*.45
allegory and allusion xx, 7, 19–21, 28–9,
263
symbolism of breasts 8, 21, 270*n*.23
Allied forces in Italy 108–9, 114
Alma-Tadema, Sir Lawrence 42
Almost America (TV series) 253–4
Altri tempi (film) 149
Amarcord (film) 197, 198–9, 207
America
appeal of Italian stars in 157–9
and Fascist monopoly on foreign
films 103, 109
influence in mass consumption era
170
influence on modern woman 81–2,
83–4
postwar influences 108–16, 127
view of Italy 161–3, 185
see also Hollywood films
Americano Rosso (film) 253
Amica (magazine) 192
amour de Swann, Un (film) 195
Andall, J. 228
Andreotti, Giulio 156, 192
Andress, Ursula 179
Annigoni, Pietro: *La bella italiana* 164,
165
Anselmi, Michele 209
Antelling, Mara 61
anthropology 54, 55–7
ideal of Italian beauty 56–7
Antonelli, Laura 201–4, *202*
Antonioni, Michelangelo 120, 136,
185–6
Appartement, L' (film) 248

Archibugi, Francesca 213
Arcuri, Manuela xiii, 257–60, *258*
Ardigò, Achille 176
Arena, Maurizio 176
Arensi, Flavio 231–2
Arianna (magazine) 192
Ariosto, Ludovico 3
Armani, Giorgio 242, 260
art
and images of Italy 1–4
inspired by feminine beauty xv, 11,
26–7
Miss Italia painting competition
163–4, *164*, *165*
peasant girl models on Capri *31*, 52
and Risorgimento 19–25
see also Renaissance art
art-house films 185–6, 189, 205–11
artificial beauty
Church warnings 128–9
and cinema 83–4
Communist dislike as bourgeois
137
Fascist disapproval 92, 94–6, 101,
103
in mass consumption era 172–3, 179
modern woman of interwar years
82–3, 86–7
Parisian women of the nineteenth
century 60–1, 78
on television 233, 236–7
see also cosmetics
Artusi, Pellegrino 57
Aspesi, Natalia 173, 210
Assisi Underground, The (film) 219–20
Astérix et Obélix: Mission Cléopatre
(film) 249
Atanasio, Padre 128
Augias, Corrado 246, 256
Azeglio, Massimo Taparellu, Marchese d'
16, 19

Bacchelli, Riccardo 122
Bagnasco, Arnaldo 236
Bagnomaria (film) 257–8
Baldini, Antonio 122
Balzac, Honoré de 60
Bambola (film) 238
Banfi Malaguzzi, Daria 86
Banti, Alberto 31
Barbara, Paola 103–4
barbarism of south 53–4
Barbieri, Paolo 250
Bardot, Brigitte xviii, 170, 189
Bariatinsky, Prince Alexander 65, 71
Barthes, Roland 171, 255–6
Bartolini, Elio 151, 165
Bartolini, Luigi 164
Beaton, Cecil 59, 69, 78, 174, 264
beauty *see* feminine beauty
beauty contests
    birth of 72–4, 76
    Church opposition to 126, 127–8
    Communist contests
        stelline dell'Unità 130–1
        Vie Nuove contest 131–6, *132*, *136*,
            137–8, 140
    and ethnicity of contestants 223–32
    film career aspirations of contestants
        and Communist contests 133, 134,
            136, 138, 140
        film stars of 1950s 155–6, 158, 159
        Miss Italia contest 119–21, 123–4
        and starlet status 159
    film magazine competitions 84
    Grandi Firme contest 91–2
    in postwar Italy 108, 116–21
    see also Miss Italia contest
'bella abissina' 99
bella di Lodi, La (film) 178
bella italiana xvii, xxiii, xxiv–xxv, 34, 261
    and ethnicity 225–32
    Fascist appropriation of 97–8, 101–3
    Lina Cavalieri as 59
    in mass consumption era 179–90
    postwar backlash against Hollywood
        glamour 113–14
    present-day incarnations 245–60
    radio discussion on 122–3
    see also beauty contests; Miss Italia
        contest
bella italiana, La (*Domus* supplements)
    96–8, 112–13
'bella Rosina', 'la' *see* Vercellana, Rosa
bella vita, La (film) 253
bell'Antonio, Il (film) 186
Belle Otero, La 60, 64, 76
bellezza d'Ippolita, La (film) 151, 165
Bellucci, Monica xv–xvi, xvii, xviii, 244,
    246–52, *247*, 264
Bembo, Pietro 3
Ben-Ghiat, Ruth 99
Benjamin, Walter 138
Berlusconi, Silvio 205, 233, 234
Bernari, Carlo 136
Berte, Loredana 193
Bertini, Francesca 83, 85
Bertocchi, Lucia 138

Bertolucci, Bernardo 200, 211
Bevilacqua, Alberto 235–6
Beynet, Michel 90
Biagi, Enzo 75, 228, 254
Bianco, rosso e ... (film) 219
Bicycle Thieves (film) 133, 136
Bidone, Il (film) 199
Bini, Alfredo 180
black immigrants in Italy 223, 224, 228
    Miss Italia winner in 1990s 223, 224–9
Blasetti, Alessandro 134, 136, 149
Boccaccio, Giovanni 3, 38
Boccaccio 70 (film) 172, 183, 248
Boccasile, Gino 81, 89, 90, 91, 110, *113*
body
    contemporary obsession with 245
    see also physical beauty; thinness
'body-landscape' 145–6, 147
Bogart, Humphrey 157
Boiardo, Matteo Maria 3
Boldini, Giovanni 40, 58, 75, 78
Bologna: women of 27, 122, 207
Bolognini, Mauro 175, 181, 188
Boncristiano, Silvia 231
Bongiorno, Mike 193
Borelli, Lyda 83
Borgese, Leonardo 164
Borgia, Lucrezia 38
Borrani, Odoardo: *Il 26 aprile 1859* 22,
    24
Bosé, Lucia 119, 120–1, *120*, 143, 147
Bossi, Umberto 229, 230–1, 232
Botticelli, Sandro 3, 38
Bouchet, Barbara 201
Boy on a Dolphin (film) 161, 162
Bracco, Roberto 72
Bram Stoker's Dracula (film) 248
Brand, C. P. 4
Brass, Tinto 205–11, 231, 238
breasts
    and allegorical females 8, 21, 270*n*.23
    contemporary appeal of Ferilli 254
    film stars of 1950s 154, 156, 158, 159,
        162–3
    meanings attributed to xxi–xxii
    and national beauty xxii, 101
Breen, Joseph 146
Brilli, Attilio 16
Brin, Irene 83–4
Bronzino, Il 3
Brothers Grimm, The (film) 249
Browning, Elizabeth Barrett 9
Browning, Robert 9
Brunetta, Gian Piero 109
Bulgari, Anna Maria 134
Burns, John 114

café-chantant, Il (magazine) 75–6
Calamai, Clara 103
calendar photo-shoots xvii, *241*, 250,
    255, 258–9
    Miss Italia calendar 266–8, *267*, *268*
Caligula (film) 205
Calvino, Italo 144–5
Calzini, Raffaele 85, 92, 94, 97–8, 112
Campagnoli, Edy 140

Campari, Giuseppe 79
Canale, Gianna Maria 119, 124
Candiani, Carla 103
Canova, Antonio 19–20
Canzone d'amore (film) 86
Capa, Robert 145
Capri: peasant girl models *31*, 52
Capriccio (film) 205, 208–9
Caprioglio, Debora 205, 209–210
Carabinieri (TV series) 259
Carati, Lilli 201
Cardarelli, Vincenzo 118–19
Cardinale, Claudia xvi, 171, 185–90, *187*,
    and Fellini 198
    in *Il Gattopardo* 167–8, *168*
    as Miss Italia judge 225
Carducci, Giosuè 35–6
Carmen di Trastevere (*Carmen '63*)
    (film) 181
Carol, Martine 197
Carrà, Carlo 164
Carrà, Raffaella 233
Carrano, Patrizia 259
Casanova (film) 197
Caselli, Caterina 178
Casiraghi, Ugo 137, 139–40
Cassel, Vincent 249
Casta, Laetitia 243–4
Castellina, Luciana 282*n*.42
Catholic Church
    and feminine beauty xviii, xix, 28, 49,
        127–31
        condemnation of *Riso amaro* 146–7
        disapproval of 1950s stars 168–9
        maternal beauty 93
        opposition to beauty contests 126,
            127–8
        and Parietti's views 237
        repressive role 262
        view on porn stars 216, 217
    and political parties 125, 126
    role in postwar civil society 125, 126
    and scientific study 55
Catholic Cinema Commission 146–7
Cattaneo, Franca 173
Cavalieri, Lina 58–9, 62–79, *63*, *67*, *69*,
    246, 264
    film career 67–8, 78–9
    as Italian beauty 59, 68–70, 72–3, 79
    Lollobrigida plays on screen 58, 151,
        152
    operatic career 65–7, 70–1, 77
Ceccani, Palmira 74
Cecchelli, Carlo 99
Cecchi, Emilio 87
Celentano, Adriano 195
censorship 92, 146–7, 192, 211
C'era una volta il West (*Once Upon a
    Time in the West*) (film) 186, *187*
Chanel, Coco 81–2
Chanler, Robert W. 71
chiave, La (film) 205, 206
Chiti, Ugo 240, 242, 243
Christian Democrats
    alliance with Catholic Church 125,
        126

Christian Democrats (*cont.*)
  and cinema 133, 156, 192
  Cuccarini's support 233
  and feminine beauty 126, 129
  and mass consumption era 170
Chronicle of a Death Foretold (film) 195
Church *see* Catholic Church
Ciano, Galeazzo 89
Cicciolina (Illona Staller) 211–14, *213*,
  215, 218
Cicciolina amore mio (film) 213
Cicciolina e Moana ai mondiali (film)
  214
'cicisbeishib' 3
cinema
  American films in postwar era 108–16
    'pin-up girls' 109–12
  art-house films 185–6, 189, 205–11
  Communist support for Italian
    cinema 133
  in Fascist era 103–6, 109
    Hollywood stars and artificial
      beauty 83–4
  imitation of American model 85–6
  Italian actresses in international
    cinema 157–63, 180, 190, 195,
    243, 248–50
  and literature 164–8
  sex films 200–18, 238
  see also actresses; historical films;
    Hollywood films; neo-realist
    cinema; star culture
Cinema Illustrazione (magazine) 84,
  85–6
ciociara, La (*Two Women*) (film) 155,
  182–3
citizenship
  of immigrants 224–5
  and women xxi
città delle donne, La (film) 197, 199–200
Ciuffini, Sabina 193
civil society: postwar rebuilding 125
Cléry, Corinne 201
Colombino, Molino 127
colonialism
  'colonial gaze' 162
  Ethiopia 98–9, 226–7
  miscegenation fears 99
  see also immigration in globalisation
    era
Colonna di Sermoneta, Princess Vittoria
  77
Comencini, Luigi 203
Commesse (TV series) 253–4
Communism
  and feminine beauty 125, 126,
    137–41, 237
    and beauty contests 129–36, 137–8,
      140
  and popular culture 126, 129–30,
    138–41
  and women's liberation 194
Con gli occhi chiusi (film) 210
consumerism *see* mass consumption and
  ideals of beauty
Conte, Maria Stella 191

Corcos, Vittorio 58
Cordelia (Italian writer) 40
Corradini, Enrico 72
Corriere della sera (newspaper) 89, 113,
  121, 229
Corriere Lombardo (newspaper) 114
corruzione, La (film) 181
Così fan tutte (film) 205, 210
cosmetic surgery 236–7, 251
cosmetics 60, 61
  adverts in Communist press 139
  Cavalieri's beauty business 79
  Church disapproval 128–9
  influence of cinema 83–4
  in mass consumption era 172–3
  and modern woman 82
  see also artificial beauty
costume films *see* historical films
Crawford, Joan 83–4, 158
Craxi, Bettino 214–15
Cremona, Luigi 46
criminology: deviance and ugliness 54–5
'crisis-woman' 88–9, *88*
Crispi, Francesco 46, 274*nn*. 51, 64
Cristaldi, Franco 186
Croce, Benedetto 37–8
Cronaca di un'amore (film) 147
Cruz, Penelope xvi, 213
Cuccarini, Lorella 226, 233–4, 235
Cucinotta, Maria Grazia xv–xvi, 224,
  238–44, *241*
culture of beauty xvi–xvii, xix

Da Verona, Guido 88
D'Agostino, Roberto 217
Damiani, Donatella 200, 201
dancing
  Church disapproval 127, 128
  and Communist ideology 131
  de Staël's *Corinne* 8–9
D'Annunzio, Gabriele 34, 41–8, 83, 89
  on Lina Cavalieri 58, 71
  and Eleonora Duse 46–8
  Il fuoco 48
  La Gioconda 48
  on 'Medusan beauty' 41–2
  Il Piacere 42–3
  politics and race 44–6
  on Queen Margherita 35
  Il trionfo della morte 43–4, 45
  Le vergini delle rocce 45
Dante Alighieri 3, 37
David, Arianna 225
De Amicis, Edmondo 36
De Filippo, Eduardo 183, 219, 221
De Filippo, Titina 185
De Giorgio, Michela 28, 127
de Lamartine *see* Lamartine, Alphonse
  de
De Luca, Lorella 176
De Napoli, V. 37, 39–40
De Roberto, Federico 167
De Rose, Francesca 232
De Sanctis, Francesco 18
De Santis, Giuseppe 134, 143, 146, 147,
  196–7, 253

De Sica, Vittorio 118, 152, 154–5, 183,
  185
de Staël *see* Staël, Mme de
decima vittima, La (film) 179
Del Boca, Angelo 227
Del Buono, Oreste 202
delfini, I (film) 186
Della Palma, Diego 226
Dellera, Francesca 205, 209
Demaria, Cristina 235
Deneuve, Catherine xxii
Denis, Maria 103, 104–5, *104*
Desiderando Giulia (film) 207
d'Este, Isabella 38
deviance and ugliness 54–5
di Carrara, Marina 231
Di Lazzaro, Eldo 94
Diamante, Cleo 76
Diario di un vizio (film) 253
Diaz, Laura 121, 282*n*.42
Digby, Kenelm 4
Dillian, Irasema 104
discourse *see* male discourse on
  feminine beauty
Diva Futura 212, 213, 214, 215
Divina creatura (film) 203
divorce referendum (1974) 191, 192
Divorzio all'italiano (film) 177
Dobermann (film) 248, 249
Dolce Vita, La (film) 170–1, 172, 197,
  198, 199
dolci inganni, I (film) 177
Domenica del Corriere, La (magazine)
  108, 113–14
Domenichino: *The Sibyl* 5, 6, 8
domestic sphere: women's place in art
  22, 23
Domus (magazine): *Bella italiana* 96–8,
  112–13
Donatella (film) 180
Donna, La (magazine) 73, 78
donna del fiume, La (film) 152
donna più bella del mondo, La (film)
  151, *152*
'donna-crisi' 88–9, *88*
D'Onofrio, Edoardo 135
Drago, Eleonora Rossi 119, 124, 163
Dudovich, Marcello 80–1, 82, *83*
Duranti, Doris 103, 104
Duse, Eleonora 46–8, *47*, 61, 66
Dyer, Geoff 249
Dylan, Bob 185

economic growth and mass
  consumption 170
8½ (film) 197–8, 200
Ekberg, Anita 170–1, 172
Elena of Montenegro 46
Elisabetta, Empress 40
emancipation of women 265–6
  in interwar years 81, 82
    Fascist reversal 87–8
    male discourse on 86–9, 100–1
    and Signorina *Grandi Firme* 91
  in mass consumption era 176
  permissive society 191–4

and porn stars 218
in postwar era 107, 116
American promotion of 114–15
women in politics 121–2, 218–19, 221
and women on television 235
women's liberation movement 193–4
see also feminism
Enciclopedia Italiana 89
English rose beauty 42–3
entertainment industry
and feminine beauty xix, 58–79
and postwar politics 126
see also beauty contests; cinema; press;
television
Epoca (magazine) 115–16
Era notte a Roma (film) 181
erotic beauty
Cavalieri's mystique 75
contemporary appeal of Ferilli 254–6
in D'Annunzio's work 42, 43–4, 46
de Lamartine's heroine 15–16
fin-de-siècle *Parisienne* 60, 78
foreign actresses 176–7
Italian film stars of 1950s 145–69
appeal of Italian stars abroad
157–63
peasant girl ideal 87
sex appeal of American stars
Italian actresses abroad 157–63, 190
Italian actresses in contrast to xvi
Italian version in *Riso amaro* 145–7
postwar 'pin-up girls' 109–12
and promotion of Italian beauty
112–16
Signorina *Grandi Firme* 89–90, *90*,
110, 205
soubrette type on television 233–5
stars of 1970s onwards xi, 191–2
in sex films 200–18, 238
see also *maggiorate fisiche* type;
physical beauty; sex
erotic comedies 201
Erté 59, 69, 78
Ethiopia
female bodies 98–9
Italian colonialism 98–9, 226–7
ethnicity
and feminine beauty xxiv, 55–7
black Miss Italia winner in 1990s
223, 224–9, 237
television's preference for blondes
172, 173
immigration in globalisation era
223–32
see also racial theory
Europe
Italian images in European culture
1–2
view of Italy and Italians 1–19
Grand Tour 2–4
in literature 4–16, 23–5
on physical beauty 61
and unified Italy 26–7
Eva (magazine) *93*, 96, *97*
'exotic' beauty
actresses in Fascist era 104–5

colonial subject 99
Italian women as xi, 229
eye colour aesthetics 52

Faccetta nera (song) 99
Fachinetti, Federico 195
Faeti, Antonio 90
Falchi, Anna 226
Famiglia cristiana (Catholic weekly) 127,
128–9
Fanfan la tulipe (film) 150
Fantastica Moana (film) 215
Farnese, Giulia 38
Fascism
colonialism 98–9, 226–7
and feminine beauty 80–1, 92–106
disapproval of modern woman
87–9, 92, 100–3
Fellini's nostalgia 198–9
see also *Gente Nostra*; Miss Padania
contest; Mussolini, Alessandra
fashion models
Bellucci as model 246, 248, 250
as role models 179, 226, 233
fashionable beauty
Bellucci and Dolce & Gabbana 250
Fascist disapproval 87–9, 92, 100–3
in mass consumption era 175, 179,
180
modern woman in interwar years
81–6
in the nineteenth century 40–4, 75–6
Lina Cavalieri 59, 77–8
Queen Margherita as role model
40–1, 61
Parisian women and fashion 60–1, 78
see also artificial beauty
Fedigrotti, Isabella Bossi 234
Fellini, Federico 188, 196–200, 207, 215,
256
La Dolce Vita 172, 197, *198*, 199
and Tinto Brass 209
feminine beauty
definitions of xxiii–xxiv
and national identity xviii–xxiii
feminism 199–200, 235
women's liberation in Italy 193–4,
265–6
see also emancipation of women
femmes fatales 42, 44, 47, 71, 83–4, 88,
249
Fenech, Edwige 201, 257–8
Ferida, Luisa 104
Ferie d'agosto (film) 253
Ferilli, Sabrina xvii, xviii, 252–7, *254*, *256*
Ferrara, Rosina 52
Ferreri, Marco 253
Ferrero, Anna Maria 175, 181
Ferrero, Guglielmo xx–xxi, 55, 56, 262
Ferri, Fabrizio 250
Ferri, Katia 171
fertility see mothers; reproduction
FHM (magazine) 240
film magazines: photographic
competitions 84
Finck, Henry 52

Fini, Gianfranco 286*n*.45
Fininvest 205, 233
flappers 80, 81, 88
Flash Gordon (film) 195
Florence
and Grand Tour 2
women of 27, 122
Florio, Donna Franca 61–2
foreign beauty
appeal in mass consumption era
172–3
as comparative for Italian beauty xxiv
foreign actresses in Italian cinema
170–1, 172, 176–7
Fortini, Franco 284*n*.73
Foscolo, Ugo 20
Fougère, Eugenie 64
Fraccaroli, Antonio 103
France
fashion influence 81–2
and Italian nationalism 4–16
Marianne figure xxii–xxiii, 243–4, 263
as model for unified Italy 27
women of 56, 57
Parisienne woman 60–1, 78
Franco, Fulvia 121, 123
French Revolution 6–7
Frontoni, Angelo 193
Fryer, Paul 77
Fuller, Margaret 30
Futurist condemnation of modern
woman 82–3

Gabel, Scilla 140
Galiena, Anna 205, 210
Galleria (cultural supplement) 87
Gallian, Marcello 103
Gamba, Giuliana 210–11
Garbo, Greta 58, 83–4, 110, 158
garçonne type 80, 81
Garibaldi, Anita 30
Garibaldi, Giuseppe 28, 263
women in literature of 29–32, 49
Garnett, Edward 48
Garofalo, Anna 114–15, 116, 160
Gattopardo, Il (*The Leopard*) (film)
166–8, 186, 188
Gautier, Théophile 26–7
'gender ideology' in media 194
Generale Della Rovere, Il (film) 181
Genna, Giuseppe 217
Genoa: women of 4
Gente (magazine) 196, 242
Gente Nostra (magazine) 93–4, *94–6*, *96*,
103
Gentile, Giovanni 89
Germi, Pietro 177
Ghio, Carol 231
Ghione, Emilio 68, 75
Giachetti, Fosco 134
Gigliozzi, G. 38
Gilda (film) 109, 110, 112
Ginger e Fred (film) 215
Ginsborg, Paul 255, 257, 259
Gioi, Vivi 104
Gioia (magazine) 192

Giorgi, Eleonora 193
Giorgi, Paolini 76
giornata particolare, Una (film) 219
Girlanda, Elio 177
Girotti, Massimo 134, 136
Glaviano, Marco xvi, 248
Gli indifferenti (film) 165, 186
globalisation era 223–44
goddess imagery
    foreigners on Italian women 27
    and national identity 7, 8, 28
Godly, Conrad 258
Goldoni, Carlo 206
Goncourt brothers 26
Gonda, Greta 199
Gonin, Francesco: *Lucia Mondella 17,*
    18
Goretti, Maria 127
GQ (magazine) xv, 250
Grable, Betty 109, 110, 111, 158
Gramsci, Antonio 167
Grand Hotel (film) 83–4
Grand Hôtel (magazine) 138, 139
Grand Tour and images of Italy 2–4
Grandi, Serena 205, 207, *208*, 209
Grandi Firme, Le (magazine) 91–2, *161*
    beauty contest 91–2
    Signorina *Grandi Firme* figure 81,
        89–92, *90*, 110, 205
    'Signorina *Grandi Firme*' song 91
Grassi, Alice 232
Grazia (magazine) 103–4, 116, 172–3,
    192
Grazzini, Giovanni 189–90
Greco, Emilio 179
Grignaffini, Giovanna 145, 156
Guareschi, Giovanni 137
Guarnieri, Silvio 154, 159, 168
Guccione, Bob 205
Guendalina (film) 177
Guerrazzi, Francesco Domenico 16
Guiccioli, Alessandro 35
Guida, Gion 110
Guida, Gloria 201, 212
Gutwirth, Madelyn 7, 9
Guzzanti, Sabina 216

hair colour
    and anthropological ideal 56–7
    blonde Miss Italia winner 173
    dark hair of *bella italiana* xvii, 34
    dark-haired peasant girls after
        unification 48–54
    and Fascist ideal 98
    fashion for blonde hair in the
        nineteenth century 40–1, 42,
        61–2, 69
    Italian actresses abroad 159
    literary Italian heroines 9, 15, 17–18
    and mass consumption era 171–2,
        179, 186
    in men 46
    and models of beauty 34
    Queen Margherita 35, 36, 37, 38
    and social class 61–2
Halsman, Philippe *153*, 158

hard-core pornographic films 211–18
Hardy, Françoise 179
Harlow, Jean 84
Hayek, Salma xvi
Hayez, Francesco 28, 264
    I bacio 21
    La ciociara 21, *22*
    La meditazione 21, *23*
Hayworth, Rita 109–10, 111, 140
Heller, Joseph 114
historical films 181–2, 248, 249
    Brass's sex films 206, 209, 210
    film star roles of 1950s 143, 148, 149,
        163
    Il Gattopardo 166–8
    see also nostalgia
historical novels 16–19
Hollywood films
    artificial beauty of Hollywood stars
        83–4, 95–6
    in Communist press 139–40
    Communist support for Italian
        cinema 133
    Fascist opposition to 95–6, 97–8, 103
    influence on Italian cinema 85–6
    parts in films made in Italy 161–3
    in postwar era 108–16
Hyams, Joe 160
Hyams, Leila 84
Hyde, Frank 52

identity *see* national identity
ideology and feminine beauty 125–41
    Fascism 80–1, 92–106
    see also politics
Ieri, oggi, domani (film) 183, 185, 240
Illustrazione italiana, L' 39, 49–52, *51*, 92,
    94, 164, *230*
immigration in globalisation era 223–32
    citizenship status of immigrants
        224–5
    southern migration to north 223–4
Indian Hunter, The (film) 175
industrialisation
    and mass consumption era 170, 176
    and modern woman in Fascist era 80,
        81–2
innocente, L' (film) 203
intellectuals
    postwar radio discussion 122–3
    and Queen Margherita 38
    see also male discourse on feminine
        beauty
international cinema and italian
    actresses of 1950s 157–63, 180, 190,
    243
Invernizio, Carolina 68
Io e mia sorella (film) 194
Io la conoscevo bene (film) 178
Irréversible (film) 249
It Started in Naples (film) 162
'Italia' (Italian national figure) xxii–xxiii,
    19–20, *20*, 28–9, *29*, 54, 231
Italian beauty *see bella italiana*
Italian Film Export 159
Italiani (film) 243

Italy
    American view of 161–3, 185
    European view of 3–4
        after unification 26–7
    see also national identity; north/south
        divide

jewellery
    Cavalieri's fondness for 76–7
    Fascist disapproval 101
Jones, Verina 18
Jotti, Nilde 121, 282*n*.42
Just One Night (film) 243

Kessler sisters 193
King, R. 228
Kinski, Klaus 209
Koll, Claudia 205, 210
Komasova, Anastasia 232
Koscina, Sylva 201
Krieger, Rob 227, 229, 242

Ladri di biciclette (*Bicycle Thieves*) (film)
    133, 136
Lamartine, Alphonse de 4
    Graziella 14–16, 161
Lampedusa, Giuseppe Tomasi di: *Il
    Gattopardo* 166–7
language and objectification of women
    xxvi
Lanocita, Arturo 160–1
Last Tango in Paris (film) 211
Lattuada, Alberto 177, 181, 197, 206
laureati, I (film) 243, 257
Lavoro (trade union magazine) *146*,
    147
left-wing politics 125
    Antonioni's bourgeois cinema 185–6
    Church opposition to 126
    hostility to sex appeal in films 146
    Parietti's left-wing stance 237
    see also Communism, and feminine
        beauty
Legend of the Lost (film) 161
legs
    and American sex appeal 111, 113–14
    appeal of Signorina *Grandi Firme* 89,
        90–1, *90*
Leonardo da Vinci 3
    Mona Lisa and Eleanora Duse 48
Leopard, The (film) 166–8, 186, 188
Leopardi, Giacomo: 'All'Italia' 20–1
Levi, Carlo 136
liceale, La (film) 212
lieu de mémoire xix
Lisi, Virna 171–2
literature
    and cinema 164–8
    European views of Italy and Italians
        4–16, 23–5
    Italian writers on Italy 16–19
    medieval poetry and feminine beauty
        3
    postwar view of Italian women
        114–15
Lizzani, Carlo 145

Lollobrigida, Gina xvi, xx, 124, 142, *148*, *150*, 154, 156–7, 174, 185, 264–5
  as Cavalieri in *La donna più bella del mondo* 58, 151, *152*
  early roles 147–51
  as international star 157, 158–9, 160, 162–3
  as Italian beauty 160
  in *La romana* 151, 165
  and Miss Italia contest 119, 120, 225
  'Lollopalooza' appellation 162–3
Lombardi, Pia Colini 128
Lombroso, Cesare xx, 54–5
Longo, Luigi 135
Loren, Sophia (*née* Sofia Scicolone) xvi, xx, 84, 124, 142, 151–5, *153*, 156, *184*, 197, 265
  as aunt of Alessandra Mussolini 220–1
  Cucinotta as successor to 240, 242, 244
  history films and popularity 181, 182–5
  as international star 157–8, 159, 163, 171, 181
    early parts in American films 161, 162
  unconventional beauty 160–1
  as Miss Italia judge 225
  and Miss *Vie Nuove* contest 138
Lotta, La (Communist weekly) 131
Love Party 214, 215
Lualdi, Antonella 175, 181
Luci del varietà (film) 199

Maccari, Mino: *Cocktail* 88
'Macchiaioli' painters 21–2
Macciocchi, Maria Antonietta 141
Macellaio (film) 238
'madamismo' 99
Maggiorani, Lamberto 136
maggiorate fisiche type 149, 150, 168–9, 175, 207
Magnani, Anna 156, 158, 161, 185
  and postwar national identity 123, 124
  traditional beauty xvii–xx
make-up *see* cosmetics
Malaparte, Curzio 141
male discourse on feminine beauty xxv, 265
  American view of Italian stars of 1950s 158, 162–3
  on Cavalieri's body 75
  Communists on beauty contests 137
  in D'Annunzio's work 43–4
  despair at modern woman in Fascist era 86–92, 100–3
  Fellini's cinematic discourse 197–200
  Futurists on modern woman 82–3
  on Mangano in *Riso amaro* 144–5
  Miss Padania requirements 231–2
  Moravia on Cardinale 188–9
  Notari's Fascist view of 100–3
  radio discussion in postwar era 122–3
  scientific discourse 54–7

sex films of 1970s onwards 205–18
and Signorina *Grandi Firme* 89–91
Stendhal on Italian women 10–14
Malena (film) 248–9, 251
Malizia (film) 201–3, *202*
Manconi, Luigi 218
mandragola, La (film) 181
Mangano, Silvana 124, 142, 163, 174–5, 197
  in *Riso amaro* 143–7, *144*
Manon Lescaut (film) 67–8
Mantegazza, Paolo 44, 55–7
Manzoni, Alessandro: *I promessi sposi* 17–19, 28
Marchesi, Concetto 135, 141
Margherita, Queen (Margherita of Savoy) 33, 34–40, *36*, *39*, 46, 54, 263
  fashion influence 40–1, 61
  as feminine role model 39–40
Margherita (fashion magazine) 40
Marianne (French national figure) xxii–xxiii, 243–4, 263
Marinetti, F. T. 72, 82–3, 100, 101
Marini, Armida 76
Marini, Valeria 226, 228, 234–5, *236*, 238
Marotta, Giuseppe 122, 162, 183
Marriage Italian-style (film) 183, 185
Martinelli, Elsa 175, 180, 193
Martini, Rosanna *117*, 118, 123, 263
maschietta type 80, 81
Masciotta, Edelfa Chiara 266–8, *266*, *267*
Masi, Stefano 206
Masino, Paolo 92
mass consumption and ideals of beauty 59, 170–90, 263
  see also advertisements
mass culture *see* popular culture and Communism
Massa, Francesco 207–8
Massaie Rurali organisation 94
Mastroianni, Marcello 183, 199–200
maternal femininity *see* mothers
Matrimonio all'Italiana (*Marriage Italian-style*) (film) 183, 185
Matrix Reloaded, The (film) 249
Matrix 2, The (film) 249
Max (magazine) 250, 255
Maxim (magazine) xv
Mazzocca, Fernando 19
'Medusan beauty' 41–2
Meloni, Alessandra 225
men
  enjoyment of physical female beauty xx–xxi, 89–90
  men's magazines xv–xvi, 240, 250
  see also male discourse on feminine beauty
Mendez, Denny 223, 224, *225*, 227–9
Menichelli, Pina 83
Mentana, Enrico 228–9
Meredith, George 23–5
  Emilia in England/Sandra Belloni 23–4
  Vittoria 24–5
Merlini, Elsa 86, 89
Michetti, Francesco Paolo 58, 78
Milan: women of 61, 122

Milani, Milena 192–3
Milo, Sandra 198
Mina (singer) 178
Minuzzo, Nerio 179
Miranda, Isa 163
Miranda (film) 205, 206–7, *208*
Mirigliani, Enzo 223, 225–6, 267
Mirigliani, Patrizia 267
Miss Camicia Verde 231
Miss Italia (film) 149–50
Miss Italia contest xxvi, 108, 116–21, *117*, *119*, *120*, 238
  blonde winner 173
  calendar photos 266–8, *266*, *267*
  Christian Democrat support for 126, 129
  and Communists 133, 134
  and ethnicity of contestants in 1990s 223, 224–9, 237
  and film careers of contestants 119–21, 123–4
  and Northern League 229, 230
  painting competition 163–4, *164*, *165*
  and public morality 121
  wholesome intentions 118
Miss Padania contest 224, 229–32
Miss *Vie Nuove* contest 131–6, *132*, *136*, 137–8, 140
Miti, Michela 201
Moana (Moana Pozzi) 212, 214–17, *216*
Moana l'insaziabile (film) 215
models *see* calendar photo-shoots; fashion models
modernisation and feminine beauty xxiv–xxv
  Catholic reservations on modern life 127–9
  modern woman in interwar years 80–106
    Fascist disapproval of 87–9, 92, 100–3
modesty
  and beauty contest entrants 119, 120–1, 140
  in Catholic view of beauty 28, 127, 128–9
  and literary heroines 18
  and star system 158
Moe, Nelson 50, 52
moglie più bella, La (film) 194
monarchy: establishment of 34–40
Mondaini, Sandra 171
Monroe, Marilyn 139, 158, 171
Montand, Yves 134
morality
  Church and feminine beauty 127–31
  public morality and Miss Italia contest 121
Morante, Elsa 134
Morasso, Mario 53–4
Moravia, Alberto 134, 151, 182, 188–9
  Racconti romani as films 164–5
Morin, Edgar 159
Moscoloni, Zelinda Vittoria 73
Mosso, Angelo 53

Most Beautiful Woman in the World, The
  (film) 58
mothers
  contemporary appeal of Ferilli 256–7
  Fascist maternal ideal 92–3, 101
  Fellini and mother/prostitute
    representation of women 197–8
  as symbols of nationhood xxii, 7,
    19–20
Motion Picture Code of America 146–7
Motterle, Tamara 231
Mulvey, Laura 162
Muratore, Lucien 66–7, 68
Murtas, Illaria 228
Mussolini, Alessandra 218–22, *220*
Mussolini, Benito 92, 93
Mussolini, Romano 219
Musu, Marisa 131, 134, 138, 282*n*.42
Muti, Ornella (Francesca Revelli) 191–2,
  194–6, *195*, 242, 244, 251

naked body *see* nudity
Naples
  and Grand Tour 2–3
  inspires Mme de Staël 5
  and Loren's screen persona 152,
    160–1, 265
  women of 122, 221
Napoleon I, emperor of France 5, 7
national identity
  and feminine beauty xviii–xxiii, 7–8,
    46, 262–4
  beauty contests 72–4, 223, 224, 227
  in Fascist era 88
  Fellini's mother/whore
    representation 197–8
  and films and film stars of 1950s
    142–57, 264–5
  'Italia' imagery xxii–xxiii, 19–20, *20*,
    28–9, *29*, 54, 231
  Italy as female figure xvi, 7, 19,
    20–1, 243–4
  Italy as maternal figure xviii, 7,
    19–20
  Lollobrigida and Loren 160
  in mass consumption era 179–85,
    263
  painting competition 163–4
  in post-unification Italy 48–54
  in postwar era 107–8, 123–4
  in Risorgimento 1, 18, 19–25
  see also bella italiana; Miss Italia
    contest
  and French literature 4–16
  and Nature 19, 21
'natural' beauty of Italians 26, 47, 50, 61,
  62, 262
  Bellucci's support for 251
  Communist approval 137
  contemporary appeal of Ferilli
    253–4
  Eleonora Duse 47
  erotic appeal of Ornella Muti 191
  film stars of 1950s xvi, 142, 160–1
  'body-landscape' 145–6, 147
  in literature 15

Loren as paradigm of *bella italiana*
  265
  Miss Padania requirements 231, 232
  Queen Margherita 34
Nature
  'body-landscape' 145–6, 147
  and national identity 19, 21
  and peasant girl type 45, 50
Nazzari, Amedeo 137–8
Neera 47, 48, 61
Negri, Toni 287*n*.74
neo-realist cinema
  Anna Magnani in postwar films of
    123–4
  and beauty contests 145
  Communist support for 133
  and female body 145
  and traditional beauty xvii–xviii
Never So Few (film) 162
Newsweek (magazine) 158
Niceforo, Alfredo 55
Noce, Teresa 282*n*.42
Noi Donne (Communist weekly) 134
Non c'è pace tra gli ulivi (film) 147
Nora, Pierre xv
Noris, Assia 104, 105
north/south divide 33–4
  Fascist portrayal of rural south 93–4
  and mass consumption era 170–1
  and Northern League 229–30, 231,
    232
  race theory and Italian nationalism
    44–8
  representations of southern peasant
    beauty 33, 48–54
  sexual fixation of southern men xxi
  southern migration to north 223–4
Northern League 224, 228, 237
  Miss Padania contest 229–32
nostalgia
  evoked by looks of Bellucci 248, 249
  in Fellini's films 199
  of north for south 33, 52, 185
  and *Il Postino* 238–40
  in sex films 202, 203, 206–7, 209,
    210
  and traditional beauty xxiii–xxv
  see also historical films
Notari, Umberto 71, 72, 75, 78, 100–2
notte brava, La (film) 175
nudity
  Bellucci's ease with 250
  in 1970s cinema 200–5
  colonial subject 99
  desires of Cardinale's fans 189
  fantasies about Lina Cavalieri 75
  Ferilli's popular appeal 255–6
  Ornella Muti 196
  and star system 158
  see also pornography in permissive
    society
Nuti, Francesco 195, 196

objectification of women xxv, xxvi
  American view of Italian actresses
    162

Communist misgivings over *Vie
  Nuove* contest 140
Moravia on Cardinale 188–9
soft porn films 203
on television 235
see also male discourse on feminine
  beauty
Oggi (magazine) 108, 196, 242, *254*
Once Upon a Time in the West (film)
  186, *187*
ordinary girls
  and Miss Italia contest 225–6, 267–8
  in neo-realist cinema xvii–xviii
  as pin-ups in postwar era 108,
    113–14, 115–16
  popular appeal of Sabrina Ferilli
    253–4
  and *Vie Nuove* contest 138
ore, L' (magazine) 157
Oro di Napoli, L' (film) 152, 155, 160,
  183
Oscar (film) 195
Otero, Carolina *see* Belle Otero, La
Ottaviani, Achille 237

Padania, La (newspaper) 232
Padanian ethnic group 230
  see also Miss Padania contest
Pagannini (film) 209
painting competition and Miss Italia
  163–4, *164*, *165*
Pajetta, Gian Carlo 135
Pampanini, Silvana 118–19, *119*, 123,
  157, 163, 256
Panaro, Alessandra 176
Pane, amore e ... (film) 152
Pane, amore e fantasia (film) 150, 154,
  156
Pane, amore e gelosia (film) 150
Panorama calendar xvii, 258–9
Panzini, Alfredo 82
Paoli, Gino 177
Paolo, Dria 86
Paprika (film) 205, 209
Parietti, Alba 227, 235–8, *236*
Parisienne woman 60–1, 78
parliament: women in 121–2, 212, 214,
  218–19, 221
parmigiana, La (film) 177
Parole di una donna (radio programme)
  114–15
Parsi, Maria Rita 257
Parvo, Elli 118, 199
Pasolini, Pier Paolo 141, 188, 200, 204
  Amado mio 110
  Ragazzi di vita 175
Passion of the Christ, The (film) 249
Pater, Walter 48
Pavignon, Contessa Vera di 76
Pavoni, Arnaldo 71, 79
peasant girl types *50*, *51*, *53*, *95*, *96*, *97*
  emancipation in mass consumption
    era 176
  as erotic ideal 16, 87, 206
  as Fascist ideal 88, 93–6
  and film star roles of 1950s 142–57

Riso amaro 143–7
  as Italian ideal after unification 48–54
  in literature 16, 17, 18, 45
  northern 'folklorisation' of south
    48–54, 94
  popularity in nineteenth-century
    press 33, 62
Pellegrini, Isabella 8
Pellicani, Michele 135, 139, 140
permissive society in Italy 191–4
Petrarch 3, 37
Petri, Elio 179
Philbin, Mary 84
photographic images
  Lina Cavalieri 64, 75
  see also calendar photo-shoots; 'pin-
    up girls'
physical beauty 262
  anthropological study 55–7
  appeal of Italian stars abroad xv–xvi,
    157–63
  Bellucci's natural approach 249, 250,
    251
  Cardinale on her body 188–9
  Catholic view of 127, 128–9
  Fascist ideal 92
  Fellini's view 198–9
  film stars of 1950s 144–5, 154, 156,
    162–3
    maggiorate fisiche 149, 150, 168–9,
      175, 207
  foreign view of Italian figure 61
  fuller figure of sex film stars 207–8
  in mass consumption era 179–80
  and Miss Italia contest 119
  Miss Padania requirements 231–2
  Miss *Vie Nuove* contest 133–4, 140
  sexual fixation of Italian men xx–xxi,
    89–90
  television *soubrettes* 234–5
  thinner bodies in mass consumption
    era 174–5
  see also beauty contests; erotic beauty
Piccini, G. 70–1, 75, 77
Picking Up the Pieces (film) 243
Pieri, Giuliana 42
Pietragrua, Angela 10
'pin-up girls' 110–12
Pirelli calendar 250
Pittigrilli 88, 89, 91, 173
plastic surgery 236–7, 251
Playboy (Italian edition) 193, 202–3,
  204, 220, *220*
Playmen (magazine) 193, 205
Podestà, Rossana 163, 165–6
poetry and feminine beauty xix, 3
Poiret, Paul 81–2
politics
  and feminine beauty 125–41, 262–3
    dark-haired beauty after unification
      48–54
    Miss Padania contest 229–32
  women in parliament in postwar era
    121–2, 265–6
    Cicciolina 212, 214
    Alessandra Mussolini 218–19, 221

see also Christian Democrats;
  Communism; Fascism
Poliziano 3
Ponti, Carlo 151
Ponti, Eduardo 219
pop music and film 177–8
popular culture and Communism 126,
  129–30, 138–41
pornography in permissive society 193,
  198
  erotic soft porn 192, 200–18, 238
  hard-core films 211–18
positivism 54
poster art 80–1, 82, 117
Postino, Il xv, xvii, 239–40
Pougy, Liane de 60
Poveri ma belli (film series) 176, 260
Pozzi, Moana 212, 214–17, *216*
Prati, Pamela 237
Pratolini, Vasco 165–6
Pravo, Patty 178, 193
Praz, Mario 9, 41
press
  Communist press 131–3, 135, 139
  and feminine beauty
    and birth of beauty contests
      72–4
    and Lina Cavalieri 71–2, 74–5
    Church opposition to beauty
      contests 127–8, 128–9
    Fascist portrayal of peasant girl
      ideal 93–6
    and modern woman in Fascist era
      80–1, 87, 88–96
    popularity of peasant girl types in
      the nineteenth century 33,
      49–52, 62
    in postwar era 108
    postwar promotion of Italian
      beauty 112–16
    and television stars 238
  male-dominated 194
  and permissive society 192–3
  see also advertisements
Pride and the Passion, The (film) 161,
  162
Primato artistico italiano, Il (magazine)
  86
primitive associations of south 2, 53–4
prostitutes
  actresses as courtesans 60, 62, 64, 76
  early contact of Italian men xxi
  in films 151, 175
  mother/prostitute representation of
    women 197–8
  state-run brothels 114, 192, 209
Proust, Marcel 61
provinciale, La (film) 165
Pugliese, Sergio 172

Qualcosa di biondo (film) 206

race laws 99, 102
racial theory
  Fascism and Italian race 98–103, 226
  and Italian nationalism 44–8

and Northern League's Miss Padania
  contest 230–2
scientific study 54, 55–7
see also ethnicity
racism in children 227
Radcliffe, Anne 4
Radical Party and Cicciolina 214
radio: male discourse on women in
  postwar era 122–3
ragazza con la valigia, La (film) 186
ragazza di Bube, La (film) 186
ragazza di Trieste, La (film) 194
ragazza Novecento type 80, 81
ragazze di San Frediano, Le (film) 165–6
Ragazzi di vita (film) 175
RAI television 172, 205, 210, 233, 234,
  237
Ralli, Giovanna 165–6, 181–2, *182*, 254
Rappaport, Erika Diane 59
Ravera, Lidia 245
Regina dei fiori (TV series) 259
'Reginella campagnola' (song) 94
regional beauty 33, 56, 122–3, 261
  Fascist praise for 94, 98, 102
  see under individual cities
Renaissance art
  Fascist appropriation 96–8, 102
  inspired by feminine beauty xix, 11,
    263
  social class and breasts xxi–xxii
Renzi, Renzo 160, 207
Repaci, Leonida 137
representation of women xviii–xix, xxv
  Fellini and mother/prostitute
    representation 197–8
reproduction
  abortion campaigns 193–4
  and nationalism xxii, 46, 89, 92–3
  see also mothers
Revlon Fire and Ice campaign 163
Ricci, Antonio 215
Ricciuti, Vittorio 185
Ricordati di me (film) 251–2
Riffa, La (film) 248
Ringgold, Gene 109
Ripa, Cesare: *Iconologia* 19, *20*
risaia, La (film) 180
Risi, Dino 203, 226, 248
Riso amaro (film) 143–7, *144*, 180
Risorgimento
  feminine symbols xxii, 1, 2, 18–19
  in art and literature 19–25
  in *Il Gattopardo* 166–8
Riva, Lorenzo 260
Roberts, Mary Louise 82
Robotti, Paolo 135
Rocco e i suoi fratelli (film) 185–6, 189
Rochet, Charles 57
Rogopag (film) 180–1
Roma (film) 197, 209
Roma città aperta (film) 123
Roma football club 255–6
romana, La (film) 151, 165
Romance (film) 58, 277n.84
Romano, Ruggiero xx
Romanticism: images of Italy 1–2, 4, 8

Rome
    and Grand Tour 2
    growth of film industry in 157
    Poveri ma belli films 176
    women of 4, 27, 41, 42, 44, 122, 264
        beauty contest 74, 76
        Lina Cavalieri as exemplar 59, 72–3
Rosa, Giovanni Titta 122–3
rosa di Granata, La (film) 68
Rosi, Francesco 177
Rosina *see* Vercellana, Rosa
Rossellini, Roberto 181
Rossetti, Dante Gabriel 42
Rothenburg, Nina 194
Rousseau, Jean-Jacques 22
Rudini, Carlo di 62
Rudorff, Raymond 60
Rusconi, Marisa 156
Russo, Carmen 201, 204–5, *204*, 257–8

Sabato, domenica e lunedì (TV film) 219,
    221
Salinari, Carlo 46
Salon Kitty (film) 205
Salvatori, Renato 176
Samperi, Salvatore 201, 210–11
Sandrelli, Stefania 171, 177, 178–9, *178*,
    180, 205, 206
Sanminiatelli, Bruno 122
Sargent, John Singer 52
    Head of a Capri Girl 31
Sassard, Jacqueline 177, 197
Savoy, House of 36–7
Scajola, Toti 179
Scarfoglio, Edoardo 149
Schiaffino, Rosanna 175, 180–1, 193, 197
Schicchi, Riccardo 212, 215
Scicolone, Maria 219
Scicolone, Sofia *see* Loren, Sophia
science and beauty 54–7
Scoccimarro, Mauro 135
Scorza, Carlo *100*
Scott, Sir Walter 16
Secchia, Pietro 135
seconda moglie, La (film) 243
Sedotta e abbandonata (film) 177
segretaria privata, La (film) 86, 89
Selvaggio, Il (magazine) 88–9, *88*
Sennett, Richard 8
Senso 45 (film) 205, 210
Serao, Matilde 61, 62, 68, 77
Sette (magazine) *111*
    Signorina *Sette* 112
Settimelli, Emilio 82
sex
    in Italian films
        controversy over *Riso amaro*
            146–7
        portrayal by foreign actresses 176–7
        soft porn films 192, 200–18, 238
    liaisons with Italian women 3–4,
        15–16
    permissive society in Italy 191–4
    sexual fixation of Italian men xx–xxi,
        89–90
    see also erotic beauty; physical beauty

sexual passion
    and allegorical figures 8
    American view of Italian actresses xvi,
        161–3
    Catholic view of physical beauty 127
    foreign actresses in 1960s films 176–7
    and literary heroines 8–9, 13–14, 18,
        43–4, 53
    Lollobrigida's film roles 149, 151
    stereotype of southern Italian women
        53
sfida, La (film) 175
Sheldon, Edward 277*n*.84
Shrimpton, Jean 179
Sicily: European view of 3
Sighele, Scipio 32
Signor Quindicipalle (film) 253
signora di notte, La (film) 207
signora senza camelie, La (film) 120, 147
Signoret, Simone 134
Signorina *Grandi Firme* figure 81, 89–92,
    90, 110, 205
signorine buonasera on television 172
Sissi 40
Skofic, Milko 148
Snack Bar Budapest (film) 208
social class
    and breasts xxi–xxiii
    Communist ideal of working-class
        girl 137
    and films of 1950s 147, 152
    and hair colour 38, 61–2
    lack of social hierarchy 11–12
    and northern view of south 33, 48–54
    postwar rise of lower-class beauty
        107, 123–4
    see also peasant girl types
Socialism and feminine beauty 125
soft porn 192, 200–18, 238
Soldati, Mario 136, 208–9
Sole delle Alpi, Il (magazine) 230
soliti ignoti, I (film) 189
Solomon and Sheba (film) 162
sorpasso, Il (film) 177
soubrette type on television 172, 233–5
southern Italy
    and Grand Tour 2–3
    see also north/south divide
Spaak, Catherine 176–7, 191, 197
Spadini, Armando 87
'spaghetti westerns' 179
Spinazzola, Vittorio 158, 160, 161, 185,
    189
sposa della morte, La (film) 68, 78
Staël, Mme de xxiv, 4, 10, 14
    Corinne ou de l'Italie 5–9, 15
Staller, Illona *see* Cicciolina
Stampa, La (newspaper) 32
star culture
    American stars of postwar era 109–12
    in Communist press 139–40
    and Communist *Vie Nuove* contest
        137–8
    in Fascist era 85–6, 103–6
        competition for future stars 84
        and peasant ideal 95–6, 97–8

Italian film stars of 1950s xvi, 142–69,
    181, 263, 264–5
    Bellucci on comparisons with
        250–1
    international stardom 157–63, 180
    starlet status 158–9
    see also actresses
state and feminine beauty xix
state-run brothels 114, 192, 209
stelline dell'Unità 130–1, 137
Stendhal xxiv, 4, 10–14, 26
    De l'amour 11
    La Chartreuse de Parme 12–14
    Rome, Naples, Florence 10–11
stereotype of Italian woman xxiii–xxiv
    in American films 162, 163
    French view of 9, 16, 26–7
    Graziella as peasant girl 16
    northern 'folklorisation' of south 50,
        52, 94
Stevens, Sacheverell 4
Storaro, Vittorio 201
Strada, La (film) 199
Stragliati, Carlo: *Episodio delle Cinque
    Giornate* 23, *25*
striptease
    Ferilli's *Roma* performance 255–6
    in Miss Padania contest 232
Stuparich, Gianni 123
Sturani, Enrico 89–90
subordination of women xx, 60
    in Risorgimento 2, 46
    and art 22
    and science 54
    see also objectification of women
supplente, La (film) 212
Symons, Arthur 48

Tabet, Paola 227
Taine, Hippolyte 27
Tampieri, Giuseppe: *Adriana 164*
Tassinaro, Il (film) 219
Tavolato, Italo 82
Tegani, Ulderico 69
television
    blonde predominance 172
    contemporary actresses on 253–4
    erotic actresses on 205, 210, 215–16
    image of feminine beauty on 233–8,
        245
    soubrette type 172, 233–5
Tempo (magazine) 108, 115, *115*
    and Miss Italia contest 116, *117*, 118,
        119, 120–1
Tennyson, Alfred, Lord 42
'terror-novels' 4
Tettamanti, Ampelio: *Portrait of a rice
    weeder 164*
Theed, Liliana 42–3
thinness
    as anti-Fascist 89, 92
    in mass consumption era 174–5
Time (magazine) 157–8, 185
Tissot, Ernest 40
Titian 3, 122
Togliatti, Palmiro 130, 135, 140

Tommaseo, Niccolò 49
Tortora, Enzio 287*n*.74
Toscani, Oliviero 248
Totò (actor) 121
Totò al Giro d'Italia (film) 121
Tozzi, Federico 210
traditional beauty xvii–xviii
    appeal to Fascism 80, 86–7, 93–4
    Cuccarini on television 233–4
    Cucinotta in *Il Postino* 238–9, 240,
        242
    maternal femininity xxii
    and modernisation xxiv–xxv
    postwar alternative to Hollywood 108
    retreat to in 1990s xviii, 224
    see also peasant girl types
Travaso delle idee della domenica, Il
    (magazine) 76
Tribuna Illustrata, Il (magazine) 76
tricolour flag and women in art 22, 23
Trieste: women of 121, 123
Troisi, Massimo xvii, 239, 240
Tu ridi (film) 253
Tutte le provocazoni di Moana (film) 215
Twiggy 179
Two Brides, The (film) 68
Two Women (film) 155, 182–3

ugliness and deviance 54–5
Ultimo tango a Parigi (*Last Tango in
    Paris*) (film) 211
Umberto I, king of Italy 34–5, 37, 54
Under Suspicion (film) 248
Union of Italian Women (UDI) 121
Unità, L' (Communist newspaper) 132,
    144
urbanisation
    and mass consumption era 176

and modern woman in Fascist era 80,
    81–2
Usova, Olga 77
Uzanne, Octave 60

Vaghe stelle dell'Orsa (film) 186
Valentina, ragazza in calore (film) 215
Valeri, Diego 122
Valle, Anna 225
Valli, Alida 103, 105–6, *105*
Vattimo, Gianni 229
Venere imperiale (film) 151, 163
Venice: women of 26–7, 94, 101, 122
Venturi, Maria 205
Venturi, Sara 232
Vercellana, Rosa ('La bella Rosina') 34,
    35
Verde e azzurro (newspaper) 71–2
Verdone, Carlo 194, 196
Verga, Giovanni 53, 167
Vergani, Orio 117, 118
Verona: women of 4
Vespucci, Simonetta 38
Viaggi, Tania 231
Viaggi di nozze (film) 257
Vie Nuove (left-wing weekly) 131–2
    beauty contest *132*, 133–6, *136*, 137–8,
        140
    and popular culture 139–40, 141
Villani, Dino 116, 117–18, 119, 121,
    163
Villani, Romilda 84
Virzì, Paolo 253
Visconti, Luchino 118, 120, 134
    Il Gattopardo 167–8, 186, 188
Viscontini, Mathilde 10
Vita coi figli (film) 248
Vitali, Alvaro 201

vitelloni, Il (film) 198
Vitti, Monica 185–6, 188
Vittorini, Elio 284*n*.73
Vittorio Emanuele II, king of Italy 34
Viva l'Italia (film) 181
voglia matta, Il (film) 177
Vogue Italia (magazine) 242
voluntary associations 125

Warner, Marina 8, 28
wet T-shirt element to Miss Padania
    231–2
White, Alice 84
White, Jessie 24, 30
Wilhelm I, Kaiser 25
Willson, Perry 94
Winchell, Walter 162–3
Woman of Impulse, A (film) 68
women *see* emancipation of women;
    male discourse on feminine beauty;
    objectification of women;
    subordination of women
women's liberation in Italy 193–4,
    265–6
World is Not Enough, The (film) 243
Wright Mills, C. 111, 116

Yalom, Marilyn xxi, 156
youth culture in mass consumption era
    176–9
Yuval-Davis, Nira 59

Zanotti, Ena *138*
Zanotti, Ivana *138*, *139*
Zapponi, Bernardino 209
Zavattini, Cesare 92, 116, 118, 133, 136,
    183
Zincone, Giuliano 228